Plato and Heidegger

Plato
and Heidegger

In Search of Selfhood

Henry G. Wolz

Lewisburg
Bucknell University Press
London and Toronto: Associated University Presses

Associated University Presses, Inc.
4 Cornwall Drive
East Brunswick, New Jersey 08816

Associated University Presses Ltd.
69 Fleet Street
London EC4Y 1EU, England

Associated University Presses
Toronto, Ontario, Canada M5E 1A7

Library of Congress Cataloging in Publication Data
Wolz, Henry G.
Plato and Heidegger : in search of selfhood.

Bibliography: p.
Includes index.
1. Plato.   2. Heidegger, Martin, 1889–1976.
I. Title.
B395.W82   184   79-19974
ISBN 0-8387-5003-6

Printed in the United States of America

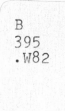
to the memory of my sister and my parents

Contents

Acknowledgments

It would be futile to try to determine the many influences from which I have profited and the stimulations I have received during discussions with students both undergraduates and graduates and in conversations with colleagues at official and social gatherings. Some names, however, remain indelibly fixed in my memory. Professor John H. Randall, Jr. of Columbia University, in typical Socratic fashion, called my attention to the dramatic elements in Plato's dialogues without spelling out their significance. The editorial skill of my friend and former colleague Professor John J. McDermott of Texas A & M University helped me expose the early versions of my ideas to public scrutiny in professional journals. Professor John B. Noone of Queens College frequently suspended the function of his sharply critical mind and used words of praise when he felt that encouragement was sorely needed. Our daughter Ursula sacrificed precious vacation days to undertake the tedious task of typing rough drafts from tape recordings. My wife Barbara generously relieved me of the duties which in the American household are traditionally assigned to the male. Mrs. Leona Beck, without a word of complaint, typed and retyped various chapters; and when she left for a warmer clime, Mrs. Ann Sands and Mrs. Gladys Passoa, our departmental secretaries, took care of last minute changes. I feel indebted to Mrs. Cynthia Fell, Associate Director of Bucknell University Press for her efforts on my behalf, and I would also like to express my thanks to the anonymous reader from whom I received many useful suggestions. Last, but by no means least, I must acknowledge a great debt of gratitude to Mrs. Barbara Noone, who at a crucial stage in the preparation of the manuscript volunteered invaluable assistance.

In addition I would like to thank the following publishers for granting permission to reprint material:

Harper and Row, Publishers, Inc. (from *Being and Time*, translated by John Macquarrie and Edward Robinson, New York, 1962)
Cambridge University Press (from *Plato's Phaedrus* by R. A. Hackforth)
Penguin Books Ltd. (from "Phaedo" in *Plato: The Last Days of Socrates*,

translated by Hugh Tredennick, Penguin Classics, revised edition 1969, pp. 107–17, 127–39. © Hugh Tredennick, 1954, 1959, 1969)

The Bobbs-Merrill Company, Inc. (from *Plato's Protagoras*, revised by Martin Ostwald, edited by Gregory Vlastos, © 1976)

Oxford University Press (from *The Republic of Plato*, translated by F. M. Cornford, 1941)

J. M. Dent & Co. Ltd. (from the *Lysis* by Plato in the Everyman's Library Series)

Acknowledgment is also gratefully made to the editors of the following journals for permission to reprint material previously published:

The Journal of the History of Philosophy (McGill University) (July 1967): 205–17

The Personalist (University of Southern California) (Spring 1965):157–70

Philosophy and Phenomenological Research (University of New York at Buffalo) 30 (March 1970):323–53

The Review of Metaphysics (Yale University) (December 1963):214–34

Southern Journal of Philosophy (Memphis State University) 12 (Winter 1974):493–511

Introduction

In practically every age, someone will try to show that Plato's dialogues contain the seeds of the currently popular philosophy. Both the richness of Plato's thought, and the manner in which he presents it, offer untold possibilities in this direction. The dialogue form enables Plato to put forward opposite points of view without committing himself to either; and the dramatic approach allows him to stimulate rather than indoctrinate, to provide hints rather than straight answers. Today, these attempts to read modern philosophy as a "series of footnotes to Plato," to use Whitehead's well-known phrase, have lost their novelty. Through their all too frequent repetition, the reader has become surfeited and refuses to allow himself to get stirred up, except perhaps to scorn and parody, of which the following may serve as an example.

> Taylor's ultimate purpose, he made clear, was to show that Plato, rightly understood, proves the soundness of the Christian faith. Such an enterprise is, in fact, quite the usual thing for an interpreter of Plato to undertake. Paul Natorp, the leader of the Marburg School, wrote a big book to show that Plato was really a Neo-Kantian. Several learned works were written in the old days to prove that Plato was a Social Democrat attacking the capitalistic system. Raphael Demos, who long taught Greek philosophy at Harvard, wrote a large book arguing that Plato was a disciple of Whitehead. Another Harvard man, John Wild, wrote one to show that Plato was a follower of St. Thomas. . . . For a time I myself lived in daily fear lest some instrumentalist would prove that Plato was really a disciple of John Dewey. Indeed, a student once started a paper to show just that. Bur fortunately he had to leave for the wars.[1]

Who, in the face of such mockery, would dare make another attempt? Unless he had very substantial reasons, he could not hope to escape ridicule. In the case of the Plato-Heidegger relationship, there are such reasons.

Understandably, serious misgivings may be felt about the attempt to relate Plato and Heidegger, an ancient Greek and a contemporary philosopher, for it means to bridge a time gap of over two thousand years. Gerhard Krueger,[2] however, believes that our age has moved closer to the spirit of Socrates than many a previous period. Philosophy, in his view, has become less sure of itself, more self-critical, and beginning with Kierkegaard and Nietzsche has lost interest in abstract constructs and eternal verities. As a result, many modern philosophers, not unlike Socrates, have turned to the complexities of the concrete human existence which defies systematization. Krueger thinks it is time that philosophers take the interpretation of philosophy out of the hands of philologists and historians who tend to avoid the substance of Plato's philosophy and instead busy themselves with Plato the man as poet and educator, with his interest in politics and religion, with the authenticity, the chronology, and the literary forms of his work. If Krueger is right, then the present philosophic atmosphere is propitious for a new approach to the dialogues of Plato.

One would expect Heidegger to be exceptionally well suited for this new approach. Heidegger has an almost uncanny ability to enter the thought of another thinker and carry this thought beyond the limits set by its author. This is particularly noticeable in his "Die Metaphysik als Geschichte des Seins."[3] Moreover, he early experienced a kinship with the Greeks. In "My Way to Phenomenology" he relates how he had difficulty with Husserl's phenomenology until he learned how to "see." "However, the clearer it became to me," he says, "that the increasing familiarity with phenomenological seeing was fruitful for the interpretation of Aristotle's writing, the less I could separate myself from Aristotle and the other Greek thinkers."[4] In fact he found that "what occurs for the phenomenology of the acts of consciousness as the self-manifestation of phenomena is thought more originally by Aristotle and in all Greek thinking as *aletheia*, as the unconcealment of what-is-present, its being revealed, its showing itself."[5]

For Plato, too, understanding is a kind of "seeing." This should become abundantly clear in the subsequent discussion of the Socratic method. Heidegger himself says that in Plato's philosophy "seeing" is essential, a seeing which is not possible without light.

The kinship between Plato and Heidegger extends beyond the phenomenological method to the subject matter itself. Socrates' interest in selfhood is too well known to need elaboration. At this point it should suffice to recall Socrates' remark in the *Phaedrus:* "I must first know myself, as the Delphian inscription says; to be curious about that which is not my concern, while I am still in ignorance of my own self, would be ridiculous."[6] Heidegger, on his part, in his search for the "meaning of Being in General," finds it necessary to start with an inquiry into selfhood, a task to which his famous early work, *Being and Time*, is devoted.[7]

Despite the common interest in regard to method as well as subject matter which Heidegger shares with Plato, Heidegger has not been as successful in interpreting the dialogue as he might have been. In fact he levels some serious criticism against Plato, not all of which, as we shall see, is wholly justified. Perhaps the most serious of this criticism has to do with *aletheia*. In his earlier writings, Heidegger translates this Greek word as truth in the sense of unconcealment. Later he reserves it for the opening or clearing which makes truth possible. "Aletheia, unconcealment as the opening of presence," he writes, "is not yet truth. . . . Rather . . . it first grants the possibility of truth."[8] Parmenides is said to have had a flash of insight into *aletheia* as opening; but neither he nor any other thinker tried to inquire further into it.[9] Plato, according to Heidegger, shares this shortcoming with the other Greek thinkers. Although he regarded understanding as a kind of "seeing" and realized that "seeing" requires light, he failed to grasp that light in turn needs the opening in order to illuminate entities and thus let them show themselves in their being. Plato, so Heidegger contends, no longer even mentions *aletheia* as the opening; instead he turns to ideas, especially the *Idea of the Good,* for the being of entities, and thereby sets in motion the long process in Western Metaphysics which, with Nietzsche's *Will to Power,* culminates in the total oblivion of Being.

This criticism does not militate against the intimate relationship between Plato and Heidegger. For it is directed, not against the Plato which emerges from a careful analysis of the dialogue, but against the Plato of the Platonists who, with Heidegger, read Plato too literally and thereby make his thought not only incompatible with Heidegger's *Dasein* analytic, but with the spirit of the Socratic method as well.[10] The real test of how it stands with Plato and Heidegger is a pragmatic one. The crucial question to ask is this: What will happen if we view the dialogues from Heidegger's perspective and at the same time take their dramatic aspects into account? Does this approach justify itself if by its means it can be shown that numerous passages, and in some instances entire dialogues, which have plagued commentators make perfect sense, and that many of the so-called Platonic doctrines assume an astonishingly new appearance and significance? And if in addition it reveals that Plato frequently drops hints which suggest that he is aware of the deeper level on which Heidegger moves and which constitutes the natural development of his thought, can we then still reject this approach out of hand simply because it yields results which do not agree with the traditional interpretation? It may even happen that when read together these two thinkers are found to illuminate each other, inasmuch as Heidegger provides the ontological underpinnings for the views expressed in the dialogues, and that Plato, in turn, furnishes illustrations and thereby enriches the barren ontological structures of *Being and Time* and makes them more accessible. But their respective shortcomings will also come into focus. In fact, we will try to show that Plato, perhaps because of the restrictions imposed upon him through his use of the dialogue form as a medium, usually does not carry the inquiry as far as it should be. The dialogues, on their part, show that Heidegger misunderstands Plato, because he does not pay sufficient attention to their dramatic aspects. Had Heidegger become aware of the hints in the dialogues which point in the direction of his own inquiry, he could not have assigned to Plato the place which he did assign to him in his "Die Metaphysik als Geschichte des Seins." Furthermore, Heidegger's contention that the traditional substance ontology has held uninterrupted sway in Western metaphysics to this very day, encounters a stumbling block in Plato's dialogues. For the paradoxes of the *Lysis*, for instance, find their solution only in the recognition that a substance ontology is inadequate for a conception of the human mode of being. The tradition appears unbroken only on an excessively literal reading of the dialogues and a failure to see that for Plato the paradox is one of the most effective means of teaching by indirection.

Before we can enter into a fruitful discussion of the philosophy of these two thinkers, it will be essential that we familiarize ourselves in greater detail with their respective methods of inquiry. Only so can we hope to gain proper access to their thoughts. To this end, three steps will be required: (a) an interpretation of the Socratic method, which was intended for oral instruction; (b) a determination of the adaptation of the Socratic method to Plato's purposes, that is, to the composition of dialogues addressed to an unknown audience; (c) an inquiry into the relation between Plato's dialogues and the phenomenological approach.

A. *THE SOCRATIC METHOD*

Nothing seems to be better known than this method; for not only is it clearly illustrated in the "early dialogues," but Plato, through the mouth of Socrates, describes it explicitly in the *Apology* and the *Theaetetus*. This very sense of familiarity with the Socratic method, however, has made inquiry into its implications seem unnecessary. Often it is thought to be no more than Socrates' habit of interrogating one of his companions or whoever might be willing "to try a fall with (him) in argument."[11] To ask questions might have been sufficient for Socrates, who was in oral contact with his interlocutor; to produce the same stimulation of thought in a written dialogue, addressed to a wider audience, required a considerably more sophisticated mode of approach.

Many commentators fail to distinguish sufficiently between the two phases of the method as described by Socrates. According to the *Apology* (30–31), the method serves in the main to bring about an awareness of one's ignorance without which the desire to know enjoys a pseudosatisfaction and does not set inquiry in motion. This purely destructive phase of the Socratic method, which is symbolized by the gadfly, must, however, be followed by the more constructive phase described in the *Theaetetus* (149ff), for which the midwife serves as a symbol. This does not simply irritate, for it is applied to a mind which has overcome the stagnant, dogmatic stage and, like that of the young mathematician Theaetetus, is now eager to know and ready to offer suggestions for a possible solution of the problem at hand. To assist in the formulation, development, and critical examination of these ideas is the function of this second phase. In neither case does the teacher make a positive contribution but is dependent for suggestions on the intelligence of the student. In the first phase he endeavors to set this intelligence free, if it is bound by false beliefs; in the second he tries to prevent it from coming prematurely to a halt. So Socrates does not feign modesty when, speaking as a teacher, he claims that "the god compels [him] to be a midwife, but does not allow [him] to bring forth" (150C–D). Were he to present his own views, he would, because of his superiority, nip the efforts of the student in the bud. He would free him from a false or unduly narrow conception merely to bind him with another, albeit a more adequate one, and his intellectual midwifery would come to naught. [12]

B. *PLATO'S ADAPTATION OF THE SOCRATIC METHOD*

Without doing violence to his method, Socrates, through skillfully directed questions, might conceivably help the young man under his charge to reach a conclusion at least temporarily acceptable, and thus avoid a purely negative outcome of the discussion. But could Plato, the author of dialogues, avoid such an outcome and still preserve at least the spirit of the Socratic method? Simply to record the conversation which took place between Socrates and his disciple would be out of the question. While Socrates' partner to the discussion could be made to think his own thoughts, the reader of Plato's dialogues would do no more than follow the thought processes of another and find the conclusion ready-made at the end. Since Plato wanted to stimulate and direct thought by the written rather than the spoken word, he had to find means of adjusting the Socratic method to the new medium.

In order to achieve in writing what Socrates aimed at orally, Plato uses various dramatic devices, myths, paradoxes, logical fallacies and outright contradictions. Well known as this fact is, it is often not sufficiently taken into account by some Plato scholars when interpreting the dialogues. This is very odd, for the dialogues, as we shall see later, abound in difficulties and present insurmountable obstacles to a literal interpretation.

Plato himself makes it quite clear that we should read the dialogues critically and with great caution. In the *Theaetetus*, for instance, as in many other places, he has Socrates confess to his ignorance. "I am not at all wise," he is made to say, "nor have I anything to show which is the invention or birth of my own soul, but those who converse with me profit" (150D,J). So it is not primarily for the discovery of the views of either Socrates or Plato that we should go to the dialogues, but to be helped to formulate our own. Socrates' function is not to indoctrinate but to stimulate. "It is quite clear," he continues, "that they never learn anything from me; the many fine discoveries to which they cling are of their own making. But to me and the god they owe their delivery" (150D,J). To bring about this delivery, Socrates may express and even defend views which are meant to challenge the reader and which cannot even remotely be called his own. In the *Symposium*, Alcibiades points to the need of penetrating beneath the surface of Socrates' utterances. "His words," he says, "are like the images of Silenus which open; they are ridiculous when you first hear them." But the effort, he promises, is highly rewarding, for "he who opens the bust and sees what is within will find that they are the only words which have a meaning in them . . . abounding in fair images . . . and extending to the whole duty of a good and honourable man" (221E–222A). Alcibiades is intoxicated, but he has enjoined Socrates to object if he does not tell the truth and Socrates is significantly silent. In the *Republic*, Adeimantus suggests that Socrates often deceives his listeners, and that he who follows him uncritically is a fool. "When you talk in this way," he complains, "your hearers feel a certain misgiving: they think that because they are inexperienced in your method of question and answer, at each question the reasoning leads them a little farther astray, until at last these slight divergences amount to a serious error and they find themselves contradicting their original position. . . . They feel they are being cornered and reduced to silence, but that does not really prove them in the wrong" (6. 487 B–C). Socrates, it seems, does not hesitate to employ sophistry when it suits his purpose. It is, of course, the sophistry which the Stranger in the *Sophist* describes as of "noble lineage [he gennaia sophistike]" and which "within the art of education [constitutes] the examination confuting the vain conceit of wisdom" (231B). Often the one to be instructed must be shocked into thinking for himself. This is why Socrates, in the *Republic*, goes so far as to say that "reflection is provoked when perception yields a contradictory impression. . . . When there is no such contradiction, we are not encouraged to reflect" (7. 523B–C).

After so many warnings in so many of the dialogues, one might wonder how so much of what Socrates said could ever have been taken literally without any effort being made to penetrate to the deeper meaning of his words. This may in large part be due to the difficulty the reader encounters in resisting the magic spell of the author of the dialogues. It is a tribute to Plato's gifts as a dramatist that again and again, often against their own better judgment, interpreters are charmed into taking the characters of the dialogues as real persons of flesh and blood and the dialogues themselves as reports of meetings which actually took place. This attitude is visible in many subtle ways. It shows itself, for instance, in the form of excuses which are offered for Socrates' logical mistakes through the reminder that he was, after all, engaged in a live debate and arguing on his feet;[13] it is implied in the attempt to blame the inconclusiveness of a dialogue on the fact that the answer which Socrates could have given would have been misunderstood by his interlocutor and therefore was withheld;[14] it shines through the tendency to use the existence of serious, and to us obvious, logical errors in the dialogues as an indication of Plato's lack of logical acumen. In all these cases the question should rather be asked: Why did Plato make Socrates commit the error or withhold the answer, and what effect on the reader did he thereby intend to produce?

If the characters in the dialogues are taken as real, then the situation in turn may be regarded as historical rather than dramatic. The interpreter may then be bogged down with questions on which nothing vital depends. He may ask, for instance, why Euthyphro waited until 399 B.C. before prosecuting his father for a murder which could not have taken place after 404 B.C. He may wonder why Euthyphro's father did not consult his own son, who was a religious seer, instead of seeking advice from the diviners in Athens. He may be astonished to find Socrates engaged in a futile discussion with the stupid Euthyphro, "when we should expect to find him in conversation with Athenians who could assist him in his trial."[15] Or he may wonder what happened to Hippocrates, who contributes so much to the charm and liveliness of the early part of the *Protagoras,* for he vanishes without a trace as soon as the debate between Socrates and Protagoras gets under way. (Presumably because by this time the reader is supposed to have taken his place.) Or we might encounter a difficulty in Socrates' admission in the opening scene of the *Republic* that he went to the Piraeus not only to pray but also in order to watch the procession. Piety is compatible with the traditional character of Socrates, but curiosity is not. And we might then, with one commentator,[16] try to overcome the difficulty by attributing the curiosity to Glaucon, whom Socrates allegedly had to gratify in order to make him listen to his teaching. We might also take note of the fact that nothing is subsequently said of the dinner which Adeimantus had promised. Why was Socrates denied his evening meal, we might ask, and is it not in a way connected with his curiosity? "Is he being punished by others or by himself for an act of self-indulgence?"[17] It is true Plato cannot take the same liberties with Socrates that Sophocles takes with Creon, who appears as a different character in three different plays, namely, as liberal-minded in *Oedipus Rex,* as a stubborn old man in Antigone, and as an outright villain in *Oedipus Coloneus.* But neither is he bound to a rigid conception; one need only compare the otherworldly Socrates in the *Phaedo* with the fun-loving Socrates in the *Symposium.* There is no reason why Plato cannot suggest the many forces to which a man is exposed and between which he must often choose, by depicting Socrates as under the influence of curiosity and piety, the attraction of a promised meal and good conversation, the spectacle of a horse race with torches, the desire to return to Athens and the opposite desire to remain and please his friends. Once these various factors have played their part and helped to create that "mixture of compulsion and persuasion, of coercion and reason"[18] which gives rise to the problem of justice, they are cleared away to make room for others which serve different purposes. The conversation in the *Republic* could go on even while dinner was being served, and if Plato had wanted to suggest that Socrates was deprived of his evening meal, he could have done so easily enough. The recollection of things which he has decided to forget or leave in the background, useful as it may at times be, has to be handled with great caution, lest it become an interference with his manipulation of characters and events and turn into an attempt to improve on the skill of the artist which, in the case of Plato no less than in the case of Sophocles, is a presumptuous and foolish undertaking.

Plato's dramatic or indirect approach places a heavy burden on the reader. He knows that he is basically confronted with philosophy, although it appears in dramatic garb, and that he is expected to exercise his critical abilities. In fact the dramatic aspects of the dialogues have as one of their functions to keep him intellectually alert and to prevent him from following too readily the thought processes of Socrates. But since they are also intended to give direction to his thought after it has been stirred up, he must at the same time hold himself responsive to their promptings, know when to give up his resistance and to follow their lead. In the modern reader, the critical intelligence is likely to be developed, for that is the fashion of the time. Whether he possesses the sensitivity required to recognize a dramatic device and entrust himself to its direction—this is a more questionable assumption. Many of those who talk about Plato's dramatic approach to philosophy still sin in the direction of mistaking signs for goal posts, of taking for doctrines what are merely challenges or hints pointing beyond themselves, of being content with discovering fallacies without probing into their revealing functions, of noting the clash between opposed positions without becoming aware of the insight which emerges from the clash.

If the dramatic or indirect approach to philosophy causes such difficulty, and, as history has shown, leads so easily to misunderstandings, why should Plato have preferred it to an explicit exposition? The reason lies in his conception of understanding as a kind of seeing. And as you can only help a person see for himself, so you cannot make him understand. The difficulty of transmitting knowledge from one person to another is suggested in the *Symposium*. "How I wish," exclaims Socrates mockingly as he sits down beside a reputedly wise man, "that wisdom could be infused out of the fuller into the emptier man, as water runs through wool, out of the fulle cup into an emptier one" (175D–E). In the *Republic* the same thought is expressed, but now significantly by means of a light metaphor. "We must conclude," remarks Socrates, "that education is not what it is said to be by some, who profess to put knowledge into a soul which does not possess it, as if they could put sight into blind eyes" (7. 518D). The light metaphor is used in great detail when Socrates introduces the *Idea of the Good:*

You may have the power of vision in your eyes and try to use it, and colour may be there in the objects; but sight will see nothing and the colours will remain invisible in the absence of . . . the sun. . . . It was the sun, then, that I meant when I spoke of that offspring which the Good has created in the visible world, to stand there in the same relation to vision and visible things as that which the Good itself bears in the intelligible world to intelligence and to intelligible objects.[19]

From the analogy it becomes clear that Plato conceives truth as an event. It is the kind of event one experiences when catching the point of a joke, or discovering a proof, or suddenly understanding the motive for a mode of behavior which a moment ago appeared wholly incomprehensible. This is most clearly stated in the Seventh Letter, where Plato speaks of an insight which "suddenly, like a blaze kindled by a leaping spark, is generated in the soul and at once becomes self-sustaining" (341C–D).

C. THE RELATION OF PLATO'S DIALOGUES TO THE PHENOMENOLOGICAL APPROACH

For Heidegger, too, communication is an attempt to share a sight, a vision. Heidegger in fact reports that he had difficulties with some of Husserl's writings until he realized that "Husserl's teaching took place in the form of a step-by-step training in phenomenological seeing," and until Heidegger himself "practiced phenomenological seeing, teaching and learning. . . ."[20] And in the introduction to *On Time and Being* he advises the reader "not to listen to a series of propositions, but rather to follow the movement of showing."[21]

Demonstration in the sense of showing is very prominent in *Being and Time*. Heidegger, to mention but one example,[22] begins with the discussion of an ordinary tool or ready-to-hand, a hammer for instance. He has the reader imagine the tool broken or missing, and then points to the world or referential context which comes to view as the tool falls out of the referential context. The tool is now seen as a mere thing, or present-at-hand, while the world is found to consist of a series of "in-order-to" ending in a "for-the-sake-of," which is a purpose set up by an individual. An ordinary life situation is thus being lit up so that it reveals different modes of being, namely, ready-to-hand and present-at-hand, which are not usually distinguished in philosophical discussion, and world as a significant aspect of man, opening the way for further analysis.

Heidegger can, therefore, be said to agree with Plato that things are known to be true when they are lit up, when they become manifest by entering into the light. As indicated before, however, Heidegger carries his inquiry beyond that of Plato by speaking not only of the light but also of the clearing which is needed by the light if it is to illuminate things. This *going beyond* will be found to be the most significant characteristic of Heidegger's relation to Plato, and it will also be found that Plato, through seemingly casual remarks, frequently foreshadows Heidegger's more fundamental concerns.

Heidegger's phenomenological method, no less than Plato's dramatic approach, has led to many serious misunderstandings. His difficulties are not identical with those of Plato, but they spring from the same source, namely, the endeavor to make the reader see, rather than convince him through logical arguments. Since Heidegger deals with phenomena, or aspects of them, which are far removed from common sense, his problem is to find the proper words to serve his purpose. Everyday language becomes inadequate and still cannot be wholly dispensed with. Frequently he uses ordinary words, giving them a different meaning. *Care*, for instance, does not mean worry in his writing, but expresses the structure of the human mode of being. The familiar voice of *conscience* is not directed to specific acts, but calls upon an individual to take possession of himself. *Death* does not refer to that all too familiar event, but to the willingness to face death as an imminent possibility. Some words are used in their original meaning. *Existence*, for instance, derived from *ex-sistere*, to stand out, means projection rather than reality. At times he finds it necessary to coin new words, such as *Dasein*, for the human mode of being, *temporality*, to distinguish his more basic conception of time from the ordinary one; *historicality*, as distinguished from history, *fallenness* to express loss of selfhood, *thrownness* to indicate man's abandonment in the world and his dependence on things encountered in the world. Although Heidegger defines the various usages and meanings of the words in question, many a reader tends to forget, especially in the case of words with ordinary meanings. The common sense meaning intrudes itself, everything is thrown into confusion and the critic unwittingly finds himself fighting a straw man instead of Heidegger.

The chief cause of misunderstanding, however, especially of the later writings, is lack of patience on the part of the reader. When standing before a famous painting, or listening to a great poem, or reading about an advanced theory in mathematical physics, Heidegger warns in the introduction to *Time and Being*, one would not expect to grasp their meaning at once. And so in some of his writings too, he claims, one should have to abandon any claim to immediate intelligibility."[23] One is strongly reminded of the *Seventh Letter*, where Plato says that "acquaintance comes only after a long period of attendance on instruction in the subject itself and close companionship" (341C–D).

Finally, a difficulty must be mentioned which confronts both Plato and Heidegger, namely the circularity inherent in their mode of presentation. It is true of the dialogues as of any work of art that the design of the whole rests on the details, but it is also true that the details derive their meaning and significance from the design of the whole. The parts of a dramatic dialogue, therefore, cannot be properly understood and evaluated without some notion of the main insight at which its author aims; and yet the basic insight is accessible only by way of the parts. This inherent circularity of a dramatic dialogue precludes a formal, logical approach.[24] The reader can only hope that by holding himself open and susceptible to the influence which the dramatic skill of the author brings to bear on him, the insight will somehow occur and the truth will dawn upon his mind, truth being understood as an event in the sense described above. Once some kind of insight has been gained, then testing and verification can take place. For if the insight is genuine, it will bring into focus the various phases of the dialogue, including some of the byplay which is often left out of account as unphilosophical. The reader must, therefore, be on the alert and ready to search out the truth which may lie hidden behind myth or allegory, formal demonstration, and even fallacy and paradox. Above all, he must not mitigate, but rather sharpen, the conflict between opposing views, in the hope that if they are struck together like steel and flint, they might emit a spark of truth which can be nurtured until it bursts into flame.

Heidegger's investigation also moves in a circle. His basic aim is to seek out the meaning of Being in general. To this end he inquires into the specifically human mode of being. But only when Being in general is known can the human mode be fully understood. Thus that which is to be proved and that on which the proof is based are dependent on each other. In logic such a proof is said to move in a "vicious circle." Heidegger does not deny the circularity, but insists that it is not a "vicious" circle. "We cannot 'avoid' a 'circular' proof in the existential analytic," he contends, "because such an analytic does not do *any* proving *at all* by the rules of the 'logic of consistency' " (363). We do in fact have an understanding of Being, he says; otherwise entities could not become manifest to us. But this understanding is vague and unconceptualized. So the proof which is needed is not one which lays down an axion from which a sequence of propositions is deductively derived; it is rather one which proceeds from the implicit to the explicit, from the vaguely known to the clearly conceptualized. In this sense, his whole enterprise can be said to be circular. "For the whole question of Being," according to Heidegger, "is nothing other than the radicalization of an essential tendency-of-Being which belongs to Dasein itself—the pre-ontological understanding of Being" (35).

It would hardly seem necessary to point out that Plato too must presuppose a vague understanding of whatever he is trying to convey. Otherwise his various dramatic devices, that is, the paradoxes, extremes, contradictions, would be of no avail, for they can only hint at but not impart the truth. But while the circularity is implicit in the dialogues, in *Being and Time* it is made explicit; it is shown to be not only unavoidable but fully justified, in fact demanded by the subject matter at hand.

A brief explanation may be appropriate, giving the reasons for the selection of particular dialogues and their arrangement in a specific order.

The most crucial problem a man faces is the choice and the preservation of genuine selfhood. It is this problem which gets the citizen involved in the conflict between obedience to the law and the assumption of personal responsibility, both of which are necessary characteristics of good citizenship. This conflict is presented in paradoxical form in the *Crito*. A similar paradox confronts the pious man in the *Euthyphro*. How can he do the will of the gods and still make his own decisions as to what is right and wrong? These conflicts, however, could not arise if a man were incapable of taking charge of himself. The distinction between authentic and inauthentic selfhood is introduced in the *Lesser Hippias* under the guise of the voluntary evildoer who, paradoxically, is declared to be better than the one who does evil involuntarily. The second-best method in the *Phaedo*, on Socrates' own admission, does not yield certainty, based as it is on tentative hypotheses. And yet the final proof for the immortality of the soul speaks of insight into essences and necessary connections, as if certainty were possible. Is Plato warning the reader not to yield to the tendency of regarding arguments which support strongly felt desires as fully convincing, to regard a reasonable faith, freely adopted, as firmly established dogma, to let an authentic faith slip into inauthenticity? Of all the dialogues, the *Protagoras* and the *Republic* are perhaps the most challenging to the present inquiry, and to omit them would smack of an attempt at evasion, for both contain doctrines which seem wholly irreconcilable with genuine selfhood. In the first we find Socrates advocating an ethical determinism through his insistence that "no man willingly pursues evil," and the ideal city envisioned in the second would despoil its citizens of all responsibility, with the exception of one or a few rulers. And finally, the trilogy on love and friendship, constituted by the *Lysis*, the *Symposium*, and the *Phaedrus*, presents a variety of pitfalls encountered in interpersonal relations. They are half concealed and half revealed in the paradoxes which Socrates creates out of the clash between an appropriate and an inappropriate conception of man in the *Lysis*, excessive materialism and excessive spiritualism in the *Symposium*, exclusive self-regard and overindulgent devotion to others in the *Phaedrus*.

It is generally recognized that Plato does not supply the reader with ready-made answers. At best he helps him find the answer for himself through appropriately placed hints. Now if we look at the dialogues from the perspective of Heidegger's philosophy, we find that the inquiry does not come to rest, even if we have managed to resolve the paradoxes. For there is always a deeper level which calls for further exploration. And to our astonishment we discover that Plato throws out hints which unmistakably point in the direction of this deeper level on which Heidegger's philosophy moves. Because of the place which Heidegger assigns to Plato in his "Metaphysik als Geschichte des Seins," we must conclude that he was not aware of these hints. Be that as it may, the fact remains that in all the dialogues here considered, Heidegger takes up the problem where Plato leaves it and carries it a significant step farther. At the end of the *Crito*, for instance, it might be asked: Why should a man assume an irksome responsibility when he has the choice of simply and comfortably following the dictates of the law? Heidegger answers this question through an original analysis of the "call of conscience." Euthyphro is said to be a theologian, but we are never told what theology really is. Heidegger makes up for this deficiency through a discussion of theology in its relation to philosophy in general and phenomenology in particular. Heidegger's *Dasein* analytic makes it clear in what sense Socrates, in the *Lesser Hippias*, can regard the voluntary better than the involuntary evildoer, although the former may rightly be subjected to severe punishment, while the latter may not. If we are to heed Socrates' advice in the *Phaedo* not to allow our faith to become dogmatic or inauthentic, we must first be made aware of the possibility of authenticity, especially since, as Heidegger maintains, we are all initially inauthentic. Plato lets us witness the dying of Socrates; Heidegger shows how this experience evokes anxiety which, if we open up to it and do not convert it into fear, uncovers our genuine self and thus offers us the choice of taking hold of it or letting it slip back into the old disguises. Socrates' warning in the *Protagoras* against the threat to selfhood in too rigid and uncritical adherence to a tradition, presupposes an answer to the question of how a tradition which is past can affect the present and the future. Heidegger solves the problem by introducing his notion of historicality, which is really temporality, a more basic notion than the conventional conception of time. Temporality, in turn, leads to transcendence, which plays a vital part in Socrates' establishment of the *Idea of the Good* in the *Republic* and underlies the discussions in the Trilogy. It is a movement from *what is* to *what might be*, i.e., from *what is* to *what is not*. And so in the end it becomes necessary to ask the bewildering and, it seems, logically impossible question: What is this *Nothing* and what role does it play in man's awareness of himself? A preliminary answer to this question is given in Heidegger's *What is Metaphysics?* The search for a fuller understanding has occupied Heidegger to the very end of his life.

Before beginning the actual discussion, it might be well to issue a word of warning against excessive expectations, that is, against the hope of arriving at a definite conception of selfhood. That Plato's dialogues never reach a final conclusion is a fact too well known to require confirmation. Furthermore, Heidegger has shown and Plato has repeatedly suggested that man is essentially potentiality and therefore cannot be assigned a definite nature, possessed of fixed qualities. It is true that Heidegger devotes his early work *Being and Time* to an analysis of the human mode of Being, and it is to this work that our inquiry will in the main restrict itself. But as he himself said in a letter which appears in

William J. Richardson's *Heidegger: Through Phenomenology to Thought*, his early work can be fully understood only in the light of the later writings, and these in turn presuppose a careful reading of the early ones. Now in the later writings the emphasis has shifted from the being of man to Being as such.[25] Being, he says, needs man to manifest itself, and man on his part does not come into his essence until he is "appropriated" by Being. At the end of his life, Heidegger was still on the way in his quest for the meaning of Being. As long as the goal which he set up lies in the future, a fully realized conception of man is not possible.

NOTES

1. John Herman Randall, Jr., *Plato: Dramatist of the Life of Reason* (New York: Columbia University Press), pp. 16–17.

2. Gerhard Krüger, *Einsicht und Leidenschaft*. 3rd ed. (Frankfurt am Main: Vittorio Klostermann, 1963), pp. x–xv111.

3. Martin Heidegger, "Die Metaphysik als Geschichte des Seins," in *Nietzsche*, vol. 2, 2nd ed. (Pfullinger: Neske, 1961), pp. 399–437.

4. Martin Heidegger, "My Way to Phenomenology," in *On Time and Being*, trans. Joan Stambough (New York: Harper & Row, 1972), p. 78.

5. Ibid. p. 79.

6. Unless otherwise indicated, quotations from Plato's dialogues refer to the translations in *The Collected Dialogues of Plato*, ed. Edith Hamilton and Huntington Cairns, Bollingen Series 71 (Princeton, N.J.: Princeton University Press, 1971).

7. Martin Heidegger, *Being and Time*, trans. John Macquarrie and Edward Robinson (New York: Harper & Row, 1962). Unless otherwise indicated, quotations from Heidegger's works refer to this edition.

8. Martin Heidegger, "The End of Philosophy and the Task of Thinking," in *On Time and Being*, p. 69.

9. Ibid. p. 67.

10. For the same reason, commentators who are said to be close to Heidegger were not helpful. Hans-Georg Gadamer *(Platos dialektische Ethik und andere Studien zur platonischen Philosophie* [Hamburg: Felix Meiner Verlag, 1968]) gives a detailed analysis only of one dialogue, the *Philebus*, which is not included in the present investigation; Gerhard Krüger *(Einsicht und Leidenschaft*, dritte durchgesehene Auflag [Frankfurt am Main, 1968]) deals only with the *Symposium;* Hartmut Buchner *(Eros and Sein* [Bonn: H. Bouvier & Co., 1965]) restricts himself to a small portion of the *Symposium*, 199c–212c3. It is true, these authors make extended references to other dialogues. But this is a risky procedure when interpreting a dramatic dialogue where the meaning of a passage frequently emerges from a clash of ideas rather than an explicit statement. The same can be said of Jacob Klein *(A Commentary on Plato's "Meno."* [Chapel Hill: N.C.: University of North Carolina Press, 1965]). He favors the dramatic approach but gives it more of an historical and philological emphasis. Typical examples of this can be found on pp. 40 and 44. All this is not meant to deny the fact that these authors make significant contributions to an understanding of Plato and that their books are well worth reading. More will be said about them in notes at appropriate places.

11. *Theaetetus* 169B,J.

12. Gilbert Ryle acknowledges only the destructive phase: "the rule-governed con-catenation of questions, answerable by 'yes' or 'no,' which are intended to drive the answerer into self-contradiction . . . this is what should be meant by 'the Socratic Method' " (p. 199). This restriction causes him to see inconsistencies in the *Theaetetus*. "Here," he says, "Plato seems to be sitting on the fence. He is representing Socratic dialectic as being at one and the same time elenctic and solution-hunting, as thesis-demolishing and thesis-establishing. . . . Nor does the modest Theaetetus display 'conceit of knowledge' requiring for his soul's good Socratic puncturing." *Plato's Progress* (Cambridge: Cambridge University Press, 1966), pp. 120–21. Socrates does not give an exposition of the "Socratic Method" either in the *Apology* or in the *Theaetetus*. He uses one phase of it or the other, in accordance with the demands of the dramatic situation. In the *Apology*, he sees his exposure of the ignorance of some of his fellow-citizens as the reason for the hostility against him; in the *Theaetetus* he helps a young man form a clearer conception of a problem which had occupied his mind and thus leads him in the direction of the solution of the problem.

13. Cf. Plato's *Protagoras*, ed. with an Introduction by Gregory Vlastos (New York: Liberal Arts Press, 1956), p. xxxvi.

14. Cf. Paul Friedländer: "And when there is no reply to the question by Socrates, 'What, then, is the chief thing among the many and beautiful things that the gods do?' we may surmise that Plato's Socrates would have replied: 'the good.' We also know that this good for him occupies the highest place and that in the presence of Euthyphro it cannot be discussed without being misunderstood and desecrated." *Plato*, vol. 2 (New York: Random House, 1964), p. 89.

15. Frederick Rosen, "Piety and Justice: Plato's Euthyphro, *Philosophy: Journal of the Royal Institute of Philosophy*, vol. 43, no. 164 (1968): 105–116.

16. Leo Strauss, *The City of Man* (Chicago: Rand McNally & Co., 1964), p. 65.

17. Ibid., p. 64.

18. Ibid.

19. Cf. also: "Nous meant to the Greek 'intellectual vision,' and the verbs associated with it, like *theorein*, or *eidenai*, are sight words, conveying the flavor of 'seeing' something. The function of *nous* is to lead to theoria, the kind of aesthetic spectacle properly beheld in a 'theatre,' the natural abode of theoria. Ultimately, when Greek culture became very much aware of its central aims, as in Plato, the function of nous was seen as leading to a beholding of human life in the world as a transparently intelligible dramatic spectacle. It is such an *aesthetic nous* that Aristotle is trying to bend to his own purposes, more scientific if in the end no less ultimately aesthetic." John Herman Randall, Jr., *Aristotle* (New York: Columbia University Press, 1960), p. 90, note 13.

20. Martin Heidegger, "My Way to Phenomenology," in *On Time and Being*, p. 78.

21. *On Time and Being*, p. 2.

22. *Being and Time*, p. 102.

23. *On Time and Being*, p. 1.

24. Sartre acknowledges a similar circularity when he speaks of a "totalizing investigation" and refers to a "heuristic principle 'to search the whole in the parts' " (p. 28). He commends Karl Marx, of whom he reports that "if he subordinates anecdotal facts to the totality (of a movement, of an attitude), he also seeks to discover the totality by means of fact" (pp. 25–26). Jean-Paul Sartre, *Search for a Method*, trans. Hazel E. Barnes (New York: Alfred A. Knopf, 1963).

25. "J. Man sagt, Sie hätten Ihren Standpunkt gewechselt. F. Ich habe einen

Standpunkt verlassen, nicht um dagegen einen andern einzutauschen, sondern weil auch der vormalige Standpunkt nur ein Aufenthalt war in einem Unterwegs. Das Bleibende im Denken ist der Weg. Und Denkwege bergen in sich das Geheimnisvolle, dass wir sie vorwärts und rückwärts gehen koennen, dass sogar der Weg zurück uns erst vorwärts führt." "Aus einem Gespräch von der Sprache zwischen einem Japaner und einem Fragenden," in Martin Heidegger, *Unterwegs zur Sprache,* 3rd ed. (Pfullingen: Neske, 1965), pp. 98–99.

Plato and Heidegger

1

Crito: The Paradox of Civic Virtue and the Call of Conscience

Plato always begins with a concrete situation: Socrates debating with visiting Sophists, such as Hippias or Protagoras; meeting friends at a religious festival and accepting an invitation for supper and discussion; talking to the boy Lysis in a palaestra; attending a banquet to celebrate the victory of a young playwright; taking a walk into the countryside with his friend Phaedrus; meeting the theologian Euthyphro on his way to court to answer an indictment; discussing with his friend Crito whether he should or should not run away; conversing with his companions on the day of his death until it is time to drink the hemlock. Man's world as it is lived soon recedes into the background and a philosophical problem comes to the fore. Unlike Descartes, however, Plato never cuts himself loose from the world. It is true, Descartes also starts with ordinary experience: the sight of a piece of wax before and after it has been subjected to heat, an individual who doubts. But at the end, the physical world has been reduced to pure extension, and man is essentially no more than a thing-which-thinks. To break out of this self-encapsulation, Descartes must call upon the goodness and veracity of God. Plato, by contrast, proceeds as if he were heeding Heidegger's warning that "Being-in-the-world is a unitary phenomenon . . . which must be seen as a whole. . . . But while it can not be broken up into contents which may be pieced together, this does not prevent it from having several constituent items in its structure" (78). These items can be described and analyzed separately, provided their connection with each other is always kept in mind.

Heidegger does not set out from as rich a life situation as Plato. He does not, for instance, show us the craftsman at work. But he does begin with the tool or ready-to-hand which the craftsman uses. He points to its dependence on the material out of which it is made and on nature which supplies the material, to its relationship to other tools, to the object it is to produce, and to the user of the

29

object. Thus he shows man to be enmeshed in an intricate web of relationships. Sometimes he starts with a traditional philosophical position, not in order to lead it to a more abstract one, but to root it in a more fundamental experience. Thus he shows, for instance, that the correspondence theory of truth presupposes *aletheia* or unconcealment; or he grounds history in historicality, time in temporality. Anxiety and conscience, it is true, call man back from his lostness in the world, but merely in order to let him reenter it more authentically.

Plato's *Crito* offers a relatively simple, but very effective, illustration of Plato's starting point, of his particular use of the Socratic method, and also of the way in which he points beyond his own position toward further questions for which Heidegger is found to seek the answer.

The dialogue can be said to move on three levels. The first deals with a purely personal problem: Should Socrates, whom the Athenians have condemned to death, try to escape or should he stay and face execution? Does he owe it to his friends, his wife, and especially to his children, that he should make every effort to survive? Or does his mission demand that he submit to the sentence, although it is clearly unjust? Before long, Socrates raises the more general, the philosophical, question: How can a good citizen be both responsible and law-abiding? Cities can not exist without laws, but blind obedience to the laws means to shirk personal responsibility. Finally we are confronted with an ontological problem: How must man be constituted so as to be capable of assuming responsibility?

Plato does not provide a direct answer to the problem posed by the paradoxical nature of good citizenship. He does not even state the paradox explicitly. Instead, he has Socrates move from one extreme to the other, from the exclusive appeal to personal responsibility to the demand for total submission to the dictates of the law. Then he helps the reader resolve the paradox by offering a number of hints. But not all of these hints are reliable; in fact only one of them is. To the ontological aspect of the problem he devotes only a few casual remarks. For a fuller treatment of it we must turn to Heidegger.

I

The perfunctory reader of the *Crito* is likely to conclude that the dialogue contains nothing more than a description of an episode in the life of Socrates and thereby fail to experience its real impact. To him Socrates seems to be plying his usual trade, asking questions and subjecting the answers he receives to the test of logical analysis.

In this manner the two friends determine the effects which Socrates' escape or death is likely to have. Crito's objection to Socrates' resolve to remain and die rather than escape are easily overcome early in the dialogue, and from then on there is no serious conflict of ideas or minds. Crito is no match for his friend's intellectual acumen or for his eloquence, and as the discussion progresses Socrates' speeches grow longer and longer, while Crito's share in the conversation reduces itself to a few words expressing assent. In fact Socrates is, and has been from the beginning, beyond argument. "This, dear Crito," he says at the end, "is the voice which I seem to hear murmuring in my ears, like the sound of the flute in the ears of the mystic; that voice I say, is humming in my ears, and prevents me from hearing any other. And I know that anything more you may say will be in vain. Yet speak, if you have anything to say. . . ." "I have nothing more to say," replies Crito (54D).[1]

Beneath the surface of this beautiful picture of calm deliberation in the face of death and the agreement of two minds on this fatal issue, the intellectual traps are scarcely concealed. But in order to discover them we must come to the realization that it is not so much Socrates talking to Crito as it is Plato who, through Socrates and Crito, addresses and challenges the reader.

The dialogue presents a vital problem in a concrete setting. Socrates is in jail, awaiting the return of the sacred ship from Delos, upon the arrival of which he is to die. Crito has gone to the house of detention at the break of dawn to inform his friend that the ship has been sighted and that the fatal hour draws desperately near. He finds him fast asleep, utterly unconcerned about his impending death. When Socrates awakes, Crito urges upon him the need to reach a final decision. He informs him that arrangements for his escape have been made and assures him that he need not worry about the financial cost of engineering the escape. His own ample fortune and that of others are at his disposal; and if he fears that his flight will cause trouble with the authorities and lead to fines and confiscation of property, and perhaps even banishment, he can accept the help of his foreign friends whom the city cannot touch. Crito's acquaintances in Thessaly will be only too glad to give him refuge and protection. Socrates, he continues, owes it to himself to save his life, as well as to his children, for whose upbringing and education he is responsible, while by dying he will merely play into the hands of his enemies who are intent upon his destruction. The whole affair, he complains, is a disgrace to all those involved in it; the case should never have been allowed to come before the courts, the trial itself was poorly managed, and now to refuse to avoid the fatal outcome when it can be so easily forestalled would be a crowning folly.

Crito manifestly has his friend's best interests at heart. But a good will may be mistaken and promote the wrong cause. So Socrates appropriately issues a warning. "Dear Crito," he says, "your zeal is invaluable, if a right one; but if wrong, the greater the zeal the greater the danger" (46B). The will alone, no less than strong feelings or impulses, no matter what their source, are treacherous guides, and it is therefore not surprising that Socrates, the paragon of virtue and wisdom, should appeal to reason:

between clan and polis, which, according to some modern commentators, is said to be the main theme of Sophocles' *Antigone*. But now we see oursleves faced with a much more acute conflict, a rift within the very core of the idea of civic virtue. For Socrates has surreptitiously changed the conflict from one between family and state to one between reason and responsibility on the one side, and obedience to law on the other. Not everyone is so devoutly attached to clan or family that he feels compelled to place himself in opposition to the state. This new strife, however, leaves no one untouched. The behavior of every citizen tends in fact to fluctuate between the two poles mentioned, and recent history has shown how easy it is to yield to one at the expense of the other, that is, to insist on the correctness and infallibility of one's own judgment and refuse compromise, or to submit blindly to the will of a leader.[2]

Leading us by turns into seemingly contradictory and equally unacceptable positions, Plato has succeeded in shocking our thought processes into action. At this stage it becomes necessary to search out the hints by means of which he gives them direction. In the spirit of the Socratic method, these too must be used with caution. They may be a trap, instead of a way out of the difficulty. Thus, for example, under the pretext of mitigating their harshness, Socrates quotes the imaginary laws as saying:

> We further proclaim to any Athenian by the liberty which we allow him, that if he does not like us when he has become of age and has seen the ways of the city, and made our acquaintance, he may go where he pleases and take his goods with him. (51D)

Although he has just pointed out the dependence of the individual on the state, the deep roots which tie him to his native city, Socrates now speaks in the name of the laws as if the individual could simply be transplanted from one country to another. One can imagine the benefits conferred upon one of the great Athenian tragedians by being allowed to emigrate to a barbarian country and take his talents with him. Granted that in some instances leaving the city might constitue the lesser of two evils, for Socrates, as he himself maintains a few paragraphs later in the dialogue,[3] and as he emphatically declared during the trial,[4] it would be worse than death. Hence permission to leave the city, in many cases, would not provide an acceptable alternative to blind submission.

A hint may contain a partial truth and still not advance the main issue, such as the following:

> But he who has experience of the manner in which we order justice and administer the state, and still remains, has *entered* into an implied contract that he will do as we command him. (51E)

If we take the meaning of the term *contract* without qualification, then we must say that a man can never enter into such a contract without forfeiting his status as a moral being. For to bind himself in advance to obedience, without knowing the effects such obedience will or is likely to have in the concrete situation, is to consent implicitly to the most heinous crime. For even the best of laws may, in its application, inflict serious harm on an innocent individual.

There is, however, a limited area in which a contract is possible. Since we are all sorry judges when our own interests are at stake, the members of a community may agree to have the accused judged by his peers. The evidence used to determine guilt or innocence will, of course, be circumstantial and the resulting sentence will rest on probability only. For to say that the accused had a motive, that his footprints matched those found at the scene of the crime, etc., merely means that on the assumption of his guilt all these facts fall into a coherent pattern. The testimony of a witness may be based on mistaken identity, and even confessions can be false. So at best it can be concluded that if the accused is not guilty, then we are faced with a very unusual coincidence of circumstances. But if sentences are based on various degrees of probability, then from time to time an innocent individual will be convicted. Since there is no alternative to the use of circumstantial evidence, we must, in the interest of the security of the community, be willing to run that risk. We cannot, however, in fairness agree to this "manner of ordering justice" and then withdraw from the agreement when we are the accused. If, therefore, as in the case of Socrates, "the state has injured us and given us an unjust sentence" (50C), *that fact alone,* in any event, is not sufficient to justify our escape; and if we nevertheless run away, we will have broken the agreement. But even then we would not be bound absolutely, for breaking the agreement might still, under certain circumstances, be the lesser of two evils and hence the proper object of choice.

Finally, we may encounter a suggestion which contains the germs of a possible solution, as for example the following:

> We [the laws] do not impose [our commands] rudely, but give him the alternative of obeying or convincing us. . . . (52A)

At first glance, this hint seems to create a problem instead of suggesting a solution. The laws we are familiar with can be obeyed or disobeyed. But what is the nature of the laws with which Socrates imagines himself in conversation and which, as an alternative to being obeyed, must be convinced? Are we to regard them as standing for the lawgivers or those who administer the laws? Then the suggestion would refer to an option open to Socrates in the past, when he was on trial, but not now in jail, at the moment when he has to make a decision. Furthermore, Socrates might have justice on his side and still fail to convince the lawgivers or administrators. Should he then turn against justice and obey in the face of injustice?

We frequently speak of "convincing reason," and if Socrates says that the laws ought to be "convinced," is he intimating a close relationship between reason and law? Now it is true that reason, in its quest for justice aims at the "just right" or "mean" in the concrete situation. In order to achieve it, it would, ideally speaking, have to consider all the relevant factors, determine all possible consequences of the contemplated act, and to assign to each factor and to each consequence its correct value. But does not the law or the legislator making the law have the same ideal objective? Thus ideal reason and ideal law have the same function and to that extent can be considered identical, and to *convince* the law would be the same as to *convince* reason.[5] The ideally wise man would need no law; his reason would be sufficient as a guide. And the ideal law would need no correction and could be relied upon to prescribe the right course of action. Real laws, however, and reason as found in an actual individual fall short of perfection and of their ideal goals. Reason may be hampered in its operation by self-interest and prejudice, and strong desires may overpower it instead of being subject to its control. Impartial laws will therefore have to be instituted to exercise the necessary restraints upon the selfish impulses of individuals.[6] Legislators, however, cannot foresee all future contingencies, and the laws they promulgate tend to become rigid and often will be at odds with the continually changing situations to which they are meant to apply.[7] They may work an injustice in their application and thereby produce results which are the very opposite of what the lawgiver intended. And so when reason recognizes that the distance between what the law aims at and what it achieves under certain circumstances is too great, the individual not only may, but ought to, suspend the enforcement of the law and act according to the dictates of his reason.[8] But this suspension should not be undertaken lightly, for every violation of a law is harmful since it tends to undermine the order without which a community cannot exist. A measure of injustice must be accepted, and the intelligent man is under obligation to curb his desire for the most rational solution possible and admit an irrational element into his calculation. If Socrates, therefore, is able to convince the imaginary laws or unprejudiced reason that setting aside the judgment of the Athenians is the lesser evil, then he has a right to run away. Socrates, however, feels that the injustice he suffers is not enough to warrant such a drastic step. And since he feels he cannot *convince* the laws, he is morally bound to accept the other alternative, namely to *obey* them.[9]

Thus the two extremes, that is, of unqualified individual responsibility and unconditional surrender to law, have been avoided, while the truth which they contain has been preserved. On the one hand, the radical freedom of the individual which Socrates advocated at the beginning of his argument has been curbed, because the sheer brute fact that a law exists must be included among the factors to be considered when reaching a decision and given considerable weight. On the other hand, the law no longer calls for unquestioning obedience, as stated in Socrates' conclusion, for its weight is to a large extent determined by its relation to other factors relevant to the situation.

It is obvious that the dialogue does not yield a rule which can serve as a guide for the solution of moral problems. Nor will we ever find the expert to which Socrates pretends to refer when he urges that we follow "not the opinion of the many but of the one who has understanding" (47D). For no one can tell him who has to make a decision how great a value he is willing to attach to his life, his family, or his country. Far from facilitating the quest for the correct answer and the right decision, the analysis of the dialogue has made the task appear more difficult; and Crito's simple plea addressed to Socrates that he should save his life while time permits has turned into a problem so complex that no certain answer is possible. Nor is the discussion concerned with abstract ideas of interest only to the intellectual. For the impulse of the family to protect its members at all cost, of the ruler to have his will, and even of reason to accept nothing but what is rational—these are real forces which tend to confuse moral judgments and obstruct justice. But he who allows himself to suffer the therapeutic effects of the Socratic method as employed in the *Crito* has gained a keener awareness of what is involved in a moral decision. And while he may have lost a false sense of security, he has gained in human dignity, for he has given himself a better chance of reaching decisions which are genuinely his own and for which he can assume full responsibility.

II

Both the personal problem of Socrates—whether he should or should not run away—which gave rise to the discussion, and the development of the paradoxical nature of virtue which occupies the main body of the dialogue, presuppose that man is capable of assuming responsibility for his behavior. Can the assumption of responsibility be simply taken for granted, or should it not also be subject to philosophical analysis? What, if anything, does Plato have to say in answer to these questions?

Plato hints at the direction such an inquiry might take through the image of the sleeping Socrates. When Socrates awakens, the following exchange takes place:

> Crito: I have been watching with amazement your peaceful slum-
> bers. . . . I have always thought you to be of a happy disposition;
> but never did I see anything like the easy, tranquil manner in
> which you bear this calamity.

Socrates: Why, Crito, when a man has reached my age he ought not to be repining at the approach of death.
Crito: Yet other old men find themselves in similar misfortunes, and age does not prevent them from repining. . . . (43B–c)

We are not so much told as shown that Socrates will not allow fear of death to divert him from his chosen course. And so when the objection is raised that if we refuse to do their bidding "the many will kill us" (48B), Socrates replies that "not life but the good life is to be chiefly valued" (Ibid.). Such a man will always have death as an alternative to any course of action that someone may try to force on him, and therefore never loses his freedom of choice.

Uncontrolled emotions are not the only threat to a man's authenticity, that is, to his ability to make genuine moral decisions. A very common one is illustrated by Crito's plea, urging his friend to run away while there still is time:

Oh! my beloved Socrates, let me entreat you once more to take my advice and escape. For if you die I shall not only lose a friend who can never be replaced, but there is another evil: people who do not know you and me will believe that I might have saved you if I had been willing to give money, but that I did not care. Now, can there be a *worse disgrace* than this—that I should be *thought* to value money more than the life of a friend? For the many will not be persuaded that I wanted you to escape, and that you refused. (44B–C) (Italics added.)

Obviously worse than the mere appearance which Crito fears would be the actual disposition to shun the expense of saving a friend's life. The reader familiar with Heidegger is reminded of *das Man* or the "they-self." It is a mode of existence in which the individual allows the anonymous group to fashion his opinions and determine his actions. The dialogue does not contain anything like the carefully worked out description found in Heidegger's *Being and Time*. But Plato does point to the chief characteristic of "the many," *(hoi polloi)* who lack both resolve and understanding, who drift and operate in the dark. "They would be as ready," Socrates remarks contemptuously, "to restore people to life, if they were able, as they are to put them to death—and with as little reason" (48C).

It is well known, of course, that powerful emotions often override a man's better judgment and that many find peer pressure irresistible. But few will take the trouble to ask what makes such surrender possible. The next exchange between the two friends allows a brief insight into Plato's thoughts on the matter:

Socrates: Why, my dear Crito, should we care about the opinion of the many? . . .
Crito: But you see, Socrates, that the opinion of the many must be regarded, for what is now happening shows that they can do the greatest evil to anyone who has lost their good opinion.

Socrates: I only wish it were so Crito, and that the many could do the greatest
          evil; for then they would also be able to do the greatest good—and
          what a fine thing that would be! But in reality they can do neither
          . . . and whatever they do is the result of chance. (44C–D)

At first glance, Socrates' reply to Crito appears paradoxical if not downright
absurd. One would expect him to wish that the many could do good. Instead he
wishes the opposite, and furthermore argues as if doing good in some way
depended on doing evil. Is not the good man simply the one who does good
deeds and the bad man the one who does evil? With Socrates' reply to Crito, the
distinction between the good and the bad man seems to become blurred if not
altogether obliterated. It requires little reflection, however, to come to understand that if the many could perform a genuinely evil act, that is, an act for
which they could be held accountable, then that act would have to spring from a
free choice. They would be blameworthy because they chose the evil, although
the good was accessible to them. Conversely, those who do a morally good deed
become praiseworthy because they chose the good although they might have
chosen the evil. Thus the good men and the evil are united in their capacity for
doing either good or evil. It is this capacity which makes both moral, be it
morally good or morally evil. The unthinking many are neither; they are amoral.
In Heidegger's terms, they are inauthentic, because their acts, and ultimately
their selves, are not their own. So we get a distinction on a deeper level, namely
between authenticity and inauthenticity. And only after a man has become
authentic, that is, after he has freed himself from inner and outer pressures, can
we speak of him as morally good or morally evil. In a sense, therefore, it is true
to say that the unthinking many are inferior to the morally evil man, for they are
inauthentic while he is authentic. Socrates' wish that the many could do the
greatest evil appears paradoxical only if we refuse to follow Socrates as he moves
from the level of morality to the underlying conditions for its possibility.[10]

III

Crito and Socrates are intimate friends. But despite Crito's closeness to an
obviously authentic human being, Plato portrays him as inauthentic, that is
under the dominance of the "many," of what Heidegger calls "das Man," the
"they-self." Authenticity and inauthenticity are not specifically named in the
dialogues, but they often underlie a discussion and are the key to its meaning.
Listening to Socrates, however, has done Crito little good in this respect. Is
Plato merely reporting an historical fact, or is he trying to convey something of
the nature of authenticity and its opposite? In view of the dramatic character of
the dialogue, the latter is the more likely alternative. Plato might well have

agreed with Heidegger's observation that initially we are all inauthentic, for in our early years all important decisions are made for us. But if a man has never experienced authenticity, how can he become aware of it? And if he lacks awareness, teaching and learning it seem impossible, whether we believe with Plato that all learning is a kind of recollection or with Heidegger that teaching succeeds only in making explicit what is already implicitly known.

Heidegger seeks a solution to this problem through an analysis of the "call of conscience." Conscience, he says, calls the self back from its lostness in the world and presents it with the possibility of authentic selfhood. At first glance, this undertaking seems very odd indeed, especially as long as we think of conscience as ordinarily understood. Before we can evaluate it, we must listen to his reasons and try to see conscience as he sees it.

He begins by carefully observing the phenomenal facts of the case. The call is a form of discourse, and though it is without vocal utterance, it reaches the individual, or *Dasein,* unfalteringly. Conscience gives no information, allows no debate, does not tell a man specifically what to do in a concrete situation. But by appealing to the individual without regard to his profession, his social status, his achievement, all those things which relate him to his fellowmen, it brings the individual back to himself from his lostness in the "they-self":

> The sort of Dasein which is understood after the manner of the world both for Others and for itself, gets *passed over* in this appeal; this is something of which the call to the Self takes not the slightest cognizance. And because the Self of the they-self gets appealed to and brought to hear, the "they" collapses. But the fact that the call *passes over* both the "they" and the manner in which Dasein has been publicly interpreted, does not by any means signify that the "they" is not *reached too*. Precisely *in passing over* the "they" (keen as it is for public repute) the call pushes it into insignificance (Bedeutungslosigheit). But the Self, which the appeal has robbed of its lodgement and hiding-place, gets brought back to itself by the call. (317)[11]

What remains after the individual has been stripped of all that with which he has illegitimately identified himself? Everything actual has been eliminated and nothing is left, according to Heidegger, but sheer potentiality-for-being.

The caller, too, refuses to be identified with anything found in ordinary experience. It appears simply as call and nothing else. The call does not come from others. It springs up within me, and yet it is not within my control. Often when I try to suppress it, it persists. This is why it has been identified with the voice of God. But we must not try to explain conscience in terms of an alien power, says Heidegger, unless we have exhausted all possibilities accounting for it in terms of our own selves.

From the seeming indefinitness and emptiness of both caller and called, Heidegger concludes that in calling, Dasein calls itself out of its lostness in the world back to its genuine self:

Nothing speaks against this; but all those phenomena which we have hitherto set forth in characterizing the caller and its calling speak for it. (321)

Then Heidegger tests his interpretation of conscience against his conception of the human mode of being, or Dasein. He rejects the Aristotelian categories as improper ways of speaking about man and instead uses what he calls existentials. The most basic ones are *thrownness, existence,* and *fallenness.* Man is thrown into the world, endowed with certain capacities, and made dependent on things in the world for the realization of these capacities. He develops his capacities by projecting possibilities or goals into the future. This projection Heidegger calls *existence,* using the term in its original meaning of "standing out." Unwilling to face himself as sheer potentiality, man tends to understand himself in terms of what he encounters in the world, as a special kind of thing, and more specifically in terms of the possibility he has realized, such as craftsman or professional, businessman or politician. But this covering up of his real being is never quite successful, for the very effort to disguise it betrays awareness of it. As all self-deception, it is haunted by the truth about itself.

It can now be seen how compatible Heidegger's view of conscience is with his idea of man:

In its "who" the caller is definable in a "wordly" way by *nothing* at all. The caller is Dasein in its uncanniness [*Unheimlichkeit,* literally; *not-at-homeness*]: primordial, thrown Being-in-the world as the "not-at-home"—the bare "that-it-is" in the "nothing" of the world. The caller is unfamiliar to the everyday they-self; it is something like an alien voice. What would be more alien to the "they," lost in the manifold "world" of its concern, than the Self which has been individualized down to itself in uncanniness and been thrown into the "nothing"? It calls, even though it gives the concernfully curious ear nothing to hear which might be passed along in further retelling and talked about in public. But what is Dasein even to report from the uncanniness of its thrown Being? *What* else remains for it than its own potentiality-for-Being as revealed in anxiety? How else is "it" to call than by summoning Dasein towards this potentiality-for-Being, which alone is the issue? (321)

What precisely does the called hear in the call? It is generally agreed, according to Heidegger, that the call addresses Dasein as "schuldig." The terms "Schuld" and "schuldig" have many meanings in German and to translate them as "guilty" is misleading. They can be used in such expressions as: "having debts," "owing respect," "incurring guilt for breaking a law or a contract," "being the cause for a loss or suffering in another." Perhaps the most general English equivalent would be "having responsibility for something" or "making oneself responsible." Now if "being schuldig" is a genuine phenomenon, then, says Heidegger, it must be sketched out in Dasein itself. In the case of owing something, being indebted or being responsible for something, there is involved a failure or lack caused in the being of the other, and this failure or lack is rooted in the being of the one who has made himself "schuldig." The debtor, for instance, has NOT lived up to his responsibility, as a result of which the other is NOT yet in possession of his property. Or one man does NOT have the respect of another, because the other does NOT grant him the respect which he deserves. Because of this twofold NOT, Heidegger defines being "schuldig" as "being the null basis of a nullity."

Heidegger than proceeds to show that this same twofold NOT appears at the very core of the Dasein structure, namely in thrownness and existence, the two principal existentials. Thrownness is the given, the endowment, on the basis of which Dasein projects its goals. Dasein must take over this basis; it must make it its own. But it cannot wholly make it its own, because the basis is not of its own making. "It never exists *before* its basis, but only *from* it, and *as this basis*," says Heidegger, "and thus 'being-a-basis' means NEVER to have power over one's ownmost being from the ground up"; in other words, he continues "it has been *released* from its basis, *not through* itself but *to* itself, so as to be *as this basis*" (330). NOT also appears in the projections rooted in the thrownness. Dasein can realize one of its possibilities only by not choosing others. Thus both the basis of the projection and the projection itself are permeated by a NOT; that is, thrownness is the "null basis of *a nullity*." But this has earlier been offered as a definition of *Schuld* (responsibility, indebtedness, guilt, cause). Hence Heidegger ventures the conclusion:

> Dasein's Being means, as thrown projection, Being the basis of a nullity (this being the basis is itself null). This means that *Dasein as such is schuldig* if our formally existential definition of Schuld is indeed correct. (331)

This formal definition appears odd and its relevance questionable; but it loses its strangeness as soon as we reflect on the realities to which it refers. If Dasein were in complete control of itself, if it had been released "through itself," it would be godlike, *causa sui;* if it were not "released to itself," as an "entity whose Being has to take over Being-a-basis" (330–31) and realize the capacities provided by this basis, it would not contribute to its being and could not be a self at all. Similarly, if in choosing one possibility it would not have to forgo others, that is, if in the end all its possibilities were realized, then its freedom to choose would have little if any significance. Thus Heidegger's seemingly odd definition of Schuld, as "being the null basis of *a nullity*," shows itself present in the very essence of Dasein, and it is found to be the "existential condition for the possibility of the 'morally good' and for the 'morally evil'—that is, for morality in general and for the possible forms which these may take factically" (332).

The content of the voice of conscience now becomes clearer. As the voice of the suppressed self as thrownness, it calls upon the self lost in the they-self to take possession of itself, that is, to assume responsibility for the "potentiality-for-Being" which it is. And the appropriate response to this appeal is the most basic choice of all, the choice of one's own self. This determination, to hold oneself responsible for one's thrownness and all the subsequent choices which are based on it, Heidegger calls *resoluteness*. This resoluteness does not mean to cling stubbornly to a resolve one has made. It rather means to hold oneself open and responsive to whatever demands the current situation may make. And it is quite compatible with the withdrawal of a particular resolve, should circumstances require it.

If Heidegger's interpretation is rightly regarded as more basic than the ordinary one, then it must be able to explain why and where the ordinary conception goes awry.

We ordinarily speak of the voice of conscience as reproving us for an act done or left undone, or else warning us against an act which we are inclined to perform. According to this view, conscience makes its appearance *after* the deed is done or willed. In Heidegger's interpretation it precedes the act. For how could we experience an act as morally wrong, unless we had first assumed responsibility for our acts in resoluteness? It is true, the voice refers back, but not simply to the deed done, "it calls beyond the deed which has happened, and back to the Being-guilty [Schuldigsein] into which one has been thrown, which is 'earlier' than any indebtedness [Verschuldung]" (337). That the common understanding should be disinclined to go beyond the deed to the condition for its possibility, is attributable to its reluctance to face the uncanniness of Dasein's abandonment to itself as "potentiality-for-Being" of which it is to take possession.

Nor does Heidegger see his failure to distinguish between a good and a bad conscience as a cause for criticism. If the bad conscience tells a man that he is evil, then a good conscience would let him say that he is good. "Who else can say this than the good man himself," Heidegger asks, "and who would be less willing to affirm it?" (338). In the complexity of human relations, how can we ever be sure that we have not failed our fellow men in some respect?

The common notion that conscience is merely negative also seems to militate against Heidegger's interpretation. Conscience in Heidegger's view, however, appears negative only if you expect from it information as to what specific act we should perform under given circumstances. This, of course, it is unable to do. But in as much as it reveals Dasein in its true being as "thrown projection" and presents it with the possibility of choosing itself, it functions in a manner which is preeminently positive.

If we now ask, by what right Socrates should urge his friend Crito to disregard the opinion of the "many," we can, in Heidegger's terms, give the answer. We can say that Socrates merely reminds Crito of his own conscience, which calls upon him in his lostness to the "many" to take charge of his own being. And we can now also understand why Socrates in the *Crito*, and in most if not all other dialogues, does not give a definite solution to the problem under consideration. The self-possession, or resoluteness, according to Heidegger, cannot *become rigid* . . . but must be *held open* for the current factical possibility" (355). We can see this illustrated as we recall to mind the way in which Socrates moves from the concrete problem with which he is confronted to the broader consideration of the relationship between obedience to law and personal responsibility. He shows, by implication, that neither law nor the outcome of our own reflections alone can be relied upon as infallible guides. By having Socrates move from one to the other, Plato dramatically places before us the task of striking a precarious balance between the two, a task which only the individual in the concrete situation has a chance of performing with any measure of success. And when Heidegger maintains that "the situation cannot be calculated in advance" (355) is he not echoing Plato's words to the effect that "the difference of men and actions, and the endless irregular movements of human things, do not admit of any universal and simple rule, and no art whatever can lay down a rule which will last for all time." With the changing situation many of a man's values are bound to undergo some transformation. To stay alive and to take care of his children's education, as Crito urges, might have been essential to Socrates in his younger years. Now he recognizes that few years of life are left to him in any event, even if he should escape. Now the promotion of his mission may appear to him as of much greater significance than his survival. This surrender of old attachments to new ones is expressed by Heidegger's statement that "resoluteness is the freedom to give up some definite resolution, and to give it up in accordance with the demands of some possible situation or other" (443). In the light of these considerations it is quite possible that Socrates, who died in conformity with the law, and Aristotle who, confronted with the same charge of impiety, is said to have run away in defiance of it, were both on the side of freedom and justice. For the violation of one and the same law will carry different weight according as it is brought about by an old moral teacher whose mission may be enhanced by his death, or by a great scientist with possibly many years of fruitful work ahead of him, not to mention the disgrace the Athenians would have suffered, had they been allowed to "sin a second time against philosophy." To be ready to face whatever new demands are made by the community in which we live, by our fellowmen and our own needs—this is liberalism in its most genuine sense. It is conferred upon all men, but only as a possibility. Its realization is a man's most urgent and most worthy task, for only through it can he become a moral being. This is what Socrates briefly suggests in the *Crito* before entering upon the discussion of a moral problem, and it is also what Heidegger never tires of insisting upon in *Being and Time*.

NOTES

1. All quotations from the Crito refer to *The Dialogues of Plato,* trans. B. Jowett (New York: Random House, 1937), vol. 1.

2. "In our time there are conflicts between what the state demands and our democratic ideals under which each individual is supposed to act as if he alone is responsible for the perpetuation of rights and justice in society." Christoph Schwerin, "The Officers' Plot: German Foes of Hitler," *New York Times,* 20 July 1974.

3. "Will you then flee from well-ordered cities and virtuous men? and is existence worth having on these terms?" (53C).

4. *Apology* 37C–D.

5. A dramatic dialogue, no less than a play, should be self-contained and its interpretation ought not to depend on elements found in other dialogues. But Plato not infrequently reveals in later dialogues what he has left half-concealed in the more dramatic earlier ones. To seek *additional* support by referring to such explicit utterances and thereby strengthen an interpretation would not seem to do violence to the self-sufficiency of the dramatic dialogue. Thus the identification of ideal reason and ideal law, which is merely suggested in the *Crito,* is made unequivocally by the Athenian in the *Laws:* "We must do all we can to imitate the life which is said to have existed in the days of Cronos, and, as far as the principle of immortality dwells within us, to that we must harken, both in private and public life, and regulate our cities and houses according to law, *meaning by the very term 'law', the distribution of mind."* *Laws* 4.714. (Italics added)

6. With the proviso and for the purpose mentioned in note 5, above, attention is called to another passage in the same dialogue which stresses the corrective function of the laws in regard to reason: "For if a man were so divinely gifted that he could naturally apprehend the truth, he would have no need for laws to rule over him; for there is no law or order which is above knowledge, nor can mind, without impiety, be deemed the subject or slave of any man, but rather the law of all. I speak of *mind, true and free,* and in harmony with nature. But *there is no such mind* anywhere, or at least not much; and *therefore we must choose law and order, which are second best.* These look at things as they exist for the most part only, and are unable to survey the whole of them." *Laws* 9.875. (Italics added)

7. "Im voraus, vor der konkreten Situation des Handelns, zu wissen, was man zu tun hat, um ein rechter Mensch zu sein, und damit seiner selbst gewiss zu sein, diese Forderung kann keine Wissenschaft vom menschlichen Sein und Handeln übernehmen." Hans-George Gadamer, *Platos dialektische Ethik* (Hamburg: Felix Meiner Verlag, 1968) pp. 177–78.

8. In the *Statesman,* Plato, on a literal interpretation, advocates one-man rule in preference to the rule of law when he has the Stranger say: "There can be no doubt that legislation is in a manner the business of a king, and yet the best thing of all is not that the law should rule, but that a man should rule, supposing him to have wisdom and royal power." (294) In view of the passage which immediately follows the above, this reference to one-man rule can be regarded as an apophantic device which points away from itself to something else; that is, the supremely wise man with his capacity for infinite adjustability serves as a mirror which reflects the rigidity of the law:

> The law does not perfectly comprehend what is noblest and most just for all and therefore cannot enforce what is best. The difference of men and actions, and the endless irregular movements of human things, do not admit of any universal and simple rule. And no art whatsoever can lay down a rule which will last for all

time. . . . But the law is always striving to make one;—like an obstinate and ignorant tyrant, who will not allow anything to be done contrary to his appointment, or any question to be asked—not even in sudden changes of circumstances, when something happens to be better than what he commanded for someone (ibid., 294).

And from the inflexibility of the law follows the obligation of a citizen to correct the law when it deviates too much from justice: "Any individual, or any number of men, having fixed laws, in acting contrary to them with a view to something better, would only be acting, as far as they are able, like the true statesman" (ibid., 300).

9. From what has gone before it should be obvious that Socrates cannot be absolutely certain that he has made the right choice. Most, if not all choices, have a seamy side and result in some evil or injury for the one who chooses or those affected by the choice. Not all of these consequences can be foreseen. The precept, therefore, which DeVogel abstracts from the Crito, as one of the first principles of the philosophy of Socrates, namely, that "we may never do wrong in any respect," would seem to be incapable of fulfillment. C. J. DeVogel, *Greek Philosophy*, vol. 1, *Thales to Plato*, 2nd ed. (Leiden: Brill, 1957), p. 144.

10. This is a theme to which Socrates devotes himself in the *Hippias Minor*.

11. All quotations from Martin Heidegger refer to *Being and Time*, trans. John Macquarrie and Edward Robinson (New York: Harper & Row, 1962).

2

Euthyphro: Piety and the Examined Life

The paradox presented in the *Crito* reapears in the *Euthyphro*. For piety, like good citizenship, shows seemingly incompatible characteristics. The pious man is expected to do the will of the gods; but if he does, he becomes inauthentic, for the authentic man must make his own decisions. And if piety is incompatible with authenticity, which, as we have seen in the *Crito*, is the condition for the possibility of morality, how can piety be a moral excellence? Furthermore, if it is true, as Socrates maintains later in the dialogue, that "no good that we possess but is given to us by the gods" (15A), do we not have to regard the *ability* to choose one's own self, that is, to become authentic, as a gift of the gods? Would not the unwillingness to develop that potentiality be a rejection of the gods' gift, offend the gods and constitute an act of impiety? So it appears that we are caught in a dilemma: We cannot escape impiety, whether we obey or disobey the gods, whether we do what the *gods* command or what *we* think is right.

In contrast to the previously considered dialogue, the dramatic movement of the *Euthyphro* is much more variegated. Piety and justice appear almost indistinguishably intermingled at the start; then they are sharply separated by Socrates, who in the end leads the reader in the direction of a synthesis of piety and justice on a higher level, but stops short of actually performing it. At the same time we witness a repeated fluctuation between concrete act and abstract idea or principle, between moods of playfulness or irony and deep earnestness, between myth or superstition and logical analysis. Instead of Crito, the loyal friend who deserves respect for his concern about the safety of Socrates, we now meet Euthyphro, whose stupidity makes him a convenient butt for the Socratic irony. Since the subtle arguments which Socrates puts forth are beyond Euthyphro's ken, the reader is challenged, on pain of being made the real object

47

of the irony, to pick up the thought where Euthyphro has dropped it and carry it forward on his own.[1]

Socrates and Euthyphro meet while both are on their way to a court of justice, Socrates in order to answer an indictment for corrupting the young and for impiety, Euthyphro to prosecute his father for murder. Euthyphro, however, is not so much interested in bringing about justice as he is in cleansing himself from the "pollution" which he claims is caused by associating with a man who has committed a crime and goes unpunished. It appears that one of the family's field laborers killed a domestic in a fit of drunken passion. Euthyphro's father, not knowing what to do with him, sent to the diviners in Athens for advice. In the meantime he bound the man hand and foot and threw him in a ditch, where he left him completely unattended so that the man died. Euthyphro now accuses his father of murder. To the objections of his family that "a son is impious who prosecutes his father," he replies with an appeal to the behavior of the gods. "Do not men," he argues, "regard Zeus as the best and most righteous of the gods?—and yet they admit he bound his father (Cronos) because he wickedly devoured his sons and that he too punished his own father (Uranus) for a similar reason" (5E–6A,J).[2]

"Good heavens!" exclaims Socrates in mock astonishment, "is your knowledge of religion and of things impious so very exact, that, supposing the circumstances to be as you state them, you are not afraid lest you too may be doing an impious thing in bringing an action against your father?" (4E,J). And when Euthyphro assures him of his expertise in matters of piety, Socrates begs to be accepted as his pupil, so that he can hide behind the authority of a master when answering his accuser in court.

Piety, after all, is a moral excellence and it is therefore not surprising that Socrates, as in the *Crito*, should offer instances of inauthenticity, suggesting indirectly that authenticity is a condition for the possibility of morality and is presupposed in any genuine moral discussion. The instances are three in number: Euthyphro's father expecting "experts" to tell him how to solve a moral problem; Euthyphro appealing to the behavior of the gods in justification of his own; Socrates ironically seeking to shift responsibility for his actions to the one who has taught him. A fourth is added later when Socrates pretends to look to a logical definition for the answer.

Now if Euthyphro's assurance does not spring from blind faith he must be able to give an account of it, that is, offer a definition. But Euthyphro, not being very bright, needs first to be told what a definition is:

> Is not piety in every action the same? And impiety, again—is it not always the opposite of piety, and also the same with itself, having, as impiety, one notion which includes whatever is impious. (5D,J)

And then Socrates describes the function of a definition, which when found would make moral judgments so simple and so reliable:

Tell me what is the nature of this idea, and then I shall have a standard to which I may look, and by which I may measure actions, whether yours or those of any one else, and then I shall be able to say that such and such an action is pious, such another impious. (6E,J)

One may question whether Socrates' implied method of arriving at a definition is at all feasible. How can we discover the element common to all pious acts, unless we already know what piety is? As Heidegger says apropos of a work of art: "One might think that what art is can be gathered from an examination of actual works of art. But how can we be certain that we are indeed basing such an examination on art works if we do not know beforehand what art is?"[3]

Nevertheless, Socrates' request for a definition has, in the minds of many commentators, created the impression that we are witnessing a passage from *mythos* to *logos*. Of course, the definition is not actually found, but this is said to be attributable to the Socratic method: Socrates means us to find the definition for ourselves. As against the doctrinaire position of Euthyphro, his logical approach is very alluring. Out of the deep darkness of superstition, one feels transported into the clear light of reason, where precise standards take the guesswork out of moral judgments. The fact, however, that we have left behind not only superstition but the concrete situation as well should give us pause. As we have seen in the *Crito*, it is the concrete situation which presents the alternatives between which a moral man must choose. Frequently, the choice is not between good and evil, but between the greater and the lesser good, or the greater and the lesser evil. Just what will turn out to be the greater good or lesser evil, only the given circumstances can reveal.[4]

Have these thoughts, which were set in motion by Socrates' request for a definition, led us astray, or do they find support in the text?

Socrates provides at least a hint to the effect that he considers the rule or definition not wholly adequate and that the concrete situation must be taken into account. For when shortly thereafter Euthyphro appeals to a rule or principle, namely, that both gods and men all agree that the wrongdoer ought to be punished, Socrates replies that this is not what people usually argue about. "They argue," he says, "about the fact of who the wrongdoer is, and what was done and when" (8D).

If we can trust this hint of Socrates, then his request for a definition was ironical, its purpose being to expose the groundless certainty which Euthyphro claims to possess in matters of religion and morality. And since Euthyphro learns nothing from the encounter with Socrates, Plato is really addressing the reader. By pitting one extreme against the other, he is trying to make him see that it is not enough to abjure superstition and adjure reason, for the appeal to a rule divorced from life can spring from as ruthless an attitude as one inspired by superstition. And just as Euthyphro's unshakeable conviction is unjustified since it implies an impossible familiarity with the will of the gods, so intellectual certainty in moral matters presupposes a definition which the world in which we live does not allow.[5]

Unless we forget that we are dealing with a dramatic dialogue, we can see that the presentation of extremes, with a mere suggestion for the discovery of the mean between them, is an effective way of involving the reader and making him an active participant in the inquiry, as the Socratic method demands. During the remainder of the dialogue, Socrates will in fact create several paradoxical situations by allowing incompatible positions to come into collision with each other.

Euthyphro, who, of course, is unaware of any of the difficulties stirred up by the discussion, responds to Socrates' call for a definition by referring to his own act. "Piety," he says, "is doing as I am doing; that is to say, prosecuting anyone who is guilty of murder, sacrilege, or any similar crime—whether he be your father or mother, or whoever he may be—that makes no difference; and not to prosecute him is impiety" (5D–E). And he justifies his own act by referring to individual acts committed by Zeus in regard to his father Cronos, and by Cronos in regard to his father Uranus. Thus Euthyphro, in his attempt to give an account of his action, does not rise at all above the concrete situation, while Socrates, through his insistence on a definition, would wholly dispense with it.

Socrates' error or excess, as we have seen, is left for the reader to correct; that of Euthyphro is exposed by Socrates. He reproaches him for giving an instance of a pious act when he was asked for the common characteristic by reason of which pious acts are pious.[6] Euthyphro then complies, with a statement which contains such a universal element: "Piety," he says, "is that which is dear to the gods, and impiety is that which is not dear to them" (7A).

This version of the definition, however, does not stand up to criticism. Euthyphro has admitted that the gods differ and even quarrel among each other. When men quarrel, says Socrates, then it is not about such things as number, or size, or weight, for such disagreements are settled by counting, measuring, or weighing. But they do quarrel "when the matters of difference are the just and unjust, good and evil, honorable and dishonorable" (7D). And if the gods quarrel at all, is it not likely that they quarrel about these same matters?[7] How then can you be sure that you are preforming a pious act? One god may agree with you that you ought to prosecute your father and another may condemn you for doing so. So one and the same act may be pleasing and displeasing to the gods. "Upon this view," Socrates concludes, "the same thing will be pious and impious" (8A, J).

In a seeming attempt to avoid these difficulties, Socrates proposes that the definition be amended to read: "Piety is what all the gods love, and impiety is what they all hate" (9E). Through an analysis of this new version, Socrates manages to create a rather complex paradox which some interpreters, presumably because of their insistence on a purely logical approach, have found so obscure and conceptually ambiguous as to defy any attempt at explanation. Basically, Socrates operates with two extremes: on the one hand he depicts the moral aspect of an act as intrinsically determined, as a quality which the act possesses and which is independent of outside factors, just as a body might be circular or rectangular in shape; on the other hand he presents it as extrinsically determined, as absorbed, so to speak, in its relation to something else, as one and the same food might be found tasty by one person and tasteless by another.

Socrates opens the new phase of the discussion with the question: "Is that which is holy loved by the gods because it is holy, or is it holy because it is loved by the gods?" (10A, F). Euthyphro does not understand, and Socrates offers an explanation which in the end shows the second half of the alternative, that is, piety as extrinsically determined to be the logical implication of the proposed definition.

In order to elucidate the relationship between that which is being loved (philoumenon) and that which loves (to philoun), Socrates offers a series of examples:

> We speak of being carried and carrying, of being led and leading, of being seen and seeing; and . . . in all such expressions the two parts differ one from the other in meaning. . . . Then, too, we conceive of a thing being loved and of a thing loving, and the two are different. (10A, F)

To bring out the difference between the members of each pair, Socrates uses the passive participle for the first member (pheromenon, agomenon, horomenon, philoumenon) and the active participle for the second member (pheron, agon, horon, philoun).

By reason of this contrast between the active and the passive participles, one is tempted to see here a causal relationship between one element and the other, the agent producing an effect on the patient. But the diversity of the examples used does not allow it. Can the act of seeing, for instance, be said to change the thing seen? Once suspicion is aroused, one cannot even be sure whether the first two examples are meant to point to a causal relationship. It is true that a thing may be altered when it is being carried, but the general intent when carrying is to leave the thing unharmed, like eggs in a basket. The same can be said of leading or guiding a blind person, for instance, or a frail old lady across the street. Of course, a general may lead his army to slaughter, but then he is considered unsuccessful in the performance of his function. On the other hand, there are occasions when the act of seeing does affect the object seen. As Sartre points out, a man peeping through a keyhole is likely to experience an acute sense of embarrassment when detected, and the young Hippocrates in the *Protagoras* blushes when he becomes aware that Socrates "knows" him to be ignorant of what a Sophist is, to whom he is so eager to entrust his spiritual welfare. Similarly, being loved may cause elation, or embarrassment, or even disgust in the person loved. But all these effects are attributable directly to the awareness of the state of being seen, known, or loved, and only indirectly to the corresponding act itself. When such an awareness is lacking, or when it is impossible, as in the case of love proceeding from the gods, the presence or absence of the state cannot be detected through observation of the thing or person in question. In the case of *carrying* and *leading* it can be argued that there is a causal effect inasmuch as the thing in question undergoes at least a change of place. But if Socrates wanted to illustrate causal relations, he could have chosen more effective examples, and he certainly should not have used *seeing* at all. The variety of the examples employed in the familiar *epagoge* or induction prevents the quick perception of a common element. Through the pairs *carrying* and *being carried, leading* and *being led,* we are made to think of a causal relationshp, merely to have it blotted out through the pair *seeing* and *being seen,* which points to the complete indifference on the part of the second member with reference to the first. Far from suggesting a causal relationship, the examples used and the manner in which they are used, seem to warn us against such an interpretation. But if the two factors do not function as cause and effect, how are they related? And if the causal relationship is not the element which all the examples share, what is the common characteristic at which the Socratic *epagogé* aims? There can be no doubt that the passive factor in each instance suffers something which is imposed from without. In the first two instances (being carried and being led) these imposed states may not, and in the third instance (being seen) the state cannot, have any effect on the thing on which it is imposed. The state in which the thing finds itself is grounded not in its own being but in that of another thing over which it has no control. It is this type of state which is suggested by the *epagoge*. The crucial question now is: Does Socrates make significant use of this notion of a state imposed from without on a thing on which it leaves no visible effect?

With the next step, however, Socrates seems to throw everything into confusion. For he now replaces the active participle of each pair, namely, *pheron, agon, horon,* by the respective singular inflective passive form, namely *pheretai, agetai, horatai.* But although we are now faced with two passive factors, Socrates insists on the dependence of one on the other. For instance, the *pheromenon,* as before, is the dependent or grounded element; its ground, however, is no longer the *pheron,* the active factor, but the *pheretai,* another passive factor:

> A thing which is carried [pheromenon] is a carried thing because it is carried [pheretai]. And a thing which is led [agomenon] is such because it is led [agetai]. And a thing which is seen [horomenon] is so because it is seen (horatai). (10B, F)

While before Socrates spoke of the cause of the state on the one hand, and the thing on which the state is imposed on the other, he now seems to distinguish between the state and the thing of which it is the state. If this is so, we could regard the *pheromenon*, for instance, as *the thing in its state of being carried*, and the *pheretai* as its *being carried*, that is, the state in abstraction. The *pheromenon* and the *pheretai* would then both be correctly expressed in passive forms. For the first suffers the state and the second is caused by the active principle but has not causal efficacy on the thing of which it is the state. It could then be said that the *thing in its state*, considered as a totality, is dependent on the state, and Socrates would be right in declaring the relationship in which they stand to each other as irreversible:

> Not because a thing is in a state of being seen [horomenon] is it seen [horatai], but on the contrary it is a seen thing [horomenon] because it is seen [horatai]; not because it is a thing in a state of being led [agomenon] is it led [agetai], but because it is led [agetai] is it a thing being led [agomenon]; not because it is a thing in a state of being carried [pheromenon] is it carried [pheretai], but because it is carried [pheretai] is it a thing in a state of being carried [pheromenon]. (10B, F)

Socrates now generalizes the relationship between the two factors by using *becoming* and *undergoing*. The processes involved are to be understood, however, in the sense indicated by the *epagoge;* that is, whatever the causes may be which set them in motion, they remain completely external determinations of the thing in question:

> If anything becomes or undergoes, it does not become because it is in a state of becoming, but it is in a state of becoming because it becomes [gignomenon hoti gignetai, middle forms of an intransitive verb], and it does not undergo because it is a thing which undergoes, but it is a thing which undergoes because it undergoes [paschon hoti paschai, active forms whose meaning is rendered in the passive]. (10C, F)

Socrates next likens becoming and undergoing to loving:

> Is not that which is beloved [philoumenon] a thing which is either becoming [gignomenon] or undergoing [paschon]? And is not this case like the former ones: Not because it is a beloved thing [philoumenon] is it loved [phileitai], but because it is loved [phileitai] is it a beloved thing [philoumenon]. (10C, F)

Let us now briefly survey the elucidation which Socrates has offered the uncomprehending Euthyphro after presenting the alternative of whether "the holy is loved by the gods because it is holy, or whether it is holy because it is loved by the gods" (10A). Using the words carrying and leading, Socrates reminds us of causality by opposing the active and the passive participles, but at the same time he minimizes the significance of the relationship through the meaning of the words which, as we have seen, represent at best a "mild" form of causality in terms of a change of place. The next example, seeing, actually forbids us to regard causality as the relationship which Socrates has in mind. Then he interiorizes the terms of the relationship by expressing both in passive forms, thus reducing them to aspects of one and the same thing. Now if we regard one aspect as the *thing in a state*, considered as whole, and the other as *the state itself*, then we can understand why Socrates stresses the dependence of the first on the second, and the irreversibility of the relationship.[9] And we can also see why he replaces the active participle used at the beginning of the elucidation with a passive form. For first he speaks about the acts of carrying, leading, seeing, which are efficacious in bringing about the state of being carried, led, or seen respectively; subsequently he refers to the state in relation to the thing of which it is the state. Now both terms of this relationship are passive, for the states of being carried and being led may not, and the states of being seen and being loved cannot, have any effect on the thing of which they are the states. The state in each case is a completely external determination of the thing in question.

Now the significance of the elucidation for an understanding of the proposed definition becomes clear. If the holy is that which is loved by the gods, then an examination of the holy act will reveal nothing of the nature of holiness, for the state of being loved, which, according to the definition, constitutes the holy, has left no visible mark on it. To understand the holy we must go, not to that which depends on it, but to that on which it depends, namely, an act of love which springs from the will of the gods. This means we must abandon philosophic inquiry into holiness in favor of theology. Holiness or piety becomes the exclusive concern of prophets and soothsayers, and Euthyphro's father was right in seeking their advice instead of deciding for himself when he was faced with the problem of how to deal with the man who had killed one of his slaves.[10]

Socrates now returns to the alternative presented to Euthyphro at the beginning of this phase of the discussion, namely, that either the holy is loved by the gods because it is holy, or it is holy because it is loved by the gods. It is obvious that his elucidation dealt only with the second half of the alternative by developing the implications of what it means to be in a state of being loved. And it is now clear that in view of his proposed definition, Euthyphro ought to choose the second alternant which roots the holy as a state of being loved in an act of the gods, and not the first which makes it a quality in the thing or act. Nevertheless, Plato lets Euthyphro choose the first alternant, which renders it easy for Socrates to convict Euthyphro of inconsistency between his former choice of a definition and his present choice among the two alternants:

If that which is dear to the gods [theophiles] and that which is holy [hosion] were identical, my dear Euthyphro, then if the holy [hosion] were loved [ephileito] because it is holy [hosion], that which is dear to the gods [theophiles] would be loved [ephileito] because it is dear [theophiles], and if that which is dear to the gods [theophiles] is dear [theophiles] because it is loved [ephileito], then that which is holy [hosion] would be holy [hosion] because it is loved [phileisthai]; but now you see that the opposite is the case, showing that the two are entirely different from each other. For the one becomes lovable from the fact that it is loved, whereas the other is loved because it is in itself lovable. (10E–11A,F)

Euthyphro has admitted that the holy is loved by the gods (L) because it is holy (H):

(1)   L because H

Since he has also defined the holy (H) as that which is in a state of being loved by the gods or dear to the gods (D), Socrates can substitute D for H in (1):

(2)   L because D

The analysis of what it means to be in a state of being loved by the gods or dear to the gods has shown that that which is dear to the gods is dear (D) because it is loved (L):

(3)   D because L

Socrates now substitutes H for D in (3):

(4)   H because L

(1) and (4) now show H and L to be and not to be the reason for each other; likewise according to (2) and (3) L and D are and are not the reason for each other.

Why should Plato set up such an obvious trap which it is so easy for Socrates to close? It does not improve the image of Socrates' cleverness, and Euthyphro's lack of acuity has already been amply demonstrated. We therefore expect to find more than a thoughtless admission which leaves one participant to an eristic debate open to attack by another.

In reality Socrates is made to launch an attack not so much against Euthyphro as against the basic moral or religious attitude which he represents. Socrates inquires into the nature of holiness, a virtue or excellence attributable to men living in the world; Euthyphro turns to the gods for justification of moral behavior and loses sight of the world:

And Euthyphro, it seems that when you were asked what holiness is you were unwilling to make plain its essence, but you mentioned something that has happened to his holiness, namely, that it is loved by the gods. But you did not tell as yet what it really is. (11A–B,F)

The gods do not speak to men directly, if they speak at all. Tiresias in the *Antigone,* for instance, has to rely on signs, such as the cries of birds and the behavior of the sacrificial animals on the altar. Similarly Euthyphro turns to ancient tales to discover the wishes of the gods. But neither signs nor legends reveal the *reason* why a given act is pious or impious. They only tell that, as a matter of fact, the gods are pleased or displeased. Thus Tiresias and Euthyphro, while regarding piety as a moral excellence, would base it on brute facts when it should spring from rational insight, for without such insight responsibility, and therefore genuine morality, is not possible. Plato gives expression to this basic contradiction in their attitude by having Euthyphro assent to both parts of the alternative, incompatible though they are. If the holy is holy because the gods love it, and thus rooted in the will of the gods, then blind obedience is demanded of the pious person, and piety ceases to be a moral excellence; but if there is a moral excellence in the act, knowledge of which is a prerequisite for moral conduct, then even the gods must submit to it and the holy is not holy because they love it, but it is loved by them because it is holy.[11]

Euthyphro's position has thus been exposed as inconsistent with itself. But Socrates, too, seems to have reached an impasse. One would assume that he could choose the alternant which regards the pious as something in itself,[12] independent of the will of the gods, and thereby rescue the inquiry from the clutches of theology. It is true, as we have seen,[13] that a definition based on the characteristic common to pious acts, even if it could be found, would by itself alone not be a reliable guide for moral action.[14] But we might perhaps be served by a definition or something like it, which would tell us whether an act is good or bad, and then a careful scrutiny of the concrete situation, in which the act is to be performed would reveal whether it is the greater good or the lesser evil. Has not Socrates himself hinted at such a solution when he remarks that in a court of law people do not argue about the principle that the wrongdoer ought to be punished, but about such things as "who the wrongdoer is, what he did, and when" (8D)?

Unfortunately, far from breaking the deadlock, we have merely moved to an extreme which is opposite to that of Euthyphro. To root piety in the will of the gods, as Euthyphro did, is to ruin it as a moral excellence. If it is to be a moral excellence, then, as any of the other virtues, it must be the outcome of a search, by critical intelligence, for the greater good or lesser evil. But is not this complete secularization of this particular virtue absurd? For what is piety if it is unrelated to the gods? And if Socrates entertained such a secularized conception of it, would not then the charge of impiety be justified, a charge which, according to the dialogue, he is on his way to answer in court?

Again Socrates resorts to paradoxes to mend the rift which the discussion has created between religion and morality and to guide the reader toward a conception which preserves piety as a moral excellence without divorcing it altogether from the will of the gods. This task is reserved for the next and last section of the dialogue.

In the opening scene, it will be recalled, justice and piety, the secular and the religious, appeared inextricably intertwined. Socrates was on his way to a court of law to answer a charge of impiety, when he encountered Euthyphro, who thought he was performing a pious act by bringing his father to justice. Socrates is now made to face the problem of determining the proper relationship between piety and justice.

Socrates begins by prodding Euthyphro into subsuming the two virtues under a broader term, so that the confused amalgamation at the beginning of the dialogue gives way to a clean separation:

> Holiness is a part of justice. . . . It is the part which has to do with the service of the gods; the remainder is the part of justice which has to do with the service of mankind. (12E)

This division of justice, upon examination, is found to have disturbing consequences. Service or care *(therapeia)*, Socrates suggests, may mean the care which professional trainers give to animals, such as horses or dogs, or herdsmen to cattle. In all these cases "the care is given for the good and welfare of the object that is served." And if this is so, asks Socrates, "are you prepared to say that when you do a holy thing you make some deity better?" (13B–C). "No, no, that was surely not what I meant," replies Euthyphro. Instead he suggests that *therapeia* refers to the kind of service "that slaves give to their master" (13D).[15] Of course, this service which men render the gods must have some purpose. Now the purpose of the physician is to produce health, that of the shipwright to make ships, that of the builder to build houses, and the service which the slaves or helpers render assists in achieving these various purposes. "Tell me, I adjure you," Socrates urges, "what is that supreme result which the gods produce when they employ our services?" (13E). "They do many things and noble," Euthyphro answers evasively. And when Socrates persists and wants to know "what these many fine and noble things are which the gods produce" (14A), Euthyphro falls back on what is basically his original definition: "If anyone knows how to say and do things pleasing to the gods in prayer and sacrifice, that is holiness" (14B).

Quite surprisingly, and to all appearances without good reason, Socrates now reproaches Euthyphro as if he believed he knew and had been about to give the answer, but then had wilfully withdrawn:

> Surely, Euthyphro, if you had wished, you could have summed up what I asked for much more briefly. But the fact is that you are not eager to instruct me. That is clear. But a moment since, you were on the point of telling me—and you slipped away. (14B–C)

In fact the passage reads as if the answer had been given, in a roundabout way, without quite coming to the point.

All along Euthyphro appeared to be only too glad to oblige Socrates with the right answer if he only knew how. So the reproach against him is pointless. If it is meant to be ironical, then it is somewhat crude, and useless to boot, for it will not arouse Euthyphro from his mental lethargy. But the irony would be to the point if it were addressed to the reader who has probably followed this part of the argument without effort, condescendingly amused over the stupidity of Euthyphro. The answer is right in front of you, Socrates now seems to challenge the reader, and unless you are resigned to regard yourself another Euthyphro, you had better bestir yourself.

At this point even literalistically inclined interpreters venture to go forward on their own. According to Paul Friedländer, the great work which the gods accomplish with our help is "the good, to which we will be introduced in the *Republic*, the *Timaeus* and the *Laws*."[16] "We also know," he concludes, "that for Plato's Socrates the good occupies the highest place and that in the presence of Euthyphro it cannot be discussed without being misunderstood and desecrated."[17] It would be difficult, however, to imagine a play in which the author postpones the denouement to a later work because its complexity would not be in keeping with the simplicity of his characters. Nor does it seem any less preposterous to credit Plato with such meager resources that he could not construct a dramatic dialogue which is a self-contained whole. Perhaps a confession of ignorance would be more appropriate than the use of such desperate hermeneutic devices. A. E. Taylor is more reasonable when he ventures the opinion that "we shall not go far wrong if we say that the 'great and glorious work of god' is to be the source of order and good in the universe, and that we 'contribute under god' to that work in the degree to which we bring order and good into the little 'world' of our own personal life and that of the society to which we belong."[18] Could not the gods, however, have ordered our lives, both private and public, as they have ordered the lives of bees and the beehive, and be much more successful than we could ever hope to be? On this view, our service to the gods would not be essential and ultimately without real significance. Furthermore, Taylor refers for confirmation to the "*Phaedo* and elsewhere,"[19] instead of first pointing to evidence in the dialogue at hand. If we have to range so far afield for an answer, why does Socrates say to Euthyphro: "You were on the point of telling me—and you slipped away" (14B–C), as if the answer were right in front of us and we could see it if we only paid sufficient attention?

Heidegger's notion of authenticity may help us overcome the difficulty, provided it is supported by the text or at least does not run counter to it. According to Heidegger, man does not merely realize certain possibilities, certain talents or capacities given to him. He can make, or refuse to make, a more profound choice, namely, the choice of his selfhood. As Heidegger expresses it in *Being and Time*:

> Dasein . . . *can*, in its very Being, "choose" itself and win itself; it can also lose itself and never win itself; or only seem to do so. But only in so far as it is

essentially something which can be *authentic*—that is, something of its own—can it have lost itself and not yet won itself. As modes of Being *authenticity* and *inauthenticity* . . . are both grounded in the fact that any Dasein whatsoever is characterized by mineness. (68)

This genuine selfhood can be attained only if a man makes his own decisions, for only then can his acts and ultimately his life be his own. And only if he thus takes possession of himself can he assume responsibility for himself and constitute himself a moral being. Authenticity is thus seen to be the condition for the possibility of being moral at all, be it morally good or morally evil.

In the light of this notion of authenticity, we can now see that Plato, at the very beginning of the dialogue, gave us a hint as to how we might answer the question which Socrates so persistently puts before Euthyphro, or rather the reader. For there he placed before us inauthenticity incarnated in the figures of Euthyphro, who justified his acts by appealing to ancient tales about the gods, and Euthyphro's father, who was willing to let the diviners decide his moral problem. By contrast, we found Socrates, all through the dialogue, asking questions about piety and justice so that he might act more intelligently and build for himself a life which is more genuinely his own and, with the help of others, a society more worthy of free and responsible human beings. In other words, what is so close to us that it tends to be overlooked is Socrates himself, the paragon of the authentic man.

What, it may be asked, has the strictly secular endeavor of the authentic man to do with the gods? What assurance do we have that it is meant to play a part in the final stages of the *Euthyphro,* which deal with piety? By now we should be sufficiently familiar with Socrates' way of handling a problem that it will not come as a surprise to us if instead of an explicit answer we are once more confronted with a paradox. Socrates constructs it out of the seemingly insignificant addition—"in prayer and sacrifice" (14B)—which Euthyphro has made to his previous definition of piety as "doing what is pleasing to the gods." Through prayer, says Socrates, we ask the gods for what we need from them, and through sacrifice we give them what they need from us. "I take it," he adds, "there would be no art in offering anyone a gift of something that he did not need" (14E). But what could they possibly gain from us which they could not obtain for themselves?—Euthyphro, as so often, fails to come forward with an answer. He slips back into his original definition that piety is that which is pleasing to the gods. Thus the discussion has returned to its starting point. Socrates would begin it all over again, but Euthyphro claims to be in a hurry to leave. So the dialogue ends and we, the readers, are left with the problem: Either all sacrifice is meaningless, or there must be something which we, and we alone, can give the gods.

Earlier Socrates has said that "no good that we possess but is given us by the gods" (15A). Now what is the most precious of these gifts? As we have seen, the inquiring Socrates, to whom "the unexamined life is not worth living" (*Apology* 38A), implied it, and Haemon of Sophocles' *Antigone* states it explicitly: "The gods, my father, have bestowed on man his reason, noblest of all earthly gifts." This gift is merely a tool, and the recipient of such a gift can best honor the giver by making a proper use of it. It is through reason, together with free will, without which reason would be of no value, that an individual constitutes himself as a responsible and genuine human being. This unique being is the "*pagkalon ergon*, the supreme result which the gods produce when they employ our services" (13E). And in the production of this result, the individual's contribution is indispensable. For the gods can give man only the capacity for authentic existence. Its realization must strictly be the individual's. And only with its realization are the conditions for the possibility of morality satisfied. Man's moral behavior is all the more significant because he cannot rely on tradition, as Euthyphro mistakenly does; nor can he deduce the proper course of action by a secure logical process from fixed principle or standard as Socrates ironically suggest at the beginning of the dialogue. Even the conventional appeal to the will of the gods would be a surrender of authenticity. For as the argument at 10A–11B has made abundantly clear, such an appeal would involve blind obedience. But not even the gods can do the impossible, i.e., demand such obedience and still hold men accountable for their actions. With nothing more basic than his free resolve, man must find his perilous way in an ever changing world, guided merely by a limited experience and the dim light of reason which the gods have seen fit to bestow upon him. This seeming withdrawal of the gods and their abandonment of man to the world is a necessary ingredient in the production of the *pagkalon ergon*. For while human life is thus doomed to uncertainty, anxiety and frustration, it is also a life in which courage and dignity have the greatest opportunity to manifest themselves; and it is here that genuine selfhood is born and that a society of free and responsible individuals comes into being. And so men do the will of the gods, not by looking to soothsayer, divine law, or ancient tradition, but by turning to the world and living as intelligently and responsibly as they can. This is why Socrates in the *Apology* can say: "And so I go about the world, obedient to the god, and search and make inquiry . . ." (23B). And when Phaedo calls Socrates of all men he has known "the bravest, the wisest, and the most upright man" (118A), he could also have called him the most pious.

The dialogue ends with a living paradox of tragic dimensions: it leaves Socrates, the most genuinely pious of the Athenians, on his way to answer the charge of impiety, brought against him by men who, through their blind fanatical zeal, prove themselves guilty of impiety. The *Euthyphro* thus exhibits a matchless unity of philosophy, history, and high drama.

Since Heidegger's conception of the authentic self has helped us solve the riddle of the *pagkalon ergon*, it is not difficult to surmise where Heidegger's sympathies would lie in a dispute between a theologian who demands blind obedience to the will of the gods and a philosopher who insists that a moral person must make his own decisions, based on reflection and rational inquiry. But in taking a stand against theology, Heidegger is confronted with more formidable opponents than Socrates. For the Christian theologians with whom he has to contend far outrank the unsophisticated Euthyphro, who models his behavior after some legendary tales about the gods.

In *Being and Time* Heidegger does not specifically deal with the relationship of philosophy and theology. There are about a dozen references to theology, but only a few give some hint as to his position in the matter. One such reference follows his distinction between the ontological discipline philosophy, which inquires into Being, and the ontic disciplines dealing with entities and facts about them. Now it is not a little surprising that he should list among the ontic disciplines not only mathematics, physics, and biology, but theology as well. (B. & T. pp. 29–30) Are we to assume that Heidegger regards theology as a positive science? Then he would make a radical distinction between philosophy and theology, and break with the tradition which links the two, in as much as both are said to deal with man and his world, one based on faith and revelation, the other on reason and free inquiry.

How can theology, however, find a place among the positive sciences? When the fundamental concepts of such sciences are questioned, the inquiry, according to Heidegger, leads to the determination of the realm of being of the entities with which a particular science is concerned. "Only after this area has been explored," he says, "do these concepts become genuinely demonstrated and 'grounded' " (B. & T. p. 30). Scientific inquiry, therefore, when pursued to its limits in the direction of the determination of its ground, leads naturally into ontology. But how can the basic terms of theology, such as sin, cross, son of God, rebirth, be grounded in this manner? For Heidegger, ontology is possible only as phenomenology (B. & T. p. 60) and by phenomenology he means "letting that which shows itself be seen from itself in the very way in which it shows itself from itself." (B. & T. p. 58) Are we not faced here with an unbridgeable gap between theology and the positive sciences—at least as Heidegger understands them? For how can entities from which the basic concepts of theology are drawn be made to manifest themselves in their being to rational inquiry, if they are accessible only through faith and revelation?

Fortunately we need not speculate about Heidegger's thoughts in the matter for he clearly expressed them in a speech delivered in 1927 and 1928, and published in 1970 under the title *Phaenomenologie und Theologie*, dedicated to Rudolf Bultmann, the famous biblical historian and theologian.[20] In this speech, Heidegger asks the following questions: What makes a science a positive science? What is the *positum* of theology? What are the characteristics of theology as a positive science? What, if anything, can philosophy contribute to theology?

Heidegger's task is aggravated by the fact that both philosophy and theology at the present time move in such diverse and at times conflicting directions that neither is capable of being brought under a common denominator. But unless this can be accomplished, there seems to be no possibility of establishing a significant relationship between them. Heidegger tries to overcome the difficulty by having recourse to "an ideal construction of the ideas of both disciplines" (Ph. & Th. p. 13), that is, by determining their relationship in terms of the possibilities which they both offer.

Every science, in Heidegger's view, deals with entities belonging to a realm determined by a specific mode of being. These entities are already accessible and familiar in a prescientific way. Science develops this vague knowledge by working out a proper method and a suitable conceptual apparatus. The realm of entities which a particular science encounters and which it uses as the objects of its inquiry is its *positum* and makes the science in question a *positive* science.

It might be thought that the *positum* of theology is Christianity with its history, its institutions, its various organizations and its rituals. Heidegger rejects this idea on the ground that theology itself is part of Christianity. He would rather seek the *positum* in that which makes Christianity possible, namely the Christian faith. (Ph. & Th. p. 18.) By Christian faith he understands a mode of human existence which is brought about not by a free choice but is determined by that which is revealed through faith, namely, the crucified God who through his sacrifice causes the believer to be reborn. This revelation, which becomes accessible only through faith, does not simply convey information about past or future events, but permits the believer to enter a history beginning with the advent of Christ and ending with his second coming. Theology must therefore be regarded as basically an historical discipline. The mode of existence of this new man, reborn through his faith in Christian revelation, is the *positum* of theology, and its elucidation and conceptualization is the basic task of theology. (Ph. & Th. p. 23.) From this *positum* theology must draw its proper mode of procedure and only through it can it claim to be an autonomous discipline.

We can now see the reason why in *Being and Time* he speaks in one and the same breath of theology and such disciplines as mathematics, physics, and biology, as if they were members of the same class. And we can now also understand the cryptic remark to the effect that "theology is seeking a more primordial interpretation of man's Being towards God, prescribed by the meaning of faith itself and remaining within it" (B. & T. p. 30).

Has he not, however, severed all ties between theology and philosophy? The other ontic sciences, as we have seen, when questioning their basic concepts, are led to a consideration of the realm of being of the entities of their concern and thus move into the ontological discipline, philosophy. But how can philosophy contribute to the elucidation of such basic theological concepts as sin, crucified God, rebirth, etc., which are admittedly accessible only through faith?

Heidegger concedes that philosophy does not ground the concepts of theology as it does those of the natural sciences. He also grants that religion does not stand in need of philosophy, nor does the believer. But he insists that theology requries the aid of philosophy, in a fundamental but uniquely restricted way.

To make his point, Heidegger fastens upon the notion of rebirth. By accepting revelation, the believer undergoes a transformation from the old to the new man, from the sinner in the eyes of God to one who is saved through divine grace. But transformation is not annihilation. Something of the old man is retained in the new; in any event, the rebirth starts with man in so far as he exists at all. But the elucidation of the human mode of being, which theology takes for granted, is the task of philosophy.

Heidegger does not, however, allow philosophy to become as closely linked to theology as it is to the other positive sciences. This he makes clear through a reference to the notion of sin. Only the believer, he says, can exist as a sinner, and philosophy cannot elucidate the notion of sin. It cannot even show that sin is a possible mode of existence. But it can point out that if it is to be interpreted and conceptualized theologically, then the theologian must go back to the notion of *Schuld,* in the sense of responsibility, accountability, guilt. The clarification of this phenomenon and its determination as an essential characteristic of Dasein, is a problem for philosophy, as Heidegger has shown in *Being and Time,* division 2, chapter 2. Sin, he insists, cannot be derived from *Schuld;* philosophy can only indicate the general realm within which the pre-Christian content of sin must maintain itself. Heidegger therefore summarizes the relationship of theology and philosophy as follows:

> Philosophy is the possible, formally indicating ontological corrective of the ontic, i.e. pre-Christian content of the basic concepts of theology. Philosophy, however, can be what it is without in fact functioning as such a corrective. (Ph.&Th. p. 32)

So it appears that a basic concept of theology, sin (not to mention rebirth), presupposes *Schuld.* This in turn is rooted in conscience which, according to *Being and Time,* calls Dasein from its lostness and dispersion in its daily concerns back to itself as sheer potentiality for being, and thus offers it an opportunity to take possession of itself.

Now we can appreciate the sharp contrast between philosophy and theology. The former seeks to help the individual to achieve genuine selfhood; the latter demands that he surrender his self as a prerequisite for entering the Christian mode of existence. Small wonder that Heidegger should call theology the "deadly enemy" of philosophy and call a Christian philosophy a "wooden piece of iron" (Ph.&Th. p. 32).

To dwell at length upon the basic similarity of Plato and Heidegger in the matter discussed seems almost superfluous. Both thinkers show the incompati-

for a definition of piety. Of five articles which have appeared in reputable professional journals, three pride themselves on the discovery of fallacies in Socrates' arguments. One author recommends the reading of the *Euthyphro* because one "may learn to be forewarned against some common fallacies and debating tricks in moral disputes" (P. T. Geach, "Plato's Euthyphro," *The Monist* 50 [July 1966]: 369). Another believes that Socrates refutes Euthyphro's unacceptable view of religion knowingly "by an illogical argument" (Robert G. Hoerber, "Plato's *Euthyphro,*" *Phronesis* 3 [1958]: 102). And a third concludes in regard to a significant passage in the dialogue (10A–11B) that "Socrates was so unclear about the conceptual definitions required to clarify the ambiguous text that no coherent account is possible" (John H. Brown, "The Logic of *Euthyphro* 10A–11B," *Philosophical Quarterly* 14 [Jan. 1964]: 13). A fourth essay goes to great length in its effort to reestablish the correctness of Socrates' reasoning. But the theme of the dialogue is then seen as nothing more than an attempt to teach Euthyphro a very primitive but basic "lesson in good definition" by making him aware of "the thing-sort and part-whole distinctions " (Albert Anderson, "Socrates' Reasoning in the *Euthyphro,*" Review of Metaphysics 22 [March 1969]: 479). A fifth tries to make the controversial passage 10A to 11B intelligible by disregarding an important distinction which Socrates makes and then comes to the conclusion that "if a moral concept M is such that there is an authority whose judgment whether or not something falls under M is decisive and is rationally grounded, then 'M' cannot be defined in terms of that authority's judgment" (S. Marc Cohen, "Socrates on the Definition of Piety: *Euthyphro* 10A–11B," *Journal of the History of Philosophy* 9 [January 1971]: 13). This simply means that the essence of a moral act cannot consist in blind obedience to an authority, no matter how wise and competent that authority may be. This is not exactly a world-shaking discovery. It tells us very little about a moral act in general and nothing specifically about piety as a moral excellence.

Despite their predilection for the logical, most modern interpreters have shied away from the argument which occupies the very center of the dialogue and deals with the question of whether "that which is holy is loved by the gods because it is holy, or whether it is holy because it is loved by the gods " (10A–11B). Some pay no attention to it at all, one regards it as altogether unintelligible (John H. Brown, "The Logic of Euthyphro 10A–11B" Philosophical Quarterly 14 [Jan. 1964]: 13), and another devotes just a few lines to it, saying that "Euthyphro has great difficulty following this part of the argument," and, although claiming to give an interpretation of the dialogue as a whole, simply concludes that "this part of the dialogue ends in confusion " (Frederick Rosen, "Piety and Justice: Plato's Euthyphro," *Philosophy: Journal of the Royal Institute of Philosophy*, vol. 43, no. 164, pp. 111–12). Only one author of an article attempts a detailed analysis of the argument in question. But he manages to make it intelligible only at the cost of disregarding a significant distinction which Socrates introduces (S. Marc Cohen, "Definition of Piety," p. 6, line 7).

Another crucial passage is usually passed by in silence or given a very superficial explanation. It is the paradox resulting from the definition of piety as that part of justice which consists in a service to the gods. If our service is not to be useless, it must contribute something which the gods all by themselves cannot achieve. Plato seems to hint that the answer to this question is decisive for the successful outcome of the discussion, for he asks again and again, "what is that supreme result [pagkalon ergon] which the gods produce when they employ our services?" (13E). And then, to underscore once more the crucial stage which the inquiry has reached, he pretends that Euthyphro could give him the required answer, if he only were willing (14B–C).

To ignore a paradox made so conspicuous is bound to be fatal to an understanding of the dialogue. For the paradox is one of the chief devices of Plato, who does not try to convince the reader through logical argument but wants to help him see for himself. In other words, the approach is not so much logical as phenomenological, and if logic is used at all, then it is in the service of phenomenology, understanding phenomenology in Heidegger's sense as that which makes manifest, i.e., "lets that which shows itself be seen from itself in the very way in which it shows itself from itself" (Martin Heidegger, *Being and Time,* trans. John Macquarrie and Edward Robinson [New York: Harper & Row, 1962], p. 58).

2. Unless otherwise indicated, quotations from the *Euthyphro* refer to the translation by Lane Cooper in *The Collected Dialogues of Plato,* ed. E. Hamilton and H. Cairns, Bollingen Series, 71 (Princeton, N.J.: Princeton University Press, 1971).

3. Martin Heidegger, *Vom Ursprung des Kunstwerkes* (Stuttgart: Philipp Reclam, 1960), p. 8.

4. "In der Front standhalten wird im allgemeinen als Tapferkeit angesehen, aber es kann eine Taktik sein, durch ein scheinbares Fliehen die feindliche Front aufzulockern und dann zu vernichten. Also ist nicht dieses Standhalten als solches das Wesen der Tapferkeit; denn das Fliehen ist in diesem Falle auch tapfer." (Hans-Georg Gadamer, *Platos dialektische Ethik und andere Studien zur platonischen Philosophie* [Hamburg: Felix Meimer Verlag 1966] p. 43.)

5. Plato says so explicitly in a later dialogue: "The difference of men and actions, and the endless irregular movement of human things, do not admit of any universal and simple rule. And no art whatsoever can lay down a rule which will last for all time " (*Statesman* 294B,J).

6. P. T. Geach calls Socrates' insistence on a definition and his refusal to accept examples to elucidate the meaning of a term, a "style of mistaken thinking . . . which may be called the Socratic fallacy, for its *locus classicus* is the Socratic dialogues " ("Plato's *Enthyphro*" p. 371). "We know heaps of things," he says, "without being able to define the terms in which we express our knowledge. Formal distinctions are only one way of elucidating terms; a set of examples may in a given case be more useful than a formal definition " (ibid.).

Albert Anderson ("Socrates Reasoning," pp. 462–65), has given a detailed refutation of Geach's view. One might add that Socrates is not so much interested in establishing the meaning of a term as of exposing the impossible conditions which would have to be met before the absolute certainty which Euthyphro claims to possess about moral matters would be justified. For this reason he seems right in rejecting examples and insisting on a definition.

7. P. T. Geach here accuses Socrates of establishing a false dichotomy between "factual questions, for which there is a definite and accepted decision procedure, and moral questions, for which there is no such procedure" ("Plato's *Euthyphro,* " p. 373). Against Geach, Albert Anderson argues that "there is nothing in the Euthyphro which indicates that Socrates tries to make such a distinction, or that he thought that one kind was essentially undecidable. Nor is it necessary that Socrates sustain such a distinction in his argument against Euthyphro" ("Socrates' Reasoning," p. 468). ". . . the fact that the gods quarrel sometimes, if not always, is sufficient to make it probable that they may not be agreed that Euthyphro's action is pious." (ibid., p. 469).

8. S. Marc Cohen ("Definition of Piety" p. 6) takes an easy way out of the difficulty by simply reading the inflected passive in an active sense: "If we are to understand the earlier distinction between active and passive participles to have any bearing on the later distinction between two passive forms, we must, I think, give the inflected passive . . . an active sense." But if the passive can be read in an active sense, then why did Plato bother to replace the active by the passive?

9. This interpretation would not violate the equivalence in meaning which, according

to Robert G. Hoerber, is maintained by Aristotle who "recognizes *badizon esti* as equivalent to *badizei*, and *hygiainon esti* as equivalent to *hygiainei* (*Physics* 185b 25–30; *Metaphysics* 1017a 28–30)" ("Plato's *Euthyphro*," p. 103). For both terms refer to the same aspect, once conceived in isolation and once in conjunction with the thing to which it belongs.

10. The approach of P. T. Geach to this phase of the argument serves as an illustration of how not to read a Platonic dialogue. Instead of taking the conflict between the obvious difference among the examples on the one hand, and the aim of the Socratic *epagoge* on the other, as a challenge, he simply denies the possibility of a common element. "The assimilation is certainly wrong," he says, "for among grammatically transitive verbs, verbs like 'know', 'love' and 'see' are logically quite different from verbal expressions that something is shifted or altered" ("Plato's *Enthyphro*," p. 379). Making no further effort at discovering a hidden sameness among the examples used, he finds the replacement of the active form by a passive form completely unintelligible (ibid., p. 378). "Fortunately," he says, "there is no need for us to try and solve this problem; for the supposed parity of reasoning between 'carried' and 'loved' just does not exist " (ibid., p. 378). Apparently satisfied with having found a flaw in the argument, he regards "the remainder of the dialogue . . . of less interest" (ibid., p. 380), and recommends the reading of the *Euthyphro* because, among other things, one "may learn to be forewarned against some common fallacies and debating tricks in moral disputes" (ibid., p. 369).

11. According to Robert G. Hoerber, Socrates' elucidation "involves a straw man which Plato builds up and then proceeds to knock down . . ." ("Plato's *Euthyphro*," pp. 102–3). The first set of pairs of agents and patients, in the view of Hoerber, imply causation. Socrates is then said to pass surreptitiously to two pairs which involve no causation. Euthyphro mistakenly assumes that "agency and causation are involved also in the second set of pairs" and as a result makes the wrong choice "by which Socrates can overthrow easily the altered definition" (ibid., p. 103). It is difficult to see what good would be accomplished through the deception of Euthyphro. His fanatical zeal remains unshaken at the end of the dialogue. If it were meant as a dramatic device to guide the thought of the reader in the direction of an insight, then the commentator should make clear what that insight is. Hoerber, however, seems to take the deception at its face value. "Euthyphro's views on religion do not meet the standards of Plato and Socrates; hence the definition must go, even if by an illogical argument" (ibid., p. 102). It would certainly be odd for a philosopher to employ dishonest, that is, immoral, means in refuting a false definition of a moral virtue.

12. According to John H. Brown, the first alternant, which says that "the holy is loved by the gods because it is holy" cannot be interpreted to mean that the holy is "loved by the gods for its own sake." "Such a reading," he says, "does not fit the epagoge. None of the instances preceding the general principle accept it. It is nonsense to say that anything is in a state of being carried, led or seen for itself" ("Logic of *Euthyphro*," p. 10). Brown fails to see that the epagoge serves to elucidate only the second and not the first alternant.

13. See pp. 3–4, supra.

14. John H. Brown is of the opinion that Socrates believes the first part of the alternative to be true and the second, which expresses the view of Euthyphro, to be false. Brown also seems to feel that Socrates tries to prove this by a logical argument: "No argument suggested by the text would be logically compelling against Euthyphro given what we can legitimately infer about Euthyphro from the dialogue" ("Logic of *Euthyphro*," pp. 1, 8). It now appears that the second alternant is not so much false as inconsistent

with the conception of piety as a moral excellence; nor is the first simply true, according to Socrates, at least not as long as it is understood as a quality of the act, isolated from the situation in which the act is performed.

15. Cf. A. E. Taylor: "We have to remember that the word *therapeia* was in use in two special connections. It was used of the cult of a deity by his worshipper . . . or of a great man by his courtiers, and of the 'tending' of men or animals by professionals such as physicians, and grooms" (*Plato: The Man and His Work* [London: Methuen & Co. 1949], p. 154).

16. Paul Friedländer, *Plato,* vol. 2 (New York: Random House, 1964), p. 88.

17. Ibid., p. 89.

18. Taylor, *Plato,* p. 155.

19. Ibid.

20. Martin Heidegger, *Phaenomenologie und Theologie* (Frankfurt am Main: Vittorio Klostermann, 1970).

3

Lesser Hippias: Beyond Good and Evil

The *Lesser Hippias* is of special interest to the present inquiry. For its meaning has persistently escaped the efforts of the elite in Platonic scholarship. Yet when the dialogue is viewed in the light of Heidegger's Dasein analytic, the fog which envelopes it dissolves and its truth shines forth in unmistakable clarity.

In this dialogue, Plato comes closest to a specific discussion of authenticity without violating the dictum that a dramatist must not teach except by indirection. Socrates defends the view that the voluntary evildoer is better than the involuntary one and makes several unsuccessful attempts to convince Hippias, the famous polymath. The word "better" refers to the ontological level. The voluntary evildoer knows what he is doing and has freely decided to do the deed. He is therefore responsible for it and to that extent a genuine or authentic self. The involuntary evildoer cannot be held accountable, for his act is not his own, and to that extent he is inauthentic. The distinction between the two is ontological, because it refers to two different modes of being, namely, authentic and inauthentic selves. By using the term "evil," Socrates seems to speak not from an ontological but from a moral point of view. Hippias, despite his acuity, gets confused and does not comprehend. Maybe we had better say: Plato does not let him comprehend. Is Plato trying to suggest that even highly intelligent people fail to see, or perhaps refuse to see, the difference between the moral and the ontological, that is, between morality and the condition for its possibility?

By a strange coincidence, the famous commentators, such as Taylor, Shorey, Friedänder, Grube et al., also fail to see the distinction. These same scholars tend to interpret the dialogues too literally; but in the case of the *Lesser Hippias*, where Socrates' pronouncements can almost be taken at face value, they insist that he does not mean at all what he says explicitly. For while he speaks of a voluntary evildoer as if he did exist, he really implies that such a being is impossible. The dialogue, in their view, would therefore give an indirect proof of what they regard as well-established Platonic doctrine to the effect that all wrongdoing is involuntary. Socrates himself is said to give a clear indication of his real intention when a few lines from the end of the dialogue he qualifies the conclusion that the voluntary evildoer is the better man by adding: "If there be such a man" (376B).[1] In Taylor's view, with which the major commentators are in agreement, "the insinuation plainly is that there really is no such person as the man who does wrong on purpose, and that the paradox does not arise simply because there is no such person."[2]

It is not immediately evident, however, that there can be no voluntary wrongdoer. Nor does the remark "if there be such a man" seem to constitute incontrovertible evidence of Socrates' real view on the matter. The same qualification appears earlier in the dialogue in connection with the geometer who masters his science. "If there be a man who is false about diagrams," says Socrates, "the good man will be he, for he is able to be false, whereas the bad is unable" (367E). May not the geometer in the classroom deliberately design errors which the student is meant to uncover, and may not one surveying land falsify his findings in favor of a poor peasant at the expense of a rich landowner on whom he thereby voluntarily inflicts an evil or injury?

Furthermore, there are several other restrictions which Socrates imposes on the position he defends in the dialogue. It seems somewhat arbitrary to seize upon one (". . . if there be such a man . . .") and regard it as a clear sign that he does not wish to be taken seriously, when there are others pointing in the opposite direction. About the middle of the dialogue, for instance, he confesses to be "sometimes of the opposite opinion." But at the same time he insists that "just now [he] happens to be in a crisis of [his] disorder at which those who err voluntarily appear to [him] better than those who err involuntarily." He blames his present "state of mind" on the previous argument but again insists that it "inclines [him] to believe that in general those who do wrong involuntarily are worse than those who do wrong voluntarily" (372D–E). There is nothing in these statements which would allow us to regard one as the real view and the other as a mere pretense. At the end of the dialogue the same indecisiveness occurs. When Hippias expresses his disagreement with Socrates' position, Socrates replies: "Nor can I agree with myself." But then he adds: "Yet that seems to be the conclusion which, as far as we can see at present, must follow from the argument" (376B–C).

In the light of the Socratic method it is quite conceivable that the hesitations are meant as a challenge to the reader not to follow Socrates uncritically, but to examine his paradoxical claim and see for himself what measure of truth or falsehood it contains. But in the spirit of the same method the practically unanimous agreement among modern commentators that Socrates himself rejects the position which he ostensibly defends in the *Hippias Minor* should also and perhaps first of all be subjected to a careful scrutiny.

The question which above all others one feels compelled to ask is why the voluntary evildoer should be an impossibility. In the opinion of Paul Friedländer, Socrates' claim that the voluntary is better than the involuntary evildoer, is "wrong and indeed criminal according to common usage and valid legal principles; according to Socrates it is meaningless, because it is self-contradictory."[3] But just how does the contradiction arise? Perhaps one might reason as follows: The voluntary evildoer, as Socrates maintains, has knowledge and power which the involuntary evildoer lacks. Therefore, the first is in control and knows what he is doing, while the second is not in control and the act is not really his own at all. Hence the voluntary evildoer is superior to the involuntary. But it is this same superiority which makes the voluntary evildoer guilty before the law, just as the inferiority of the involuntary evildoer makes him less guilty or not guilty at all. "Surely," says Hippias, "there is a great excuse to be made for a man telling a falsehood or doing an injury or any sort of harm to another in ignorance. The laws are obviously far more severe on those who lie or do evil voluntarily, than those who do evil involuntarily" (372A). So it seems that if we admit the possibility of a voluntary evildoer we must say that he is better for the same reasons that make him guiltier, while the involuntary evildoer is worse for reasons that make him less guilty or guiltless. In other words, the better is guilty because he is better; the worse is guiltless in so far as he is worse. And since it is better to be guiltless than to be guilty, we can sharpen the paradox by saying that the better man is worse because he is better, and the worse is better because he is worse.

The reluctance to run the risk of getting entangled in such perplexities might understandably have induced a strong urge among interpreters to deny the voluntary evildoer the right to exist. And since this denial amounts to what is generally regarded as well-established Platonic doctrine, they would have to feel no qualms about yielding to this feeling. But whatever their ultimate motives, they do in fact appeal to this doctrine to justify their belief that Socrates himself rejects the position which he seems to advocate in our dialogue.

This raises the inescapable question of the validity of this doctrine as Platonic. Before we have examined its credentials in this respect, we have no right to appeal to it in an attempt to resolve the paradox of the *Hippias Minor*.

Is it possible that the "doctrine" constitutes a belief which was generally held in Greece, or at least in Athens, and that it is not necessary to establish it as specifically Platonic? "Euripides in his *Medea*, addressing himself to this question," so Professor Gregory Vlastos reports, "declares flatly for the negative." Medea comes to the realization that the only way to hurt Jason is to murder her children. She is fully aware of what she is doing, and she knows that she will inflict greater suffering on herself than on him. "I know the evil I am about to do," she declares. And yet she carries out her fateful decision. "So here on the stage before our eyes," Professor Vlastos concludes, "Euripides gives Socrates the lie."[4]

Not even the dialogues themselves seem to be in full agreement on the issue. As we have seen, Socrates' paradoxical wish in the *Crito* that the many could do the greatest evil, implies not only Socrates' belief in the possibility of a voluntary evildoer, but his recognition that the capability of doing evil voluntarily is the condition for the possibility of being moral. Furthermore, Alcibiades, in his eulogy of Socrates in the *Symposium*, depicts himself as a voluntary evildoer. It is true, Alcibiades is intoxicated, but he has challenged Socrates to correct him if anything he says is not strictly in accordance with the truth, and Socrates remains significantly silent:

> This Marsyas has often brought me to such a pass that I felt as if I could hardly endure the life which I am leading (as Socrates you will admit); and I am conscious that if I did not shut my ears against him and fly as from the voice of the siren, my fate would be like that of others—he would transfix me, and I would grow old sitting at his feet. (216A)[5]

Here the ill-famed Alcibiades is shown to resist with all his might the attraction of the good life exemplified by Socrates and to persist, with full awareness, in his own evil ways.

The view that the doctrine under consideration is Platonic appears now rather dubious. It therefore becomes imperative to cast a critical eye on its *locus classicus* in the *Protagoras*.

The doctrine is mentioned for the first time in the exegesis of a poem by Simonides, and it is extracted by what Taylor calls "an impossible punctuation."[6] The passage in question reads: "But he who does no evil voluntarily I praise and love" (345D).[7] Socrates insists on placing the comma after *evil* instead of after *voluntarily*, because, he says, "no wise man will allow that any human being errs voluntarily or voluntarily does evil and base actions; but they are very well aware that all who do evil and base things do them against their will" (345D–E). This appeal for support to the "wise men" need not be taken any more seriously than the obviously satirical remark in the *Hippias Minor* where he confesses that he "hardly ever has the same opinion as they have," and asks: "what proof of ignorance can be greater than to differ from wise men?" (372B–C).

Next the doctrine appears as one of two extremes in a discussion on the power of knowledge. Socrates asks Protagoras whether he agrees with the many who hold that "a man may have knowledge, and yet the knowledge which is in him may be overmastered by anger, or pleasure, or pain, or love, or perhaps by fear—just as if knowledge were nothing but a slave and might be dragged about by all these other things" (352B–C). Since Protagoras charges a high fee and guarantees success, he cannot accept the view which would declare knowledge worthless. Nor can he admit the true state of affairs, namely that knowledge sometimes wins the upper hand and that sometimes the passions override a man's better judgment. He boasts that if a young man associates with him "on the first day he will be in a position to return home a better man than he came" (318A). This boast implies a guarantee in regard not only to the quality of his teaching, but also to its acceptance by his pupil and the latter's willingness to carry it into practice. Young children, as he has said earlier in the dialogue, can be "straightened by threats and blows like a piece of bent or warped wood" (325D). No such disciplinary measures can be applied to the young Athenians who flock to him, and Protagoras therefore feels compelled to assent to the other extreme which Socrates offers, namely, that "knowledge is a noble thing and fit to command in man, which cannot be overcome and will not allow a man, if he only knows the good and the evil, to do anything which is contrary to what his knowledge bids him do" (352B–C). Thus the "doctrine" appears as a consequence of Protagoras's boast rather than as a belief of either Socrates or Plato.

Finally, Socrates recalls the "doctrine" just prior to his attempted demonstration of the unity of courage and wisdom. As already suggested above, it is really a presupposition of the boastful claim of Protagoras. How can he guarantee to make a man better by instruction, unless in the face of a clearly perceived good the student is determined in his choice? Socrates exposes the preposterous character of this claim by making its presupposition the premise of an argument which ends in an absurd conclusion. To the premise that no man willingly pursues evil, he adds the definition of fear as "the expectation of evil" (358D). The argument then proceeds as follows:

> Do cowards go where there is nothing to fear, and the brave where there is much to fear?
> Yes, Socrates, so men say.
> Very true, I said. But I want to know against what do you say that the brave are ready to go—against fearful things, believing them to be fearful things, or against things which are not fearful?
> No, he said; the former case has been proved by you in the previous argument to be impossible.
> That again, I replied, is quite true. And if this has been rightly proved, then no one goes to meet what he thinks fearful. . . .
> He assented.
> And yet the brave man and the coward alike go to meet that about which they are confident; so that, in this point of view, the cowardly and the brave go to meet the same things. (359C–E)

The conclusion contradicts experience, and Protagoras himself is made to exclaim:

And yet, Socrates, that against which the coward goes is the opposite of that against which the brave goes. The one, for example, is willing to go to battle, and the other is not willing. (359E)

The playfulness of its introduction in connection with the interpretation of a poem by Simonides, its presentation as one of two extremes, its use as a premise in an argument which leads to an absurd conclusion—all this surely does not lend support to its accreditation as a doctrine seriously entertained by Plato. And if the view that no man willingly pursues evil is itself in conflict with the commonsense view of what distinguishes the coward and the brave, how can it be used to resolve the paradoxical conclusion of the *Hippias Minor* that the voluntary is better than the involuntary evildoer, which in its turn is said to conflict with common sense and even valid legal principles? If, with Taylor and those who follow him, we deny that there are voluntary evildoers, on the ground that they would be both better and not better, then we avoid the disturbing conclusion of the *Hippias Minor*. But we escape one trap merely in order to fall into another, for by maintaining that there are only involuntary evildoers, we lose the distinction between the coward and the brave as indicated in the *Protagoras*. Letting "V" stand for the voluntary evildoer, and "B" for better, then interpreters of the *Hippias Minor* can be said to argue as follows:

$V \supset (B \cdot \sim B)$ Premiss or theme of the H. M.

$\sim (B \cdot \sim B)$ Tautology

$\sim V$ Conclusion (There are no voluntary evil-doers)

But then they would have to argue in the *Protagoras* (letting "B" stand for brave):

$\sim V \supset (B \cdot \sim B)$ Premiss

$\sim V$ From Hippias Minor

$B \cdot \sim B$ Conclusion

So that they would be as much in difficulty as before. In other words, they find themselves in an exegetical quagmire from which only a radically different interpretation has a chance of extracting them.

Before attempting a new approach, we should make sure that we have a clear conception of the nature of the dilemma in order to see whether and in what direction there is a possible way of escape. As noted before, the difficulty is occasioned by a conflict between the conclusion of the *Hippias Minor* to the effect that the voluntary is better than the involuntary evildoer, and common sense which holds the opposite. If we let "V" stand for voluntary evildoer, "$\sim V$" for nonvoluntary or involuntary evildoer, "B" for better than, the paradox can be formally expressed as follows:

1. $(x)(y)[(V_x \cdot \sim V_y) \supset B_{xy}]$ Hippias Minor
2. $(x)(y)[(V_x \cdot \sim V_y) \supset \sim B_{xy}]$ Common sense view
3. $(x)(y)[(V_x \cdot \sim V_y) \supset (B_{xy} \cdot \sim B_{xy})]$ 1, 2
4. $(x)(y) \sim (V_x \cdot \sim V_y)$ 3
5. $(x) \sim V_x \, V (y) \, V_y$ 4
6. $\sim (\exists_x) V_x \, V \sim (\exists_y) \sim V_y$ 5

The conclusion leaves us a choice between:

(a) There are no voluntary evildoers.

(b) There are no involuntary evildoers.

Now (b) clearly violates experience, for much harm is done unintentionally. This seems to leave us with (a), and since this has long been regarded as a Platonic doctrine, it is understandable that it should have been taken as the indirectly established theme of the *Hippias Minor*. Unfortunately, however, we have found that in the *Protagoras* Socrates derives absurd conclusions also from (a), not to mention the fact that it is contradicted by passages in the *Symposium* and the *Crito*. This makes the claim that (a) in a Platonic doctrine altogether untenable.[8] And since, as noted before, it also violates common sense, we have no reason to accept it. In fact, it becomes like (b) an impossible choice. But if we reject both alternants of the alternative which constitutes the conclusion of a valid argument, we must, to remain consistent, find fault with premises. Now the only chance of breaking the deadlock seems to be offered by an examination of line (3) of the above argument. If it could be shown that B in B_{xy} and $\sim B_{xy}$ refers to different aspects or levels of reality, then there would be no contradiction in the consequent of the conditional proposition and the embarrassing alternative in the conclusion would not arise.

In order to help the reader in the discovery of the distinction necessary to resolve the paradox, Plato, in accordance with his method, ought to give some hints. The problem now is, where to find them. Of course, we could go back to the *Crito* where Plato refers to authenticity and inauthenticity, to the latter by showing Crito in bondage to the opinion of the many; the former by having Socrates point to the capability of doing both good and evil as the condition for the possibility of morality (44D). There is nothing wrong in drawing upon other dialogues for suggestions to resolve a paradox, provided that these suggestions are tested against specific statements in the dialogue under consideration. But it would be preferable to derive them directly from the dialogue in which the paradox appears. Before making an attempt in that direction, let us see whether the notions of authenticity and inauthenticity help us remove the logical difficulties which we encounter.

The argument has left us with a choice between two equally unacceptable statements, namely, one according to which all men are voluntary evildoers, and another which maintains that no man does evil voluntarily. With the distinction between morality and the ground of morality, i.e., between the moral and the condition for its possibility, we can escape the dilemma. It will be recalled that Socrates in the *Hippias Minor* claims that the voluntary evildoer is better, while common sense regards the involuntary evildoer as better. Now we see that the combination of the two propositions does not lead to a contradiction, since the word "better" refers to two distinct levels. In the case of Socrates, it is applied to the individual who, because he is said to possess knowledge and power, has met the prerequisites for being moral, whether morally good or morally evil; in the case of common sense it is applied to the man who is guiltless, that is, not morally evil because, lacking control and awareness, he is not moral at all. Just because the voluntary evildoer is moral, he is called to account and declared guilty, and perhaps subjected to severe punishment. The involuntary evildoer is not punished and the forgiveness granted to him stamps him, at least in regard to this particular act, as amoral. So punishment can be a recognition of worth, that is, of authenticity. This is what Dante acknowledges in the *Inferno* when he allowed the Trimmers, who refused to make decisions and take sides, neither into heaven nor into hell. That they should not have merited heaven is obvious: they performed no good deeds. Since they did no evil deeds either, one would expect Dante to say that they did not have to go to hell. Instead he says they were not worthy of it:

> Heaven chased them forth to keep its beauty from impair; and the deep Hell receives them not, for the wicked would have some glory over them. (Canto 3, ll. 40–43)

We need not have gone to the *Crito* for hints as to the solution of our logical difficulty. For all through our dialogue Socrates speaks of the voluntary evildoer as having knowledge and power, and his opposite, the involuntary evildoer, as lacking it. Once we see the contrast between the voluntary and the involuntary evildoer as a contrast, not between the morally good and the morally evil, but between the authentic or moral, and the inauthentic or amoral, we have found the key to the resolution of the paradox which Socrates constructs in the *Hippias Minor*.

The authentic man, having the *capacity* to do good as well as evil, cannot be said to be morally good or morally evil in any enduring sense, and therefore cannot be tagged with fixed moral qualities. But this is precisely what Hippias does in answer to Socrates' question about the relative worth of the heroes. He claims that Homer meant "Achilles to be true and simple, and Odysseus to be wily and false" (365B). Now it is obvious that if Achilles were always or for the most part truthful, regardless of circumstances, he would be a fool, nor could Odysseus always or usually be wily or false without becoming an utter failure in his alleged attempts to practice deception. Instead of correcting Hippias, Socrates encourages him to widen the dichotomy and to assert that "the true man is not the same as the false" (365C) and that in fact they "are the very opposite

of each other" (366A). Socrates now proceeds to construct a paradox by making
them identical. He induces Hippias to admit that in order to practice deception
the false must possess a certain power which permits a man to do "that which he
wishes at the time when he wishes" (366B), and they must also have a certain
"cunning and a kind of prudence" (365E). In other words, they have knowledge
and therefore are not ignorant but in a sense wise, so that "the false are powerful
and prudent and knowing and wise in those things about which they are false"
(366A). Therefore, Socrates concludes, "the false are to be ranked in the class
of the powerful and wise" (366A). We know now, of course, that the same could
be said not only of the genuinely false, but also of the genuinely true.

Since Hippias has said earlier that the true and the false are opposites,
Socrates could now spring the trap and infer that according to Hippias the true
man is powerless, imprudent and ignorant. But he is interested in leading to a
new insight, not in winning a forensic victory, and he therefore gives the
argument a different turn. Speaking of Hippias's skill as a calculator and
arithmetician, they both agree that as the greatest expert in the field, he would
be best able to tell the truth about numbers. "But would you not also," Socrates
asks, "be the best and most consistent teller of a falsehood, having always the
power of speaking falsely as you have of speaking truly, about these same
matters, if you wanted to tell a falsehood, and not to answer truly" (366E–
367A). A man who is not an expert, on the other hand, might "sometimes
stumble upon the truth, when he wanted to tell a lie, because he did not know"
(367A).

Socrates then recalls Hippias's previous admission to the effect that "he who
is false must have the ability to be false" (367B). And now, he says, we have
discovered that you as an accomplished arithmetician also have the ability to
speak falsely, together with the ability to speak truly. From these two assertions,
Socrates draws the startling conclusion:

> Who, then, is discovered to be false at calculation? Is he not the good man?
> For the good man is the able man, and he is the true man.
> Do you not see that the same man is false and also true about these same
> matters? And the true man is not a whit better than the false, for indeed he is
> the same with him and not the very opposite, as you were just now imagining.
> (367C–D)

Immediately thereafter we are furnished the key to the solution of the paradox.
Socrates first speaks of "the good and wise geometer who has this double
power," and who is "*able* to be false" (367E). Then referring to the astronomer
he begins by describing him as "*able* to be false" but concludes that "in
astronomy also the same man will *be* true and false" (368A). Socrates thus
completely disregards the distinction between the *ability* to be false and *actually*
being false, between the scientist's control over his science which enables him

to put it to whatever use he chooses, and his actual misuse of it. The flagrant disregard of the distinction may reasonably be regarded as Plato's way of calling attention to it, for with its aid we can resolve the paradox. We can see now that when Socrates identifies the false with the true by way of the able and the good, he does not mean that the morally evil who practices deception is morally good. He must rather be understood to say that the *false* must have control over his science, he must be *good* at it or competent, and therefore a genuine or *true* scientist. From the moral level Socrates has moved to its ground, namely, to conscious control. Now even the seemingly absurd statement to the effect that "if Odysseus is false he is also true, and if Achilles is true he is also false" (369B) contains an element of truth. For if the one is genuinely false, he must also have the capacity of being true; and if the other is genuinely true, he must be capable of being false. The true and the false are not the same *simpliciter*, but *secundum quid;* they share the double power of speaking truly and falsely.

Hippias has been quite willing to concede that the good or competent arithmetician, geometer or astronomer is best at speaking falsely, and who, if he does speak falsely, does so voluntarily and is therefore better than the one who speaks falsely involuntarily. But when Socrates extends the principle to all human activities, that is, when he asks "whether voluntary liars . . . are not better than the involuntary," Hippias balks:

And how, Socrates, can those who intentionally err, and voluntarily and designedly commit iniquities, be better than those who err and do wrong involuntarily? Surely there is a great excuse to be made for a man telling a falsehood or doing an injury or any sort of harm to another in ignorance. And the laws are obviously far more severe on those who lie or do evil voluntarily, than on those who do evil involuntarily. (371E–372A)

The objection shows that Hippias has not followed Socrates to the deeper level where the voluntary evildoer is better because he is responsible. He moves wholly on the level of morality, where the involuntary evildoer is better in as much as he deserves a less severe punishment or none at all. If Socrates were speaking on the level of morality, he would agree with Hippias. This is why Socrates says: "Sometimes I am of the opposite opinion . . . but just now I happen to be in a crisis of my disorder at which those who err voluntarily appear to me better than those who err involuntarily" (372D–E).

After a brief interval, during which Hippias must be coaxed into continuing the discussion, Socrates makes a second attempt to lead him to that deeper level. There are good runners and bad runners, he says, and we distinguish them by the way they run. He who runs slowly is said to run ill and is called a bad runner; conversely, the good runner is one who runs quickly and therefore well. "In a race, and in running," Hippias admits, "swiftness is a good and slowness an evil quality" (373D). And yet two runners may run equally slowly

and therefore badly, and in running badly perform a disgraceful act; nevertheless, one must be called better than the other because "he does this bad and
disgraceful action voluntarily" (373E) while the other does it involuntarily. One
runs badly, although he could, if he so chose, run well; the other can only run
badly because his nature or constitution does not allow him to do otherwise.
What is true of running can, of course, also be said of wrestling and "any other
bodily exercise." (374A) In each case, the one who is in control of his action is
superior to the one who is not. Socrates then turns to the various bodily organs:
feet, eyes, voice; to instruments, both inanimate, such as rudder, bow, lyre,
flute, and animate, such as horse and dog; and from instruments he turns to the
user. He speaks of the mind (psyche) of the archer, the lute- or flute-player, the
physician. In all cases, that which makes voluntary ill use possible is better
than that which necessarily produces bad results.

Once more Socrates tries to extend the principle from special skills to human
living in general. "Would we not desire to have our own mind in the best state
possible?" (375C), Socrates asks, and to this Hippias agrees. But then comes
the crucial question:

> Will our minds be better if they do wrong and make mistakes voluntarily, or
> involuntarily? (375D)

Again Hippias demurs:

> Oh, Socrates, it would be a monstrous thing to say that those who do wrong
> voluntarily are better than those who do wrong involuntarily. (375D)

Hippias still thinks that in declaring the evil voluntarily done better, Socrates
regards it as morally good. This would indeed be monstrous, since it is clearly
morally evil. But Socrates calls it better because it is under the control of the
doer and therefore moral, while the evil involuntarily done is not under control
and therefore not moral at all but amoral.

It is astounding that so many modern interpreters should side with Hippias
and object to the extension which Socrates here attempts. "Knowledge of the
good," says A.E. Taylor, "is . . . the only knowledge which cannot be put to
wrong use; every other kind of knowledge can be abused, and is abused when it
is put to bad use . . ."[9] According to Friedländer, "the just soul, acting in
accordance with its own nature, cannot do wrong, and that nobody acting in
accordance with his own nature would voluntarily do wrong."[10] Justice,
according to these men, seems to be a fixed quality which, when a man
possesses it, draws him irresistibly toward the good. But how can such a man
still be called free and responsible and therefore moral?[11] And if a competent
scientist wilfully uses his skill for an evil purpose, is he not precisely
accountable and therefore moral because he also has the power to use it for a

good purpose. It is this twofold power which is the ground of morality and to which Socrates now directs his attention.

Rather abruptly he introduces power and knowledge as somehow related to justice. It cannot be denied, of course, that in order to act justly a man must know what the just is and he must have the power to perform the act. Power and knowledge are not justice; they are, as we have seen in connection with the scientist, the necessary conditions for its possibility. Their possession makes a man capable of performing a just act. Since Hippias has been unwilling or unable to distinguish between the act and its ground or necessary condition, Socrates himself now disregards the distinction; and instead of saying "is made possible by" or "is made capable of," he simply says "is":

> *Is* not justice a power, or knowledge, or both? . . .
> If justice is a power, then the soul which has the greater power *is* also the more just. . . .
> And if justice is knowledge, then the wiser will *be* the juster soul, . . .
> And if justice be power as well as knowledge—then will not the soul which has both knowledge and power *be* the more just. . . . (375D–E) [Italics added]

Earlier it has been found that "the soul which has the greater power and wisdom is better able to do both good and evil in every action" (375E). And if it "acts ill, it acts voluntarily by power and art" (376A). But power and art, or knowledge, now turn out to be "either one or both of them . . . elements of justice" (376A). So the implied conclusion is that the soul, when it does wrong voluntarily, does wrong with elements of justice, namely, power and knowledge. But how can elements of justice possibly be contributing factors to doing evil?

The absurdity disappears if, instead of saying: knowledge and power make the soul more just, we say, they make it more *capable of acting justly*. Of course, they make it also more capable of acting unjustly. But this is precisely the ability which the moral man must possess and the amoral lacks, namely to choose between the morally good and the morally evil act. Otherwise his behavior could be called neither meritorious nor worthy of blame. Thus by correcting the fallacy in the argument of Socrates, we are led to the truth he meant to convey.

Hippias is blind to the relevant distinctions and unable to see beyond the paradox. It is understandable, therefore, that he should brush all reasoning aside and bluntly assert: "There I cannot agree with you" (376B). It is less obvious why Socrates should add: "Nor can I agree with myself" (376B).

What does it mean to disagree with oneself? Socrates, as we have seen, has proceeded from the outer to the inner, from the ability of instruments to perform both well and ill, to conscious control over such instruments, and finally to the ability of the psyche or self to perform good *and* evil acts. Again and again he has brought into view the possibility of choosing to act with knowledge and power, that is, to exist as an authentic individual. Not unless he makes or has made that choice is Socrates at one with himself. And even the reader who has successfully followed the arguments of Socrates has gained little unless he too takes this final step and seizes hold of this most basic possibility. For only by refusing to let others make his decisions for him, can he acquire that knowledge and power which, according to Socrates, makes his soul capable of justice or, in modern terminology, his self a genuine self.

The choice in question is not, of course, a completely free choice. Plato, at least as far as the *Hippias Minor* is concerned, has nothing to say about this. Heidegger, however, calls attention to the fact that the individual can take possession of himself only as what he already is. He has been "thrown" into the world, into a specific culture, and has been endowed with certain capacities and talents, and deprived of some others. Heidegger, therefore, calls the possibility of taking hold of oneself a "thrown possibility":

> Possibility, as an *existential*, does not signify a free-floating potentiality-for-Being in the sense of the 'liberty of indifference' (libertas indifferentiae). In every case Dasein . . . has already got itself into definite possibilities. As the potentiality-for-Being which it *is*, it has let such possibilities pass by; it is constantly waiving the possibilities of its Being, or else it seizes upon them and makes mistakes. But this means that Dasein is Being-possible which has been delivered over to itself—*thrown possibility* through and through. Dasein is the possibility of Being-free *for* its ownmost potentiality-for-Being. (p. 183)[12]

Hippias, as we have seen, was quite willing to grant that all sorts of specialists, such as arithmeticians, geometers, astronomers, if they are competent, possess the ability of using and misusing their skill. But whenever Socrates turned to the moral man and maintained that he too possesses this "double power," that is, of acting rightly and wrongly, Hippias disagreed. This is surprising, for Hippias, unlike Euthyphro, is far from stupid. In fact he is a famous polymath of no mean accomplishments. Why, then, his stubborn refusal to acknowledge a fairly obvious truth?

One of Heidegger's essential characteristics of the human mode of being, namely fallenness, sheds some light on this aspect of Hippias's behavior in the dialogue. It suggests, not a lack of understanding on the part of Hippias, but an unwillingness to face himself as he really is. For if it is not possible to call Achilles simply honest and true, and Odysseus wily and false, the suspicion arises that man is not basically an entity endowed with definite qualities. But why should this realization be so disturbing?

As Heidegger points out, we usually understand ourselves in terms of what he calls our concernful dealings with things encountered in the world and in terms of our relationship with others. We see ourselves as craftsmen or professionals,

as parents or friends. We are at home in these concerns and these roles. We feel
we know who we are. But when these concerns lose their significance in anxiety,
in the face of disaster, the individual seems to have lost hold of himself. He
finds nothing stable to which he might cling and with which he might identify
himself. In Heidegger's terms, he is then thrown back upon himself as sheer
"potentiality-for-Being." He no longer feels at home with himself and tries to
flee from this uncanniness. (Heidegger's term is *Unheimlichkeit,* literally,
not-at-homeness):

> When Dasein "understands" uncanniness in the everyday manner, it does so
> by turning away from it in falling; in this turning away, the "not-at-home" gets
> "dimmed down." . . . That kind of Being-in-the-world which is tranquilized
> and familiar is a mode of Dasein's uncanniness, not the reverse. *From an
> existential-ontological point of view, the "not-at-home" must be conceived as
> the more primordial phenomenon.* (P. 234)

Even the fleeing, however, implies an understanding of himself, no matter
how vague this understanding may be:

> Only to the extent that Dasein has been brought before itself in an ontologi-
> cally essential manner through whatever disclosedness belongs to it, *can* it
> flee *in the face of* that in the face of which it flees. . . . That in the face of
> which Dasein thus shrinks back must, in any case, be an entity with the
> character of threatening; yet this entity has the same kind of Being as the one
> that shrinks back: it is Dasein itself. (Pp. 229–30)

Socrates' discussion with Hippias can now be seen as an attempt to stop him
in his futile flight and to call him "all the way back to [his] naked uncanniness,"
and by taking him "back from [his] *'worldly'* possibilities, he at the same time
gives [him] the possibility of an *authentic* potentiality-for-Being" (P. 394).

Plato does not let Socrates succeed in budging Hippias from his position,
despite the obviousness of the arguments employed. He thereby indicates the
firm grip which inauthenticity may have even on a highly intelligent individual.
In fact Hippias's very achievements facilitate his flight from his true self. In this
condition, says Heidegger, "one is what one does" (p. 283) and Hippias's
activities are remarkable, both in quality and diversity. He is not only a skilled
orator, a poet and a prose writer, but also an accomplished craftsman who once
went to the Olympic games arrayed and adorned with articles of his own making.
Proudly he tells Socrates: "Since the day when I first entered the lists at
Olympia I have never found any man who was my superior in anything" (364A).
No wonder that Socrates' arguments did not prevail against such self-confidence
and assurance.

While Plato, however, merely hints at the way in which men tend to hide from
themselves, Heidegger describes the condition in considerable detail. He points
out that human beings fall captive not only to the roles which they play in the
world, but also to the group to which they happen to belong. This bondage,

according to Heidegger, has certain characteristics, of which *tranquillization*, *disburdening*, and *distantiality* are the most significant. We feel assured when we share our beliefs with others, when we approve what they approve, condemn what they condemn. "We take pleasure and enjoy ourselves as *they* take pleasure; we read, see and judge about literature as *they* see and judge . . . we find shocking what they find shocking" (p. 164). Thus the individual self becomes submerged in the group, the "they-self," of which it is a part. The insecurity of human life is dimmed down and we experience a *tranquillizing* sense of belonging. The surrender to the "they-self" *disburdens* the individual of the agonizing task of having to make decisions in the complex and uncertain situations of human existence. The "they-self," says Heidegger, "can be answerable for everything most easily, because it is not someone who needs to vouch for anything. It 'was' always the 'they' who did it, and yet it can be said that it was 'no one' " (165). The third characteristic, *distantiality*, is the most relevant to our dialogue. We measure ourselves, according to Heidegger, in terms of the distance which separates us from others, "whether that difference is merely one that is evened out, whether one's own Dasein has lagged behind the Others and wants to catch up in relationship to them, or whether one's Dasein already has some priority over them and sets out to keep them suppressed (p. 163–64). Hippias feels superior to other people, and in this superiority he sees his worth. He does not realize that through his pride in this superiority he has fallen victim to a most subtle and stubborn bondage. One can perhaps best visualize that dependence if one imagines what would happen to Hippias if someone defeated him at Olympia, or if young men grew up endowed with talents equal to his own, or if he came to a country where most people were on his level of achievement. Most likely he would feel shattered in his selfhood, even if his capabilities had undergone no change whatsoever.

Hippias, as he appears in the dialogue, creates a false sense of security by attributing to himself and to others a measure of stability incompatible with the human mode of being. He identifies himself with his achievements, believing himself to *be* a polymath and to *be* a victor at the Olympian games; he forgets that these are roles he has chosen to play, that he was free to develop other capabilities in quite different directions, and that the chooser and the role chosen are not the same. And when dealing with others he assumes, as shown in his characterization of Achilles and Odysseus, that they have fixed qualities which make judgments about them easy and reliable. Socrates' repeated efforts to budge him from his position leave him unmoved. Nor is Plato any more successful with the interpreters of his dialogue, for they too, as we have seen, speak with Friedländer of the *nature* of the just soul and its *inability* to do wrong, and thus side with Hippias instead of Socrates. They too refuse to face themselves as what they basically are, namely potentiality-for-being, and fail to realize that even their selfhood is something to be achieved rather than conferred upon them ready-made at birth.

Socrates' verbal assault on Hippias has been as ineffectual as Crito's long and intimate association with Socrates. And it is doubtful whether an analysis of the "call of conscience," similar to that of Heidegger, would have done any good. Rational arguments alone seem too weak to arrest men's headlong flight from their own selves. This is why Heidegger calls upon an emotion, namely anxiety, "as a distinctive way in which Dasein is disclosed" (228). Was Plato familiar with the revelatory function of this powerful emotion? Since anxiety is said to arise in the face of the possibility of imminent death, it should, if anywhere in the dialogues, show itself in the *Phaedo*.

NOTES

1. All quotations from the *Hippias Minor* refer to the translation by B. Jowett in *The Collected Dialogues of Plato*, ed. E. Hamilton and H. Cairns (Princeton, N.J.: Princeton University Press, 1961).

2. A. E. Taylor, *Plato: The Man and His Work* (London: Methuen & Co., 1949), p. 37. Paul Shorey: "A few lines from the end of the dialogue, however, Plato warns the observant reader by a reservation. The one who errs voluntarily is the good man, if there is anyone who errs voluntarily. But it is a fundamental Socratic doctrine, which Plato himself holds in some sense to the end, that no man does err voluntarily." *What Plato Said* (Chicago: University of Chicago Press, 1933), p. 89. G. M. A. Grube: ". . . the Hippias Minor . . . is an apparent *reductio ad absurdum* of the equation 'virtue is knowledge' in its simplest form. . . ." *Plato's Thought* (Boston: Beacon Press, 1961), p. xii. Rosamond Kent Sprague: "The good man has the power to err, but cannot by the very description of his nature, have the desire to do so. . . . Plato gives us the key to all this when he says in Socrates' next to the last speech, 'if there be such a man'; we are to infer that there is none." *Plato's Use of Fallacy* (New York: Barnes and Noble, 1962), p. 76. Also, Paul Friedländer, Plato, 2. (New York: Random House, 1964), p. 143; p. 366, note 4.

3. Friedländer, Plato, 2:144.

4. *Plato's "Protagoras,"* ed. with an Introduction by Gregory Vlastos (New York: Liberal Arts Press, 1956) p. xliv.

5. All quotations from the *Symposium* refer to *The Dialogues of Plato*, translated by B. Jowett, vol. 1 (New York: Random House, 1937).

6. Taylor, *Plato*, p. 256.

7. All quotations from the Protagoras refer to *Plato's "Protagoras,"* ed. with an Introduction by Gregory Vlastos (New York: Liberal Arts Press, 1956).

8. The doctrine of the impossibility of voluntary evildoing is not restricted to the *Protagoras*. It is mentioned also in the following dialogues: *Charmides* 173; *Gorgias* 460B–D, 486C, 509E, 5–7; *Laches* 198; *Meno* 77B–78B, 87, 89; and *Laws* 731C, 860D. This essay has merely tried to show that in the *Protagoras*, where it appears in its most elaborate form, the doctrine is used ironically, as a presupposition of the boast of Protagoras, and carried to absurd consequences. If this attempt has been successful, then the doctrine can no longer be attributed to Plato. It should not be required that its nonliteral use in all other instances be demonstrated. Nor would it be possible to do so in a short essay. Since we are dealing with dramatic dialogues it would be necessary to show what specific function the doctrine plays in the discussion in question. The burden of proof would rest with those who still insist on regarding it as a Platonic doctrine.

Since the reference to *Laws* 9.860 ff., is often quoted in support of the view that Plato upheld the doctrine to the very end of his life, a suggestion may be in order. It will be recalled that in the *Hippias Minor* Socrates says that while "sometimes [he] is of the opposite opinion, . . . just now those who err voluntarily appear to [him] to be better than those who err involuntarily" (372E). We interpreted this to mean that when he speaks of authenticity, the voluntary appears better than the involuntary evildoer, but that the opposite is true when it is a question of the morally good or the morally evil. The Athenian in the *Laws* places a similar temporal restriction on his belief in the doctrine when he says: "I in particular am bound *at this moment* to accept the position . . . that those who commit wrongs act against their own will" (860D). "At this moment" he is a legislator who believes that his function is "to educate his fellow citizens rather than lay down the law to them" (857E). (It is perhaps significant that at 731C, where the doctrine is also mentioned, the Athenian again speaks precisely as a teacher: "But as concerns the transgressions of those who commit wrong, but reparable wrong, we must first of all rest assured that no wrongdoer is so of deliberation.")

The law, according to the Athenian, "will both teach and constrain" (862D). Constraint alone, of course, will not work. It is not possible to have a law enforcement agent behind every citizen. So the legislator, of necessity, must also be a moral teacher, and such teaching is based on the belief that if the law presents a good to an individual clearly enough, the individual will pursue the good by obeying the law. Now we see the difference between the Athenian and Protagoras. The latter guarantees success, and this guarantee presupposes that the doctrine holds universally and necessarily for all men. The former can be satisfied if it holds for the most part. For him it is a hope, a faith that there is something in *most* men that will respond to a call for fairness or justice. He knows that the teaching of the law will not always have the desired effect and that he must then resort to compulsion. While he acts on this faith, he does not hesitate to speak of homicides due to passion as "partially voluntary and partially involuntary" (867A), of "intentional and unintentional assaults" (874D), or about "acts . . . done with intent, in outright wickedness, and of deliberate design" (896E). Unless we see the distinction between the ideal as an object of faith and reality which often puts this faith to a severe test, we will have to regard the following as a startling and inexplicable repudiation of the doctrine of the impossibility of voluntary evildoing:

> Mankind must either give themselves a law and regulate their lives by it, or live no better than the wildest of wild beasts, and that for the following reason. There is no man whose natural endowments will ensure that he shall both discern what is good for mankind as a community and invariably will be both able and willing to put the good into practice when he has perceived it. It is . . . hard to perceive . . . that it is to the advantage of community and individual at once that public well-being should be considered before private. Again, even one who has attained clear perception of this principle . . . if subsequently placed in a position of irresponsible autocratic sovereignty, would never prove loyal to his conviction. (875A–B)

9. Taylor, *Plato*, p. 38.

10. Friedländer, *Plato*, 2, pp. 143–44.

11. The belief that according to Socrates "virtue is knowledge" and "no man willingly pursues evil" is so deep-rooted that some have objected to this question as *un-Socratic* and also as contrary to Aristotle's doctrine of *Hexis* in NE. In this connection my attention has been called to David Furley, *Two Studies in the Greek Atomists*, 2, "Aristotle and Epicurus on Voluntary Action" (Princeton, N.J.: Princeton University Press, 1967). Professor Furley maintains that "we do not find in Aristotle the 'free volition' dear to later ethical philosophers" (p. 225). This might arouse the suspicion that we have been reading modern ideas, namely the notion of authenticity, into some of Plato's writings.

In answer to this it might be said that Aristotle describes men's actions as they are "always or for the most part" (aei e hos epi to poly). Admittedly, all men's actions are determined to some extent, and perhaps for the most part, by dispositions of various degrees of rigidity, by the culture into which they were born, by their families, their friends, their fellow citizens. Plato recognizes this when he presents Crito, a close friend of Socrates, as determined by the opinion of the many. "Can there be a worse disgrace than this—that I should be thought to value money more than the life of a friend?" he has Crito complain. But Socrates reprimands Crito and urges him not to yield to group pressure. This seems to imply that he regards Crito as not necessarily determined, strong as the pressure might be. Of course, there may be other pressures which are irresistible. So a man can be held accountable only to the extent to which he is in control. Francesca and Paolo da Rimini, the adulterous lovers, are in the second circle, while Lucifer, initially closest to God and the most powerful and intelligent, is at the bottom of Dante's Hell. Plato seems to be fully in agreement with this when he has Socrates in the *Hippias Minor* base justice on knowledge and power, this same justice which according to Cornford is for the Greeks the virtue "covering the whole field of the individual's conduct in so far as it affects others." (*The Republic of Plato*, translated with an Introduction and Notes [Oxford, N.Y.: Oxford University Press, 1945], p. 1).

Professor Furley, interpreting Aristotle, maintains that "the freedom of an action, for Aristotle, does not depend on his being able to choose otherwise at the time of the action. The act might still be liable to praise or blame, even though his character were so rigidly determined that he could not possibly in the circumstances choose otherwise" (Greek Atomists, p. 226, n. 15). This can be granted if we understand it to mean that the individual in question, though no longer responsible for the actions determined by his rigid disposition, is responsible for having allowed the disposition to get out of control. This would seem to be implied in Professor Furley's statement that "man's responsibility for his actions depends on the claim that his dispositions are created *by himself*, not on the degree to which his dispositions are now unfixed" (ibid.). In this case, the responsible choice, that is, "the ability to choose otherwise at the time of the action," is simply being pushed farther back. William James warns against the danger of losing control over habits by recommending to "keep the faculty of effort alive in you by a little gratuitous exercise every day" (*Principles of Psychology*, vol. 1, ch. 4 [New York: H. Holt & Co., 1890], p. 123).

Plato was fully aware of the danger of even good habits. This is shown by the character in the *Myth of Er* who chooses the life of a tyrant fated to devour his own children. He had good habits, and in a good community he managed to lead a good life. As a result he spent a thousand years in heaven. But when he finally was confronted with a crucial choice, he failed miserably. Socrates blames his failure on the fact that he had "become virtuous from habit without pursuing wisdom" (*Rep.* 10. 619, trans. Cornford, p. 357). But if Plato had such a low opinion of "virtue from habit," as evidence by the *Myth of Er*, he must have had an even lower opinion of the "virtue of nature" of which Friedländer speaks in his attempt to interpret the *Hippias Minor:* "The just soul, acting in accordance with its nature, can do nothing wrong" (see note 10).

12. All quotations from Martin Heidegger refer to *Being and Time*, trans. John Macquarrie and Edward Robinson (New York: Harper & Row, 1962).

4

Phaedo: Faith, Authenticity and Death

Anxiety in the face of imminent death hovers like a dark cloud over the dialogue from beginning to end, from the removal of the chains before Socrates' friends arrive in his cell early in the morning, to the drinking of the hemlock when the sun is about to set. Is it conceivable that Plato, when writing the *Phaedo*, was wholly unaware of anxiety and gave no expression to the singular revelatory power of this mood? Anxiety, according to Heidegger, as distinguished from fear, reduces an individual's daily concerns to insignificance, so that there is nothing left with which to identify himself while the anxiety lasts.[1] After the mood has passed, he can return to the world from which he has temporarily withdrawn either as a genuine self or again slipping into the old disguises. For the mood does not make him authentic, but merely offers him an opportunity for self-possession.

In the face of a firm belief in life after death, anxiety loses its revelatory power. If anxiety arises at all, it is quickly overcome. The world may fail a believer in view of the insignificance of all it has to offer, but he can project beyond this world to the next and concern himself with its possibilities instead of facing himself stripped of everything except his potentiality.

Does this mean that genuine selfhood is possible only for the nonbeliever? Then Socrates would be doomed to inauthenticity, for as early as the trial and as late as the day of his death he expressed the belief that his existence does not come to an end with the death of his body. This would be the case only if Socrates' belief were a dogmatic belief, a belief which claims to be in possession of the truth. If, on the other hand, his belief is a free belief, then it is the result of a choice between two alternatives, i.e., between the possibility of annihilation and that of continued existence. Such a belief is based on the awareness that choosing one alternative does not make the other false and therefore would not destroy the revelatory function of anxiety. The task of Socrates in the *Phaedo* would then be to give his friends hope for an afterlife without letting that hope be perverted into a firm conviction.

Far from speaking about moods of any sort, many commentators concern themselves exclusively with the elaborate proofs which Plato offers for the immortality of the soul. They rightly point out that these fill the main body of the dialogue, and some even insist that the final proof was "thoroughly satisfactory and conclusive" to its author.[2] If these proofs were to constitute the chief content of the dialogue, then the ravages of time would seem to have spared hardly anything of value to the modern reader. In an age when the very term soul is suspect and serious thinkers are impressed with the ambiguity of the human mode of being,[3] a proof for the immortality of the soul is likely to be viewed as little more than an historical oddity. But even on logical grounds the proofs are commonly found wanting.[4]

In the belief that such proofs are no longer of interest in our age, some commentators go to the other extreme and try to turn our attention away from the strictly philosophical parts of the dialogue and urge us to look for the dramatic in the byplay, the atmosphere, the concrete situation in which the discussion takes place. And there the dialogue is said to yield a rich harvest. What could be more moving, we are told, than the picture of Socrates calmly conversing with his friends on the day on which he is to die? What more dramatic than the cheerfulness with which he sets the poison-filled cup to his lips while his friends cry out in pain and sorrow so that he has to rebuke them for their lack of self-control? What more tense than the last moments when he walks about the cell as long as his legs support him, and then lies down to await the fatal effect of the hemlock—until, immediately after his request to sacrifice a cock to Asclepius, the convulsive movement of his body indicates the end. Of the two questions which Echecrates asks at the beginning of the narration: "How did the man die, and what did he say?" only the first would seem to be still worthy of an answer. The division of the dialogue into the valuable and the antiquated has led one scholar to print the philosophical part in smaller print, so that "people who are interested in the importance of Socrates to the world need not struggle through passages of a difficult argument on immortality, which would not convince any modern reader of its truth . . . and is not necessary to an appreciation of Socrates."[5]

Perhaps the difficulty with the interpretation of the *Phaedo* arises from the total neglect of anxiety, a neglect which in turn blinds the reader to Socrates' attempt not to let faith in a hereafter interfere with the possibility of authentic selfhood which this mood reveals. An occurrence at the very center of the dialogue lends support to this contention. Narrating the events of the last day in the life of Socrates to Echecrates, Phaedo speaks of the doubts voiced by the two Pythagoreans against the arguments offered in favor of the immortality of the soul. The speculations of Socrates had led his listeners to the consoling conclusion that the soul is immortal, and all were satisfied, except Simmias and Cebes. The objections raised by these bright young men exploded like a bombshell in the midst of the intellectual and emotional contentment which had fallen over the company. Only a moment ago there prevailed conviction and a sense of security; now all is confusion and turmoil. The argument appears damaged beyond repair and the efficacy of reason shaken in its very foundation:

> Phaedo: All of us, as we afterwards remarked to one another, had an unpleasant feeling at hearing what they said. When we had been so firmly convinced before, now to have our faith shaken seemed to introduce a confusion and uncertainty, not only into the previous argument, but into any future one; either we were incapable of forming a judgment, or there were no grounds of belief.
> Echecrates: There I feel with you—by heaven I do, Phaedo, and when you were speaking, I was beginning to ask myself the same question: What argument can I ever trust again? For what could be more convincing than the argument of Socrates, which has now fallen into discredit? (88C–D)[6]

Why should an attack upon an intellectual argument cause such an emotional upset? And why should it shake the confidence of most of those present not only in this but in any future argument? Phaedo and Echecrates, perhaps unwittingly, put their finger on the reason: ". . . we had been so firmly *convinced* . . ."; ". . . what could be more *convincing* than the argument of Socrates?" (88C–D).

Even a brief glance at the arguments makes it evident that they are incapable of producing the certainty which would justify a sense of conviction in the minds of the audience. For the evidence introduced in support of the claim that the soul is immortal consists, not of empirical facts, but of scientific and philosophic doctrines. Such a procedure cannot *establish* a belief, but only show that it is not incompatible with certain other beliefs.

According to the first doctrine so used, "everything which has an opposite is generated from that opposite and from no other source" (70E). And there are always two processes moving from one opposite to the other, from the large to the small, for instance, and from the small to the large, so that we speak of decrease and increase. This is said to be true of all other processes of generation, such as "separating and combining, cooling and heating, . . . sleeping and waking" (71B–C). Now life and death are well-known opposites, and one of the two corresponding processes, namely dying, is all too familiar. "Shall we omit the complementary process," Socrates asks, "and leave a defect here in the law of nature?" (71E). Should we not rather conclude that "the living come from the dead no less than the dead from the living . . . and that the souls of the dead must exist in some place from which they are reborn?" (72A).

If the law of opposites could be established as a universal law, then the conclusion would necessarily follow. If it is merely a generalization based on observed facts, then the opposites of life and death might well constitute an exception. In any event, Socrates offers no serious proof for the doctrine of opposites, since no one raises any objections to it.

The evidence which Socrates uses in the second instance is the theory of recollection. It is enthusiastically received by the two Pythagoreans. In fact it is introduced by Cebes, and Simmias asks for an explanation only because he has forgotten the supporting arguments and wants "to have this doctrine of recollection brought to his own recollection" (73B,J). We speak of recollection, says Socrates, when the presence of an object suggests another object, especially if that object has not been seen for a long time or has been forgotten. The recalled object may be similar to or quite different from the one which recalls it. A portrait of Cebes may remind us of Cebes, but so may Simmias, since the two are frequently found together; and even a piece of clothing, or a musical instrument, a material thing, may recall a human being, such as its possessor for instance. Now it is a common experience that when we speak of two concrete things, such as sticks or stones, as being equal, we mean that they are more or less equal, or equal from one point of view and unequal from another. In other words, "they seem to us to be equal not in the sense of absolute equality but to fall short of it in so far as they only approximate to equality" (74D). The perception of equality as approximate, however, presupposes the presence of the idea of absolute equality as a standard of comparison. So the perceived equality of concrete things brings to mind a radically different equality, which is not directly perceived. Now we have sense perception of concrete things at the time of our birth, but no knowledge of these absolute realities and since only sense perception recalls the absolute standards to our minds, the standards themselves must have been known to us before birth. And so Socrates is ready to conclude:

> If all these absolute realities, such as beauty and goodness, which we are always thinking about, really exist, if it is to them, as we rediscover our own former knowledge of them, that we refer, as copies to their patterns, all the objects of our physical perception—if these really exist, does it not follow that our souls must exist too even before our birth, whereas if·they do not exist, our discussion would seem to be a waste of time? Is this the position, that it is logically just as certain that our souls exist before our birth as it is that these realities exist, and that if the one is impossible, so is the other? (76D–E)

Simmias and Cebes accept the conclusion about the prenatal existence of the soul, but claim that its existence after death has not been proven. Socrates answers by recalling the proof based on the theory of opposites, according to which the living come from the dead. And if this is so then the soul "must exist after death, if it must be born again" (77D).

It is ingenious to look at sense perception as if it were a case of recollection. For sense perception seems to give more than it can account for in terms of itself alone. These absolute ideas, as we have seen, are not perceived by the senses, but without them the sense objects and their relations would not be recognized as imperfect or relative. If this puzzling fact tends to disturb us, we need only think of any ordinary case of recollection where a present object is also able to bring to mind a radically different object which is not present. Thus the less familiar or puzzling process, knowledge occasioned by sense perception, is explained or at least made less perplexing by being described in terms of the more familiar, namely recollection. Furthermore, if we think of the acquisition of knowledge as a recollection, we will be less inclined toward indoctrination. For just as we can only assist another in recalling what he has forgotten, so we cannot, as Socrates persistently maintains, convey to another the knowledge which he does not possess but only stimulate him in his effort to acquire it for himself. Thus the theory which conceives coming to know or learning on the analogy of recollection is a useful theory. But in every analogy it is important not to overlook the disanalogy, for the two things or processes conceived analogically are not identical and hence have differences as well as similarities. Recollection does presuppose the previous experience or knowledge of the object forgotten. The recognition in sense perception of things as relative, however, functions merely AS IF the mind had a prior knowledge of absolutes; and as Socrates admits only "if these realities exist, does it follow that our souls must exist too even before our birth" (76D–E). Furthermore, Socrates offers what he believes to be facts in support of the theory of recollection, and then uses this theory in support of his belief in the immortality of the soul. The belief which he is trying to establish is therefore not at one but at two removes from experienced reality.

If Socrates' faith were to rest on such arguments as those based on the theory of opposites and the doctrine of recollection, it would be frail indeed. At best they succeed in producing a temporary harmony in a man's outlook, but should a serious change in philosophical or scientific doctrine occur, the work of reconciliation would have to be done all over again.

The third argument purports to eliminate the fear of death, a fear which springs from a materialistic conception of the human soul. "You are afraid, as children are," Socrates mocks his two friends, "that when the soul emerges from the body the wind may really puff it away and scatter it, especially when a person does not die on a calm day but with a gale blowing" (77D–E). The problem is to determine whether the soul is material and whether the kind of destruction we witness in connection with a body does really apply to it:

> We ought, I think, said Socrates, to ask ourselves this. What sort of thing is it that would naturally suffer the fate of being dispersed? For what sort of thing should we fear this fate, and for what should we not? When we have answered

this, we should next consider to which class the soul belongs, and then we shall know whether to feel confidence or fear about the fate of our souls. (78B)

Socrates compares the objects of sense perception, that is, of the bodily organs, with the objects accessible only to the mind. The first, which he calls visible, are subject to continual change; the second, the invisible, such as absolute beauty or equality, "remain always constant and invariable, never admitting any alteration in any respect or in any sense" (78D). Furthermore, he says, when the soul in its inquiry relies on sense perception it becomes confused, but obtains wisdom when it occupies itself with the absolute realities. And finally, it is the function of the soul, as it is of the divine, to lead and govern, and of the body to follow and obey. From all this he infers and his friends agree that "the soul is most like that which is divine, immortal, intelligible, uniform, indissoluble, and ever self-consistent and invariable, whereas the body is most like that which is human, mortal, multiform, unintelligible, dissoluble, and never self-consistent" (80B). All that Socrates ventures to conclude is that "while it is natural for the body to disintegrate rapidly . . . the soul is quite or very nearly indissoluble" (80D). At best the soul can be regarded as midway between the objects of sense experience and the absolute realities; and Socrates would be the last to declare the soul unalterable, for it is he who never tires of urging men to promote the virtue of their souls and to prevent their wickedness.

So far Socrates has done all the thinking for his friends, or Plato for his readers, and all they have had to do was to follow him. But a teacher who regards all learning as a kind of recollection could be expected to engage his students sooner or later more actively in his inquiry. The stimulation for such engagement is furnished by a claim of Socrates which immediately follows but far exceeds the modest conclusion he has drawn from the argument:

> The soul goes away . . . to the true Hades or unseen world . . . to that place which is, like itself, invisible, divine, immortal and wise, where, on its arrival, happiness awaits it, and release from uncertainty and folly, from fears and uncontrolled desires and all other human evils, and there, as they say in the mysteries, it really spends the rest of time with God. (80D–81A)

This is a dream rather than an argument, a dream which carries to their ultimate consummation men's desires for happiness, for certainty and wisdom, for self-possession, for security and for freedom from all evil. And just as in the *Crito* Socrates soundly asleep in the face of his imminent death exhibits his freedom from fear, so in dreaming Socrates *demonstrates* man as capable of reaching beyond himself, as a transcending being, "whose essence," as Heidegger would say, "is his existence" and who is thus quite different from a material thing.

If there is such a gap between the human and the nonhuman mode of being, why is it necessary for Socrates to go to great lengths in persuading his friends that fear based on a material conception of the human soul or self is unwarranted? Why are men so bent upon seeing themselves as what they are not? For this transcendence is apparent not only in connection with man's highest aspirations, as in Socrates' "dream," but also in his most ordinary, everyday activities, i.e., when he projects goals and uses tools to realize these goals and thereby tries to satisfy his daily needs. And when he reflects upon himself, he finds, as Heidegger maintains, that whatever he claims to be, whether craftsman or professional, soldier or politician, reveals itself as a project, as a choice he has made, and that the chooser, his real self, remains an enigma. In order to escape this disturbing thought he lets himself become absorbed in his concernful activities; he tranquillizes himself by turning away from himself to the things he deals with and suppresses the distinction which separates him from the nonhuman, until he sees himself more or less as just another thing. This would seem to be the reason why Socrates can say that the soul which concerns itself with physical things is "so beguiled by the body and its passions and pleasures that nothing seems real to it which cannot be touched and eaten and drunk and used for sexual enjoyment" (81B). And since men not only can but must develop habits, their mode of behavior assumes a certain rigidity and predictability not unlike those of things, especially if they yield to these habits and let them control their behavior. The condition of such souls, which have fallen captive to their own life styles, Socrates describes mythically in terms of reincarnation. They are said to become so "permeated by the corporeal" that upon their release from the body they are "weighed down and dragged back into the visible world . . . and through their craving for the corporeal, which unceasingly pursues them, they are immersed once more in the body" (81C–E). In their new existence, Socrates maintains, they take on the shapes of various animals, such as hawks and wolves and donkeys, which is simply Socrates' way of saying that these people have lost their specifically human mode of being. For just as animals simply act out their various natures, and are driven by their several instincts and impulses, so these people are under the control of such vices as "gluttony or drunkenness . . . or irresponsible lawlessness and violence" (82A). And not only passion and vices can take possession of a man, but also seemingly good and useful habits:

> The happiest people, and those who reach the best destination, are the ones who have cultivated the goodness of an ordinary citizen—what is called self-control and integrity—which is acquired by habit and practice, without the help of philosophy and reason. . . . They will probably pass into some other kind of social and disciplined creature like bees, wasps and ants, or even back into the human race again, becoming decent citizens. (82A–B)

Even the most law-abiding citizen, whose behavior is dictated by inflexible habits, so Socrates ironically suggests, is not basically different from the most ferocious animal.

Freedom and self-control are not natural gifts bestowed on some and denied to others. In the early stages of their lives, all men are unfree. "Every seeker after wisdom knows that up to the time when philosophy takes over his soul is a helpless prisoner, chained hand and foot in the body" (82D–E). And without being aware of it, the individual himself has fashioned the chains which keep him shackled. "The imprisonment is ingeniously effected by the prisoner's own active desire, which makes him first accessory to his own confinement" (82E–83A) ". . . because every pleasure or pain is a sort of rivet with which it fastens the soul to the body and pins it down and makes it corporeal" (83D). And just as Heidgger maintains that from the initial state of fallenness, which some men never overcome, the individual must wrest his authenticity, so according to Socrates, philosophy makes the soul aware of its condition and persuades it to throw off its bondage by yielding to the body only when necessary. It makes it "reflect that the result of giving way to pleasure or fear or desire is not as might be supposed the trivial misfortune of becoming ill or wasting money through self-indulgence" (83C–D). For nothing less is at stake then genuine selfhood. He can allow his desires and passions and habits to control him, or he can reach beyond himself and "by contemplating the true and divine and unconjecturable and drawing inspiration from it" (84A) let it be the guide for the direction of his life. Thus the dream of human self-fulfilment, exhibiting man's transcendence or existence, and the myth of reincarnation which shows his potentiality for loss or gain of selfhood, testify to the inadequacy of categories drawn from material things for an understanding of the human mode of being. More effectively than logical arguments, they demonstrate that whatever the nature of the soul, it cannot be said to be material, and whatever its ultimate fate "it can have no grounds for fearing that on its separation from the body it will be blown away and scattered by the winds, and so disappear into thin air, and cease to exist altogether" (84B). Dream and myth thus help to allay, not any kind of fear of death, but at least that kind which arises out of conceiving man as just another material thing.

Socrates' inquiry into the nature of the soul, however, whatever the form in which it is conducted, and whatever its value, reveals itself upon analysis to be quite incapable of yielding anything approaching certainty, a fact of which Plato himself seems to have been fully aware. For he has neither Socrates nor the Pythagoreans entertain any illusions about the probative force of the arguments. "I fancy," says Cebes, even before the discussion gets under way, "that it requires no little faith and assurance to believe that the soul exists after death and retains some active force and intelligence" (70B). Socrates does not promise to establish these formidable truths but merely suggests that they "converse a little on the probabilities of these things" (70B,J), and at the end of the first group of arguments he admits that "there are many points still open to suspicion and attack, if one were disposed to sift the matter thoroughly" (84C,J). And these remarks of Socrates are followed by a pointed characterization on the part of Simmias of any argument applicable to the subject on hand:

> I think, just as you do Socrates, that it is very difficult if not impossible in this life to achieve certainty about these questions. (85C)

The sharp contrast between the liberal temper of those actively engaged in the discussion and the dogmatism produced in the minds of the rest of the company tends to call the reader's attention away from the question of immortality and direct it to the interaction of intellect and feeling. "A mood always has its understanding," says Heidegger, "even if it merely keeps it suppressed. Understanding always has its mood" (182). Thus the first "act," which ends with the shock produced by the objections raised against the arguments, presents us with the spectacle of men who are overeager to secure their hopes, who greedily reach out for the most illegitimate means of converting their subjective desires into objective truths. Here the intimate involvement of drama and philosophy, of mood and understanding is unmistakable. For the *pathos* of the protagonists, the dismay they suffer when seeing their dearest hopes irreparably shattered, is the outcome of an *intellectual* flaw. They have surrendered their critical powers to the fervent hope for life everlasting, and their acute sense of frustration is simply a measure of their credulity. In the defense of their faith they have allowed themselves to fall victim to intellectual rigidity; they have attached it too firmly to scientific and philosophical doctrines. Such attachments are dangerous, for if in the course of time these tentative structures crumble and make room for more spacious mansions, their faith dies with the old, when it should be free to seek a more suitable habitation in the new.[7]

At this point of the dialogue it is now possible to say with considerable justification that Socrates is far from trying to *convince* his friends of the immortality of the soul. On the contrary, he is making every effort to forestall a false sense of security which would choke off anxiety and block the road to genuine selfhood.

In view of such efforts Socrates is rightly made to give primary attention to the effects produced by the arguments rather than their defense against the objections. For his task is twofold: He must destroy their false sense of security while maintaining their faith in immortality. This is how Phaedo describes his reaction:

> I can assure you, Echecrates, that Socrates often astonished me, but I never admired him more than on this particular occasion. That he should have been ready with an answer was, I suppose, nothing unusual, but what impressed me was, first, the pleasant, kindly, appreciative way in which he received the

two boys' objections, then his quick recognition of how the turn of the discussion had affected us, and lastly the skill with which he healed our wounds, rallied our scattered forces, and encouraged us to join him in pursuing the inquiry." (88E–89A)

The cure consists in an exposition of Socrates' method of inquiry, demonstrating both its effectiveness and its limitations. But before he can gain their ear, he must restore their confidence, administer first aid, so to speak. In an attempt to accomplish this, he draws an analogy between their condition and that of people who place an unquestioning trust in their friends, believing them to be "absolutely truthful and sincere and reliable" (89D), merely to be disillusioned later on. Similarly, the uncritical acceptance of the conclusion of an argument as certain and unshakable truth may cause the kind of disappointment which has occurred in the present case and may eventually create a distrust in any intellectual argument. In other words, as excessive confidence in our fellowmen may lead to its opposite, namely misanthropy, so the lack of critical acumen in discussion may end up in misology.

The detailed exposition of Socrates' method is found in his refutation of the objection of Cebes, but his answer to Simmias already contains at least implicitly some of its essential features. Simmias compares the soul to the attunement of an instrument. Such an attunement would belong to the class of invisible things and therefore, according to Socrates' earlier argument, would have to be regarded as capable of surviving the destruction of the instrument, which is clearly absurd. "If the soul is really an attunement," he concludes, "obviously as soon as the tension of our body is lowered or increased beyond the proper point, the soul must be destroyed, divine though it is—just like any other adjustment, either in music or in any product of the arts and crafts" (86C).

In his reply, Socrates first points out that the attunement theory is in conflict with the theory of recollection. According to this theory the soul exists before its entry into the body, and if the soul were an attunement, one would have to say that "it is composed of elements which do not exist" (92B). Both theories cannot be entertained together, and Socrates urges Simmias to make a choice between them. Simmias regards the theory of recollection well established and opts in its favor. Next Socrates asks Simmias to agree that a soul cannot be more or less a soul. Now when we speak of a wicked soul we mean that its various desires and impulses are not attuned to each other, while those of the good soul are. How shall we describe this goodness and wickedness? Shall we say that "the good soul is in tune, and not only is an attunement itself, but contains another, whereas the bad soul is out of tune and does not contain another attunement?" But we have already admitted, he says, that no soul can be more or less a soul, and therefore if it is an attunement then it cannot be more or less an attunement. "So on this theory," Socrates concludes, "every soul of every living creature will be equally good" (94A). Finally, the attunement theory is incapable of giving an adequate account of human experience. The attunement of an instrument is completely dependent on the tensions and relaxations of its elements and can never go against them, while the soul controls the impulses and desires of the body, "sometimes by severe and unpleasant methods like those of physical training and medicine, and sometimes by milder ones, sometimes scolding, sometimes encouraging . . . as though it were quite separate and distinct from them" (94D).

The attunement theory proposed by Simmias has failed to meet three principal conditions which any good hypothesis must satisfy, for it is incompatible with an established theory, it lacks inner consistency, and it is contradicted by observable facts. Its incompatibility with an accepted theory does not, of course, make it necessarily false; such incompatibility merely shows that both theories cannot be true together. It is also obvious that neither inner inconsistency nor disagreement with observable fact of a hypothesis makes its rival hypothesis necessarily true. They do not even make the hypothesis under consideration necessarily false. For a different formulation might avoid the absurd consequences and such a restructuring of the hypothesis might succeed in rendering harmless the facts which seem to be in conflict with it. If the refutation of Simmias's objection is any indication of the method which Socrates will presently expound, then no more than various degrees of probability are attainable through it, and the sense of conviction felt by the silent partners to the discussion is wholly unjustified, not only with regard to the arguments actually used, but any argument based on the method. The very imperfection of the method, however, makes it possible for the investigator to adopt a flexible position. He need not shun objections and can readily surrender the less to the more adequate hypothesis. In fact, if he is sincere in his quest for truth, he will welcome opposition, since this either serves to fortify the stand taken or leads to a more satisfactory one. Phaedo, therefore, need not have been astonished at "the pleasant, kindly, appreciative way in which Socrates received the young men's objections" (89A).

Cebes' objection is based on a materialistic conception of the human psyche. He grants that "the soul existed before it took on this present shape . . . that it is stronger and more durable than the body . . . and far superior to it" (87A). But all that, he claims, does not prove that it is indestructible. Just as a weaver might outlive many coats he has made and still be outlasted by the last coat, so the soul, weakened by many reincarnations, might ultimately succumb, and the kind of death we are facing on earth might mean the final annihilation of the soul.

Socrates, after some time spent in reflection, remarks on the difficulty of answering Cebes. "It involves," he says, "a full treatment of the cause (ten aitian) of generation and destruction" (95E). In other words, he proposes to discuss not only Cebes' objection, but the general why and wherefore, or the nature of explanation as such.

From now on up to the death scene at the end of the dialogue, Plato makes heavy demands of the reader. He has Socrates argue that explanation in purely materialistic terms is faced with insurmountable obstacles, not only, as in the case of Cebes' objection, when dealing with the human psyche, but when attempting to account for any event whatsoever. Next he has him develop his own method and project it against an ideal mode of explanation so that it reveals its strength as well as its weakness, thus healing the "wound" struck by the previous arguments and avoiding the excesses both of overconfidence and of despair in reason. At the same time Plato tries to involve the reader who must not be allowed to follow Socrates' argument passively. To this end he has Socrates first present his method as operating with tentative hypotheses and then he has him offer a seemingly rigorous proof for the immortality of the soul in which these same hypotheses appear miraculously transformed into the essences of things. The reader has no assurance that the views expressed by Socrates are really his own or those of Plato, any more than a character on the stage can be relied upon to act as the spokesman of the playwright. He would be well advised to maintain a critical attitude throughout and heed the warning which Socrates addresses to his friends at the opening of the second "act," namely to agree with him only when they feel he speaks the truth and to oppose him with all their might when they believe he is not. "You must not allow me," he says, "to deceive you . . . and leave my sting behind when I fly away" (91C).

Socrates begins by relating how in his youth he was taken in by the "nature philosophers" who sought for principles of explanation among physical things. "Is it when heat and cold produce fermentation that living creatures are made? Is it with the blood that we think, or with the air or the fire that is in us?" These are the kind of questions, he says, which agitated him. But instead of seeing more clearly he seemed to become more confused; or rather, becoming aware of the distinction between factual juxtaposition and causal or necessary connections, he recognized that what he took to be an explanation was no explanation at all:

> I had understood some things plainly before, in my own and other people's estimation, but now I was so befogged by these speculations that I unlearned even what I had thought I knew, especially about the cause of growth in human beings. Previously I had thought that it was quite obviously due to eating and drinking—that when, from the food which we consume, flesh is added to flesh and bone to bone, and when in the same way the other parts of the body are augmented by their appropriate particles, the bulk which was small is now large, and in this way the small man becomes a big one. (96C–D)

Then, he says, he heard of a book by Anaxagoras who maintained that "it is mind that produces order and is the cause of everything" (97C). The description of his expectations from the book provides him with an opportunity to outline what he thinks would be the ideal method. And this model can later be used as a standard for the evaluation of his own method which he calls "second-best."

Anaxagoras, he thought, would tell him, for instance, whether the earth was flat or round, and then he would prove to him why it was necessarily so and finally why it was best that it should be so. "It never entered my mind," he says, "that a man who asserted that the ordering of things is due to mind would offer any other explanation for them than that it is best for them to be as they are. I thought that by assigning a cause to each phenomenon separately and to the universe as a whole he would make perfectly clear what was best for each and what is the universal good" (98A–B).

The enormity of the expectations of Socrates is obvious. They presuppose that the universe is radically intelligible, that it is governed by a single princple which gives meaning and significance to the whole as well as to every part of the whole, and that this principle is accessible to the human understanding. "On this view," he says, "there is only one thing for a man to consider, with regard to himself and to anything else, namely the best and highest good" (97D).

It is hardly surprising that when Socrates read the book he found that his "wonderful hope . . . was quickly dashed" (98B), for Anaxagoras referred to "causes like air and ether and water and many other absurdities" (98C). Socrates had earlier indicated the failure of the attempt to find successful principles of explanation on the same level with the things to be explained. And if the method failed to shed light on such physical processes as the growth of the human body, it was not likely to be more successful when dealing with the complexities of human behavior. One might just as well, Socrates continues, try to explain his sitting in jail in terms of bone structures and muscle movements, instead of mentioning the main cause, namely the fact that both the Athenians, in their momentous decision to condemn him, and he, in his resolve not to escape but to remain and suffer death, were motivated by the *idea* of what they thought best. Without bones and muscles he could not do what he thinks is right, but to call them the cause is to confuse the condition without which the cause could not operate, with the cause itself (98E–99B).

Since he could not discover the cause of things for himself nor learn it from anyone else, he decided in desperation to work out his own "makeshift approach" or "second-best" (deuteros plous) (99C):

> I was afraid that by observing objects with my eyes and trying to comprehend them with each of my other senses I might blind my soul altogether. So I decided that I must have recourse to theories (eis taus lògous kataphugonta) and use them in trying to discover the truth about things. (99D–E)

While Socrates was determined to turn from concrete things to *logoi*, that is, to a higher level, in search for principles of explanation, he could not, of course, hope to reach "the good," the all-embracing ultimate principle—to agathon kai deon chundein kai sunechein.[8] All he could do was to set up some tentative hypotheses which might prove fruitful:

In every case I lay down the theory which I judge to be soundest, and then whatever seems to agree with it—with regard either to causes or to anything else—I assume to be true, and whatever does not I assume not to be true. (100A)

The principle postulated derives its value from its ability to bring order into observed phenomena and must in turn fit into a larger pattern:

I cannot afford to give up the sure ground of principle. And if anyone assails you there, you would not mind him, or answer him until you had seen whether the consequences which follow agree with one another or not, and when you are further required to give an explanation of this principle, you would go on to assume a higher principle, and a higher, until you found a resting-place in the best of the higher; but you would not confuse the principle and the consequences in your reasoning. (101D–E,J)

In a whole in which everything depends on an ultimate principle, nothing can be known with absolute assurance until the ultimate principle is known. Whatever partial order Socrates' hypotheses might bring about could prove inadequate or illusory on a broader view.[9] And a clear awareness of this possibility should go a long way toward forestalling any temptation toward overconfidence. But these hypotheses do establish patterns which are workable at least for the time being. Furthermore, the appeal to hypotheses rather than things as principles of explanation manages to evade some of the sophistical paradoxes which might induce the inexperienced to lose confidence in reason. You would not say, for instance, he warns, that one man is taller than another "by a head" and that the other is shorter by the same. For you would then be faced by the objections of the eristics (hoi antilogikoi): "First that the taller should be taller and the shorter shorter by the same, and secondly that the taller person should be taller by a head, which is a short thing, and that it is unnatural that a man should be made taller by something which is short" (101A–B). You would rather say that "it is by largeness that large things are large and larger things larger, and by smallness that smaller things are smaller" (100E). Nor would you say that through mere juxtaposition do one and one become two, and that the division of one, that is the opposite process, also produces two (97A). Instead you would maintain that "you recognize no other cause for the coming into being of two than participation in duality, and that whatever is to become two must participate in this, and whatever is to become one must participate in unity" (101C). In similar fashion you would hold that what is "beautiful . . . is beautiful because it partakes of absolute beauty" (100C). It would seem that Socrates neither gives nor intends to give an *actual* explanation; he merely describes the *type* of explanation, namely explanation by means of theories. This may be the reason why he calls the simple appeal to the idea of beauty in order to explain beautiful things "safe," in as much as it avoids the paradoxes of the eristics and the danger of misology, but also "foolish" because it does not make clear how the presence of absolute beauty in the beautiful thing—that is, the relation between explanatory principle and thing to be explained—must be understood. He merely insists that explanation of the sensory must be by means of the non-sensory:

> I cling simply and straightforwardly and no doubt foolishly to the explanation that the one thing that makes that object beautiful is the presence in it or association with it, in whatever way the relation comes about, of absolute beauty. I do not go so far as to insist upon the precise details—only upon the fact that it is by beauty that beautiful things are beautiful. This, I feel, is the safest answer for me or for anyone else to give. (100D) . . . You would loudly proclaim that you know of no other way in which any given object can come into being except by participation in the reality peculiar to its appropriate universal. (101C)

With the careful exposition of his second-best method of inquiry, Socrates should have helped his friends in making themselves immune against the twin threat of overconfidence and despair. For the method is capable of establishing or detecting partial orders which for the most part facilitate the management of affairs both private and public. But the patterns are partial at best and therefore subject to correction and liable to obsolescence.

If the philosophical part of the dialogue had come to an end at this point, the *Phaedo* could never have been used as evidence of the growing dogmatism in the outlook of Plato. But it would also have left the reader in the position of a passive onlooker. Having observed the attitude of Socrates' friends, he may even smile complacently at their naiveté, and instead of making him wary and watchful, the observation is likely to instill in him a false sense of his own superior wisdom. This temptation is all the greater if, as here, he is able to identify himself with the wiser heads of the group, namely Socrates and the two Pythagoreans who never forget the uncertain character of the conclusion offered by the arguments. To bring about a genuine awareness of the difficulty attending any attempt to secure one's faith, the problem must be interiorized so that it becomes a conflict in the mind of the reader.[10] This, as we hope to show, is the real purpose of the final proof.

Socrates is now made to behave as if he had fallen victim to the insidious tendency of overtaxing the results of a rational argument, a tendency against which only a little while ago he himself had sounded the alarm. He argues as if in the face of his impending death he were making frantic efforts to secure his faith beyond the reach of any possible doubt. For when Socrates puts his method to the test in the final demonstration, an abrupt and disconcerting change of attitude takes place. The obvious modesty and open-mindedness which pervades the discussion of the method, gives way to the most rigid dogmatism in its application. The freely chosen postulates, which were to serve as tentative, temporary principles of explanation, turn out to be the familiar forms or ideas, and these, in the mind of the reader, are invariably associated with the absolute and the eternal:

> What I mean is this, said Socrates, and there is nothing new about it. I have always said it; in fact I have never stopped saying it, especially in the earlier part of this discussion. As I am going to try to explain to you the theory of causation which I have worked out myself, I propose to make a fresh start from those principles of mind which you know so well—that is, I am assuming the existence of absolute beauty and goodness and magnitude and all the rest of them. If you grant my assumption and admit that they exist, I hope with their help to explain causation to you, and to find a proof that soul is immortal. (100B)

The argument which follows presupposes an insight into the essences of things which the preceding discussion on method would not have led one to expect. Hence the care with which Socrates prepares the listener, or Plato the reader, for what is to come. In answer to an objection, Socrates distinguishes between opposite things and the opposite itself. In the former argument, he says, we were talking about "things in which opposites are inherent and which are called after them, but now about the opposites which are inherent in them and which give their name to them" (103C,J). Of the opposite *things* it could be said that they are generated one from the other, but "the opposites themselves would absolutely refuse to tolerate coming into being from one another" (103C). Socrates likewise distinguishes clearly between an accidental and a necessary quality or characteristic.[11] Simmias is bigger than Socrates and shorter than Phaedo, "not because he is Simmias but because of the height which he incidentally possesses, and conversely the reason why he is bigger than Socrates is not because Socrates is Socrates, but because Socrates has the attribute of shortness in comparison with Simmias' height" (102B–C). In other words, Simmias is bigger than one of his friends and shorter than another, not because of his or their natures, but because of an accidental relation in which they stand to each other.[12] The stage is now cleared for a discussion, not of contingent relations between concrete things, but necessary connections between essences.

Socrates then proceeds to argue not only that opposites exclude each other, but that anything necessarily related to one of two opposites also excludes the other opposite. The examples he uses are fire and heat, snow and cold, three and odd, to which he later adds disease and fever. There is general agreement among commentators on the main part of the demonstration for immortality, and this has been conveniently summarized as follows:

> Just as fire is that which, when it is present in a body, makes that body hot, so soul is that which, when it is present in a body, makes that body living. And just as fire is necessarily possessed by heat and cannot under any cir-

cumstances become qualified by what is opposite to heat—namely, cold—so soul is necessarily possessed by life and cannot under any circumstances become qualified by what is opposite to life—namely, death. Finally, just as that which cannot be qualified by the even is uneven, so that which cannot be qualified by death is deathless. Soul, therefore, is deathless.[13]

Commentators disagree on the short second part of the argument (106A–E), which Socrates thinks necessary in order to prove that the undying or immortal is also imperishable. Those interpretations which do not do violence to the form of the argument agree that it is strictly demonstrative in character and that it implies an insight into the essences of things, the eternal forms, and the necessary connection between them.[14]

This change from a liberal to an illiberal spirit in the *Phaedo,* at the point where Socrates introduces the forms, has not gone unnoticed.[15] But since traditionally the theory of ideas and the belief in the possibility of attaining infallible certainty are thought to be so much more "Platonic" than the type of method discussed by Socrates, the latter receives but scant attention or is explained away by the most devious means. One commentator, for instance, passes it by with a comment expressing some puzzlement as to its relevance;[16] another sees in the whole passage a transition from "Socratism" to "Platonism," as if the latter with its alleged dogmatism were an outgrowth of or improvement over the former rather than its opposite;[17] a third attributes the difficulty to forgetfulness on the part of Plato that he is dealing with a "second-best" method,[18] or to his indecision as to whether he should regard certainty as attainable or not.[19]

The cavalier treatment given to the method explicitly set forth by Socrates finds its justification in the embarrassment of the interpreters rather than in the actual text. For far from being casually introduced, Socrates, as we have seen, shows it to be the outcome of a long experience. And the care with which Socrates develops his methodological reflections must be taken as an indication of the importance which Plato attaches to them. Simply to ignore them would be the height of arbitrariness. But it would be just as irresponsible to deny that immediately thereafter, in the final proof, he proceeds as if his postulates were the result of a clear insight into the essences of things, an insight which the method does not allow,[20] and that he thereby exhibits the naive trust in human reason which, according to his own warning, is liable to lead to disaster. At this point Plato denies us the luxury of simply following the thought processes of Socrates. We are either confronted with a riddle, or we must call on our own critical resources.

Despite their difference it is possible to draw an analogy between the first group of arguments and the final demonstration. Through the former, as we have seen, Socrates tries to establish consistency between the faith in immortality and current philosophic and scientific speculations. Some of his friends, impelled by the urgency of deeply felt needs, had mistakenly passed from a sense of encouragement by the outcome of the argument to a feeling of certainty, in the face of repeated warnings by Socrates and the two Pythagoreans that such certainty was not possible. In the final demonstration he now makes, or pretends to make, the similar error of believing himself in the possession of intuited essences, despite the fact that the method he expounded clearly allowed no more than postulates. What the warnings of the active participants to the discussion were to the earlier arguments, the exposition of the method is to the final proof. Thus both the first and the second "act" of the *Phaedo* illustrate analogous, but illegitimate and fruitless, attempts to discover a secure ground on which to build a faith. The shock experienced by the friends of Socrates at the end of the first "act" is paralleled in the second by the puzzlement of the reader when confronted with the irreconcilability of Socrates' method as *advocated* and the same method as *practiced,* or more specifically, the earlier claim to *mere probability* and the later promise of *infallible certitude.*[21]

The shock and the puzzlement may be regarded as two instances of *pathos,* each of which should result in its corresponding *epiphany.* The first leads to the realization of the true function of such arguments, namely to introduce a measure of order into a man's mind by showing that his basic beliefs are not incompatible with each other. Once the believer is made aware of the true nature of the tools at his disposal for such purpose and the dangers which lurk in too close an alliance between religious and scientific or philosophical doctrines, there is no reason why he should not yield to the urge for reconciliation, which has been said to be "a necessary part of religious faith for the intellectual."[22] For he will thereby avoid the agony of having to maintain the desperate kind of faith which is in opposition to what his age has chosen to raise to the level of irrefutable fact.[23] The second pathos should destroy the false hope that a religious faith can be purged of all doubt by a logical argument. While the arguments of the first part of the dialogue appear rather feeble and loosely constructed, that of the second part gives the impression of being conducted with great rigor and therefore capable of carrying conviction. But when we examine the illustrations of necessary connections which Socrates offers, doubts begin to arise as to just how seriously they should be taken. As long as he refers to mathematical entities and claims, for example, that three is inseparably tied to oddness, we may experience no difficulty. The relation between fire and heat, snow and cold, is so constantly found in ordinary experience that many a reader may be reluctant to question it.[24] But does fever or abnormally high body temperature invariably indicate disease as Socrates maintains? (105C).[25] And if we are uncertain about bodily phenomena, how much more cautious do we have to be about the complex human self. But perhaps we have been unduly perturbed over an unfortunate selection of examples which, at the time of Socrates, may have been quite acceptable because of a failure to recognize that necessary connections are discoverably only in analytical statements and never in statements about physical facts known through sense perception; or some familiarity with contemporary philosophy and literature, which often question the applicability of the traditional categories to a reality capable of choosing its own mode of being,[26] may have misled us into reading modern conceptions into the reflections of Socrates.

An important part, however, if not the whole of Socrates' mission, consisted in inducing people to change their way of life, and the drunken Alcibiades in the *Symposium* tells how difficult it was not to succumb to his persuasive powers (215E–216A). Both Socrates' attempt to reform and Alcibiades' resistance to it presuppose at least a measure of freedom, which seems to preclude a fixed essence of the soul and the possibility of gaining an insight into it. Furthermore, the ideal mode of explanation which Socrates expected to find in the book of Anaxagoras, also serves to expose the false claim to certainty which Socrates ostensibly makes in the final demonstration. Since the elements in this ideal scheme derive their meaning from their position in the whole, nothing can be said with certainty about the particular as long as the structure of the whole remains unknown. In view of these considerations it is difficult to understand how anyone can maintain that "all the evidence suggests that Plato himself regarded this argument as sound."[27] It seems more reasonable to hold that its purpose is to impress upon the reader how impossible it is to meet the conditions which a rigorous demonstration yielding certainty would demand, namely, insight into the very essences of things.[28] Simmias has said as much earlier in the dialogue:

> I feel myself (and I dare say you have the same feeling), *how* hard or rather *impossible is the attainment of any certainty about questions such as these* in the present life. And yet I should deem him a coward who did not prove what is said about them to the uttermost, and whose heart failed him before he had examined them on every side. For he should persevere until he has achieved one of two things: either he should discover, or be taught the truth about them; or if this be impossible, *I would have him take the best and the most irrefragable of human theories, and let this be the raft upon which he sails through life*—not without risk, as I admit, if he cannot find some word of God which will more surely and safely carry him. (85C–D,J) [Italics added.]

Thus neither science, nor philosophy, nor logic can provide a secure and unshakable ground for the hope of immortality. Relentlessly Socrates has removed all the props and crutches, until the believer must stand on his own feet, if he is to stand at all. Nothing is left but faith. But such faith should be reasonable and it should be authentic, that is, not impelled by fear of deep-rooted desire alone. It should be based on a resolve capable of freely choosing between hope and despair. Only then can whatever a man chooses be genuinely his own.

The question of the *free resolve* is introduced casually and almost playfully early in the dialogue under the paradoxical claim that the true philosophers "are directly and of their own accord preparing themselves for dying and death" (64A). Death, he says, "is simply the release of the soul from the body" (64C), and is not the philsopher throughout his life trying to wrest control over himself from the body? He despises "the so-called pleasures connected with food and drink . . . sexual pleasures . . . smart clothes and shoes and bodily ornaments . . ." (64D). He thereby liberates himself as far as possible from the bondage of the body. Moreover, in the acquisition of knowledge the soul succeeds best "when it is free from all distortions such as hearing or sight or pain or pleasure of any kind—that is, when it ignores the body and becomes as far as possible independent" (65C). Further evidence of Socrates' concern with independence or "freedom from" is found in his distinction between a vulgar and a genuine morality. By self-control or temperance, he says, we mean "not being carried away by desires, but preserving a decent indifference toward them" (68C). Most men, however, abstain from one kind of pleasure merely in order to be able to indulge in another which they find irresistible. These same people are courageous and face death through fear of something worse. Thus, he says, they find themselves in the absurd condition of "being made temperate through intemperance" (69A,J) and "courageous through fear" (68D,J). This exchange of one pleasure or pain or fear for another, according to Socrates, is really no virtue at all. For it is an exchange of one bondage for another, and those who practice it are still "slaves in the service of the body" (66D). Genuine virtue is based on wisdom, which he rightly calls "a kind of purgation from all these emotions" (69B). For to be wise means to be open to all voices and to receive them undistorted from the pressure of feelings, self-interest, and prejudice. But such openness is not immediately given, nor is it simply passive. It requires a strong will to break the chain of stimulus-response reactions of feelings and habits, so that the situation can show itself as it really is, that is, basically indifferent to man's highest hopes and worst fears.

If a free resolve is all that is left as a basis for Socrates' faith, does it then not become completely subjective and arbitrary? Plato seems to think that while a securely rooted faith is not possible, there are some grounds why despair need not be the only alternative.

Strangely enough, he sees the reasonableness of a freely chosen belief in immortality in our shortcomings and our frustrations.[29] Men crave a kind of happiness which the world cannot provide. For, as Diotima declares in the *Symposium*, men want "not only the possession, but the everlasting possession of the good" (206A,J), or, as Nietzsche exclaims: "Weh' spricht: Vergeh! Doch alle Lust will Ewigkeit—will tiefe, tiefe Ewigkeit!"[30] The emptiness of the goods of life must have become glaringly evident to Socrates in the face of death. All his life he sought after truth, but the proper object of this noblest of human desires, the supreme principle of intelligibility, *to agathon,* was clearly beyond his reach. "While we are in the body," says Socrates, "our desire will not be satisfied, and our desire is of the truth" (66B,J). Thus the whole being of man points beyond this life, and to try to account for it in purely human terms is to make it appear paradoxical if not downright absurd, possessed as man is of cravings which from the outset are doomed to frustration. And just as physical facts, according to his method of inquiry, can be explained only by means of principles found on a higher level, so Socrates, if he is unwilling to resign himself to his futility, must place his existence in a wider setting, that is, he must transcend life itself and speak of a life after death. He has no assurance that there is such a life. The gods are silent and the human modes of knowing in whatever form can offer no guarantee. But unlike the inhabitants of Dante's Inferno, whom certainty dooms to hopelessness, his very ignorance leaves him free to choose between resignation to the futility of human existence and belief in a better life to come in which his fondest wishes find fulfillment.

It might be objected that the keen awareness of the *prima facie* futility of human endeavors has seduced Socrates to turn his back on his present existence; that in his eagerness to secure his hopes he has taken for established truths what are merely projections of intensely felt desires; that despite his professed "love of wisdom" he has found truth too difficult to face and is trying to hide it from himself, thus leading an inauthentic existence *en mauvaise foi*. But Socrates escapes this danger to his integrity, for he never allows himself to forget that he is faced with two alternatives, and that opting in favor of one does not remove the other as a real possibility:

> If while in company with the body, the soul cannot have pure knowledge, one of two things follows—*either knowledge is not to be attained at all*, or, if at all, after death. (66E–67A,J)[31]
> For if what I say is true, then I do well to be persuaded of the truth; but *if there be nothing after death*, still, during the short time that remains, I shall not distress my friends with lamentations, and my ignorance will not last, but will die with me, and therefore no harm will be done. (91B,J) [Italics added]

And in the *Apology,* after the Athenians have condemned him to death, he muses:

> *Either death is a state of nothingness and utter unconsciousness,* or, as men say, there is a change and migration of the soul from this world to another. Now if you suppose there is no consciousness, but a sleep like the sleep of him who is undisturbed even by dreams, death will be an unspeakable gain. . . . But if death is the journey to another place, and there, as men say, all the dead abide, what good, O my friends and judges, can be greater than this? (40C–D,J)[32] [Italics added]

Arguments may or may not add weight to one alternative or the other, but they can never decide the issue in the sense of producing certainty. Ultimately, the decision rests on a free choice. And only the preservation of this freedom can prevent the leap into faith from becoming an escape.[33]

At the conclusion of the arguments, Plato the thinker makes room for Plato the poet. For the dialogue ends with a beautiful myth and with the moving description of the last moments of Socrates.

Is it conceivable, as has been maintained, that the myth has no possible connection with the rest of the discussion, and that the death scene is simply Plato's tribute to his friend and master?[34] Is it not more likely that Plato, consummate artist that he is, makes effective use of both myth and death scene in the endeavor to convey his notion of what an authentic faith should be like? On the one hand, faith is possible only in the face of uncertainty, for only in an uncertain situation must will and not reason ultimately resolve the issue. To this awareness of uncertainty, the myth is made to contribute. On the other hand, if the faith is to be an authentic faith, then the choice on which it is based must be that of an individual who has rendered himself immune, as far as possible, to all outer and inner pressures. In the achievement of that kind of freedom the death scene plays a significant role.

The myth describes the earth as expanded in two directions; to the realm familiar to the senses it adds an upper and a lower region:

> I believe that the earth is very vast, and that *we who dwell in the region extending from the river Phasis to the Pillars of Heracles inhabit a small region only about the sea, like ants or frogs about a marsh.* . . . For everywhere on the face of the earth there are hollows of various forms and sizes, into which the water and the lower air collect. But the true air is pure and situated in the pure heaven . . . and it is the heaven which is commonly spoken of as the ether, and of which our own earth is the sediment gathering in the hollows beneath. But *we who live in these hollows are deceived into the notion that we are dwelling above on the surface of the earth: which is just as if a creature who was at the bottom of the sea were to fancy that it was on the surface of the water,* and that the sea was the heaven through which he saw the sun and the other stars, he having never come to the surface by reason of his feebleness and sluggishness, and having never lifted up his head and seen, nor ever heard from one who had seen, how much purer and fairer the world above is than his own. *And such is exactly our case.* (109A–E,J) [Italics added]

And in the other direction of the experienced world, "there are diverse regions in the hollows on the surface of the globe everywhere, some of them deeper and more extended than that which we inhabit . . ." (111C–D,J).

If Socrates' reassuring words after the apparent breakdown of the initial set of arguments may be regarded as a first-aid application and the exposition of Socrates' method an attempt to heal the wound struck by the objections, then the myth near the end of the dialogue can be said to perform the function of preventive medicine. For it imagines a world which is wider than our own, and of which ours is only a small part. It points to the fragmentary character of human experience and the consequent inconclusiveness of all arguments based on it, be they in support of the significance or the absurdity of human existence. It thus creates an awareness which should exert a salutary restraint on the human understanding which, as Francis Bacon warns, "is of its nature prone to suppose more order and regularity in the world than it finds."[35] But while it cautions against a false sense of certainty, the very uncertainty which it suggests leaves room for hope.

If we look more closely at the nature and function of the myth, we shall find that it again illustrates Heidegger's contention that every understanding has its mood and every mood its understanding. It will be recalled that the arguments of the first part produced in the uncritical a false sense of security, followed by feelings of consternation and dismay at the first onslaught of serious objections against them. In the second part, the appearance of logical rigor tended to lull the critical intelligence of the reader to sleep, merely to rouse it from its slumbers by the irreducible disparity between the exposition and the application of Socrates' method of inquiry. Thus, while the arguments appealed primarily to the intellectual side of man, they also stirred up a groundswell of strong feelings. Now the myth in the *Phaedo* reverses the emphasis: it speaks directly to the emotions and yet lends itself to a logical analysis.

The myth obviously does not provide knowledge in the ordinary sense. The world it describes is purely imaginary. But it does create a *sense* of the vastness of the world, which helps to guard against both overconfidence and hopelessness. At the same time it furnishes a modicum of understanding. It does this by means of an analogy of proportionality. First we are told to imagine an experience more limited than our own, namely, that of "ants and frogs about a pond" (109A). This imaginary experience appears limited because we are aware of our own wider experience. Similarly, in order to recognize our own experience as limited, we must be able to transcend it. And because of this transcendence, we can say that what man's experience is to the frogs', a *possibly* wider experience is to man's: $M/F = X/M$. Since by hypothesis, X is a position beyond all human experience, nothing can be said about it, except that it is a possibility. We can fill the emptiness of that transempirical possibility, as Socrates does, with elements drawn from experience. But it must never be forgotten that this content is not directly experienced. The purpose of this transcendence is not to give us a new experience; it merely provides us with the point of vantage from which to survey and see more clearly our actual experience. Our experience, thus seen as limited, does not preclude the *possibility* of a wider experience in the light of which human life would become meaningful. To repeat, it provides only a possibility; but this is enough to give rise to the hope for an ultimately meaningful human existence. This hope a free man may reasonable choose to entertain—"not without risk," as Simmias warns (85D, J), for the hope in the end may turn out to be false.

Finally, the myth helps to underscore the paradoxical nature of the final proof. For this proof, which is based on insight into essences and necessary connections, now appears wedged in between the exposition of Socrates' second-best method, a method which allows for no more than various degrees of probability, and the myth which, through its presentation of a possibly wider experience than our own, makes the attainability of certain truths highly questionable. Here the reader must choose between two alternatives: he can follow those commentators who take the proof literally, as satisfactory to Plato, and disregard or dim down the significance of the method and the myth; or he can allow these two to play their proper roles and see in the final argument not a proof for the immortality of the soul, but Plato's way of exhibiting the impossible conditions, namely insight into essences and necessary connections, which would have to be met in order to rest Socrates' faith on unshakable foundations.

Socrates' method and the myth have shown that because of its inherent uncertainty the human situation offers a choice. The death scene provides an opportunity to make the choice, for whatever alternative, an authentic choice.

Before a man can make an authentic choice, he must first take possession of himself; that is, he must make himself the sole source of his actions. Very early in the dialogue, Socrates has referred to this act of self-possession through his paradoxical claim that the true philosophers "are directly and of their own accord preparing themselves for dying and death" (64C), by not allowing themselves to be "carried away by desires, but preserving a decent indifference toward them" (68C). If the description of the last moments of Socrates could be shown to confirm this notion, then the myth and the death scene would find their proper place in the dialogue and contribute to its unity.

Nothing is said explicitly about authenticity. We are told that Socrates faced death courageously and full of confidence, although he had expressed his awareness of complete annihilation and the absurdity of human existence as real possibilities. Presumably, his choice of hope rather than despair was an authentic one, which, as we have seen, presupposes an act of self-possession. Some of his friends cried out in sorrow, so that Socrates had to reprimand them. The dying man's last words, seconds before the fatal hemlock reached his heart, contained expressions of gratitude toward the son of Apollo, the healer-god Asclepius. Did Socrates feel healed, made whole in the face of death? Plato is silent, and after a few words of eulogy on the part of Phaedo, the dialogue comes to a close.

Is it again possible to show that where the dialogue ends Heidegger's analysis begins, and that dialogue and phenomenological analysis mutually enhance each other's insights? Or does Socrates' death, as the death of any man, put a final stop to philosophical inquiry? For death is totally inaccessible to the living and cannot be shared with the dying. Those who remain suffer a loss, but, as Heidegger admits, "in suffering this loss we have no way of access to the loss of Being which the dying man 'suffers' " (282). And if death is annihilation, maybe the dying man himself cannot experience it, since with his death he is deprived of any possibility of experiencing.

While death as an *event* eludes existential-ontological analysis, death as a *possibility* does not. As Nietzsche has said: "Even the thought of a possibility can shatter and transform us."[36] And not only Socrates' friends who witnessed his death as an event, but also the readers who in the course of the long discussion have come to feel close to Socrates, are bound to have experienced a keener awareness than usual of the fact that they too someday must die. It is the thought of death as a possibility which Heidegger scrutinizes, in order to uncover its extraordinary revelatory power—not about death as an event, but about the human mode of being.

When we encounter the terms "death" and "dying," we must not let the ordinary meanings intrude, but hold fast to the sense in which Heidegger proposes to use them:

> The 'ending' which we have in view when we speak of death, does not signify Dasein's Being-at-an-end (Zu-Ende-sein) but a *Being-towards-the-end* (Sein-zum-Ende) of this entity. (289)
> Let the term 'dying' stand for that *way of being* in which Dasein *is towards* its death. (291)

"Being toward death", i.e., opening up to death as an inescapable possibility, can take two basic forms: an individual can let the possibility exert its full influence and shed light on his being, or he can dim it down and try to close himself off from it.

If a man has the courage to face this possibility, how does it affect his self-awareness?

"Being-toward-death" individualizes; for death reveals itself as a possibility which belongs exclusively to each individual. *"No one,"* says Heidegger, *"can take the Other's dying away from him.* Of course someone 'can go to his death for another.' But that always means to sacrifice oneself for the Other 'in some *definite affair.'* Such 'dying for' can never signify that the Other has thus had his death taken away in even the slightest degree" (284). This individualization makes a man aware of and tends to wrench him away from the 'they-self', or the group to whose dominance he has fallen captive. And since no one and nothing can help him escape this impending possibility, the thought of it severs all relations with others, and with everything with which he has identified himself. He thus catches a glimpse of himself, stripped of all that is actual. He finds himself reduced to what Heidegger calls his "ownmost potentiality for Being."

This glimpse of himself as sheer possibility needs to be brought into sharper focus. Whenever we reach out for something possible, we do not contemplate the possible but move beyond it to its actualization. "Even in expecting," says Heidegger, "one leaps away from the possible and gets a foothold in the actual. It is for its actuality that what is expected is expected. By the very nature of expecting, the possible is drawn into the actual, arising out of the actual and returning to it" (306). In the case of "death," this skipping over the possible is checked by the very nature of this possibility. One is compelled to stay with the possible as possible because the realization of this possibility would mean the impossibility of any existence at all. Thus "death" not only draws a man away from the roles with which he tends to identify himself, but creates a keener awareness of himself as sheer potentiality.

Since understanding and mood are inseparable for Heidegger, he must ask for the specific mood which corresponds to the self-understanding brought about by "Being-toward-death." The mood in question is anxiety. It is evoked by the realization that death is not only certain but also indefinite, that is, it may occur at any moment. Anxiety is to be distinguished from fear. In fear we feel threatened by an object which draws near from out of the world. In anxiety things in the world, and others, become irrelevant. They show themselves in their "empty mercilessness" (393), and thus destroy the world in which we felt at home "shattering all one's tenaciousness to whatever existence one has reached" (p. 308). One feels rootless, concerned about oneself and yet reluctant to face oneself. But if a man musters up enough courage to let the mood of anxiety have its effect, he will experience himself as a potentiality for which he can assume or refuse to assume responsibility. In other words, he can let "the possibility of authentic potentiality-for-Being be lit up" (393).

The understanding and the mood under consideration, however, reveal only the *possibility* of authentic existence. Most people, according to Heidegger, close themselves off against the light which "death" could shed on their being. Of course, they too are certain of their death: "One of these days one will die too, in the end; but right now it has nothing to do with us" (297). They take death as an event which is still *in the future* and therefore has little to do with them *now*. Thus they extinguish or at least weaken its revelatory power. By saying "one dies", they make it a public event and thus try to cover up the threat which strikes at the very core of the individualized self. Anxiety which would face the threat is suppressed and in its stead fear arises as of an oncoming event. This fear, in turn, is considered a weakness and unworthy of a man. Thus the "many" of Plato and the 'they-self' of Heidegger tranquillize themselves and at the same time alienate themselves from their true being.

Anxiety, according to Heidegger's own admission, is a rare mood, and most people cover up its corresponding understanding. How then can Heidegger demonstrate that what he says is true? Demonstration for him means letting something show itself, pointing to an experience so that an aspect of it or an element in it is being lit up. But how can he help people see something in their experience when they turn away from that experience and make every effort to hide it from themselves? Does not his whole enterprise become rather esoteric, accessible only to the privileged few?

Heidegger solves the problem by basing his demonstration on this very turning away from a confrontation with the true self, a movement which he calls *falling:* "In falling, Dasein turns away from *itself.*" On what is this turning away based? It cannot be based on fear, because fear is a fleeing from something threatening encountered in the world. Falling, on the contrary, turns to the world in which it seeks refuge from whatever it experiences as a threat. The threatening, therefore, cannot be an entity in the world. It is Dasein itself.

> Thus the turning away of falling is not a fleeing that is founded upon fear of entities within-the-world. Fleeing that is so grounded is still less a character of this turning away, when what this turning away does is precisely to *turn thither* toward entities within the world by absorbing itself in them. *The turning-away of falling is grounded rather in anxiety,* which in turn is what first makes fear possible. (230)

The very effort to veil what anxiety tends to uncover shows that falling, the condition in which men find themselves "for the most part," implies an experience of anxiety, no matter how vague. To make an implicit awareness explicit is one of the legitimate functions of Heidegger's analytic of Dasein. Everyday "Being-toward-death" might try to attribute to death merely an empirical certainty. For we seem to know only that so far no man has lived beyond a certain age limit. This observation establishes no more than a high degree of probability and falls short of the highest certainty, "the apodictic, which we reach in certain demonstrations of theoretical knowledge" (301). But the omnipresence of anxiety, in whatever degree of intensity, shows that men are aware of death in a way which is neither empirical nor apodictic:

> Even though, in the publicness of the "they," Dasein seems to 'talk' only of this 'empirical' certainty of death, *nevertheless at bottom* Dasein does *not* exclusively or primarily stick to those cases of death which merely occur. *In evading its death,* even everyday Being-toward-the-end is indeed certain of its death in another way than it might itself like to have true on purely theoretical considerations. (302)

Socrates' statement early in the *Phaedo,* to the effect that the philosopher is always dying, now takes on a deeper meaning, whether Plato intended to convey that meaning or was himself unaware of it. For Socrates speaks of loosening the bonds which tie the individual to the pleasure of eating, or drinking, or sex, etc.

But while Socrates is concerned with a *freedom from*, Being-toward-death makes possible at the same time a *freedom to*, namely to man's own being as potentiality:

> It reveals to Dasein its lostness in the 'they-self', and brings it face to face with the possibility of being itself, primarily unsupported by concernful solicitude, but of being itself, rather, in an impassioned FREEDOM TO-WARD DEATH—a freedom which has been released from the Illusions of the "they," and which is factical, certain of itself, and anxious. (311)
> Anxiety makes manifest in Dasein its *Being towards* its ownmost potentiality-for-Being—that is, its *Being-free for* the freedom of choosing itself and taking hold of itself. Anxiety brings Dasein face to face with its *Being-free for* the authenticity of its Being, and for this authenticity as a possibility which it always is. (232)

This detachment from the 'they-self' does not isolate Dasein or make it unsocial. Neither did Socrates' independence or freedom from bodily pleasures prevent him from enjoying them. The *Symposium* shows that he could drink others under the table without adverse effect on himself. It is not the pleasures as such which he condemns, but the loss of control to which they often lead. Similarly Heidegger believes that " 'authentic Being-one's-self' does not detach Dasein from its world, nor does it isolate it so that it becomes a free-floating 'I'. . . . Authentic disclosedness . . . brings the Self right into its current concernful Being-alongside what is ready-to-hand, and pushes it into solicitous Being with Others" (344). It would seem obvious that a person driven by uncontrollable desires or impulses or overdependent upon the opinions of others, will have difficulty entering into proper social relations. How can an individual genuinely love or be loved, if his being has been dispersed and his self has lost itself in his various activities? Only a man who is truly himself can become the true friend of another. Anxiety, therefore, by individualizing Dasein, offers the possibility of self-possession, and far from leading to isolation, it is the condition for the possibility of genuine sociability.

Heidegger undertakes an intricate and highly suggestive phenomenological analysis of 'dying' as 'Being-toward-death'; Plato has Phaedo answer the second half of the question which Echecrates asks in the opening lines of the dialogue: "What did the master say before he died, and *how did he meet his end?*" (57A). It would seem that nothing more than the most tenuous connection exists between Heidegger's analysis and Phaedo's answer. And yet, as on previous occasions, a closer look reveals, not a parallelism or simple agreement, but a continuity of treatment of the same subject matter by the two authors. In other words, Heidegger supplies the ontological underpinnings which are implicit and often vaguely suggested in Plato's explicit concerns.

Plato the poet allows us, at least vicariously, to witness the dying of a man with whom we have identified and whom we have come to admire and perhaps even love in the course of the long discussion which precedes the death scene. We can sympathize with his friends who on the day following his execution will no longer be able to come to him with their problems and rely on him for advice. They and we come to the realization that as Socrates must release his hold on his entire life and on the world in which he lives, so must we progressively learn to sever our dependence on others and become master over our selves. To place the phenomenon of "dying" before us, is all the artist can do. And for Plato the moral teacher, it is enough. He thereby provides us with an opportunity to let the experience have its full impact upon us, to let it call us back from the lostness in the 'they-self', to throw us back upon our true self, of which we can then take possession. Of course, we can also refuse to do so. We can hide from ourselves as quickly as possible the uncanniness *(Unheimlichkeit)* which always pursues us in some form or other. And just because we are free to resist or yield to it, Plato can do no more than give this pursuit through the death scene a fresh impetus, and thus render the evasion more difficult. The choice must be our own. But unless we let anxiety enter our being and unless we make this choice, authenticity in general and an authentic faith in particular are not possible.

Heidegger, on the other hand, as he frequently insists, is not directly concerned with morality. He is an ontologist. He must, therefore, go beyond Plato's evocation of the phenomenon and analyze its structure. To let the death scene have whatever impact it may, is not enough for him. He must determine the nature of the anxiety which it tends to call forth, in order to see what light it sheds on the being of man. For he maintains that only if he gains a better understanding of the human mode of being can he hope to come nearer the ultimate goal of his inquiry, namely, the meaning of Being in general. While Plato's concern with an authentic faith presupposes genuine selfhood, Heidegger makes manifest how such selfhood is possible; he points out how an individual must be constituted so that he can gain or lose himself; he shows why men, for the most part, seek refuge in the unauthentic mode; and finally he makes clear how death as a possibility, by rendering the evasion of authenticity more difficult, offers the opportunity to take possession of themselves and thereby meet the condition for the possibility of morality. Thus Plato the moralist and Heidegger the ontologist, pursuing different interests and moving in different directions, can nevertheless be said to complement each other's insights. For the dialogue can be read as furnishing concrete examples of some of the abstract analyses of *Being and Time;* and Heidegger, in turn, by laying bare the structures underlying the level on which Socrates moves, provides a clearer vision of Plato's thoughts and an increased awareness and appreciation of their significance.

If we now look back upon the dialogue, we find that its philosophic crop is not so meagre or outdated as to justify the exclusive concentration of our attention "on the image of the dying Socrates."[37] Through the first set of arguments we

ile one's faith with current philosophic
s not misled into thinking that such
his faith into incontrovertible truth.
proposed by Simmias, has taught us the
ory, namely, compatibility with other
d agreement with observable facts. His
both in its strength and its weakness: its
g about a certain amount of order in a
es from the fact that it must operate with
hen attaining a measure of success, are
gs. Socrates' discussion of Anaxagoras's
ossibility of what Heidegger calls the
real connections of interaction between
ints to desires, especially the desire to
y life, and he dreams of a world in which
monstrating" man's ability to transcend
's claim that "Dasein is always 'Beyond
of behaving toward other entities which
iality-for-Being which it is itself" (236).
head-of-itself," or *existence*, and regards
uman mode of being. Socrates further
if he allows himself to be dominated by
te which is reminiscent of Heidegger's
prisonment," however, is not caused by
hen speaking about reincarnation, Soc-
tizens pass into such "social and disci-
ts." They are said to be controlled by the
which is acquired by habit and practice
eason" (82A). Now they could not fall
were not vulnerable, that is, sensitive or
ithout. And without such sensitivity or
world could not show themselves in their
as means for the achievement of human
ility of things Heidegger calls "thrown-
much to say that Heidegger's three basic
in, namely, thrownness, existence, and
lo. In any event, it is clear that far from
arious parts of the dialogue are suggestive

e common element which permeates the
d of uncertainty. This uncertainty is the
of arguments and it is reenforced by the

dismay felt by some of Socrates' companions when they found their conviction shattered by the objections raised against the arguments. It reappears when Socrates projects his "second-best" method against the ideal method, when his high expectations from the book of Anaxagoras are followed by disappointment upon reading the text. There is the puzzlement created in the mind of the reader by the conflict between the exposition of the "second-best" method which operates with tentative hypotheses, and its application in the last argument which presupposes an impossible insight into the essences of things. And finally there is the geographic myth which, through an analogy of proportionality expressed in a beautiful image, lights up the uncertainty for the last time by contrasting the possible vastness of the universe with the narrowness of human experience on which all arguments must ultimately rest.

We can now also appreciate the reason for this all-pervasive uncertainty. It is not meant to destroy the belief in an afterlife. By pointing out that man's desires reach beyond his earthly existence and that human life makes sense only in the light of a *possibly* wider experience, Socrates shows that such a faith is not unreasonable. But his main concern is not to let this faith become dogmatic. For the uncertainty does not necessarily lead to either hope or despair, but to the possibility of choosing between them.

If uncertainty is a characteristic of the situation which offers the possibility of an act of faith, then authenticity is a prerequisite of the believer. And this authenticity as a possibility, according to Heidegger, is offered by the awareness of death which calls the individual from the 'they-self' to his true self. Just as uncertainty permeates every aspect of the dialogue, so death as a possibility is present from the first to the last line. And as toward the end uncertainty is most forcefully brought home by the geographic myth, so the awareness of death reaches its greatest intensity with the actual dying of Socrates; and both the sense of uncertainty and the awareness of death tend to loosen the firm hold which man's concernful activities have over him. Plato displays his poetic, his dramatic, and his philosophical skills, using myth and logical argument, appealing to mood and understanding, and thus addressing the whole man. And he does not let up until he has touched him at the very core of his being, where he is most genuinely himself, namely, in the possibility of making himself the ultimate source of his decisions. It should now be evident how wrong-headed are the approaches of those who debate over whether or not the arguments logically establish the immortality of the soul and whether or not the proofs were satisfactory to Plato. Nor do those fare better who would simply disregard the arguments as antiquated and concentrate on the dramatic and poetic aspects of the dialogue. For all these are subservient to one single insight: the nature of an *authentic* commitment in the *uncertain* atmosphere of the human condition. Such commitment presupposes genuine selfhood which, as Heidegger has shown, is brought out most vividly before us in the face of imminent death. It is conceivable that Socrates in his final moments felt most fully at one with himself. And this may be the reason why he addressed his last words to his friend Crito, asking him to sacrifice a cock to the healer god Asclepius.

NOTES

1. Martin Heidegger, *Being and Time,* trans. John Macquarrie and Edward Robinson (New York: Harper & Row, 1962), p. 228. Unless otherwise stated, all quotations from Heidegger refer to this edition.

2. R. S. Bluck *Plato's "Phaedo,"* translated with Introduction, Notes and Appendices (New York: Liberal Arts Press, 1955), p. 23. See also the statement by Karl R. Popper: "The Socrates of the *Apology* and some other dialogues is intellectually modest; in the *Phaedo* he changes into a man who is assured of the truth of his metaphysical speculations." *The Open Society and Its Enemies* (Princeton, N.J.: Princeton University Press, 1950) p. 601.

3. Few if any contemporary philosophers would use the term soul at all, but even a consideration of the self reveals serious difficulties to the modern inquirer. The impossibility, for instance, of ascribing a fixed essence to a being capable of choosing its own mode of being is expressed by Sartre in connection with his famous notion of "mauvaise foi." "Let us note finally the confusing syntheses which play on the nihilating ambiguity of these temporal ekstases, affirming at once that I am what I have been (the man who deliberately arrests himself at one period of his life and refuses to take into consideration the later changes) and that I am not what I have been (the man who in the face of reproaches or rancor dissociates himself from his past by insisting on his freedom and on his perpetual re-creation). In all these concepts, which have only a transitive role in the reasoning and which are eliminated from the conclusion, (like hypochondriacs in the calculations of physicians), we find again the same structure. *We have to deal with human reality as a being which is what it is not and which is not what it is*" (Jean-Paul Sartre, *Being and Nothingness,* translated with an Introduction by Hazel E. Barnes [New York: Philosophical Library, 1956], p. 58. Italics added). Karl Löwith, in an interview *(Der Spiegel* 43 [1969], states the problem laconically: "Von der Seele mag niemand mehr reden, weil man nicht weiss, ob man eine hat."

4. Sir R. W. Livingstone, *Portrait of Socrates* (Oxford: Clarendon Press, 1946), p. viii. See also Paul Tillich: "Even if the so-called arguments for the 'immortality of the soul' had argumentative power (which they do not have) they would not convince existentially." *The Courage to Be* (New Haven, Conn.: Yale University Press, 1953), p. 42.

5. Livingston, *Portrait of Socrates,* p. viii. Tillich makes a similar recommendation when he says: "In discussing [Plato's so-called doctrine of immortality of the soul] we should neglect the arguments for immortality, even those in Plato's *Phaedon,* and concentrate on the image of the dying Socrates." *(Courage to Be,* p. 168) It is interesting to note that the complete neglect of the philosophical aspects of the *Phaedo* is the opposite extreme of an earlier tendency to overlook the artistic aspects, as reported by Paul Friedländer: "Hermann Bonitz wrote three quarters of a century ago in his *Platonische Studien* (1886), a work held in high esteem at the time and even in the days of my youth, that he was confining himself entirely to the presentation of the philosophical doctrine, disregarding everything pertaining to the artistic composition of the dialogue (i.e., the *Phaedo*)." *Plato I, An Introduction,* trans. H. Meyerhoff (New York: Random House, 1958), p. 232.

6. Quotations from the *Phaedo* refer to the translation by Hugh Tredennick in *The Collected Dialogues of Plato*, ed. Edith Hamilton and Huntington Cairns (Princeton, N.J.: Princeton University Press, 1971). When the Jowett translation seems preferable, the reference to the dialogue is followed by the letter "J."

7. "As history makes clear, to reduce religious beliefs and symbols to the compass of any philosophic formulation, however well established, is tragic, and indeed, in the end, fatal." John H. Randall, Jr., *The Role of Knowledge in Western Religion* (Boston: Beacon Press, 1958), p. 13.

8. For a proper understanding of the meaning of the word *to agathon* note Heidegger's explanation "*To agathon* übersetzt man durch den scheinbar verstaendlichen Ausdruck 'das Gute'. Man denkt dabei meist auch noch an das 'sittlich Gute', das so heisst, weil es dem Sittengesetz gemaess ist. Diese Deutung fällt aus dem griechischen Denken heraus. . . ." (pp. 36–37). "*To agathon* bedeutet griechisch gedacht das, was zu etwas taugt and zu etwas tauglich macht. . . . Die 'Ideen' machen daher, griechisch gedacht, dazu tauglich, dass etwas in dem, was es ist, erscheinen und so in seinem Beständigen anwesen kann. . . . Das, was jede Idee zu einer Idee tauglich macht, platonisch ausgedrückt, die Idee aller Ideen, besteht deshalb darin, das Erscheinen alles Anwesenden in all seiner Sichtsamkeit zu ermöglichen." *Platons Lehre von der Wahrheit*, 2nd ed. (Bern: Francke Verlag, 1954).

If Heidegger's interpretation is correct, as it seems to be, then Hugh Tredennick's translation of *to agathon* as "goodness or moral obligation" would be grossly misleading.

9. "Aller Logos hat . . . im sokratischen Gespräch zunächst notwendig nur den Charakter der Hypothesis. Seine 'Stärke' liegt . . . allein in seiner sachlichen Leistung, eine Mannigfaltigkeit in ihrem einheitlich selbigen Sein zu begreifen." Hans-Georg Gadamer, *Platos dialektische Ethik, und andere Studien zur platonischen Philosophie* (Hamburg: Felix Meiner Verlag, 1968), p. 52.

10. This need on the part of the reader to reach an existential awareness of the problem under discussion seems to be expressed in the opening statements of Martin Heidegger's *Platons Lehre von der Wahrheit:* "Die Erkenntnisse der Wissenschaften werden gewöhnlich in Sätzen ausgesprochen und dem Menschen als greifbare Ergebnisse zur Verwendung vorgesetzt. Die Lehre eines Denkers ist das in seinem Sagen Ungesagte, dem der Mensch ausgesetzt wird, auf dass er dafür sich verschwende" (p. 5).

11. Note also: "The point has to be made, because the force of the argument now to be produced depends on the fact that it deals with essential predication." A. E. Taylor, *Plato, The Man and His Work*. 6th ed. (London: Methuen and Co., 1949), p. 204.

12. It is, of course, understood that Plato does not speak of "relations between two persons, but [of] *properties* which one has 'toward' the other" (R. Hackforth, *Plato's "Phaedo,"* translated with Introduction and Commentary [Cambridge: 1955], p. 69, note 3). "The curious thing," Hackforth remarks, "is that Plato appears to be at least on the verge of realizing [that 'tall' and 'short' are not qualities, but relations] . . . Yet this semi-awareness of the distinction between qualities and relations is, it seems, only momentary; from 102D 5 onwards it disappears" (ibid. p. 155).

13. David Scarrow, "*Phaedo*, 106A–106E," *Philosophical Review* 70 (1961): 245.

14. For details see ibid., pp. 247–51.

15. R. S. Bluck describes the new attitude as follows: "We may note how Socrates, who has hitherto been his usual self-deprecating self ("the most stupid creature in the world," 96C), becomes almost magisterial. The language at 100B in particular is unlike that of the usual Socrates (i.e., of Socrates talking in true Socratic vein)" (*Plato's "Phaedo,"* p. 165, note 2).

16. "This hypothetical method, if our analysis of the *Phaedo* has been correct, can never attain to absolute knowledge . . . but, when we recall that [Plato] believed in the

possibility of absolute knowledge . . . *we must certainly wonder why he devoted so much space to its elaboration . . .*" Richard Robinson, *Plato's Earlier Dialectic,* Second Ed. (Oxford: Clarendon Press, 1953), p. 146. Italics added.)

17. R. S. Bluck, *Plato's "Phaedo,"* p. 165.

18. "It is well that we should be reminded that the doctrine of Forms as causes is put forward by Socrates as a second-best doctrine relative to that which he had hoped to build on the principle suggested by Anaxagoras. Nevertheless *Plato seems in our present section, and indeed throughout the rest of the argument which gives his final proof of immortality to have forgotten this*" Hackforth, *Plato's "Phaedo,"* p. 146. Italics added.

19. "Only when this first principle is reached, and the Forms are seen in their dependence on it, will the goal of all inquiry be reached. . . . *I think that Plato wavers on the question whether the goal can ever in fact be reached by any man in this life:* the earlier part of our dialogue seems to suggest that it cannot, the present passage and the Republic that it can." Ibid. Italics added.

20. The history of science offers numerous instances of this kind of overestimation of the results of inquiry. Scientific hypotheses may, at a given period of time and in regard to specific aspects of nature, appear so successful that the inquirer is tempted to regard them as revealing the nature of things. This temptation may prove irresistible when coupled with the common tendency of the scientist to allow as real only that which falls within the range of this method and conforms to his postulates, and to regard as "mere appearance" that which does not. To those who believed themselves in possession of definitive truth about the cosmos, Galileo was a dangerous heretic; and many of those who felt comfortably at home in the world of Newton must have looked upon Einstein as a subversive intruder and a disturber of the scientific peace. Nor are philosophers immune to this excess, especially when they set up norms to which things must conform before they can be acknowledged as genuinely real. Heidegger refers to Descartes as an illustration of this tendency: "The kind of Being which belongs to entities within the world is something which they themselves might have been permitted to present; but Descartes does not let them do so. Instead he prescribes for the world its 'real' Being, as it were, on the basis of an Idea of Being whose source has not been unveiled and which has not been demonstrated in its own right—an idea in which Being is equated with constant presence-at-hand" (p. 129).

21. Note the analogous conflict between superstition and rationalism in the *Euthyphro,* and between radical freedom and responsibility as against unquestioning obedience to law in the *Crito.*

22. John H. Randall, Jr., *Role of Knowledge,* p. 24.

23. Bertrand Russell describes such a faith by imagining science as capable of certifying the purposelessness of the universe. Although man is said to be "the outcome of accidental collocations of atoms" in a world indifferent to his hopes and fears, and although "the whole temple of [his] achievement must inevitably be buried beneath the debris of a universe in ruins," he is urged to maintain his faith in ideals, to worship, if only at "the shrine that his own hands have built," to accept a God even if he be "recognized as the creation of [his] own conscience." "A Free Man's Worship," *Mysticism and Logic* (New York: Doubleday Anchor Book, 1957), pp. 45, 47, 54.

24. Gadamer does not question the necessary connection between fire and heat. He misses the irony and is led to say that such necessary connection forms the basis of the "genuine proof for the immortality of the soul in the *Phaedo.*" *Platos dialektische Ethik,* p. 54.

25. *Phaedo,* 10C. Hackforth attributes the cause of the difficulty to self-deception on the part of Plato: "The refusal of a cold lump of snow to admit heat, while yet remaining snow, is a physical fact known through sense perception; whereas the refusal of 'twoness'

to admit 'threeness' and 'oddness,' and that of the soul to accept 'deadness,' are statements about implications of terms; they are in fact somewhat unnatural expressions of analytical propositions, and the final 'proof' of immortality is a disguised assertion that the term 'soul' implies as part of its meaning, the term 'alive.' But by putting all these instances of exclusion on all fours with one another, as the military metaphor helps him to do, Plato disguises—from himself, as I believe, as well as from us—the fundamental weakness of his argument" (*Plato's "Phaedo"* p. 157). To accuse a thinker of Plato's stature of confusion is always risky, for the charge may all too easily boomerang on its originator.

26. This is a problem which is of serious concern to some of the disciples of Martin Heidegger, such as Katharina Kanthack: "In Freiheit *seinkönnendes* Dasein, das sinnstiftend zum Seienden hin transzendiert und eben in diesem Transzendieren ueber sich selbst entscheidet, ist nicht 'anzunageln': weder etwas wie eine Substanz noch etwas wie Eigenschaften lassen sich hier als das irgendwie Beharrende benennen" (*Vom Sinn der Selbsterkenntnis* [Berlin: Walter de Gruter & co., 1958], p. 48). and again: "Kann aber der Mensch als dieses Freisein Unstimmigkeit oder Einstimmigkeit sein, so verliert das vom Vorhandenen abgelesene Wort 'Eigenschaft' seinen Sinn. Das Substanz-Schema zerbricht. Es zerbricht an Freiheit, zerbricht daran, dass der Mensch Seinkönnen ist" (ibid., p. 150). The problem has also found its way into literature, as seen, for instance, in Aldous Huxley's *Point Counterpoint* (New York: Modern Library, 1928), pp. 230–1. "The essential character of the self consisted precisely in that liquid and undeformable ubiquity; in that capacity to espouse all contours and yet remain unfixed in any form; to take, and with an equal facility efface, impression."

27. R. S. Bluck, *Plato's "Phaedo"*, p. 16.

28. It is interesting to note how often the lesson which Plato is trying to teach in the *Phaedo* has to be relearned: Whatever may be one's opinion as to our permanent acceptance of the analytical details of Einstein's restricted and general theories of relativity, there can be no doubt that through these theories physics is permanently changed. *It was a great shock to discover that classical concepts, accepted unquestioningly, were inadequate to meet the actual situation,* and the shock of this discovery has resulted in a critical attitude toward our whole conceptual structure which must at least in part be permanent. Reflection on the situation after the event shows that it should not have needed the new experimental facts which led to relativity to convince us to the inadequacy of our previous concepts, but that *a sufficiently shrewd analysis should have prepared us for at least the possibility of what Einstein did.* (P. W. Bridgmen, *The Logic of Modern Physics.* [New York, 1951], p. 1. Italics added.)

29. "Der Vergleich mit dem Christentum . . . ist auch hierlehrreich. Der wahre Gott wird bei Plato nicht als spontane, sich selbst offenbarende Macht—nicht als *Wille* (der fordert und begnadigt)—erkennbar, sondern ausschliesslich in der Perspektive des verlangenden Menschen: als das rettende Gute." Gerhard Krüger, *Einsicht und Leindenschaft*, 3rd ed. (Frankfurt am Main: Vittorio Klostermann, 1963), p. 180.

30. "Woe implores: Go! But all joy wants eternity—Wants deep, wants deep eternity." *Thus spoke Zarathustra*, third part, in *The Portable Nietzsche*, edited and translated by Walter Kaufmann (New York: Viking Press, 1954), pp. 339–40.

31. How easily the expression can be turned into an expression of dogmatism is shown by the following paraphrase: "Since this sort of knowledge cannot be acquired while we are associated with the body, it can be gained only when we are free of it, that is, after death." George Boas, *Rationalism in Greek Philosophy* (Baltimore: Johns Hopkins Press, 1961), p. 171.

32. R. S. Bluck notes the lack of assurance about an afterlife in the *Apology:* "From Plato's *Apology* it is clear that however much the real Socrates may have hoped for an

afterlife, or thought that there probably was one, he deliberately refrained from making any sure pronouncement on the subject" (*Plato's "Phaedo,"* p. 5). Subsequently, while discussing the nature of Plato's belief as expressed in the *Phaedo,* he remarks: "Socrates may have hoped for an after-life; Plato here shows that he himself had no doubt about it" (ibid., p. 47). From the *Apology* he cites 29A-B and 41C *ad fin.* But he does not mention 40D *ad fin.,* which seems to make the point more forcefully and might have led him to notice similar alternatives in the *Phaedo.* (See 91B above.) Of course, as long as the demonstrations, especially the final one, are taken literally, the alternatives presented by Socrates are easily overlooked, as indicated by Boas's paraphrase, quoted in note 31 above.

33. The futility of human existence appears as a frequent theme in Western thought. Significantly it has been used for opposite ends, although usually not recognized as something men are free to accept or reject. Lucretius, for instance, deduces it from his radical this-worldliness in order to subdue men's will to live and make them less reluctant to die: "Nor by prolonging life do we take one tittle from time past in death nor can we fret anything away, whereby we may happily be a less long time in the condition of the dead. Therefore, you may complete as many generations as you please during your life; none the less, however, will that everlasting death await you; and for no less long a time will be no more in being, who beginning with today has ended his life, than the man who has died many months and years ago" *(On the Nature of Things,* book 3 [Chicago: Henry Regnery Co., 1949], p. 104).

By contrast this same awareness of man's state in its stark misery serves Saint Anselm of Canterbury to drive home the urgency, if not the inescapability, of his faith in God: "What, O most high Lord, shall this man do, an exile far from thee? . . . He pants to see thee, and thy face is turned from him. He longs to come to thee, and thy dwelling-place is inaccessible. . . . O wretched lot of man, when he hath lost that for which he was made! O hard and terrible fate! . . . Wretched that I am . . . What have I accomplished? Whither was I striving? . . . I sought blessings, and lo! confusion. I strove toward God, and I stumbled upon myself. I sought calm in privacy, and I found tribulation and grief, in my inmost thoughts." St. Anselm *Proslogiun,* chap. 1, translated from the Latin by Sidney Norton Deane (Chicago: The Open Court Publishing Co., 1925), pp. 4–5.

With modern writers the pendulum has swung back again to the notion of futility as an incontestable, inescapable fact: "Vous connaissez la phrase: 'Il faut neuf mois pour faire un homme, et un seul jour pour le tuer.' Nous l'avons su autant qu'on peut le savoir l'un et l'autre . . . May, écoutez: il ne faut pas neuf mois, il faut soixante ans pour faire un homme, soixante ans de sacrifices, de volonté de . . . de tant de choses! Et quant cet homme est fait, quand il n'y a plus en lui rien de l'enfance, ni de l'adolescence, quand, vraiment, il est un homme, il n'est plus bon qu'à mourir" (André Malraux, *La Condition Humaine* [Paris: Gallimard, Le Libre de Poche 27, 1955], p. 287). The above reflections of Gisor on the death of his son Kyo give eloquent expression to the absurdity of *la condition humaine.* An unwillingness to accept the finality of this judgment forms the basis of Socrates' faith in immortality.

34. It is curious to note that Gilbert Ryle sees in this description of an imaginatively extended world, which runs from 108C to 113C, nothing but "a subsequent interpolation" which is "totally irrelevant to the subject-matter of the dialogue as a whole." *Plato's Progress* (Cambridge: Cambridge University Press, 1966), p. 227.

35. "Novum Organum", par. 45. In *Modern Classical Philosophers,* 2nd ed. compiled by Benjamin Rand (New York: Houghton Mifflin Co., 1936), p. 32.

36. *Werke.* Grossoktavausgabe, Nachlass, vol. 12 (Leipzig: A. Kröner, 1926), p. 65.

37. See Note 5, above.

5

Protagoras: Tradition and Critical Intelligence

The *Protagoras*, it seems, is wholly incompatible with freedom and hence with the notion of genuine selfhood. For Plato has Socrates declare repeatedly and in unmistakable terms that "no man willingly pursues evil or that which he thinks to be evil." Are we to understand this to mean that man *by nature* is determined to pursue the good once he believes it to be so? But what he believes to be good may appear so only because he has failed sufficiently to reflect upon its possible consequences. And yet he could rightfully blame his nature for the undesirable outcome of his behavior instead of assuming personal responsibility. In a dramatic dialogue, however, a statement considered in isolation may be seriously misunderstood. What Plato has some of his characters say or do need not have his approval; and even Socrates may, for pedagogical reasons, play the devil's advocate. Only in the light of the whole can we, with any kind of assurance, evaluate a particular part. A detailed analysis of this lengthy dialogue can, therefore, not be dispensed with.

I

As a work of art, the *Protagoras* presents itself as one of the richest dialogues. It contains myth and logical demonstration, drama and history, literary criticism and philosophical doctrine. Its most appealing aspects, at least to the general reader, are the dramatic portrayals of Protagoras and Socrates. The Sophist is shown in his boastfulness, his verbosity, his inability to match the dialectical skill of Socrates; but he is also given credit for his eloquence, his high-mindedness, his willingness, although not without some appeals to his sense of fairness, to continue the discussion even when it becomes apparent that he cannot escape defeat. Nor does Socrates emerge without blemish, as the shining example of the lover of wisdom. Protagoras, with good reason, chides him for his contentiousness; and Hippias urges him not to persist in his cramped style of discourse but "let go the reins of speech so that your words may present themselves grander and more graceful before us" (338A).[1] And most astonishingly of all, Plato allows him to suffer a crushing defeat in his first round with Protagoras.

The dialogue clearly shows Plato the dramatist at the height of his powers; but its philosophic harvest appears surprisingly meager, so meager in fact that one commentator advises that "the reader who is interested only in Plato's philosophy . . . pass over the first three quarters of it."[2] Furthermore, the philosophy which it does offer seems of doubtful quality: Most of Socrates' arguments contain glaring fallacies; the doctrine that no man willingly pursues evil offends common sense; and the hedonism toward the end of the dialogue cannot, without difficulty, be attributed to either Plato or Socrates, for it is incompatible with repeated and emphatic statements in other dialogues, while Protagoras is reluctant to admit it even as a tentative hypothesis for examination.

To find fault with a genius such as Plato, however, is always risky. This is not to say that he cannot be mistaken, but criticism should be delayed until it has been made reasonably certain that the shortcomings we believe to have discovered are not due to our own simple-mindedness. Specifically, in the case of a philosopher who is also a skilled dramatist, the fault may well lie with too literal an approach on our part, and such an approach in a highly dramatic dialogue may be expected to have particularly disastrous consequences. Before passing judgment, therefore, let us make every effort not to overlook the dramatic elements and to hold ourselves responsive to their promptings.

The dramatic elements are often so lifelike that the reader instinctively shrinks from subjecting them to a critical analysis for fear of despoiling them of their charm. This is particularly true of the opening scene of the *Protagoras*. The meaning of the scene seems obvious enough. Hippocrates, the young man who at the crack of dawn storms into Socrates' bedchamber and begs to be taken to Protagoras, typifies the intellectual curiosity of the Athenians and tends to make one disagree less violently with Aristotle's dictum that all men by nature desire to know. There is also great irony in the fact that the most eminent not only of the Athenians but of all the Hellenes of his time should be asked by one of his townsmen to take him to a foreigner who is really a considerably lesser man. And finally there is an insight into the character of Socrates who takes not the least offense at being slighted.

The reader who rests content with what so far has been offered forgets that Plato is a thinker as well as an artist, and that incidents created and remarks made may have a double function, namely dramatic and philosophical. Hippocrates' report, for instance, that he had just returned from Oenoe, where he had gone in pursuit of his runaway slave Satyrus, may be nothing more than a realistic detail to enhance the drama. But it might also have philosophical implications when taken in conjunction with Socrates' remark that "if you give Protagoras money he will make you wise too" (310D), and Hippocrates' reply that "if it depended on that he might take all that I have, and all that my friends have" (310D–E). For it might then suggest that Hippocrates' attempt to purchase knowledge is as improper as his claim to property rights over a fellow man. Socrates makes it obvious that he holds Protagoras responsible for creating the impression that knowledge is purchasable, for he describes the Sophist as "a person who deals wholesale or retail in . . . the wares of knowledge and makes the round of the cities, offering them to any customer who wants them" (313C–D). We may be sure that he will not allow this view to go unchallenged, and he at once proceeds to give a concrete demonstration of another kind of knowledge by taking the young man for a walk around the court and questioning him about his contemplated association with a Sophist for the purpose of receiving instruction. At the beginning Hippocrates feels quite certain that he knows what a Sophist is and what he may reasonably expect to gain from him. At the end of the interrogation his assurance is gone, and Socrates has good reason to chide him:

> You have quite made up your mind that you must by hook or by crook be a pupil of Protagoras, and are prepared to expend all the property of yourself and of your friends in carrying out this determination, although, as you admit, you do not know him and have never spoken with him; you call him a Sophist, but are manifestly ignorant of what a Sophist is; and yet you are going to commit yourself to his keeping. (313B–C)

From Socrates, Hippocrates has gained no more than an awareness of his ignorance and of the complexity of his undertaking. But his critical intelligence has been aroused. And while the knowledge which Protagoras may possess and be ready to impart to his pupils is not condemned, there is the clear implication that the type of knowledge to which the Socratic method leads is more basic. "For only if you know which of the wares are good and which are evil," says Socrates, "may you safely buy knowledge from Protagoras or anyone; but if not . . . then don't take risks . . . with the most precious thing you have" (313E–314A).

The opening scene thus strongly suggests that the dialogue will be found to center around these two types of knowledge, one which can be imparted and the other, being strictly the achievement of the individual, which can not.

There is a further incident which might be worth noting. When Socrates and Hippocrates reach the house of Callias, where Protagoras is staying, they are in the midst of an argument and stand talking in the vestibule until they are finished. When they finally knock at the door, the doorkeeper, who presumably has overheard the conversation, mistakes them for Sophists and refuses to admit them. It is only after some difficulty that Socrates convinces him otherwise and persuades him to open the door. This may be taken as a hint that in his conversation with Protagoras, Socrates may easily be mistaken for a Sophist. Socrates does in fact use trickery in his arguments and he reasons from premises which seemingly are his own but which in reality are implied in the position taken by Protagoras. While the doorkeeper, however, who is described as a eunuch, might understandably be fooled by the outward appearance, the intelligent reader should, without too much effort, be able to look through the deception.

Once inside, Socrates discovers Hippias and Prodicus, each surrounded by a group of listeners, and above all Protagoras who leads what appears to be a procession of admirers consisting of some native Athenians and numerous foreigners—"he, like Orpheus, charming them with his voice, and they following its spell" (315A). After watching for a moment the impressive spectacle, which stands in sharp contrast to his own unpretentious way of teaching, Socrates goes up to Protagoras and states the purpose of his visit:

> My friend Hippocrates, who is a native Athenian, . . . aspires to political eminence, and he thinks that association with you is most likely to procure this for him." (316B–C)

Socrates asks whether the discussion should take place in private or public. And when Protagoras explains at length why he has made it a policy, despite its inherent dangers, to proclaim himself openly "a Sophist and instructor of mankind" (317B), Socrates suggests that they call in the other two Sophists and their audience. After they are all seated, Socrates restates his mission. "This is my friend Hippocrates," he says, "who is desirous of making your acquaintance. He would like to know what will happen to him if he associates with you" (318A). The answer which Protagoras now gives is critical for an understanding of the rest of the dialogue, especially of Socrates' attempted demonstration of the unity of the virtues:

> Young man, if you associate with me, on the first day you will be in a position to return home a better man than you came, and better on the second day than on the first, and better every day than you were on the day before. (318A)

Socrates is not wholly satisfied with the answer and would like to know in what Hippocrates will be better, which prompts Protagoras to a more precise formulation of the object of his teaching:

> If he comes to me, he will learn . . . prudence in affairs private as well as

public; he will learn to order his own house in the best manner, and he will be
able to speak and act most powerfully in the affairs of the state. (318E–319A)

Socrates, rather bluntly, calls in question the very *raison d'être* of the Sophist's
profession before the whole gathering:

> Do I understand you and is your meaning that you teach the art of politics,
> and that you promise to make men good citizens? . . . I will freely confess to
> you, Protagoras, that I have a doubt whether this art is capable if being
> taught. (319A–B)

In support of his challenge Socrates appeals to the behavior of the Athenians.
When they meet in the Assembly only experts in the various fields, such as
architects and shipwrights, are consulted and allowed to give advice. "But when
the question concerns an affair of state, then," says Socrates, "everybody is free
to get up and give advice—carpenter, tinker, cobbler, passenger and ship-
owner, rich and poor, high and low—and no one reproaches him, as in the
former case, with not having learned and having no teacher, and yet giving
advice" (319D–E). Now the Athenians are an intelligent people and "esteemed
to be such by the other Hellenes" (319B). They would not act the way they do if
they believed that virtue can be taught. A similar oddity can be observed in the
attitude of the great statesmen toward their sons. They "gave them excellent
instruction in all that can be learned from masters," Socrates observes, "but in
their own department of politics they neither taught them nor gave them
teachers. . . ." (319E–320A). How else can this paradoxical demeanor be
explained, so Socrates concludes, except by assuming that they believe virtue to
be unteachable.

Socrates thus has shrewdly confronted Protagoras with the choice of either
declaring the behavior of the Athenian elite as absurd, or granting that virtue
cannot be taught—a most embarrassing position for a visiting foreigner who
claims to be a teacher of virtue.

Since Protagoras's professional efficacy has been called in question in the
presence of such an illustrious gathering, one would expect him to use the most
powerful means of defense at his command. Instead he dares offer his listeners a
choice. "Shall I, as an elder," he asks, "tell you as younger a myth, or shall I
argue out the question?" (320C). And when they leave it to him he decides in
favor of the myth, as if he regarded myth and argument as equally potent
instruments.

The myth presents man as a *Mangelwesen*, a being with basic deficiencies
because of negligence in the act of creation:

> When the destined time came that mortal beings should be created, the gods
> fashioned them out of earth and fire and various mixtures of both elements in

the interior of the earth. And when they were about to bring them into the light of day, they ordered Prometheus and Epimetheus to equip them and to distribute to them severally their proper qualities. Epimetheus begged Prometheus: "Let me distribute, and do you inspect." Prometheus agreed, and Epimetheus made the distribution. . . . Epimetheus, not being very wise, . . . distributed among the brute animals all the qualities which he had to give . . . and when Prometheus came to inspect the distribution, he found that the other animals were suitably furnished, but that man alone was naked and shoeless, and had neither bed nor arms of defense. Prometheus, not knowing how he could devise man's preservation, stole the wisdom of practising the arts of Hephaestus and Athene, and fire with it (it could neither have been acquired nor used without fire) and gave them to man. (320D–321D)

While animals were thus fully equipped when they started out in life, man was given the knowledge to produce this equipment himself. Prometheus thus turned the carelessness of Epimetheus into an advantage for man. For by being made to contribute to his own constitution, he was allowed to take part in the creative process, and had, as Protagoras expresses it, "a share of divinity," and was the only animal who was the "kindred of the gods" (322A).

As a social animal, however, he had to set up communities, and for that purpose the gift of Prometheus was not sufficient:

> Thus provided, mankind at first lived dispersed, and there were no cities. But the consequence was that they were destroyed by wild beasts, for they were utterly weak in comparison with them, and their arts and crafts were only sufficient to provide them with the means of life, and did not enable them to carry on war against the brutes. Food they had, but not as yet the art of government, of which the art of war is a part. After a while the desire of collective living and of self-preservation made them found cities; but when they were gathered together, having no art of government, they dealt unjustly with one another, and were again in process of dispersion and destruction. Zeus feared that the entire race would be exterminated, and so he sent Hermes to mankind, bearing reverence and justice to be the ordering principles of cities and the uniting bonds of friendship. Hermes asked Zeus [whether he should] distribute them as the arts are distributed; that is to say to a few only, . . . or [whether he should] give them to all. "To all," said Zeus, "I would like them all to have a share; for cities cannot exist if a few only share in justice and reverence, as in the arts." (322B–D)

Again, community life has not been given to man; but through the sense of justice *(dike)* and respect for others *(aidos)* he has been enabled to create such a life for himself. They are, however, given as capacities only, and a man must actualize them before he can function properly in a city. And as a prospective young craftsman needs a master, so a young citizen needs a guide for the proper development of his social *arete* or excellence. It is as such a guide for this all important task that Protagoras offers his services.

By telling the myth, Protagoras has induced his listeners to try to imagine man without a sense of justice, that is without the ability to see the rights of others at least to some extent as if they were his own and to respect these rights. This attempt has failed, and the failure has called attention to the sense of justice and regard for others as necessary conditions not only for the possibility of social living but for human life itself.

So far Protagoras has been engaged in laying the groundwork for his defense. He has shown that *dike* and *aidos* are innate in all men in the sense that men cannot be imagined without them. The question arises, however: Does Protagoras build on a solid foundation if he establishes the basic concept of the discussion by means of a myth? Especially those who hold that a myth should be used only after reason has spent its force are likely to find the procedure of Protagoras inadmissible, if not outrageous. Instead of yielding to the temptation of condemning Protagoras's procedure before it has fully gotten under way, we should remind ourselves that he has thrown out an implicit challenge. For, as we have seen, he claims that he can handle *myth* and *logos* with equal facility and effectiveness. So if any one is dissatisfied with the use of the myth, let him try his skill at establishing the basic concept philosophically, that is through reason reflecting on experience. As if to lend a helping hand, Protagoras supplies two out of the three notions essential to the argument. First he states in ordinary language the idea which has emerged from the myth, and which would have been the conclusion had he choosen to argue the point. "Is there or is there not," he asks, "some one quality of which all the citizens must be partakers if there is to be a city at all?" (324D). Answering his own question he names "justice and self-control and piety, in a word, human virtue . . . as the quality of which all men must be partakers, and which is the very condition of their learning or doing anything else" (325A). Subsequently he refers to what could be viewed as the root or the starting point of the argument:

> I would have you consider that he who appears to you to be the most unjust of those who have been brought up in laws and society would appear to be a just man and a master of justice if he were to be compared with men who had no education, or courts of justice, or laws, or any restraints upon them which compelled them to practice virtue. . . . If you were living among such men . . . you would sorrowfully long to revisit the rascality of this part of the world. (327C–D)

Protagoras here offers a comparison between the high quality of life in a community which offers many educational opportunities, such as Athens, and the low quality of life in one which offers but few or none at all. Were Socrates compelled to live in the latter, he would yearn to return to his native city in which he now finds so much to criticize. Protagoras thereby suggests that the quality of life in a community is a function of the degree to which the sense of justice of its citizens has been developed. Both comparison and correlation are susceptible to verification, and, if confirmed, can serve as an empirical basis for an argument. All that remains to be done is to establish a link between this correlation and the state destructive of human life as described in the myth. This is accomplished easily enough by carrying the correlation to the limit, that is, by a process of extrapolation: if the quality of life in a community increases or decreases to the extent to which the sense of justice of its citizens reaches a higher or lower stage of development, then, if we were to reduce the sense of justice to zero, the quality of life would also reach zero, that is, human life would become impossible.

In this progression from comparison to correlation and extrapolation, there is a steady moving away from the experienced or that which is capable of being experienced. For the comparison is restricted to a relatively small number of instances and the correlation can merely assume a continuity between the points at which observation has actually been made. Furthermore, it is not impossible that above or below the last magnitude observed there lurks a complete breakdown of the behavior pattern previously registered. Does not water contract as it is being cooled, and then at the freezing point suddenly expand? Finally, extrapolation makes a precarious leap into the unknown simply on the assumption that the behavior pattern remains essentially the same, even if the variables involved reach an upper or lower limit. At this point the question may be asked: Of what possible use can be the outcome of a procedure which depends on such precarious assumptions? Our appreciation of its usefulness may be enhanced by an illustration from physics, whose magnitudes are susceptible to precise measurement. Every one knows that friction retards motion, and that a decrease in friction increases the duration of motion, but observation of this correlation alone would never have led Newton to the formulation of his First Law of Motion. He had to imagine a state in which a moving body encountered no friction at all. And then applying the correlation between friction and motion to this imaginary state, he could conclude that with friction at zero the duration of the motion would be infinite. The term infinite alone is sufficient to indicate that we have now definitely transcended all possible human experience. If Newton's law were meant to describe and thus assist in the discovery of actually existing bodies "free from impressed force," it would be both absurd and worthless. But by referring to an imaginatively constructed ideal motion, it is neither. For this functions as a norm against which to measure and thus shed light on real motion. As Einstein and Infeld have said:

> This law of inertia cannot be derived directly from experiment, but only by speculative thinking consistent with observation. The idealized experiment can never be actually performed, although it leads to a profound understanding of real experiments.[3]

Similarly it can be said that the tale of Protagoras would serve no serious purpose if it were meant to give a description of men lacking all sense of justice. For on his own account, no such men can exist. But as an imaginatively conceived limiting idea it operates as a negative norm: any action leading in the direction of this norm or the state described in the myth is to that extent evil; any action leading away from it is ipso facto good. And thus the Protagoras myth ends up by elucidating the actual behavior of men in society, as Newton's First Law of Motion helps to understand and control the motion of actual bodies in the physical universe. The outcome of an extrapolation can, therefore, be said to be empirical in its origin, transempirical in its nature, and, in as much as it may serve as a norm or a means of elucidation, once more empirical, namely, in its function.

If this is the manner in which Protagoras could have conducted his argument, why should he have preferred "as an elder [to] speak to [the others] as younger men in an apologue or myth?" (320C). As a widely travelled man he might actually have witnessed the chaos which results from a breakdown in public morality. For the members of his audience this was perhaps no more than a remote possibility. Protagoras's task, however, was not simply to make them aware of the role which the sense of justice plays in the life of a community; as a moral teacher he had to induce men to action. He had to get them emotionally involved; he had to make them realize that the deterioration of community life is a constant, ever-present threat, and that the need for education is urgent and unavoidable. To bring about this existential awareness of the problem, Protagoras, the teacher, had to assume the role of the poet and resort to myth. Plato himself gives expression to this function of the poet in the *Ion:*

> Socrates: Are you not carried outside yourself, and does not your soul in an ecstasy seem to be among the persons or places of which you are speaking, whether they are in Ithaca or in Troy or whatever may be the scene of the poem?
> Ion: That proof strikes home to me, Socrates. For I must frankly confess that at the tale of pity my eyes are filled with tears, and when I speak of horrors, my hair stands on end and my heart throbs.
> Socrates: Do you know that the spectator is the last of the rings which . . . receive the power of the original magnet from one another? The rhapsode like yourself and the actor are the intermediate links, and the poet himself is the first of them. Through all these the God sways the souls of men in any direction which he pleases. (535B–536A)[4]

There is a second and perhaps no less important advantage of the myth over the argument. Even a cursory analysis of the result of an extrapolation usually uncovers incompatible elements. Since words based on experience are used to speak about a realm which reaches beyond experience, this is not surprising; nor is it a serious defect since the transempirical is not of interest in itself but only in so far as it sheds light on the empirical. But the use of other than mythical language may seduce the reader into a literalistic interpretation. And then the degree of credibility which would have satisfied the myth becomes wholly inadequate. The description given appears fantastic and the position of the author is discredited even before it is fully understood. Now the myth leaves no doubt that the description of an actual situation is not intended. And it thus helps to direct the attention to the human situation as it appears in the light of the myth, rather than to the myth itself.

It should be obvious by now that the traditional condemnation of Protagoras's use of a myth was hasty and unwarranted. For in the hands of a skilled writer the myth based on extrapolation can serve as a powerful instrument for making man stand away from himself the better to gain a view of himself.[5] Protagoras's myth has laid before our eyes a conception of man with which we were already vaguely familiar. It has reminded us that man is radically different from a thing; that instead of a fixed nature he has been given only potentialities, whose development he must take upon himself both as an individual and as a member of society.

Protagoras now uses the doctrine that virtue is an innate capacity in all men as a bulwark from which to launch his counterattack against Socrates. He renders the facts cited against him harmless by incorporating them in his own theory and at the same time accounts for a number of additional facts which the theory of his opponent cannot explain:

(a) As Socrates has pointed out, the Athenians in the Assembly insist on experts in all matters except when they "deliberate about political excellence or virtue, which proceeds only by way of justice and self-control" (323A). But this fact can be regarded as a consequence of the innateness of virtue just as well as of the belief that virtue cannot be taught.

(b) When a man claims to be skilled in an art when he is not, people reprimand him. But when he lacks "justice . . . or some other political virtue" (323B) and publicly tells the truth about himself, they think he must be out of his mind. For they believe that justice is so vital to the community that not even the unjust can function without at least making a pretense of it.

(c) Who would be "so foolish as to chastise or instruct the ugly, or the diminutive or the feeble?" Protagoras asks. These are defects inflicted by nature, and those who suffer from them cannot be held responsible for them. But men do hold responsible those who lack political virtue, which shows that they believe virtue to be innate in all men as a capacity which can be developed "by study and exercise and teaching" (323D).[6]

(d) The theory of punishment held by all reasonable people likewise favors the view of Protagoras over that of Socrates. For "he who desires to inflict rational punishment does not punish for the sake of a past wrong which cannot be undone; he has regard to the future, and is desirous that the man who is punished, and he who sees him punished, may be deterred from doing wrong again . . . thereby clearly implying that virtue is capable of being taught" (324B).

(e) Finally, Protagoras removes the second of the two main props from under Socrates' argument and uses it to fortify his own. This refers to the undeniable fact that the great Athenian statesmen sent their sons to riding masters and fencing masters, but did nothing to instruct them in the art in which they distinguished themselves, namely political virtue. From this, Socrates had inferred that there were no teachers of virtue and that virtue could not be taught; Protagoras on the contrary concludes that there are no *special* teachers of virtue simply because everyone teaches it:

> Mother and nurse and father and tutor are vying with one another about the improvement of the child. . . . He cannot say or do anything without their setting forth to him that this is just and that is unjust; this is noble, that is base; this is pious, that is impious; do this and don't do that. And if he willingly obeys, well and good. If not, he is straightened by threats and blows, like a piece of bent or warped wood. (325C-D) . . . All men are teachers of virtue, each according to his ability. And you say, Where are the teachers? You might as well ask, Who teaches Greek? For of that, too, there will not be any teachers found. (327E–328A)

Since virtue, though innate in all, does not appear fully developed in the child but merely as a capacity, it is quite possible that the son of a great statesman, like that of a great musician, may be less gifted and show less improvement while undergoing training, than the son of an ordinary man. And just because everybody teaches virtue, it is difficult to find a teacher who excels all the rest. "A teacher of this sort I believe myself to be," concludes Protagoras, "and above all other men help people attain what is noble and good" (328A–B).

The argument of Protagoras is in all respects superior to that of Socrates. Socrates merely asserted the theory that virtue cannot be taught and then sought to confirm it by referring to two facts or phenomena in the lives of the Athenians, namely the behavior of the members of the Assembly and the attitude of the great statesmen toward the education of their sons. Protagoras, on the other hand, carefully grounded his theory by linking it up with the innateness of virtue in the form of a capacity found in all men, which he in turn established by the skilful use of a myth based on a process of extrapolation. In the verification of this theory, he appealed not only to the Athenian elite, as Socrates did, but to intelligent people in general. And this broad approach enabled him to explain a larger number of facts and thereby exhibit the greater synthesizing power of his theory. Finally he wove all the facts used by Socrates into his own argument, thus leaving his opponent's position without foundation. With consummate skill Protagoras has thus turned the tables on Socrates, who now must choose between declaring the behavior of the Athenians or civilized people in general as absurd or retracting his earlier claim that virtue cannot be taught; that is, he is faced with the same kind of dilemma he tried to impose on Protagoras.

In the first round, Socrates has suffered a crushing defeat and Protagoras would now occupy an impregnable position if he only were true to its implications. Socrates could hardly object to his understanding of virtue as an innate capacity, nor to the manner in which he uses the myth to lead his listeners to the truth so that they can see for themselves. This conception of the nature of virtue and the function of the myth determine the role of the teacher as a mere aid in the development of the individual. Does not Socrates express the same view when, speaking as a teacher in the *Theaetetus*, he claims that "the gods compel [him] to be a midwife, but do not allow him to bring forth" (150C)? For he realizes that a student may reject the assistance and refuse to be led to the truth. A guarantee such as Protagoras offers at the beginning of his encounter with Socrates is, therefore, altogether out of the question.

Protagoras's eagerness to justify his role as a Sophist seems to becloud his vision and cause him to advocate a pedagogical doctrine which is at odds with the brilliant performance he has just given. When describing the universal education in a civilized state, he says the child is told "this is just and that is unjust . . . do this and don't do that" (325D). When he has learned to read, his elders "put in his hands the works of the great poets . . . in which are contained . . . many tales . . . of ancient famous men, which he is required to learn by heart in order that he may imitate or emulate them and desire to become like them" (325E–326A). Gymnastic and music teachers continue to shape his character and finally the "state compels him to learn the laws and live after the pattern which they furnish and not after his own fancies" (326C–D). The aim here is obviously not to help the individual develop his own particular capacities but rather to impose a ready-made mould on a diversity of individuals. The transmission of a tradition from generation to generation performs this function. Now the importance of tradition should not be underestimated, for it constitutes the wider experience of the race. Nor can it be denied that without a degree of uniformity in outlook which springs from a common tradition, community life would become very difficult, if not impossible. Tradition, however, may lose contact with reality; some of its prescribed modes of behavior may become obsolete and its accumulated store of knowledge diminish in relevancy. As the student becomes more mature, there is therefore a need for another type of education of which Socrates gave an illustration when he examined the young Hippocrates. Its aim is to develop critical intelligence, which enables the individual in crucial moments of his life to decide for himself whether and to what extent it is right for him to conform or not to conform to tradition. In this endeavor to make the student self-reliant, guarantee of success is not possible. And if Protagoras persists in furnishing such a guarantee by promising to make a man better the first day he comes to him, he must restrict the function of education to the handing down of a tradition.

Even with this truncated view of education Protagoras's boast runs into serious difficulties which Socrates, during the remainder of the dialogue, makes it his business to exploit. Of the presuppositions of the claim of Protagoras he selects three and uses each in turn as the explicit or implicit premise of an argument. The arguments ostensibly demonstrate the unity of a pair of virtues, namely justice and piety, wisdom and self-control, courage and wisdom; in reality they lead to absurd conclusions and thereby destroy the presuppositions of the guarantee and expose the emptiness of the Sophist's promise to his paying customers.[7] The three presuppositions and the reasons why they can be regarded as such are as follows:

I. Radical Separation of the Virtues

At the end of the first round Socrates expresses his willingness to accept the teachability of the virtues on the authority of Protagoras, if he can only get an answer to "a little question." He would like to know, he says, whether the various virtues are one and the same or whether, like the parts of the face, they "differ from one another in themselves and in their functions" (330A–B) so that "no other part of virtue is like knowledge, or like justice, or like courage, or like self-control, or like piety" (330B). Protagoras is bound to adopt the latter view. In order to be able to say with assurance that "this is just and that is unjust" (325D) he, as a teacher, must be in possession of clear and distinct ideas of the various virtues, and these in turn are possible only if the various virtues are separate and distinct from each other.

II. Disregard of the Difference between Abstract Idea and Concrete Act

Protagoras promises to give his pupils not only theoretical but also practical instruction, in as much as he claims to make him better and more virtuous "in affairs private as well as public" (318E). But whether it is right to perform a given act depends not only on what *kind* of act it is, but on the presence or absence of alternatives which the situation offers. Hence a master cannot tell his disciple "do this and don't do that" (325D) in the sense that one type of act will always be reliably right and the opposite type wrong. Telling a lie, though basically evil, may under given circumstances bring about a lesser evil and therefore be preferable and a morally better act than telling the truth, which is basically good. Now, then, can Protagoras guarantee success in teaching the young men to act rightly in the complex situation of a household or the hustle and bustle of a great city such as Athens? His insistence that he can implies a failure to distinguish sufficiently between the abstract idea of a virtue and the concrete virtuous act; the former can be implanted or taught, the latter is unpredictable. Socrates exposes this lack of discrimination, not by explicitly calling attention to it, but by slyly making it his own in the second argument, leaving it to the reader to uncover the error which is responsible for the absurd conclusion which the argument yields.

III. Ethical Determinism

Even if Protagoras could lay before his disciples clear and reliable rules of conduct, he would still be faced with the problem of gaining their acceptance. The child, if necessary, could be coerced. As Protagoras himself has pointed out earlier in the dialogue, he can be told that "this is just and that is unjust; this is noble, that is base; this is pious, that is impious; do this and don't do that. And if he willingly obeys, well and good. If not, he is straightened by threats and blows, like a piece of bent or warped wood" (325D). The young men who flock to him, however, and are asked to pay a high fee, could hardly be subjected to such disciplinary measures. Protagoras, therefore, cannot afford to object when Socrates proposes, as a presupposition for the third argument, an ethical determinism which he formulates as follows and which Plato scholars have seen fit to elevate to the status of a "Platonic doctrine":

> No man voluntarily pursues evil, or that which he thinks to be evil. To pursue what one believes evil rather than what is good is not in human nature. (358C–D)

Now let us see whether these three assumptions do in fact control the three arguments which Socrates offers under the pretext of attempting to prove the unity of the virtues.

First Argument: Justice and Piety

After having elicited from Protagoras the admission that, according to his view, the virtues "differ from one another in themselves and in their function" (330A–B), Socrates has an imaginary objector draw the following inferences:[8]

> Then *piety is not of the nature of a just thing,* nor justice of the nature of a pious thing, but of the nature of an impious thing (me hosion); and *piety of the nature of the not just, and therefore of the unjust, and the unjust is the impious.* (331A–B) [Italics added]

If, for the sake of simplicity, we deal only with the italicized portion of the argument, then we arrive at the unexpressed conclusion: Piety is the nature of the impious. This obviously calls for a determination of the fallacy in the argument. With this aim in view, let us examine the statements one by one:

(a) *Piety is not of the nature of a just thing*

This statement obviously means that piety or the pious, considered simply by itself, in so far as it is the pious, is not the just. In other words, if we divide our universe of discourse into Just (J) and Non-Just (Non-J), then the Pious (P) does not fall into the J class. This would certainly be true for Protagoras in view of his separation of the virtues.

(b) *Piety is of the nature of the not just*

This is an immediate inference from or the obverse of (a). Since J and Non-J are the only classes available, and P does not belong to J, then it must be a sub-class of Non-J.

(c) *And therefore of the unjust*

From a purely formal point of view, this inference claims too much. P is necessarily a subclass of Non-J, but not so of the Unjust (U). If we are content with the discovery of a logical fallacy, our analysis will have come to an end. It often happens, however, in Plato's dialogues that if the reader corrects a fallacy or reduces an excessive claim to its proper limits, he arrives at a notion which mends the break in the argument. This is true in the present case. P is not *necessarily* a subclass of U, but it might *possibly* be. In any event P and U as subclasses share membership in the same principal class:

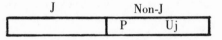

The result of the analysis may seem harmless enough. But it ceases to be so once we substitute the various virtues for the symbols. For then we find that piety is a subclass of that which is other than justice, i.e., the opposite of justice, and furthermore that it shares subclass membership with the unjust.

If we follow Socrates' hint and direct our attention to the possible rather than the necessary relationships between the various virtues and their opposites, then we can arrive at a similarly disturbing conclusion in a somewhat different way without straying from the general tenor of Socrates' approach to the problem. For if the virtues are, as Protagoras maintains, different from and independent of each other, then they can serve as substitution instances of an extensional or atomic logic. In such a logic, the conjunction is a mere juxtaposition: the presence or absence of one element makes no difference to the other. P and J, together with their opposites, can, therefore, enter into the following possible combinations:

PJ   *Non-PJ*   *P Non-J*   *Non-P Non-J*

If we now adopt a less formal point of view, that is, if note is taken of the meaning of the terms involved, then we must admit that any given member of

Non-P and any given member of Non-J *might* be not simply not-pious and not-just respectively, but impious and unjust.

With the results of the preceding arguments in mind, let us return to the scene in the house of the Athenian Callias. The members of the party assembled there, whether native or foreign, while listening to the debate between Socrates and Protagoras, might already have experienced a twinge of uneasiness at the admission that piety is associated with injustice with which it shares class membership as a subclass of the opposite of justice. This feeling might turn into one of outright alarm if it should be recalled that according to Protagoras "many a man is courageous and not just, or just and not courageous" (329E). For this implies that the separability of the virtues holds not only on the level of abstract ideas, but also in regard to concrete behavior. It is quite possible, therefore, that the basic behavior pattern of a given individual *might* have to be characterized not simply as *P Non-J* or *Non-P J*, that is pious and not-just or not-pious and just, but as pious and unjust or impious and just. In other words, it would have to be admitted that the gods *might* disapprove of a man whose behavior pattern is basically just, or approve a basically unjust mode of behavior.

The next statement in Socrates' argument underscores and gives the reason for the inadmissibility of even the *possibility* of these two combinations:

(d) *The unjust is the impious*

This statement does not follow from the preceding ones. But its function might well be to confront Protagoras with a belief of the Athenians about the nature of their gods. That the gods hate injustice, that. is, regard an unjust behavior as impious, needs no proof for an Athenian; and a foreigner and professed sophist could deny it only at the risk of being accused of impiety, which, as the fate of Socrates has shown, might be considered a capital offense. Socrates can deny the applicability of an atomic logic to ethical matters, on the ground that ethical terms are not wholly separable as such a logic demands. Protagoras, who, in view of his guarantee, advocates their separability and independence, has no such escape. He is, therefore, faced with a dilemma: He must choose either to offend the religious-ethical sensibilities of his hosts and thereby endanger his life, or to retract his position and damage his reputation.

This interpretation gains a considerable measure of plausibility from the fact that in the first round Socrates, as we have seen, tried to corner Protagoras in essentially the same way. There he sought to prove that the behavior of the Athenians, who are "esteemed a wise people by the other Hellenes" (319B), would be very strange indeed if they believed that virtue can be taught. This seemed to leave an unenviable choice for a teacher of virtue on a visit to Athens, namely the choice between declaring the Athenians unintelligent or maintaining that virtue cannot be taught. Protagoras, however, managed to escape the dilemma by showing on Socrates' own and additional evidence that the behavior of not only of the Athenians but of intelligent people in general would be even more surprising if they believed virtue could not be taught. But now, in the first argument of the second round, Protagoras is unable to break the stranglehold of Socrates, who has moved to the attack and seized upon a real weakness in the position of his opponent, namely the sharp separation of each virtue from the rest.[9] And the embarrassment caused by the new dilemma has increased in intensity, for Protagoras can now maintain his position only at the risk of facing the dangerous charge of impiety.

Second Argument: Wisdom and Self-Control

The controlling presupposition of the second demonstration, in contrast to that of the first, remains unexpressed, and perhaps not without good reason. For hardly anyone would explicitly deny the difference between abstract idea and concrete act. An implicit denial, however, is far from infrequent, especially when applying a general rule of conduct in disregard of the demands of the concrete situation, or in an argument involving classes or ideas on the one hand, and members of classes or things or actions on the other. As we shall see, the crucial fallacy in the second argument is due precisely to the failure to distinguish sufficiently between abstract idea and concrete act, the very same lack of discrimination we found implicit in Protagoras's guarantee to teach matters of practical behavior as if he were handing down a tradition or instilling an ideology. By mimicking Protagoras, so to speak, Socrates is able to draw inferences which would render all virtues completely indistinguishable one from the other. His argument may be summarized as follows:

It is agreed without argument that

(a) "wisdom is the very opposite of folly" (332A)

It is likewise agreed that men who "act rightly and advantageously" are self-controlled, and that "they who do not act rightly act foolishly, and in acting thus are not self-controlled" (332A–B). From this it is said to follow that

(b) "to act foolishly is the opposite of acting with self-control" (332B).

Now since "foolish actions are done by folly, and self-controlled actions by self-control" (332B), and furthermore since "that which is done in the same way is done by the same; and that which is done in opposite ways, by opposites" (332C), the inference is drawn that

(c) "folly is the opposite of self-control" (332E)

The Socratic *epagoge* or induction is then used to establish the proposition that

(d) "every opposite has one opposite only" (332C).

From (a) and (c) it follows that

(e) "folly is the opposite of both wisdom and self-control" (334B).

But since according to (d) "every opposite has one opposite only," the conclusion is reached that

(f) "self-control and wisdom are the same" (335B).

The term opposite (enantion), especially when used in (b) above, is crucial to the argument. Its meaning is determined by Socrates' claim that everything which has an opposite has one opposite only. To the modern reader, this statement would be true by definition. The opposite of A, for instance, simply means everything other than A, or Non-A, so that A and Non-A constitute the entire universe, or some restricted realm or universe of discourse.

Does Socrates' *epagoge,* which is used to establish the principle, support this interpretation? As Vlastos points out, "all that happens here is a reference to some instances which *exhibit the meaning of the statement* by exemplifying it rather than proving it."[10] Unfortunately, two of the three pairs of terms used for illustration are notorious for their vagueness: the beautiful and the ugly, the good and the evil. This vagueness becomes apparent when we try to classify acts under one class or its opposite. Plato seems to have been aware of it, for he has Socrates exclaim in the *Republic:* "Of all these many beautiful things is there one which will not appear ugly, or of these many just or righteous actions, is there one which will not appear unjust or unrighteous?" (442C–D). The third pair, *high and low in tone* is more amenable to the division into opposites. We can set up a certain pitch as a standard and say: every tone below that pitch will be called a low tone, and every tone at that pitch or above a high tone. Then the class of high tones can have only one opposite, namely the class of low tones, and the two classes together exhaust the universe of discourse. But while the division is possible, and although it may be convenient, its arbitrary character is also apparent.

What then can Socrates mean when he says that "wisdom is the opposite of folly" (332A)? Perhaps the line immediately following, which leads up to the opposition between folly and self-control, will give us a hint:

When men act rightly and advantageously, do they seem to you to be self-controlled?

Reflecting on the line, one feels inclined to say: why *necessarily* self-controlled? Could one not *also* have said wise? And in asking this question, one is vaguely motivated by the perception of a common element in the self-controlled and the wise, an element which becomes more conspicuous when the wise and the self-controlled are contrasted with the foolish. The wise act aims at a purpose which gives it direction and structure. The self-controlled act has the same characteristic, although the emphasis is now on wilful maintenance and preservation of direction and structure rather than possession. The foolish act, on the other hand, is aimless, purposeless, haphazard, or directed at cross-purposes. So if we make human acts our universe of discourse, then FOLLY, class F, would contain the structureless acts, while the opposite class, Non-F, would contain the structured, purposeful acts.

Now, WISDOM, i.e., the class W, can be said to be the opposite of F only if it is the sole member of NON-F, or if W and NON-F are identical. But NON-F might very well contain more than one member. It is of course possible that two elements, while sharing the characteristic which serves as a principle of division, might differ in other respects. Thus we might divide men into TALL, that is, six feet or more, and SHORT, that is, below six feet. But we might also divide them into TALL as defined on the one hand, and *medium* and *short* on the other. *Medium* and *short* would be subclasses of NON-TALL, NON-TALL alone would be the opposite of TALL. If we were to call both *medium* and *short* the opposites of TALL, and upheld the principle that everything has but one opposite, then we would have to make the absurd assertion that the *medium* and the *short* are identical.

Ordinary discourse does in fact make a distinction, no matter how vague, between self-control and wisdom. Socrates, in the *Republic*, describes wisdom as the legislative and controlling part of the soul, and self-control as the voluntary submission to that control, or as a self-imposed restraint from encroaching upon the business or function of another. Self-control [S] and wisdom [W] thus become subclasses of NON-F,

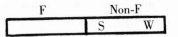

and to call each of them the opposite of F, as Socrates does, is to commit a serious logical error.

Not only does Socrates fail to make a distinction between the principal class and its subclasses, but he compounds the error by predicating of the *members* of the subclasses, foolish acts and self-controlled acts, what can be said not even of the subclasses but only of the principal classes:

> And they who do not act rightly act foolishly, and in acting thus are not self-controlled. Then to act foolishly is the opposite of acting with self-control. (332B)

But once we oppose the members of the subclasses of Non-F to F, and still maintain that everything has only one opposite, then we must conclude that all elements contained in Non-F are identical. And since F may represent only a small portion of the universe and Non-F all the rest, the conclusion becomes patently absurd.

F	Non-F	
	S	W
	s1	w1
	s2	w2
	s3	w3
	•	•
	•	•
	•	•
	sn	sn

After committing the fateful error of opposing foolish acts and selfcontrolled acts, Socrates moves upward again to subclasses and principal classes:

Foolish actions are done by folly, and self-controlled actions by self-control. (332B)

Similarly, he says, swift actions are done by swiftness, slow actions by slowness, etc. "and that which is done in the same way," he continues, "is done by the same; and that which is done in opposite ways by opposites" (332C). Now since foolish acts have been declared the opposite of self-controlled acts, Socrates can infer that folly is the opposite of self-control. Then follows the *epagoge* which, by pointing to the opposition between the beautiful and the ugly, the good and the evil, the high in tone and the low in tone, leads to the conclusion that "every opposite has one opposite only and no more" (332C), and that therefore wisdom and self-control, sharing the same opposite, ought to be the same (333B).

The manner in which the paradox comes about is now evident: Socrates establishes one pair of opposites, folly and wisdom, with at least a semblance of legitimacy on the level of ideas or classes; then he produces another pair, the foolish and the self-controlled, quite illegitimately on the level of actions or members of classes. With the aid of the principle that what is done in opposite ways is done by opposites, he moves back to classes for the assertion that folly and self-control are opposites.

At this point the reader must make an important decision. He may feel inclined to charge Socrates or Plato with incompetence, with the inability to make proper distinctions, or, more precisely stated, with the failure to perceive significant implications of the difference between acts and the corresponding classes. If he yields to this temptation, he will bring his own reflections to a halt. On the other hand, he may wish to place the argument into its proper context and take into account the boastful claim of Protagoras. If he does, then he can hardly fail to notice that Socrates' easy and unconcerned passage from one level to the other, from idea or principle to individual act, is precisely the characteristic implicit in the position of Protagoras. On the one hand the Sophist promises to teach the young man "to order his own house in the best manner . . . and to act most powerfully in the affairs of the state" (318E–319A), which involves the choice and the performance of concrete acts; on the other hand he suggests a method of teaching which is suitable only to the transmission of ideologies from generation to generation. "All men are teachers of virtue," he says to Socrates, "each according to his ability; and you say: where are the teachers? You might as well ask: Who teaches Greek?" (327E). In the solution of the urgent problems of the life of a family or a city, the wisdom of the past is a notoriously unreliable guide. Now the flagrancy with which Socrates violates the distinction between abstract principle or idea and concrete act suggests a conscious mimicry of the Sophist. It is quite in keeping with the Socratic irony and with the puckish character of Socrates that he should pretend to have fallen victim to the confusion from which his opponent suffers and then, on the basis of this confusion, draw inferences which bring the rival position to utter ruin. For far from allowing the various virtues to be conceived as clearly distinct from each other, as a prerequisite for their teachability, they would lump them all into one amorphous mass which defies intelligibility.[11]

Protagoras has been getting more and more reluctant to respond to Socrates' questions, and when Socrates begins a new argument, dealing with the relationship between self-control and justice, he seeks to escape the clutches of his opponent's dialectic by taking off on an oration. Socrates objects and a dispute ensues as to the proper way of responding to questions. Some insist that Protagoras has the right to be his own judge as to the proper length of his responses; others maintain that since Protagoras claims to be able to make long speeches as well as give precise answers, while Socrates claims skill only in the latter, Protagoras should make the adjustment. Prodicus takes occasion to introduce some of his verbal distinctions and Hippias suggests a compromise. "Do not you, Socrates," he says, "aim at this precise and extreme brevity in discourse, if Protagoras objects, but loosen and let go the reins of speech, that your words may present themselves grander and more graceful before us. Neither do you, Protagoras, go forth on the gale with every sail set out of sight of land into an ocean of words, but let there be a mean observed by both of you" (338A). At one point Socrates makes ready to leave, claiming that he has another engagement, but those present beg him to continue the discussion, and it is finally agreed upon that Protagoras should ask questions and Socrates answer.

Many a reader's sympathies will lie with the Sophist. He will be grateful—to Protagoras if he forgets that it is drama or to Plato if he remembers—for preventing Socrates from plunging into a third of his very exacting and most confusing and therefore extremely irritating demonstrations. And it will be a relief to him to learn that Protagoras assumes the role of the interrogator. For he is likely to make less rigorous demands on the attention of the listener or reader, and using him as a mouthpiece, Plato can convey the basic notions contained in the two demonstrations in a more palatable form, while at the same time carrying the argument a step forward.

In typical Greek fashion Protagoras turns to the poets for moral instruction:

> I propose to transfer the question which you and I have been discussing to the domain of poetry; we shall speak as before of virtue, but in reference to a passage of a poet. (339A)

He does not, however, accept the poets uncritically. "I am of opinion," he says, "that skill in poetry is the principal part of education; and this I believe to be the ability to understand which of the compositions of the poets are correct and which are not" (338E–339A).

It is important to note the difference between Protagoras's handling of the myth in his *Great Speech* and his present attitude toward poetry. In the former case, Plato portrayed him as highly skilled in the use of fiction as an apophantic device. Since such a device merely *points* to the truth, the listener or reader may or may not perceive it, depending not only on his perspicacity but also on his willingness. He is in a position similar to that of the proverbial horse who can be led to the water but cannot be made to drink. Clearly such a conception of truth militates against the guarantee of success which Protagoras claims for his teaching. Now the Sophist appears as the master who is in possession of the truth or some standard or norm against which the statements of the poets are to be measured. In Heidegger's terms, truth has been transformed from *aletheia* or unconcealment to *orthotes* or correctness. But since, as Heidegger has clearly shown, the former is the more basic of the two, the latter does not allow any guarantee either. And so we have another illustration of Protagoras's failure to draw the implications of his better insights, be it because of innate inability or because his boast beclouds his vision.

Protagoras then claims that his examination of a poem of Simonides has uncovered a contradiction. The poet, he says, criticizes Pittacus for maintaining that "with difficulty can a man be good," although a few lines earlier he himself has asserted that "it is with difficulty that a man can become truly good" (339D). Socrates turns to Prodicus for confirmation of the distinction he makes between being and becoming and then answers Protagoras by declaring that "Pittacus does not say, as Simonides says, that with difficulty can a man become good, but with difficulty can a man be good. And our friend Prodicus would maintain that being is not the same as becoming; and if they are not the same, then Simonides is not inconsistent with himself" (340C).

It is at least unlikely that the real Protagoras should have failed to distinguish between being and becoming. But perhaps the *dramatic* Protagoras could not be allowed to make the distinction because he guaranteed that after the first association with him, the student would *be* a better man. And unless this condition of being better could be regarded as more or less permanent, it would not be worth the high fee that Protagoras demands in payment.

Socrates now cites a passage from Hesiod, who also differentiates being from becoming in saying that "it is difficult for a man to become good . . . but . . . to maintain virtue, however difficult the acquisition, is easy" (340D). Again Protagoras does not recognize or is not allowed to recognize the distinction when he answers:

> It would reflect great ignorance on the part of the poet, if he says that virtue, which in the opinion of all men is the hardest of all things, can be easily retained. (340E)

Hesiod apparently conceived virtue as a habit (a notion which should appeal to Protagoras because of his advocacy of indoctrination and conditioning as a mode of teaching.) And it is obvious that the process of acquiring the virtue or habit may be difficult, while the habit, once established, is not only easy to maintain but often very difficult to break.

Socrates again turns to Prodicus, this time to satirize his art of making distinctions. Since *chalepon* means not only *difficult* but also *evil*, Prodicus, at the instigation of Socrates, maintains that "Simonides blames Pittacus for saying, 'it is difficult to be good,' just as if that were equivalent to saying 'it is evil to be good' " (341C). Since Prodicus has just made a useful contribution with the distinction between being and becoming, it may be assumed that the barbs of Socrates' irony are directed not at the art of Prodicus, but only at its excess. Useful as linguistic analysis may be, it makes itself ridiculous if it forgets that it functions in a world of becoming where words can change in meaning as the context changes in which they appear.

Socrates continues to lampoon the futile attempts to arrest a changing world in order to render certainty possible, when he now pokes fun, not at tradition when rightly understood and properly used, but at a tradition conceived as consisting of pithy sayings with which the young can be indoctrinated and by means of which even the most stupid people can be made to appear wise. While the Lacedaemonians, he says, are "thought to excel the other Hellenes . . . by reason of their fighting ability and their courage," they really surpass them in wisdom. "If a man converses with the most ordinary Lacedaemonian," he continues, "he will find him seldom good for much in general conversation, but at any point in the discourse he will inject some notable saying, short and terse, with unerring aim, like a sharpshooter, and the person with whom he is talking is like a child in his hands" (342D–E). And they are careful to conceal their wisdom, for if their secret became known "all men would be practicing their wisdom" (342B). Socrates then describes the ancient sages, such as Thales,

Pittacus, Solon and the rest of the Seven Wise Men as "lovers and emulators and disciples of the culture of the Lacedaemonians," and it is they, he concludes, who "dedicated in the temple of Apollo at Delphi, as the first fruits of their wisdom, the far-famed inscriptions which are in all men's mouths, 'Know theyself' and 'Nothing in excess' " (343A–B). If Protagoras were to agree with the imaginary Lacedaemonians that education consists in their being "capable of uttering such expressions" (342E–343A), Socrates seems to say, then his guarantee of success in teaching virtue might assume a measure of plausibility. But who would be so simple-minded as to believe that a mind or memory well stocked with these maxims would constitute moral excellence in the life of an individual or a community?

Turning again to Simonides, Socrates undertakes to show that it was the aim of the poet to gain fame by overthrowing one of the pithy sayings of the ancient sages, namely that of Pittacus according to which "it is difficult to *be* good" (343B). Probing deeper into the meaning of the poem, Socrates becomes serious again. This, according to Socrates, is what the poet is trying to say:

> There truly is a difficulty in becoming good, yet this is possible for a time, and only for a time. But having become good, to remain in a good state and be good, as you, Pittacus, affirm, is not possible, and is not granted to man; a god only has this blessing, "but man cannot help being bad when the force of circumstances overpowers him." (344B–C)

Resorting to his customary analogy with the arts and crafts, Socrates asks: "Whom does the force of circumstances overpower?" "The descent of a great storm," he answers, "may make the pilot helpless, or the severity of the seasons the farmer or the physician . . . not the layman, for he is always overpowered" (344C–D). Before the writer or the physician can become a bad writer or a bad physician, he must first become a writer or a physician, and he acquires his skill by learning to write well or "learning the art of healing the sick" (345A). Now circumstances may prevent him from practicing or applying his skill in a satisfactory manner, so that in that sense he becomes a bad writer or a bad physician. So likewise, Socrates concludes, "the good may become bad by time, or toil, or disease, or other accident" (345B).

In the expert, Socrates apparently distinguishes between the basic skill which can be taught, and the successful application of the skill in the concrete situation, which cannot be taught, for the practitioner may encounter unforeseen and even insurmountable obstacles. How does this apply to virtue? What is the part which can be taught? Socrates does not say, but presumably it consists of the traditional norms or values. Whether they have retained their usefulness over the years, and whether they should or should not be applied in a specific case—this cannot be taught. Who then corresponds to the layman in the arts and crafts? Are they the unthinking many who are swept now in one direction, now in another, and who, as Socrates maintains in the *Crito*, can do neither great good nor great evil, just as the layman cannot become a good or bad physician? Are they the inauthentic who are not responsible because their acts are not their own and who are therefore amoral?

The analogy with the arts and crafts has revealed a complexity which stands in sharp contrast to the simplicity of a world in which the effectiveness of moral teaching can be guaranteed. And in comparison with the master craftsman, the teacher of virtue faces even greater difficulties. For the young apprentice who comes to a master may be presumed to be desirous of learning the trade. If at any time he should become recalcitrant, threats of physical punishment can be expected to restore his initial zeal. Protagoras, on the other hand, in view of the type of students he attracts, is denied such simple means of producing compliance. He must assume, not only that what he regards as good is good in fact, but that its mere presentation to the student will be enough to bring about acceptance and to incite the student to action. Otherwise his guarantee of making a man better would be meaningless. And so Socrates, rather abruptly, now introduces the third presupposition of the position of Protagoras, the ethical determinism according to which "all who do evil and base things do them against their will" (345E). Oddly enough, perhaps to suggest its artificial character, it is derived from the poem under discussion by the positioning of a comma in the passage which says that "he who does no evil voluntarily I praise and love" (345D). The comma, according to Socrates, must be placed before instead of after the word "voluntarily," so that it reads: "He who does no evil, voluntarily I praise and love." "For Simonides," he insists, "was not so ignorant as to say that he praised those who did no evil voluntarily, as if there were some who did evil voluntarily" (345D). Since the doctrine is repeated twice, namely at 352D and 378C–D, it may be expected to play a significant role in Socrates' attack upon the position of Protagoras, despite its seemingly casual and almost arbitrary inference.[12]

When Protagoras took over the role of the questioner, the discussion lost its former rigor. Its underlying theme, however, remained the same. Socrates continued his attack on the position of Protagoras by pointing to its presupposition of a world in which the wisdom of the past is unfalteringly the wisdom of the present, as contrasted with the real world in which a man may at any time run into a problem for which there is no known precedent. The terse proverbs of the Lacedaemonians, which are thought to be applicable no matter what the situation, suggest the sharply separable and therefore clearly definable virtues as required by Protagoras, which Socrates ridiculed in the first demonstration.[13] Protagoras's inability to distinguish between being and becoming in his examination of the poem of Simonides is reminiscent of his disregard of the distinction between ideas which can be said to *be* and individual acts occurring only in concrete situations which are for ever in a state of *becoming*. It is this lack of discrimination, it will be recalled, which Socrates exploited in the second demonstration. The interpretation of the poem of Simonides has thus called renewed attention to the misconceptions which underlie the guarantee of Protagoras and which were responsible for the fallacies in the two formal arguments dealing with the unity of justice and piety, as well as wisdom and self-control respectively.[14] Through the artificial punctuation of a line in the poem of Simonides, Socrates has also introduced the third prerequisite of Protagoras's guarantee, namely the ethical determinism which Socrates is about to employ in the third formal argument dealing with the unity of wisdom and courage.

From one and the same poem, Socrates has been able to draw the most diverse inferences. Some, such as the ethical determinism, favor the position of Protagoras, others, as for instance the claim that "to remain in a good state and be good . . . is impossible," are diametrically opposed to it. This outcome discredits the statement with which Protagoras opened the present round to the effect that "skill in poetry is the principal part of education" (338E). Socrates therefore concludes that "a company such as ours, and men such as we profess to be, do not require the help of another's voice, or of the poets whom you cannot interrogate about the meaning of what they are saying; people who cite them declaring, some that the poet has one meaning, and others that he has another" (347E). And then he brings the argument back to his customary mode with the words: "Leaving the poets and keeping to ourselves, let us try the mettle of one another and make proof of the truth in conversation" (348A).

It is not surprising that at this point Protagoras should be loath to expose himself to further humiliations. And not until Alcibiades practically shames him into continuing the argument does he suggest that Socrates should ask and he would answer.

Third Argument: Wisdom and Courage

It is significant that under the guise of flattering and thereby conciliating Protagoras, Socrates opens the new round with a reminder of the boast of Protagoras:

> Do not imagine, Protagoras, that I have any other interest in asking questions of you but that of clearing up my own problems as they arise. . . . And I would rather hold discourse with you than with anyone, because I think that no man can better investigate most things which a good man may be expected to investigate, and in particular virtue. For *who is there, but you?—who not only claim to be a good man and a gentleman, for many are this, and yet have not the power of making others good—whereas you are not only good yourself, but also able to make others good.* Moreover such confidence have you in yourself that, although other Sophists conceal their profession, you

proclaim openly in the face of all Hellas that you are a Sophist or teacher of virtue and education, and are the first who demanded pay in return. (348C–349A) [Italics added]

Then he asks Protagoras whether he still holds, as he did in the beginning, that all the virtues are different from each other and have different functions like the parts of the face. Protagoras replies that he now regards "four out of the five to some extent similar, and the fifth of them, which is courage, as very different from the other four" (349D). And this, he says, can be seen from the fact that "many men are utterly unrighteous, impious, self-indulgent, ignorant, who are nevertheless remarkable for their courage" (349D).

Socrates, however, immediately takes courage out of this isolation by linking it up with confidence and by showing that confidence in turn is affected by knowledge.[15] Referring to divers and various types of fighting men he maintains, and Protagoras readily agrees, that by the courageous we mean the confident and that "those who have knowledge are more confident that those who have no knowledge, and they are more confident after they have learned than before" (350A). But are there not some, Socrates asks, who are wholly ignorant about these matters and still confident, and would you nevertheless call them courageous. "In that case," Protagoras replies, "courage would be a base thing" (350B) and inconsistent with the earlier admission that courage is a virtue and therefore wholly good.

The argument so far has shown that although courage is intimately related to confidence, the two cannot be equated. For confidence is the wider term or class and it has been acknowledged that only that part of confidence which is caused by knowledge can be said to contain courage.

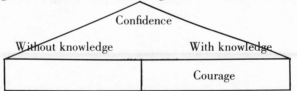

It is therefore obviously not legitimate to infer "all the confident are courageous" from the admittedly true statement that "all the courageous are confident." In fact the purpose of this part of the discussion seems to be to call attention to the fallacy which in traditional logic is known as a "false conversion."

Up to this point the argument has been consistent and easy to follow. Now Socrates throws everything into confusion:

Those who are thus confident without knowledge are really not courageous, but mad. And in the former case, on the other hand, those who are the wisest are also most confident, and being most confident are most courageous. According to this argument also wisdom would be courage. (350C)

The first sentence repeats what has been agreed upon, namely that courage must be excluded from that part of confidence which is not caused by knowledge, and thereby warns against the fallacy of a false conversion. The second sentence refers to that part of confidence which is caused by knowledge and which therefore can accommodate courage. The entire class of the confident was shown to be more extensive than the class of the courageous. The restricted class of the confident has not been shown to be more extensive than the class of the courageous, but neither has it been shown to be coextensive with it. Therefore a simple conversion would be no less fallacious than in regard to the entire class. But although Socrates has just warned against the error in regard to the entire class, he now commits it in reference to the restricted class, namely the class of those who are confident because of knowledge, by saying that "the wisest are also most confident, and being most confident are most courageous" (350C).

Protagoras in a lengthy statement now accuses Socrates of having committed the fallacy. His argument, however, is not quite to the point because, unlike Socrates, he refers, not to the restricted class, but again to the entire class of the confident before the division has been made. "I argue," he says, "that the courageous are confident, but not all the confident are courageous; for confidence may be given by art, and also . . . by madness and rage" (351A–B). But Socrates has just shown that, with reference to the whole class of the confident, the conversion is not possible. His error, on the other hand, refers to that part of confidence which is caused by knowledge.

All this is very puzzling: Socrates explains to Protagoras the fallacy of a false conversion in connection with a class A included in a class B. Then he himself commits the fallacy in connection with class A and a part of class B. Finally, Protagoras exposes the logical error made by Socrates, but again referring to all of A and all of B, when he should have spoken of A and part of B. It has been suggested that Socrates here calls attention to an error by seemingly committing it.[16] But why should Plato have him do this right after he has made him expose the error? And why should he add to the confusion by having Protagoras argue off key?

If the reader is not content with having discovered an error, and allows his own thoughts to be provoked into action, he might ask himself how Protagoras should have responded to the false conversion of Socrates. Obviously he should have pointed out that, just as previously the entire class of the confident could not be equated with the class of the courageous, so it might now be the case that the restricted class of the confident, that is, those whose confidence is caused by knowledge, cannot be equated with the courageous, because knowledge may have to be divided just as confidence had to be divided in the previous case. This would lead to a discussion and analysis of the meaning or meanings covered by the term "knowledge" in its relation to courage.

Now it is interesting to note that Socrates does in fact continue the discussion with an inquiry into knowledge. And what would have been an abrupt change in direction, now appears as a natural succession. In other words, the correction of Protagoras' misplaced objection has served as a transition from one topic to the next. For the time being, the question of various types of knowledge is kept in the background; the explicit concern at the moment is the power of knowledge. Socrates begins by confronting Protagoras with two extreme positions. The world, he says, is of the opinion that "a man may have knowledge, and yet that the knowledge which is in him may be overmastered by anger, or pleasure, or pain, or love, or perhaps by fear—just as if knowledge were nothing but a slave and might be dragged about by all these other things" (352B). This, of course, is a view which cannot be shared by a professional sophist who guarantees to make a man better the first day he comes to him. For why should young men pay a high fee for the acquisition of a kind of knowledge which cannot withstand the onrush of a blind impulse? And so when Socrates presents the other extreme and asks, "Do you think that knowledge will not allow a man, if he only knows the good and evil, to do anything contrary to what his knowledge bids him do?" (352C) Protagoras is quick to answer. "I, above all other men, am bound to say that wisdom and knowledge are the mightiest of human things" (352C–D). Thus the doctrine of the impossibility of the voluntary evildoer is introduced for the second time. Earlier, it will be recalled, Socrates derived it rather capriciously from a passage in a poem of Simonides; now it appears more explicitly as a presupposition of the guarantee of Protagoras.

The great stumbling block to Protagoras's belief in the invincibility of knowledge is a phenomenon commonly described as "overcome by pleasure." And those who do not share your view, says Socrates, will ask, "If this event is not to be called 'being overcome by pleasure,' pray tell us what it is, and what you call it" (353A). Socrates now constructs a theory of good and evil in such a way that the phenomenon in question can be called illusory. It turns out to be so primitive and narrow as to become useless for all practical purposes. It is at this point and in this context that the controversial hedonism makes its appearance in the dialogue.

Since to be "overcome by pleasure" is apparently regarded as something undesirable, the question of the relation of pleasure and pain to good and evil is being raised. Socrates first considers pleasure and pain as isolated from each other, as Protagoras had earlier tried to separate courage from the other virtues: "I say that things are good in so far as they are pleasant if they have no consequences of another sort, and in so far as they are painful they are bad" (351C). Protagoras does not at first agree, but, as previously, his objection is off key, for he disregards the qualification stated by Socrates to the effect that consequences must be left out of account:

Having regard not only to my present answer, but also to the whole of my life, I shall be safer, if I am not mistaken, in saying that there are some pleasant

things which are not good, and that there are some painful things which are
not evil, and some which are, and that there are some which are neither good
nor evil. (351D)

Since Protagoras has misunderstood, Socrates repeats his qualified statement,
namely that "things *in so far as* they are pleasant are good" (351E). Now another
misunderstanding is attributed to Protagoras, for he answers as if Socrates were
trying to identify the pleasant and the good. "If investigation proves," he says,
"that pleasure and good are really the same, then we shall agree; but if not, then
we shall argue" (351E).

Whatever the reason may be why Plato has Protagoras misunderstand
Socrates twice in succession, the reader cannot fail to notice the difference
between three types of assertions and the objects to which they refer. Socrates
attributes a quality to a subject, namely, goodness to pleasure or badness to
pain, both considered in isolation, apart from the consequences to which they
may lead. Protagoras, disregarding Socrates' specifications speaks of pleasant
things which are not good and painful things which are not evil, thereby clearly
introducing consequences. These expressions seem to contradict the statement
of Socrates, but only apparently so, for they refer to different objects, namely,
not to pleasure and pain as such, but rather to the outcome of the interactions of
pleasurable and painful experiences and their respective consequences. By
having Socrates blot out these interactions and by having Protagoras immediately restore them, Plato has in fact succeeded in calling attention to them.
Pleasures therefore may be called evil, not because they are evil in themselves,
but because they "cause disease and poverty and other like evils in the future"
(353D). Similarly, pains may be regarded as good although they cause immediate suffering, if they prevent greater evil or bring about a good outweighing
the evil of the suffering. The second misunderstanding of Protagoras underscores the difference between the simple identification of the pleasant and the
good, and the statement of Socrates that the pleasant is a good but not
necessarily the good, just as the painful is an evil, although not the evil.

Obviously, to regard pleasure and pain apart from their consequences is to
regard them in abstraction, and the identification of the pleasant with the good
and the painful with the bad is, according to Protagoras himself, subject to
debate. If we could make these two assumptions, that is, strip the pleasant and
the painful of their consequences and identify them with good and evil
respectively, then "the event of being overcome" could be rendered harmless to
the position of Protagoras by being reduced to an absurdity. For the substitution
of good for pleasure would yield the statement that "a man does what he knows
to be evil when he ought not, because he is overcome by good" (355D).

Now the ordinary man may in fact be unable to offer any standard other than
pleasure and pain; but he need only observe what he is doing when he makes a
choice to realize that he cannot afford to leave consequences out of account.

And while for a hedonist the substitution of good for pleasure and pain for evil still produces the *form* of an absurd statement, it is no longer actually absurd, as indicated by the response which Socrates places into the mouth of his imaginary representative of the ordinary man:

> That is too ridiculous, that a man should do what he knows to be evil when he ought not, because he is overcome by the good. Is that because the good was worthy or not worthy of conquering the evil? . . . How can the good be unworthy of the evil, or the evil of the good? Is not the real explanation that they are out of proportion to one another, either as greater or smaller, or more and fewer? . . . And when you speak of being overcome, what do you mean . . . but that you choose the greater evil in exchange for the lesser good? (355D–E)

And so it appears that not even a simple kind of hedonism can sustain the position of Protagoras. As long as it becomes necessary to determine the proper proportion between good and evil, or pleasure and pain, then we can no longer have recourse to the kind of knowledge which the Sophist says can be drilled into children "by threats and blows" (325D) and imparted to a person once and for all. The kind that is required constitutes a certain know-how, a knowing how to evaluate the relevant factors present in a given situation:

> And do you, like a skillful weigher, put in the balance the pleasures and the pains, and their nearness and distance, and weigh them, and then say which outweighs the other? If you weigh pleasures against pleasures, you of course should take the more and greater; or if you weigh pains against pains, you should take the fewer and the less; or if pleasures against pains, then that course of action should be taken in which the painful is exceeded by the pleasant . . . and you avoid that course of action in which the pleasant is exceeded by the painful. (356A–C)

Now we are ready to answer the question which was raised earlier, that is, whether knowledge needs to be divided as confidence had to be divided, so that it becomes false to say all those who have knowledge are courageous, as it was found to be false to say that all the confident are courageous. And Socrates' analogy of the divers and peltasts will help us to decide the issue in connection with knowledge, as it has helped in the case of confidence. The divers and peltasts can be trained in their respective skills so that they become experts. But if they were to dive or to stand and fight no matter what the circumstances, they would be fools. Their expertise merely reduces the risk; it does not eliminate it. Whether to take the risk and apply their skill, that is, whether to dive or not to dive, whether to fight or to flee from the enemy—this is a decision which each individual must make for himself. It involves an evaluation of the risk in relation to the expected outcome of the particular act. This kind of knowledge, which "has to do with excess and defect" (357A), cannot be taught, at least not in the sense in which Protagoras understands teaching.[17] It depends in large measure on keen observation of the situation and a shrewd evaluation of the alternatives it offers. It requires the kind of critical intelligence which Socrates tried to arouse in the young Hippocrates at the beginning of the dialogue before taking him to Protagoras to purchase a piece of knowledge. Now for the first time the conception of knowledge which Socrates opposes to that of Protagoras comes out into the open. But it is still tied to a hedonist theory of morality from which it must be liberated.

This emancipation occurs in the second part of the third formal demonstration, dealing with the unity of courage and wisdom. Before examining it we must deal with the first half which has for its premise the third of the presuppositions of the boastful claim of the Sophist, namely the doctrine that no man willingly pursues evil. This doctrine, it will be recalled, made its first appearance as a rather arbitrary derivation from a poem of Simonides; next it was presented by Socrates as one of two extremes in a discussion of the power of knowledge; now Socrates refers to it for the third time and just prior to the formal argument, which may plausibly be regarded as a hint to the reader to look to it as the reason for the absurd conclusion which the argument yields.[18] Socrates formulates it as follows:

> No man willingly pursues evil, or that which he thinks to be evil. To pursue what one believes to be evil rather than what is good is not in human nature; and when a man is compelled to choose one of two evils, no one will choose the greater when he may have the less. (358C–D)

After adding the definition of "fear as the expectation of evil" (358D) Socrates asks whether "if our former admissions are true, a man will pursue that which he fears when it is open to him to pursue that which he does not fear" (358D). When all agree that this would be impossible, he interrogates Protagoras as follows:

> Against what are the brave ready to go—against the same things as the cowards?
> No, he answered.
> Then against something different?
> Yes, he said.
> Then do cowards go where there is nothing to fear, and the brave where there is much to fear?
> Yes, Socrates, so men say.
> Very true, I said. But I want to know against what do you say that the brave are ready to go—against fearful things, believing them to be fearful things, or against things which are not fearful?
> No, said he; the former case has been proved by you in the previous argument to be impossible. (359C–D)

If neither the cowards nor the brave are willing to face dangerous or fearful situations, then the difference which has been said to exist between them collapses, and it must be admitted that "the cowardly and the brave go to meet the same things" (359E). But this is clearly contrary to experience and Protagoras himself feels compelled to object: "Yet, Socrates, that against which the coward goes is the opposite of that against which the brave goes. The one, for example, is willing to go to battle, and the other is not willing" (379E).

The most obvious error in the argument is the fact that the fearful is conceived as an unmitigated evil, devoid of future consequence, and that as such it determines the will. And the great puzzle is why Protagoras does not object by saying that the courageous are determined in their action not simply by the evil inherent in the fearful or dangerous situation, which according to the "doctrine" would cause them to flee, but by the desire to avoid *future* greater evil, which induces him to face the enemy. What the historical Protagoras would have said under the circumstances we have no way of knowing; but as on previous occasions the dramatic Protagoras is not allowed to object, because he is strictly held to his guarantee and its implications. This guarantee demands the doctrine, namely the belief that in the presence of good or evil, a man's will is determined to accept or reject it. The admission of future consequences of an act, however, would conjure up a host of doubts and uncertainties. Such consequences are never absolutely predictable, and even if they were, we might not be there to suffer or enjoy them. Furthermore, the consequences themselves have consequences in an unending chain, and what at one time appears to be the lesser evil or the greater good may, on a wider view, turn out to be the greater evil or the lesser good. And finally, the consequences are innumerable and to try to take account of all is to set oneself an impossible task. Therefore, a man can never wait until all the evidence has been gathered together and is absolutely compelling. Sooner or later he must stop weighing the pros and cons and be prepared to act. It often requires a strong resolve and considerable courage to cut through the uncertainties and make a decision. According to the "doctrine," the clearer the perception of what the situation offers, the stronger the power exerted on the will to act one way or the other. In reality it is quite the opposite: the more keenly we are aware of the nature of the human situation and the obscure, uncertain, and ambiguous goods or evils presented to us, the greater the experienced agony of having to make a choice.

Thus the third presupposition of the claim of Protagoras, the ethical determinism, has been shown to depend on the existence of simple, clearcut alternatives, devoid of future consequences. The alternatives, however, which are encountered in the world in which we live, are entangled in an intricate net of relationships which defies final analysis. And thus the promise of the famous Sophist, who at the beginning of the discussion proudly proclaimed himself the "instructor of mankind" (317B), stands exposed as a preposterous though unintended hoax.

which Socrates interrogates the young Hippocrates, through his debate with Protagoras, and especially in connection with the hypothetical hedonism, where it appears as the art of weighing or measuring in order to determine the greater and the less, whether it be of pleasure and pain or of good and evil. But nowhere in the dialogue is it explained, at least not explicitly, just what tradition is and how it enters our lives. In a sense, there is no need of such an explanation, for we are all familiar with tradition; we are born into it and to some extent it shapes our lives from the cradle to the grave. We cannot escape it, for we are affected by it even in rebelling against it.

This vague familiarity, no matter how intimate, is not sufficient for Heidegger. In preparation for his inquiry into the meaning of Being in general, he must form as clear as possible a conception of the human mode of being. Since tradition, this process of *handing down* which Heidegger calls *historizing*, plays such an important part, he cannot afford to leave it in the dark, for in so doing he might miss a significant aspect of the object of his investigation.

Heidegger begins his analysis with a brief look at the way in which we ordinarily speak about history. We say "something already belongs to history", which means that it belongs to the past, and no longer affects the present. But we also say, "one cannot get away from history," and thereby refer to something past, which is still effective. But whether effective or not, the historical, the remains of a Greek temple for instance, while definitely belonging to an earlier time, can nevertheless be present here and now. How is this possible? We also understand by history a form of development, when we characterize a thing or event as "having a history." Here the reference is not exclusively to the past, but includes the present. We may even stress the future as indicated by the expression "epoch making." And finally, "whatever has been handed down is as such held to be historical, whether it is something which we know historiologically, or something which has been taken over as self-evident, with its derivation hidden" (431). Again the emphasis is on the past, but the present and future are not totally excluded.

Ordinarily we equate the historical with the past, and yet, as we have seen, there are some expressions in which the present and the future play an equally important role. Is this ambiguity an adumbration of the fact that history cannot be understood in terms of our customary conception of time, according to which the three temporal dimensions are sharply separated? For on this view, only the present is real, while the past is no more, and the future is not yet. As a result, says Heidegger, "a historical being traverses the span of time granted to it between the two boundaries, and it does so in such a way that, in each case, it is 'actual' only in the 'now,' and hops, as it were, through the sequence of 'nows' of its own time" (425). The historizing of Dasein may have to be conceived in terms of the more basic notion of temporality, which lets the three temporal aspects realize themselves simultaneously.

This is in fact the conclusion in the direction of which Heidegger moves with the next step of his enquiry, as he turns from talk about the historical to the historical reality itself. An antique piece of furniture, for instance, is present here and now, yet it belongs to the past. "By what right," asks Heidegger, "do we call this entity 'historical,' when it is not yet past?" (431). It does not loose its historical character even if it is still in use. What is past, he answers, is the world in which it functioned. It was part of a "context of equipment and encountered as ready-to-hand and used by a concernful Dasein, which was-in-the world" (432). But since the world is a characteristic of Dasein, that which accounts for the historical quality of the entities is ultimately found in the Dasein which is no longer. Heidegger therefore calls Dasein primarily histori-cal, while those entities which belong to a world of Dasein are said to be secondarily historical or 'world historical'.

If the historical has been correctly rooted in Dasein then it must be subject to the same conditions which makes Dasein possible. Now Heidegger has estab-lished temporality as the basic structure of Dasein. Temporality differs from the ordinary conception of time, which reduces the past to a *'now-no-more'* and the future to a *'now-not-yet'*, and can therefore be called 'now-time'. Temporality underlies our ordinary activity. We project goals into the *future*, based on the potentialities which *have been* given, and let these goals determine what we are doing *now*. So both goals and potentialities are present, one as *futural* and the other as *having been;* they are not simply, *now-no-more* or *now-not-yet*. The recent past of a serious traffic accident as well as the prospect of a dangerous operation may make their 'presence' felt more strongly than anything 'actual' in the current situation. Temporality makes possible not only our ordinary choices, but also the most basic of all, the choice of our own selves. In the discussion of authenticity, Heidegger shows how the confrontation with its ultimate *future*, the possibility of death, can throw Dasein back upon itself, and reveal it as it *has* always *been*, namely as potentiality-for-being. As such, if offers Dasein the possibility to take possession of itself *now*. Authenticity, which results from the anticipation of death and the decision to hold oneself responsible for one's being, Heidegger calls *anticipatory resoluteness*. Through this resoluteness Dasein constitutes itself as an authentic whole embracing the three temporal ecstasies, namely, its future, its past or having been, and its present.

When Dasein thus encounters itself in its thrownness, it does so not as an isolated being, but as "Being-in-the-world." In gaining possession of itself, it also gains possession of its world. Because of its temporal constitution, it is open to the past, and, therefore, in taking over its world it also takes over the tradition which has been operative in its world from the beginning.

What precisely does Dasein hand down from the past? Ordinarily we think of attitudes, customs, laws, institutions, and such like. But he who faces his thrownness courageously and authentically, that is, in "anticipatory resoluteness," is aware that these derive their meaning from a world and are as a consequence 'world historical' or historical in a secondary sense. And he also knows that the 'past' Dasein to which this world belongs is basically "potentiality-for-Being." Hence to hand down that which is primordially histori- cal is to hand down a 'past' Dasein in its significant possibilities. This authentic handing down Heidegger calls *repetition*. "Repeating is grounded existentially in anticipatory resoluteness," he says, "and is handing down explicitly—that is to say, going back into the possibilities of the Dasein that has-been-there" (437).

The authentic individual cannot let himself be bound by the past; he does not simply actualize again a past possibility. Instead he makes "a *reciprocative rejoinder* to the possibility of that existence which has-been-there" (438). In other words, he adjusts the possibility to the demands of his own time and place. It is not enough, for instance, to discover simply what Socrates said and did, that he refused to escape when the opportunity was offered him, that he obeyed the law although the sentence inflicted was grossly unjust. Nor does it mean that because Socrates, under his circumstances, chose to obey the law, we ought always to obey it. What is significant is that Socrates freely made his decision in the light of what he thought best for himself, his family, his friends, and the state, untrammeled by fear of death or any uncontrollable impulse. It is this attitude, the possibility of acting freely in response to the demands of a particular situation, that is truly worthy of *repetition*. "Dasein's primordial historizing," says Heidegger, "lies in authentic resoluteness . . . in which Dasein *hands* itself *down*, free for death, in a possibility which it has inherited and yet has chosen" (435).

What a strange conception, some will say, which regards history as primarily concerned with the possible. Does not Aristotle in the *Poetics* distinguish between history and poetry by saying that "the one describes the thing that has been, and the other a kind of thing that might be," and therefore considers "poetry as something more philosophic and of greater import than history . . ." (1451A–1451B)? If compelled to choose between Aristotle and Heidegger, common sense would surely opt for Aristotle. For Heidegger not only maintains that history is concerned with the possible, but that in its roots it is futural rather than past. And if two of the greatest thinkers can reach such diametrically opposed conclusions, then even the intelligent layman might be well advised to leave philosophy alone and trust his own insights.

In reality the two views are more intimately related than appears at first glance. Heidegger speaks of authentic historicality, which presupposes an- ticipatory resoluteness. This in turn is based on a confrontation with death as an inescapable possibility. The resultant anxiety destroys the hiding places and unmasks the false security, thereby throwing Dasein back upon itself as sheer potentiality. But this movement to the very end of existence and back again to itself as sheer potentiality is precisely what inauthentic Dasein makes every effort to avoid. Of course, the very effort shows that it is aware of it, but it at least succeeds in dimming down this *unsettling* experience. It seeks refuge and forgetfulness in its daily activities and loses sight of the source of historicality. It restricts itself to the 'world historical,' that is, to those entities and events which are historical because they belong to a world which has been. "Accordingly," says Heidegger, "historiology, the study of history, has many branches and takes for its object the history of equipment, of work, of culture, of the spirit and of ideas" (447). It is this 'world historical' which Aristotle has in mind when he says that history is concerned with what has been. And so Aristotle and Heidegger speak of different aspects of the same history. For Heidegger, against Aristotle, is concerned with that which is primarily historical, the 'past' Dasein as "potentiality-for-Being" and in addition probes into the hidden ground of historicality in resoluteness, which, as anticipatory, springs from the future.

Does Plato, like Aristotle, stay with the 'world historical' or does the movement of the *Protagoras* as a whole point in the direction of Heidegger's conception of authentic historicality?

Seen from Heidegger's point of view, the Sophist's guarantee to make his disciples better is a clear perversion of the process of historizing. The 'past' Dasein offers possibilities from which the authentic man freely chooses those which are adaptable to his interests and needs. And the manner of the realization of these possibilities in turn determines the moral character of his behavior. Only the unfree individual lends himself to the sort of control which the claim of Protagoras implies, and such an individual would be amoral. The fact that Socrates combats the position of Protagoras through lengthy and intricate arguments would seem to indicate that he was not unaware of this perversion.

Plato moves positively in the direction of authentic historicality through the myth which he puts in the mouth of Protagoras. The myth portrays men as devoid of qualities, as having been given potentialities instead. He describes them as "naked and shoeless, having neither bed nor arms of defense" (321C). Man thus appears abandoned to himself, constrained to develop his basic potentialities or perish. Since he is not bound to any fixed nature he has the choice of taking charge of his own development and thereby constitute himself authentic, or remain in bondage to the pressure which society from his early youth has put upon him. Protagoras does not recognize the choice of freedom as a possibility, but speaks only of strengthening submission to the tradition. The very young are made to conform, by "mother and nurse and father and tutor," if necessary by threats and blows; they are conditioned through poetry and music; and finally "the state compels them to learn the laws and live after the pattern which they furnish, and not after their own fancy" (326C,D). In typical Platonic fashion, Plato lets a basically correct if rudimentary conception of man as potentiality-for-being clash with an incompatible method of developing those potentialities in the hope of making the intelligent and attentive reader aware of the possibility of what Heidegger calls historicality in the inauthentic mood.

After Socrates has thoroughly discredited the position of Protagoras, he draws away completely from tradition and moves the individual to the fore. He does this not openly but in the guise of a simplified hedonism. In the light of such a theory, Socrates can identify virtue with knowledge, meaning by knowledge the ability to weigh pleasures and pains against each other, so as to obtain an excess of the former over the latter. But only the individual himself can know what gives him pleasure and what causes him pain. In this regard he is completely self-sufficient in the here-and-now with no need of tradition to tell him what to choose. But when the paradox of the imaginary "laughing argument" suggests that tradition and critical intelligence are not as unrelated as the behavior of the two opponents might suggest. What the relationship is remains unsaid—at least as long as we persist in overlooking the image of Socrates which Plato, the artist, places before us. Throughout the dialogue Socrates has failed to adopt any definite position. He started out by warning his friend Hippocrates against the teaching of the Sophist who lectures at the house of Callias, but he takes him there none the less. He readily acknowledges defeat at the end of the first round of arguments. He denies that virtue can be taught in the way in which Protagoras proposes to teach it, but in support of his denial he argues not from his own point of view, but from premises which are implied in the claim of Protagoras and which lead to absurd conclusions. Even the hedonism is not his, but merely a device to illustrate the untenability of his opponent's position. He seems totally uncommitted, free from preconceived notions, from fixed beliefs and hardened attitudes. In this manner Socrates approaches Protagoras, the advocate of tradition. This detachment is not an end in itself; its purpose is to let the matter of the discourse show itself in its true being. Is not this attitude very similar to, if not identical with, Heidegger's anticipatory resoluteness, which is the prerequisite for an authentic choice? With anticipatory resoluteness we have reached only the determination to choose freely and authentically. Possibilities for choice are offered through tradition. But which to choose and which to reject, neither Plato nor Socrates nor anyone else can tell us. "In the existential analysis," says Heidegger, "we cannot, in principle, discuss what Dasein factically resolves in any particular case" (435). Discussion may help to clarify the situation and shed light on the possibilities which tradition has to offer, but the choice itself must strictly be our own. This is why Socrates the teacher says: "I know nothing, but those who converse with me profit."

The *Protagoras*, by general agreement, is one of the most dramatic of Plato's dialogues. As such we cannot expect it to offer explicitly stated doctrines or even openly expressed opinions of its author, who, as a dramatist, must try to reach his audience by indirection, the clash of ideas, and other such devices.

Any interpretation, therefore, can at best be accepted only "with a hesitating sort of confidence." Whatever conclusions we have drawn could have been reached without the aid of Heidegger. But in the light of his existential analytic, many hints and suggestions in the dialogue have taken on a deeper meaning, as a result of which the dialogue has gained in unity and significance. This gives rise to the perhaps not unjustified hope that we have come a step closer to the real intent of Plato. In any event, now that we clearly understand the role which Socrates' statement that "no man willingly pursues evil" is meant to play in the dialogue, the "doctrine" need no longer disturb our belief that even in the *Protagoras* Plato is essentially concerned with authentic selfhood.

NOTES

1. *Plato's "Protagoras,"* edited, with an Introduction, by Gregory Vlastos (New York: Liberal Arts Press, 1956.) All quotations from the *Protagoras* refer to this edition.

2. Introduction to the *Protagoras* in the *Collected Dialogues of Plato,* ed. Edith Hamilton and Huntington Cairns, Bollingen Series 71 (Princeton, N.J.: Princeton University Press, 1961), p. 308. Michael J. O'Brien refers to the "division of labor in the Bude edition of Plato, in which A. Corset and L. Bodin have edited the *Protagoras* as a work of art and have said that it contains no Platonic philosophy properly so-called. (Paris, 1923, p. 3)." He also quotes Wilamowitz as saying that "it is futile to search the Protagoras for 'ein wissenschaftliches Resultat' (Ulrich von Wilamowitz-Moellendorf, *Sappho and Simonides,* Berlin 1913, p. 179, No. 2)." Michael J. O'Brien, *The Socratic Paradoxes and the Greek Mind* (Chapel Hill, N.C.: The University of North Carolina Press, 1967), p. 8, no. 5., and p. 140, n. 23.

3. Albert Einstein and Leopold Infeld, *The Evolution of Physics* (New York: Simon and Schuster, 1951), pp. 8–9.

4. *Ion,* 535C–536A.

5. Plato scholars maintain that Plato resorts to myth only when he reaches the higher realms of truth from which dialectical argument and everyday language are barred. According to W. K. C. Guthrie, for instance, "myth is valuable as a means of presenting a possible account of things which we know to exist, but the exact manner of whose existence and working we must admit to be beyond our present powers of literal description." *Socrates and Plato,* The Marcossan Lectures for 1957 (Brisbane: University of Queensland Press, 1958), p. 24. Cf. also: Hermann Gauss, *Philosophischer Hand-kommentar zu den Dialogen Platos,* Erster Teil, Zweite Haeflte, "Die Frühdialoge" (Bern: Verlag Herbert Lang, 1954) p. 154. Also: Percival Frutiger, *Les Mythes de Platon* (Paris: F. Alcan, 1930), p. 185. The Protagoras myth, as we have seen, does not at all conform to this sharp separation of the function of *mythos* and *logos*. For it does not deal with some supernatural realm, but with the sense of justice as a condition for the possibility of social living. As a result, some commentators have felt compelled to declare it un-Platonic or to deny it altogether the status of a genuine myth. There are even some who, like Frutiger, go so far as to consider it merely as an attempt of a sophist to pass off a fabulous tale for a proof, with the intent of befuddling rather than enlightening the audience: "Plus spécieux que convainçant, il ne révèle à l'analyse qu'un tissu de pensées obscures et contradictoires. Aussi n'est-ce point en raison de ses qualités propres qu'il nous intéresse, mais parce qu'il nous permet de mieux saisir, par

contraste, le caractère distinctif des véritables mythes de Platon. . . . Le conte de Protagoras, et en général le mythe sophistique, vise donc plus à éblouir, l'auditeur qu'à l'instruire; c'est un tour de passe-passe, un expédient commode—trop commode—pour esquiver les difficultés d'une démonstration." Frutiger, *Mythes de Platon*, pp. 183–85.

According to Paul Friedländer, ". . . the myth is presented first, superficially, concealing rather than clarifying." *Plato*, vol. 2, *The Dialogues*, translated by Hans Meyerhoff. Bollingen Series 59 (Princeton, N.J.: Princeton University Press, 1964), p. 14. Cf. also: T. Gomperz, *Griechische Denker*, vol. 2 (Leipzig, 1896–1909), p. 215. Schleiermacher also regards the Protagoras myth as un-Platonic and complains about its "grobmaterialistische Denkungsart, die ueber die sinnliche Erfahrung nicht hinaus philosophiert." F. Schleiermacher, *Einleitung zum Protagoras*, vol. 1 (Berlin, 1817), pp. 233–34.

6. G. M. H. Grube seems to think that virtue cannot be both innate and teachable when he says: "The creation myth by which the sophist answers does not really solve the difficulty since it maintains that virtue is inborn and teachable." *Plato's Thought* (Boston: Beacon Press, 1961), p. 263. Obviously, it can be inborn as a capacity which needs development. This seems to be the view of A. E. Taylor: "The very universality of the instruction would lead to differences between individual citizens, based on their more or less marked natural aptitude." *Plato: The Man and His Work* (London: Methuen & Co., 1949), p. 245.

7. In a general discussion, without special reference to the *Protagoras*, Hans-Georg Gadamer comments: "Im allgemeinen aber führt Sokrates die Widerlegung so, dass er die gegnerische These folgerichtig bis in Konsequenzen entwickelt, bei denen die Rücksicht auf die allgemein geltende Meinung, insbesondere die Moral, dem Gegner das Festhalten an der Konsequenz seiner These unmöglich macht. Dies ist die radikalste Form von Widerlegung ueberhaupt." (*Platos dialektische Ethik und andere Studien zur platonischen Philosophie*. [Hamburg: Felix Meiner Verlag. 1968], p. 46.)

8. The argument really begins with the notorious self-predications: ". . . justice, is it just or unjust?" and "nothing can be pious if piety is not pious" (330C–D). For want of a better explanation, I would suggest the following:

To the modern reader, these statements are, of course, absurd, for they are of the same type as the statement that *redness is red*. And who would think of attributing color to an abstract idea? Still we might be prompted to ask: What, then, can be said to be just or unjust, pious or impious? If we answer a man can be so characterized, it could be objected that in order to be just or unjust he must be moral, and to be moral means to be *capable* of being both just and unjust. You cannot affix a definite moral quality to a man without destroying his freedom, the very condition for the possibility of his morality.— Shall we say that certain types of acts are just or unjust? That too is out of the question, for even lying or stealing may under certain conditions do less harm than their opposites and therefore be the right thing to do. This leaves us merely with the individual act freely chosen and performed in the concrete situation. But if a moral quality is attributable only to such an act, then the guarantee of Protagoras becomes obviously absurd.

9. G. M. A. Grube grossly oversimplifies the argument when he says: "He first attempts to force upon Protagoras the identity of piety with justice by a fallacy, the well-known confusion between a predicative judgement and one of identity, which is not finally cleared up until the *Sophist* ('piety, you say, is not like the just, it is then like the not-just, it is therefore unjust'.) 331A–B." *Plato's Thought*, p. 220. Paul Friedländer can do no more than declare the argument absurd: "Thus the inference that Socrates draws from this artificially constructed piece of nonsense is made worthless: the complete identity of piety and justice." Its only merit is said to be its superiority "to the relativistic

talk in which the baffled Sophist indulges." *Plato*, vol. 2, (New York: Random House, 1964), p. 19.

10. Gregory Vlastos, *Plato's "Protagoras*," p. xxix.

11. Grube again slurs over the real problem which confronts the reader: "With moderation Socrates' case is a little better, though his argument is still verbal, for it depends largely on the common root in the Greek words for wisdom and moderation (phronesis and sophrosyne) and its contrary (aphrosyne). To act with moderation is to act wisely; moderation and wisdom have but one opposite: folly. They are therefore the same thing. Again, this does prove that the two words, wisdom and moderation, are in Greek used at times indifferently so that the two virtues cannot be very distinct." *Plato's Thought*, pp. 220–21. For a brief discussion of the views of Taylor, Shorey, and Friedländer, see Vlastos, *Plato's "Protagoras*," p. XIX. Vlastos finds all of them unsatisfactory, and rightly so. He does not actually analyze the argument which contains the fallacy, but from the illustration which he uses to point to it, it appears that he has the correct notion. He seems to hold that the error is unintentional on the part of Plato; in any event he does not suggest any reason why Plato might have made Socrates commit the fallacy.

12. Paul Friedländer, like many commentators, regards the doctrine as typically Socratic: ". . . Socrates can impress this meaning upon the poem only by doing violence to it, combining the words falsely. The interpretation as a whole . . . is a brief sketch of what is called the Socratic ethics of knowledge. The attentive reader realizes that he is here introduced to a doctrine of essential significance even though it is concealed by a sophistic method and a capriciously deceptive interpretation" *Plato*, p. 25. For more detailed comments see note 18 below.

13. So we cannot agree with Taylor who holds that the "introductory homily on the devotion of Sparta to 'culture' . . . is manifestly the merest playful humour" (*Plato*, p. 256), or furious fun" (p. 255).

14. Taylor regards the interlude "as intended mainly to be humorous relief!" It is meant to relax the reader's attention, he says, in anticipation of the heavy demand which the subsequent arguments make upon his "powers of hard thinking" (*Plato*, p. 251). The only exception he makes refers to the doctrine that no man willingly pursues evil. "Here," he says, "Socrates is in dead earnest." But he admits that the manner in which the doctrine is extracted and Socrates' pretense that it is universally accepted by all right thinking men, "is itself merely play" (p. 256). So at least by implication Taylor recognizes in regard to a portion of the interlude what is really true of the whole, namely that it consists of a mixture of seriousness and playfulness which makes it necessary for the reader to take it seriously but not literally.

15. "When you speak of courageous men, do you mean the confident, or something else?" (349E).

16. A. E. Taylor, *Plato*, p. 258. Taylor simply disregards Protagoras's misplacement of the fallacy. Vlastos (*Plato's "Protagoras*," p. XXXIII) does call attention to it, but gives no reason why Plato should have made Protagoras commit such a strange error.

17. Vlastos correctly points to Socrates' "failure to make clear what sort of knowledge is involved, how unlike that of the aforesaid divers, cavalrymen, peltasts" (*Plato's "Protagoras*," p. XLVIII). It is typical for one who reads the dialogues literally to be content with calling attention to a difficulty without asking whether it may not have been created intentionally as a part of the Socratic method.

18. According to Paul Shorey "it is a fundamental Socratic doctrine, which Plato himself holds in some sense to the end, that no man does err voluntarily" (*What Plato Said* [Chicago: University of Chicago Press, 1968], p. 89). And A. E. Taylor implies as

much when he points out that the "well-known Socratic dictum [is] repeated by Plato on his own account in the *Laws*" (ibid., p. 37). But the context in which it appears in this late dialogue is radically different. For there he says the legislator is one who will teach the citizens "hatred of iniquity, and love of right or even acquiescence in right" (862D). It would seem obvious that to the extent to which the legislator believes that good laws will make good citizens, he believes that by merely presenting what is good, the laws will induce men to good behavior. And the Athenian is justified in saying: "I in particular am bound at this moment to accept the position . . . that those who act wrong always act against their own will" (860D). But there are always a few who do not have the good will which the legislator presupposes, and this is why there is need for law enforcement agencies. In the *Protagoras,* by contrast, Socrates makes a much stronger claim: "To pursue what one believes to be evil rather than what is good is not in human nature [en anthropou physei]" (358D). This stronger version of the dictum is, as we have seen, necessitated by Protagoras's guarantee, which cannot be satisfied with the statement that most men pursue the good if they are only made aware of it, but must maintain that all men will *necessarily* do so.

19. Taylor sees the difference between Protagoras and Socrates not as one between adherence to a tradition on the one hand, and critical intelligence taking account of the concrete situation on the other, but rather as one between relativism and absolutism: "The whole point of the identification of morality with 'knowledge' is that morality is not any more 'relative' than geometry. . . . Goodness, as Socrates understands it, is a matter not of tradition but of insight into principles" (*Plato,* p. 246). In opposition to Taylor, it must be pointed out that principles can be as rigid as a tradition and just as incompatible with a changing situation.

20. Socrates in the *Protagoras* represents only one aspect, as indicated by the following: "Even as you were telling the myth, I preferred your Prometheus to your Epimetheus, for of him I make constant use, whenever I am busy about these questions, in Promethean care of my own life in its entirety" (361D).

6

Republic: Personal Integrity in the Ideal Commonwealth

The *Republic* presents a most formidable threat to our inquiry. For while it is generally recognized that the dialogues previously considered end inconclusively and thereby allow a certain freedom of interpretation, Plato is now said to have given explicit and unequivocal expression to his conception of the ideal rule, namely, that of the philosopher-kings who, through their access to the supreme principle of intelligibility, guide the destiny of the state with unerring hand.[1] Of course, the concern with failure is not altogether absent. There is the long treatise on the aberrations from the ideal, extending over Books 8 and 9 and ranging from timocracy and the timocractic man to despotism and the despot. This fall from perfection, however, is usually regarded as enhancing the beauty of the ideal and thus made subservient to the positive approach.[2] Failure is also predominant in Book I with its fruitless attempts at defining justice. But this book is frequently rendered harmless to a literal interpretation by being declared an early dialogue, which has somehow and not quite legitimately become attached to the *Republic*.[3]

As long as we paid attention to the often neglected dramatic aspects of the dialogues so far considered, it was not difficult to establish a fruitful relationship between Plato's insights and Heidegger's concern with authentic existence in *Being and Time*. The *Republic*, however, at least as traditionally understood, seems to present an insurmountable obstacle to the establishment of such a relationship. For the philosopher-kings control all the major aspects of the lives of their subjects, namely, education, vocation, marriage, war and peace, religion and art. And such control is the very opposite of what Heidegger regards as the proper dealings between one human being and another. He distinguishes between two kinds of solicitude, which he calls *einspringen* and *vorausspringen, leaping in* and *leaping ahead*. The first solves the other's problem and unburdens him, thus holding him in a subtle bondage; the second does not "take away his 'care' but gives it back to him authentically as such for the first time" (159), in other words, it tries to help him become independent and self-reliant. "Everyday Being-with-one-another," according to Heidegger, "maintains itself between the two extremes of positive solicitude—that which leaps in and dominates, and that which leaps forth and liberates" (ibid.). Would not the rule of the philosopher-kings constitute an instance of the first, and the Socratic method an instance of the second, mode of behavior?

Buried in the *Myth of Er,* on the last few pages of the dialogue, there is, however, an incident so damaging to the literal interpretation that its advocates have persistently passed it by in silence. The story is told of a man who, when confronted with the choice of a new earthly existence, selects the life of a tyrant fated to devour his own children. Strangely enough, says Socrates, he was one of those who had lived in a "well-ordered commonwealth" (10.618)[4] and thereafter spent a thousand years in heaven. And yet he failed miserably in the proper performance of the most specific of human functions, the choice of his own life. Something must have gone radically wrong in his education, a wrong which even a thousand years in heaven could not prevent, must less a single life span in an earthly city, no matter how perfect. The *Myth of Er* is the last, but, as we shall see, far from the only attempt of Socrates to shock the uncritical reader into the awareness that the *Republic* too contains its excesses, which the reader must make it his task to ferret out.

It would be unwise to rule out Book 1 as an integral part of the *Republic,* unless there is strong evidence to the contrary. For it contains the byplay of the opening scene which, on other occasions, has provided us with important hints as to the main theme of the dialogue.

Socrates and Glaucon, one of the elder brothers of Plato, have attended a religious festival at the Piraeus, the seaport of Athens, and are about to return home. They are discovered by a group of young men, among them Adeimantus, Glaucon's brother, and Polemarchus, son of Cephalus, a rich merchant. Polemarchus urges Socrates and his companion to stay for the evening's festivities, and invites them all to his house for dinner, where, he says, they will find plenty of young men for a talk. He threatens playfully that if they refuse, he and his friends will use force. Socrates and Glaucon decide to yield.

City streets in a seaport town, religious celebration, friendly coercion, promise of entertainment, hospitality: all this suggests relation to the gods or the universe, to foreign countries, to the native city, to friends—a world in which the individual is the focal point. How far shall he yield to the pressure brought to bear upon him? How much resistance should he offer? A man may lose himself in the world about him; he may also become isolated, alienated. There lies danger of too much or too little in either direction.[5]

The religious festival, with its torchrace on horseback, and the dinner are completely forgotten, but the problem suggested in the opening scene remains. It is brought into sharper focus through Socrates' brief discussion with Cephalus. As death approaches, says the old merchant, a man is increasingly troubled by the question: Have I acted aright? The confrontation with the possibility of one's own death, as we have seen in the discussion of the *Phaedo*, is said to throw a man back upon his individual self.[6] The ambitions and goals, in which he was formerly able to seek self-forgetfulness, shrivel into insignificance; and death as an inescapable possibility is something he himself, all alone, must face. So the question of right conduct becomes an intensely personal problem: I, and I alone, am accountable for the life I lead. But this is too much responsibility for most people and Cephalus is no exception. He would seek refuge and solace in a rule: "Telling the truth and paying back anything we have received" (1.331). This, he says, is the greatest advantage wealth affords—that it allows a man to abide by such a rule. But Socrates wrecks the refuge with the simple question: "Suppose a friend who had lent us a weapon were to go mad and then ask for it back?" (1.331).

Some interpreters maintain that through this question Socrates has expressed the narrowness of the suggested rule and that the problem now is to broaden it or to seek one which is sufficiently comprehensive. But how comprehensive would a rule have to be? Breaking a trust and telling a lie are certainly wrong, as the rule maintains. But under given circumstances they may become the lesser of two evils. When would we be able to say that a given evil will never become the lesser evil and thereby the object of a responsible choice? Would we not have to be able to survey the whole history of man, both past and future? And if this is impossible, then the rule, although not without usefulness, loses its comforting reliability. The rule may tell that a given act is evil, but only the concrete situation makes manifest whether or not it is the greater or the lesser evil, and therefore the final decision is made not by the rule but by the individual. Socrates' simple question, therefore, has blocked the attempt to escape personal responsibility.

Cephalus is unable or unwilling, at this late hour, to let Socrates undermine his faith in the principle which has guided him through life. He leaves the room to attend to the sacrifice and bequeathes his share in the discussion to his son Polemarchus.

Unlike his father, whose rule seems to be based on experience, although an unexamined one, Polemarchus appeals to authority, the poet Simonides, according to whom justice means "to render every man his due" (1.332). Under the probing questions of Socrates, the rule receives a more and more precise formulation until justice is defined as "doing good to friends and harm to enemies" (1.332). This raises the question of the "sphere of action in which the just man will be the most competent to do good or harm" (1.332). In war, replies Polemarchus. But, remarks Socrates, while a ship's captain is most competent on a voyage and a physician in matters of health, the one is useless when we are on land and the other when we enjoy good health. Does it follow that the just man cannot be of help to us in times of peace? Yes he can, insists Polemarchus, namely in matters of business. But there we call in the experts of the various crafts, such as the carpenter and the shipwright, rather than the just man. So Polemarchus is forced to modify his suggestion that the just man is of use in business, by adding "when money is involved." Again, when we use money to buy and sell we appeal for help not to the just man but to the connoisseur. Polemarchus finally has to restrict the helpfulness of justice still further by saying that it comes into play when we want to deposit money for safekeeping. Socrates is now ready to draw the absurd conclusion:

> And in the same way, I suppose, if a pruning knife is to be used, or a shield, or a lyre, then a vine-dresser, or a soldier, or a musician will be of service; but justice is helpful only when these things are to be kept safe. In fact justice is never of any use in using things; it becomes useful when they are useless. And if that is so, justice can hardly be a thing of much value. (1.333)

The attempt to confine justice to a specific area has ended in an absurdity and therefore has failed.

Socrates now leads the reader toward the reason for this failure. He proceeds in a manner which we have had occasion to observe in several other dialogues. He commits an obvious fallacy in the argument. If we correct the fallacy and draw a few simple inferences we discover the reason for ourselves. The expert, says Socrates, always has a double skill: the boxer is skilled in dealing blows and skilled in warding them off, the physician can keep us from disease and produce it by stealth. Therefore the just man, who according to Polemarchus is good at keeping money safe, must also be good at stealing it. "So the just man," he concludes, "turns out to be a kind of thief" (1.333).

The fallacy responsible for the absurd conclusion is obvious. It is the failure to make a necessary distinction, namely between potentiality and actuality. The man who is good at safe-keeping need not *be* a thief; he must only be *capable of becoming* a thief, that is, in order to outwit the criminal he must possess the criminal's know-how.[7] The double skill which Socrates attributes to all experts is nothing but their *ability* to use or abuse their art. And by his paradoxical identification of the just man with the thief, he calls attention to the relationship between expertise and morality. The arts as such are neutral. But *every* expert in *every* field can be just or unjust in the practice of his art, that is, he can use it properly or improperly, for good or ill. And so it was not the fault of Socrates or Polemarchus that they could not find a "sphere of action" in which the just man is the most competent to do good to friends or harm to enemies. There really is no such sphere, for justice extends over the whole field of human activities. But the just man shares with the craftsman the *double skill,* the control over his activities. If he lacked this control, he would not be responsible for what he is doing and hence not act morally at all. And as the honest guard must be *capable* of acting like a thief, so the just man must be *capable* of acting unjustly. The just act and the unjust, if they are to be genuine, must therefore have as their source the free resolve of the individual will. It is this truth which, as we have seen, underlies the paradoxical claim of Socrates in the *Lesser Hippias* to the effect that the voluntary is better than the involuntary evildoer, for the former is at least *moral* while the latter is not. [8]

Polemarchus by this time is utterly confused. In desperation he brushes aside all that has been said and simply insists on his former statement. "All the same," he says, "I do still believe that justice consists in helping one's friends and harming one's enemies" (1.334). This provides Socrates with an opportunity to expose the weakness of the rule from another aspect. Before we can apply the rule we must first know how to separate friend from foe, and unless we discover another rule which distinguishes one from the other, we must rely on our own best judgment and thereby assume responsibility. Furthermore, the second half of the definition demands that we do harm to our enemies. Now to harm a being, Socrates maintains, is to make it "less perfect in its own special way" (1.334), and to harm human beings is to make them "worse men by the standard of human excellence" (1.334). And since justice is such an excellence, harming them would mean to make them less just. Polemarchus has agreed to all that Socrates has said, and so he must admit that according to his definition it would be the function of the just man to make men unjust. "So it was not a wise saying," Socrates concludes, "that justice is giving every man his due, if that means that harm is due from the just man to his enemies, as well as help to his friends. That is not true; because we have found that it is never right to harm anyone" (1.335).

It has been suggested that Polemarchus could have avoided defeat by denying that to harm a man is to make him worse. [9] For the Greek word *blaptein*, not unlike the English word *to harm*, may mean "to hurt" or "to make worse." Now to hurt a man, whether it be through fines or imprisonment or even by inflicting corporeal punishment, may in fact do him good. But if Socrates understood *blaptein* in the sense of "to make worse" then of course it cannot be denied that to harm is to make worse. But then Polemarchus might have asked why and how justice has this effect and what it means to make a man worse. Socrates avoids all these questions by using an ambiguous word which gives his statement the appearance of being self-evident without being tautological. Our conclusion then might be that Socrates won his point because his opponent failed to see through an ambiguity and we could characterize Polemarchus as somewhat obtuse and Socrates as intellectually dishonest.

When we take this attitude, however, we have inadvertently slipped from drama into history. We behave as if we were dealing with an actual conversation between two real people instead of a dramatic encounter between two characters who are the creations of the author.[10] It is hardly worth knowing that of two dramatic characters in a dialogue one is stupid and the other deceitful, unless we also find out why Plato made them appear as such, what purpose he thereby tried to accomplish. Perhaps the questions which the critics feel Polemarchus should have raised are questions which Plato meant to be asked and answered by the reader.

Now the remarkable thing about the present stage of the discussion is not that Socrates operates with an ambiguity which Polemarchus fails to recognize. What is startling is the fact that Socrates, after having directed all his efforts toward undermining the reliability of fixed standards in moral matters, should now come up with a general rule, albeit a negative one. So far norms of conduct proposed by others were subject to criticism by Socrates. Is it not reasonable to assume that the rule proposed by Socrates should not be accepted uncritically either; and since Polemarchus remains silent, the task of examining it falls upon the reader.

If the word *blaptein* were used in the sense of "to hurt," then, as indicated before, the rule would not stand up. But does it not appear unassailable if by *blaptein* we mean, as Socrates obviously does, "to make worse"? "By spoiling the character of one of my companions," Socrates says in the *Apology*, "I'll run the risk of getting some harm from him" (25E). And surely, one may add, it cannot be to my advantage to make even my enemies vicious.

In the argument leading up to the injunction that *it is never right to harm anyone*, Socrates has made the claim that "justice is a peculiarly human excellence" (1.334) and that to hurt a man or to make him worse is to destroy this excellence. Now we have seen in the previous argument that justice or any other virtue has, as its prerequisite, the capacity to act rightly or wrongly. One sure way of destroying the specifically human excellence, therefore, would be to rob an individual of that capacity, that is, to deprive him of his ability to choose freely. But how does one get at a man who, as Socrates says of himself in the *Apology*, does not "care a straw for death" and whom "the strong arm of an oppressive power cannot frighten into doing wrong" (32C–D, J). If even threats of physical destruction are of no avail, Socrates can rightly say that "nothing can injure me . . . for a bad man is not permitted to injure a better than himself" (30C–D, J). So even the negative rule has broken down, for it bids men to refrain from doing what cannot be done at all. But if the evil designs of the bad man cannot affect the genuinely good man, then it follows that the man who has become bad can lay the blame on no one but himself.

The defense of justice suggested by Polemarchus and his father involved activity directed toward the other: telling the truth, returning what belongs to another, doing good to friends and harm to enemies. Thrasymachus, the famous orator, who enters the discussion, reverses this direction. His problem is no longer, how can I be sure of doing what is proper with reference to the other? It is rather: how can I best serve myself provided I have the power to enforce my will? And so according to Thrasymachus, "just or right is nothing but what is in the interest of the stronger party" (1.338). The stronger are said to be those who rule, and whether they operate under a tyranny, an aristocracy, or a democracy, they make laws which are to their own advantage. For the subjects, therefore, to act justly is to obey these laws and thereby serve the interests of others. If they want to advance their own good, they can do so only by circumventing the law. To promote the welfare of others is just; to promote their own becomes unjust.

In his attack upon the rule, Socrates fastens upon the difficulty of determining one's own interests, as in the case of Polemarchus he made use of the absence of a criterion for distinguishing friend from foe. He elicits from his opponent two admissions: first, that the rulers sometimes are mistaken about their own best interests, and second, that it is right for the subjects to obey the laws laid down by the rulers. Now if, in any given case, the rulers are mistaken, they will make laws which are not in their best interests, and then the subjects will be acting unjustly no matter what they do. If they obey the laws, they will do what is not in the interest of the rulers; and if they refrain from doing what is not in the interest of the rulers, they will have to break the law.

Cleitophon tries to come to the defense of Thrasymachus by amending the definition: "He meant whatever the stronger *believes* to be in his own interest . . . is what the subjects must do" (1.345). Now while the rulers can be in error about their interests, they can hardly be mistaken about what they believe to be so, and this version of the definition would escape the dilemma. But as has been pointed out, "if the laws are bad for the subjects, the laws will lose all respectability if they are not at least good for the rulers."[11] Thrasymachus is therefore right in rejecting the helping hand of Cleitophon. Instead he tries to save his definition of justice by restricting the meaning of the word *ruler*. Just as the craftsman, viewed as the ideal embodiment of his craft, makes no mistakes, so the ruler, he says, as the ideal embodiment of the ruling art, is infallible.

In reply Socrates turns the separation of the craft from the craftsman against the view of Thrasymachus. He calls attention to the fact that the nature of craftsmanship always points away from the interests of the craftsman to the interests of those the craft serves. The physician as physician is concerned not with his own health but that of his patients; "the ship's captain, considered strictly as no mere sailor, but in command of the crew, will study and enjoin the interests of his subordinates, not his own" (1.343). And what holds true of craftsmanship also holds true of the art of government. "No ruler, in so far as he is acting as a ruler," he concludes, "will study or enjoin what is for his own interest. All that he says and does will be said and done with a view to what is good and proper for the subjects for whom he practices his art" (1.343).

It has been said that Socrates' argument is defective in as much as he merely cites a few favorable instances, namely crafts which are clearly altruistic, and then generalizes by induction to the proposition that all crafts are altruistic.[12] From this he is said to conclude by deduction that the rulers are exclusively concerned with the welfare of their subjects. Furthermore, his contention about the altruistic nature of the arts is said to look rather silly when the material on which it is exercised are animals or material things instead of human beings. Thrasymachus, in his defense against Socrates, would then be perfectly justified in overgeneralizing in his turn from a few typical counter-instances such as sheep-breeding, which is not so much interested in the welfare of the sheep as in fattening them up for the slaughterhouse.[13] Such criticism, however, tends to take the arguments out of context. Socrates is trying to show that the completely self-regarding attitude which Thrasymachus advocates is not possible. To this end he points to the nature of the arts and crafts. As he shows in more detail in the second book, their function is, through a division of labour, to provide more effectively for the various needs of the members of a social organization and thus help bring about a better life for all. If their needs were not intimately interrelated, the arts and crafts would have no reason for being. This is a truth that needs no demonstration. A few striking illustrations should suffice to recall it to memory.[14] Nor is the altruistic element lacking in those crafts which have animals or material things for their subjects. The shoemaker's craft aims at the best possible shoes and sheep-breeding at the fattest sheep or the sheep producing the most wool. But shoes and sheep are merely means, not ends in themselves. Ultimately, they are produced for the sake of human beings. They satisfy the needs, not primarily of the shoemaker and the sheep-breeder, but those of the rest of the population.[15] The fact that the crafts do not primarily supply the needs of their particular craftsman is further evidenced by his demand for wages. Through these the craftsman can obtain the products of the other crafts which cater to his needs. Socrates' argument, properly understood, thus points to the intricate interrelation of human needs and interests and thereby to the basic weakness in the definition of Thrasymachus, namely the sharp separation of one man's interest from those of his fellowmen. No man can afford completely to disregard the concerns of others, and immediate and direct self-interest is not a reliable criterion in human behavior. "In der Weltsein heisst Mitsein."

Thrasymachus, however, is unable or unwilling to see what Socrates points out to him. He has his eye fixed on a sheep-breeder who looks forward to keep the juiciest lamb chops for himself and the ruler who legislates strictly in his own interest. "The genuine ruler," he says, "regards his subjects exactly like sheep, and thinks of nothing else, night and day, but the good he can get out of them for himself" (1.343). In fact Thrasymachus's view differs from that of ordinary bad men who regard injustice as something disgraceful but are willing to sacrifice nobility and decency in order to gain an advantage. Thrasymachus has brought about a transvaluation of values, for he does not shrink from regarding injustice as an excellence, provided it is carried out on a grand scale and is not followed by any kind of punishment. Socrates therefore must undertake to discredit injustice as an excellence, and he does this by showing that it is not a source of either (a) wisdom, or (b) strength, or (c) happiness.

(a) *Wisdom*

A man engaged in tuning an instrument will try, as far as possible, to imitate the expert musician who aims at perfect attunement. He will want to do better than the man who is not a musician, but he would not try to outdo the musician. If he were to tighten the strings more than the expert would, his instrument would be out of tune. In interhuman relations, according to Socrates there also is a 'just right', at which the just man aims. The unjust, however, simply wants more, more than any other man, be he just or unjust. The object at which he aims is without limits and hence indefinable and therefore unintelligible. But if injustice has the unintelligible as its object, it cannot be the source of wisdom.

(b) *Strength*

Justice recognizes the rights and interests of others, injustice does not. The first helps to unite people, while the second is a divisive force. If people persistently disregard each other's interests, they hurt each other and become enemies. "Tell me," Socrates asks, "whether any set of men—a state or an army or a band of robbers or thieves—who were going to act for some unjust purpose would be likely to succeed, if they were always trying to injure one another" (1.351). If the unjust succeed in any enterprise, Socrates maintains, "they must have had some justice in them, enough to keep them for injuring one another. . . . Their injustice only partially incapacitates them for their career of wrongdoing; if perfect it would have disabled them for any action whatsoever" (1.352).

(c) *Happiness*

Socrates begins by establishing the principle that some things have a specific function and that the function of a thing is "the work which it alone can do, or can do better than anything else." (1.352) As illustrations he offers seeing for the eye, hearing for the ear, etc. Now the virtue or excellence of a thing consists in the excellent performance of its function. Interference with that function destroys the thing's excellence. Now as far as the human soul is concerned, Socrates mentions two functions: (1) living and (2) "such actions as deliberating or taking charge and exercising control" (1.352). Although Socrates does not explictly say so, it would seem obvious that in the case of man the two are inseparable. For a man it is not enough that he should live; to be truly human or a self he must try to make his life his own. To this end he must gain control over his bodily impulses and choose his own goals, unemcumbered by the pressure of bodily desires. Injustice, as we have seen, makes concerted effort impossible. "It will produce the same result in the individual," says Socrates, "because he will have a divided mind and be incapable of action, for lack of singleness of purpose" (1.351). But how can a man be called happy if he is frustrated in his endeavors and if he is alienated from his own self?

The discussion with Thrasymachus, like those with Polemarchus and Cephalus, ends in the typical inconclusiveness. And yet there is a positive element shining through. In his attack upon injustice, that is, in saying what it is not, or does not accomplish, Socrates gives some indication of what is involved in justice. He refers to the 'mean' between extremes as the aim of wisdom, while injustice recognizes no limits and goes to extremes; and he speaks of strength through cooperation, which injustice undermines. But both the 'mean' and cooperation occur in a situation presenting continually shifting patterns which defy prediction and make reliable rules of behavior impossible. But this very instability and uncertainty makes the assumption of personal responsibility unavoidable and thus gives significance to the performance of what Socrates calls the specifically human function, namely, that of "deliberating and exercising control" (1.352).

The two brothers, Glaucon and Adeimantus, do not share the views of Thrasymachus. Yet they feel he has yielded too readily and they propose to put up a stronger defense of injustice, not in order to convince anyone, but to provoke Socrates into offering more powerful arguments in favor of justice. Sages and poets, they point out, do not praise justice in itself but only its desirable consequences, such as high position and other advantages. These results, however, can be obtained also by one who merely appears just and is in reality unjust. And since it is generally held that the road to justice is steep and narrow, while injustice is easily attained, no man in his right mind would pursue justice if he could be assured of immunity from punishment. No man who, in possession of the Gyges ring, could make himself invisible would resist the temptation of taking unfair advantage of his fellowmen. Justice is said to be merely the result of a compromise. People soon discovered that the evil of suffering wrong outweighs the advantage of doing it; and so they made a compact, promising to act justly in order to avoid the evil of suffering injustice. On this view, justice is not a good in itself, as Socrates has earlier claimed, but "stands between the best thing of all—to do wrong with impunity—and the worst, which is to suffer wrong without the power to retaliate" (2.359). "So I want you, in commending justice," says one of the brothers, "to consider only how justice, in itself, benefits a man who has it in him, and how injustice harms him, leaving rewards and reputation out of account. . . . You must explain how one is good, the other evil, in virtue of the intrinsic effect each has on its possessor, whether gods or men see it or not" (2.366–67).

Socrates makes no attempt to comply directly with the request of the two brothers, but moves to a consideration of justice in the state. In fact, even before Adeimantus strengthens the position outlined by his brother, Socrates confesses that "so far as [he] is concerned, Glaucon has said quite enough to put him out of the running and leaves [him] powerless to rescue the cause of justice" (2.362).

What might be the reasons for Socrates' surrender or declaration of inability even before the case to be refuted has been fully stated? Have the brothers asked for the impossible? Does the request imply a conception of justice which is untenable?

Glaucon has stripped his just man of all advantages he might gain from his good reputation. In fact he has made him *appear* unjust and subjected to all the punishments which the unjust deserves. Socrates is asked to show that even under such extreme or perverse conditions, justice would be better for a man than injustice. He would, so to speak, light up justice as a quality possessed by the soul. Is it possible to conceive justice as such a quality?

As on other occasions, Socrates has dropped helpful hints even before the difficulty arose. When refuting Thrasymachus's unbridled selfishness, Socrates argued that injustice is a source neither of wisdom, nor strength, nor happiness. From this one can conclude that he regards justice, the opposite of injustice, as such a source. As the source of wisdom, it aims at the 'just right' or 'mean' in the concrete situation; as that of strength, it promotes cooperation between individuals. Justice thus functions only in the world and in conjunction with our fellow human being. What then is the effect which justice "in itself has upon its possessor when it dwells in his soul unseen of gods and men" (2.366)? The answer is suggested in Socrates' discussion of injustice as hindering and justice as promoting the specific function of the soul, namely, that of "deliberating or taking charge and exercising control" (1.352). Deliberation and exercising control are obviously beneficial, in as much as they make a man an authentic human being. But they cannot be called morally good, for they are the conditions for the possibility of performing moral acts. This, as we have seen, is the meaning of Socrates' paradoxical wish in the *Crito* "that the many could do the greatest evil, for then they could also do the greatest good" (44C–D). So the unjust man of Thrasymachus, who sets no limits to his greed but lets it run wild and unchecked, and therefore is "incapable of action, for lack of singleness of purpose and will be at enmity . . . with himself" (1.351), is not morally evil but incapable of any moral act, be it good or evil.

Justice, as it now emerges from the discussion, is not a quality of the soul such as the brothers ask Socrates to make manifest. It is rather an act of self-possession, a willingness to hold oneself open to whatever demand a given situation may make, and to assume responsibility for whatever actions one may decide upon. This willingness Heidegger calls resoluteness. "When resoluteness," he says, "is transparent to itself, it understands that the *indefiniteness* of one's potentiality-for-Being is made definite only in a resolution as regards the current situation" (p. 356). What the resolution will or ought to be cannot be expressed in terms of a general rule or idea. For the "situation cannot be calculated in advance" and the resolution, therefore, "must be *held open* and free for the current factical possibility" (p. 355). But if "resoluteness 'exists' only as a resolution" (p. 345) and the resolution in turn depends on the situation, then it is not possible to isolate or detach justice understood as resoluteness from the world and regard it as a quality of the 'soul'. This may be the reason why Socrates does not even try to answer Glaucon's question as to "what good . . . justice does to its possessor, taking it simply in itself" (2.366), and instead turns to the world in an attempt to reveal the function of justice as it manifests itself in social living.

Since we can speak of justice in relation to a community as well as to individuals, Socrates suggests that they try to discover it first in the state, where it is writ large, so to speak, and then "look for its counterpart on a smaller scale in the individual" (2.368). To this end he will build up an imaginary state from its most fundamental and simplest elements, hoping that in the process justice will somehow make itself manifest.

Socrates' imaginary state, unlike that of Thrasymachus and Glaucon, stresses not the selfishness of human nature, but the interdependence of men:

> My notion is that a state comes into existence because no individual is self-sufficient; we all have many needs. . . . And having these many needs, we call in one another's help to satisfy our various requirements; and when we have collected a number of helpers and associates to live together in one place, we call that settlement a state. (2.368–69)[16]

Nature has endowed different individuals with different capacities, and therefore the introduction of division of labor will make for greater efficiency:

> More things will be produced and the work be more easily and better done, when every man is set free from all other occupations to do, at the right time, the one thing for which he is naturally fitted. (2.370)

There will be farmers, builders, and weavers to provide for food, shelter and clothing, the most basic needs. Other craftsmen will have to be added, such as toolmakers of various sorts, together with shopkeepers and merchants who trade with foreign countries. "Where in all this will we find justice?" Socrates asks. In reply Adeimantus suggests that it might be "somewhere in their dealings with one another" (2.371).

What will be the relationship among the citizens of this newborn state? Socrates characterizes their lives as simple, healthy, and pleasant (2.372). Nothing is said about a form of government, about laws or a system of rewards and punishment to regulate their intercourse. Each member of the group simply seems to do that for which he is best fitted and spontaneously pursue both his own and the common good. There is not even a hint of conflict, as if nature herself had provided the right amount of diversity to bring about complete harmony among the activities necessary to satisfy the needs of all. A citizen in such a society could feel secure. But would it not be the security provided by the anthill or the beehive? The contribution which each individual makes is natural, ultimately attributable to nature rather than an individual's will. Would such a society still be human, that is, a society made up of individuals whose souls have the specific function of "deliberating or taking charge and exercising control," as Socrates claims in his debate with Thrasymachus? Such a society presupposes a measure of conflict. And when Glaucon complains that Socrates acts "as if he were founding a community of pigs" (2.372), he may or ought to have in mind more than the simple food which has been prescribed for the inhabitants of his city.

Socrates yields to the demands of Glaucon "to study the growth, not just of a state, but of a luxurious one" (2.372). This means a considerable expansion of the primitive state and many more services and functionaries must be added. And because the state or its neighbors may need to extend their territories, warriors will be required. In war, efficiency is of prime importance. "These guardians of our state," says Socrates, "in as much as their work is the most important of all, will need the most complete freedom from other occupations and the greatest amount of skill and practice" (2.374).

With the expansion of the state and the introduction of luxury, the natural harmonious interaction of the citizens which was present in the primitive state disappears and manmade safeguards against conflicts must be established in the more sophisticated society. This raises the problem of education, especially of the warrior class, on whose competence the life of the state depends.

During most of the rest of the dialogue, Socrates speaks of training which, when closely examined, aims not at justice but at efficiency and safety. The citizens are carefully conditioned so as to remain reliably obedient to their ruler, and the ruler is endowed with infallible knowledge, which enables him "to shape the pattern of public and private life into conformity with his vision of the ideal" (6.500). The state which emerges from the discussion not only falls short of the ideal of justice, but reduces all except the rulers themselves to a subhuman level, depriving them of their specifically human function of contributing significantly to the formation of their own lives. Thus, submission to the wisest and best intentioned rulers, just as the excessive adherence to a fixed rule of conduct, is found to be fatal to morality and hence to manhood. This broad outline of the interpretation of the *Republic* is meant to facilitate exposition. At this point, it could only be stated dogmatically; adequate substantiation, it is hoped, will be found in what follows.

The early training quite naturally consists in the main of a process of habituation. It starts with story telling, according to Socrates, and the stories must be carefully screened. For when children are young and tender, the "character is being moulded and easily takes the impress we may wish to stamp on it" (2.378). The ancient tales have to be purged of reports about crimes committed by the gods and their quarrels with each other. The divine nature should be represented as incapable of evil, and this image must be "indelibly fixed" (2.377) in the mind of the child, "if we mean our guardians to be godfearing and to reproduce the divine nature in themselves so far as men may" (2.382). The ancient heroes too, will serve as models to be imitated. Hence they must be cleansed of all unseemly behavior. "We shall do well," counsels Socrates, "to strike out descriptions of the heroes bewailing the dead, and make over such lamentations to women (and not to women of good standing either) and to men of low character, so that the guardians we are training for our country may disdain to imitate them" (2.387).

As long as Socrates speaks about early education, one can hardly quarrel with him. Young children usually develop good habits as easily as bad ones, and while they are too young to understand the reason for a particular mode of behavior, conditioning seems to be the only way. "And when reason comes," as Socrates says, "they will greet her as a friend with whom their education has made them long familiar" (2.401). Without warning, however, and with a deceptive casualness he extends the conditioning process from the young to the adult. He is still speaking about the young, who are to develop into brave warriors and who therefore must not be allowed to have their minds filled with images of the horrors of Hades. But then he suddenly remarks:

> We shall ask Homer and the poets in general not to mind if we cross out passages of this sort. If most people enjoy them as good poetry, that is all the more reason for keeping them from children *or grown men* who are to be free, fearing slavery more than death. (2.383) [Italics added]

Conditioning by means of an image is now reenforced by conditioning through action. The guardians are to be kept free from all demeaning labor, and even dramatic representation is pressed into the service of moulding character:

> Our guardians . . . if they act, should from childhood upward impersonate only the appropriate type of character, men who are brave, religious, self-controlled, generous. They are not to do anything mean or dishonorable; no more should they be practiced in representing such behavior, for fear of becoming infected with the reality. You must have noticed how the reproduction of another person's gestures or tones of voice or states of mind, if

persisted in from youth up, grows into a habit which becomes second nature. (3.395)

The dramatic arts will be seriously mangled in the service of education, and Socrates readily admits such loss. When a great and versatile performer comes to town, he says, we shall "bow down before a being with such miraculous powers of giving pleasure; but we shall tell him that we are not allowed to have such a person in our commonwealth; we shall crown him with fillets of wool, anoint his head with myrrh, and conduct him to the borders of some other country. For our own benefit, we shall employ the poets and story-tellers of the more austere and less attractive type, who will reproduce only the manner of a person of high character and, in the substance of their discourse, conform to those rules we laid down when we began the education of our warriors" (3.397).

Finally, music is called upon to induce the appropriate emotions. Of the current modes only two will be retained: "the two which will best express the accent of courage in the face of stern necessity and misfortune, and of temperance in prosperity won by peaceful pursuits" (3.399). And in similar fashion we must discover, he says, "the rhythms appropriate to a life of courage and self-control" (3.400).

It is obvious that some of the best of Greek art which has survived the ages, namely, the Greek tragedies, would have to be excluded from the city of the philosopher-kings. Their heroes, as Aristotle points out, are all possessed of a tragic flaw and therefore not suitable objects for imitation. One wonders how the conception of a commonwealth which deprives its citizens of the richest fruits of its culture could ever have been regarded as an ideal.

Perhaps it is noteworthy that the *Theory of Ideas*, which is generally held to be a doctrine seriously advocated by Plato, fits into this conditioning process so as almost to appear as an outcome of it. The Guardians are habituated to look to models in their behavior. And so in making judgments, be they moral or otherwise, they look not to the changing world in which they live and consider the possible consequences of their contemplated actions, but to a realm of immutable ideals or forms:

> We and these Guardians we are trying to bring up will never be fully cultivated until we can recognize the essential Forms of temperance, courage, liberality, high-mindedness, and all other kindred qualities, and also their opposites, wherever they occur. We must be able to discern the presence of these Forms themselves and also of their images in anything that contains them. (3.402)

There is a strange contrast between the way the rulers are selected from the larger group of prospective Guardians and their treatment after the training period is over and they have taken office. These young men, says Socrates, will be placed into terrifying situations to see whether they stand fast; they must be exposed to intense pleasures to try their ability to resist temptation. Only those who have come through these trials unscathed will be chosen as rulers, as the true Guardians. The rest, he says, "will be better described as Auxiliaries, who will enforce the decisions of the Rulers" (3.414). But having been "put to severer proof than gold tried in the furnace" (3.414) and thus given evidence of great strength of character, why should they, after their education is complete, have to be protected so carefully against possible corruption? "None of them," decrees Socrates, "must possess any private property beyond the barest necessaries . . . They alone of all the citizens are forbidden to touch and handle silver or gold. . . . For if ever they should come to possess land or their own houses and money, they will give up their guardianship for the management of their farms and households and become tenants at enmity with their fellow citizens instead of allies" (4.419). Is this a confusion on the part of the author of the dialogue or is it his way of calling attention to the difference between genuine education, which aims at inner strength and adaptability, and habituation, which produces a dangerous rigidity. As if to underscore the brittleness of a social organization which rests on conditioning, Socrates forbids "the least infraction of the rule against any innovation upon the established system of education either of the body or of the mind" (4.424). The individual is presented as completely helpless in the face of external forces, for he presumably responds with equal indifference to the good and the bad, and thus contributes in complete innocence to the establishment of a good or a bad society:

> Little by little the lawless spirit gains a lodgement and spreads imperceptibly to manners and pursuits; and from thence with gathering force invades men's dealings with one another, and next goes on to attack the laws and the constitution with wanton recklessness, until it ends by overthrowing the whole structure of public and private life. (4.424)

Much less disguised appeals to the reader's critical intelligence immediately follow, urging him not to be swept away by Socrates' seeming eagerness to construct the ideal community. They are contained in the discussion of the four virtues. The state has been established and is ready for inspection. As planned, Socrates now attempts to locate the various virtues.

WISDOM first comes into view. It is identified with the knowledge which "takes thought not for some particular interest, but for the best possible conduct of the state as a whole in its internal and external relations" (4.427). In accordance with the principle of the division of functions, it must be restricted to the Guardians.

COURAGE is the exclusive property of the Auxiliaries. Its description marks it unmistakably as the outcome of a rigorous conditioning process. For a state to be brave, says Socrates, "will mean that, in this part, it possesses the power of preserving, in all circumstances, a conviction about the sort of things that it is right to be afraid of—the conviction implanted by the education which the law-giver has established" (4.429). This is not the kind of courage which springs from a reflection unruffled by the presence of danger. The very metaphors which Socrates uses suggest that it is a practically spontaneous reaction to a certain type of situation. As wool is dyed so that it gets a fast color which no washing will rob of its brilliance, so "convictions of what ought to be feared . . . must be indelibly fixed" in the minds of the soldiers (4.429). This unthinking courage makes it evident how exclusively wisdom has been assigned to the rulers. The second class in the state is already so completely under the domination of the rulers that its members can hardly be regarded as genuinely human. Small wonder that Socrates finds it unnecessary to mention the third class, the farmers, merchants, craftsmen, etc. It is one thing to entrust the most intelligent members of the community with the highest matters concerning the state; it is quite another to deny any kind of wisdom to all the others.

TEMPERANCE, according to Socrates, differs in one respect radically from the other two virtues. While they are confined each to a specific class, temperance is said to "extend throughout the whole gamut of the state" (4.437). It is defined as "the unanimity or harmonious agreement between the naturally superior and inferior elements on the question which of the two should govern" (4.431). Consent of the governed as a necessary ingredient of the state was already recognized by Sophocles when in the *Antigone* he has Haemon reproach his father with the words: "This is no state which hangs on one man's will."

JUSTICE now emerges as the principle complementary to temperance. A genuine whole is a union of diverse parts. And if common consent binds individuals together, justice differentiates them by assigning different functions. "We have laid it down, as a universal principle," says Socrates, "that every-one ought to perform the one function in the community for which his nature best suits him. Well, I believe that that principle, or some form of it, is justice" (4.432). Needless to say, justice, like temperance, permeates the entire state.

We now have two types of virtues: wisdom and courage which are characteristic each of a specific class of citizens; temperance and justice, which are common to all. Since the latter constitute the principles of union and differentiation, it is obvious that they concern every individual in the state. Is it just as obvious, however, that wisdom and courage do not?

Courage, it was said, belongs only to the Auxiliaries. Does this mean that the Guardians do not possess courage? Paradoxically we must answer yes, if with Socrates we define courage as the soldier's fidelity to "the conviction, implanted by education which the law-giver has established . . . about the sort of things which may rightly be feared" (4.429). The courage of the Guardians, by contrast, is not based on a belief implanted in their minds by others. It is rooted in a reflection on what is or is not a risk worthy of being taken in a given situation. The courageous act of the Guardians springs from their own decision as a result of their own insight. It is an act for which they are accountable. The Auxiliaries, however, are merely vehicles of habits instilled by the rulers. Their acts are not authentic, that is, not genuinely their own, and hence not really moral at all. So it seems that if wisdom is separated from courage, courage ceases to be a *moral* excellence.[17]

A similar difference can be observed between the temperance of the Guardians and that of the rest of the population. The former, since they are in possession of wisdom, recognize themselves as superior and the rest of the population as inferior. Obviously, their consent as to who should rule and who should obey is based on insight. But on what basis do the others give their consent? Self-recognition, especially of one's own inferiority, is not easily achieved. And how are the inferior supposed to gain it if they lack wisdom altogether? Are they, like the soldiers, merely habituated? Then again their consent is not authentic and their temperance not a moral excellence. Obviously, the same questions can be raised about justice, since it requires recognition of and a willingness to perform the function for which each is best suited.

Socrates' proposal of the radical separation of wisdom from the other virtues has, therefore, led to consequences which show that such separation is really not possible. All members of the state must possess some degree of wisdom, or they cannot be considered as moral at all. The most gifted, no doubt, should devote their energies to "the best possible conduct of the state as a whole" (4.427), but to some extent this must remain the concern of all, at least as long as we conceive the state as a community of moral beings.

Whenever we go beyond an author's express statements and consider their implications, there is risk of misinterpretation. It is therefore encouraging to observe that in passing from the virtues in the state to those in the individual, Socrates himself issues a warning against the uncritical acceptance of his analysis of the virtues in the state. "We must not be too positive yet," he says, "for if we find that justice in the individual is something different, we must go back to the state and test our result" (4.434). In fact, he urges us to do with the virtues of the state as against those of the individual, what we have already done with the first pair of virtues as against the second, namely expose the flaw in the one by means of the other. "Perhaps," he suggests, "if we brought the two cases into conflict like steel and flint, we might strike out between them the spark of justice, and in its light confirm the conception in our minds" (4.434).

Before this confrontation between the two types of virtue can be brought about, Socrates must discover in the individual human being virtues which correspond to those in the state. With this end in view he conceives the individual as analogous to the state inasmuch as both are made up of heterogeneous elements which stand in need of reconciliation. As there are individuals with widely varying ambitions and capacities in the state, so there are different and often conflicting desires in the individual. It is the function of reason to bring order into this initial disorder, as the Guardians are responsible for the smooth and efficient cooperation of the various classes in the state. Socrates distinguishes between two factors on the level of the emotions. There is the blind craving, such as the desire for food or drink regardless of consequences. There is also a passionate or spirited element which makes itself felt in anger and indignation when the craving is too persistent or when reason is inclined to yield in situations where it should not. This spirited element can therefore be regarded as an ally of reason, which supports its decisions, as the Auxiliaries were said to carry out the commands of the rulers of the state. Corresponding to his conception of an ideal state, Socrates now renders a picture of a richly endowed and harmoniously developed human being who has taken full possession of himself:

> It will be the business of reason to rule with wisdom and forethought on behalf of the entire soul; while the spirited element ought to act as its subordinate and ally. The two will be brought into accord, as we said earlier, by that combination of mental and bodily training which will tune up one string of the instrument and relax the other, nourishing the reasoning part on the study of noble literature and allaying the other's wildness by harmony and rhythm. When both have been thus nurtured and trained to know their own true functions, they must be set in command over the appetites, which form the greater part of each man's soul and are by nature insatiably covetous. They must keep watch lest this part, by battening on the pleasures that are called bodily, should grow so great and powerful that it will no longer keep to its own work, but will try to enslave the others and usurp a dominion to which it has no right, thus turning the whole of life upside down. At the same time, those two together will be the best of guardians for the entire soul and for the body against all enemies from without: the one will take counsel, while the other will do battle, following its ruler's commands and by its own bravery giving effect to the ruler's designs. (4.441)

Let us now follow Socrates' advice and bring these two conceptions of virtue, that of the state and that of the individual, "into contact like flint and steel" (4.434). The clash will be violent indeed. The authentic person which Socrates has portrayed so effectively, when placed into the ideal state, would have to disown himself. For his reason must be surrendered to that of the rulers. If he qualifies as an Auxiliary, he will be allowed to support rational decisions; but they will not be of his own making. If he does not qualify, then he will be reduced to the status of the "inferior multitude whose desires will be controlled by the desires and wisdom of the superior few" (4.431). If, however, he should be allowed to maintain his integrity, if he should be received into the elite of the rulers, then his function, strangely enough, will not be to raise the subjects, as far as possible, to the level of genuine human beings, but to reduce them to dehumanized puppets which will be at his beck and call.[18] Even the Guardians must avoid emotions which tend to strengthen their sense of individuality. Strong family ties must not be allowed to develop, and therefore "no one man and one woman are to set up house together privately: wives are to be held in common by all; so too are the children, and no parent is to know his own child, nor any child his parent" (5.457). In the case of the subjects, however, insult is added to injury. They are told that the choice of a partner in marriage must be left to chance, when in reality the rulers manipulate the proceedings so that "as many unions as possible of the best of both sexes are brought about, and as few of the inferior as possible" (5.459).

What could induce the members of a community, the reader might ask, to give their consent to a form of government which robs them of their integrity as human beings? What advantage could offset such a sacrifice? It might be argued that in the state under discussion the subjects have been trained since childhood to submit to their rulers. Consent need not necessarily be free in the strict sense; it might be the result of a firmly established habit. But Plato, whatever his real views, makes it appear as if such a state had a great attraction for the young men listening to Socrates. "No doubt," says Galucon, "if our commonwealth did exist, all manner of good things would come about. . . . All we have now to do is to convince ourselves that it can be brought into existence and how" (5.471).[19]

The reason for this eagerness to establish the city which they have constructed in discourse, is suggested in Socrates' explanation why philosophers are not playing the role in their community they might be expected to play. He compares the state to a ship whose master knows nothing about navigation. He is besieged by members of his crew, who are equally ignorant, to entrust them with the helm. Sometimes, when others succeed in persuading the master, they kill them or throw them overboard. If they manage to gain control of the ship, "they make free with its stores, and turn the voyage, as might be expected of such a crew, into a drunken carousal" (6.488).

In such a state, education is held in very low esteem. The populace, at huge public gatherings, shouts its approval or disapproval, declaring as good what it likes and evil what it dislikes. Young men of great promise soon discover where the real power lies. They flock to the sophists who teach them how to manipulate the moods of the crowd, how to arouse it to anger and how to soothe it, thus learning to exploit it for their own selfish interests without regard to the welfare of the state.

The decent elements in the community become filled with anxiety as they watch "the frenzy of the multitude and see there is no soundness in the conduct of public life" (6.496). Education of the citizenry in general seems a hopeless task; "it would be great folly even to try . . . for the multitude can never be philosophical" (6.492–93); and the few gifted among the young cannot be expected to resist the powerful corrupting influence to which they are exposed.

In this mood of despair, many a good citizen is seized by a yearning for a great leader, one who can be trusted and who in his superior wisdom would know how to bring order into the existing chaos, and thus lift from the shoulders of his followers the burden of an irritating and frustrating sense of responsibility.[20]

It is in response to such a need that Socrates makes his famous proposal:

> Unless either philosophers become kings in their countries or those who are now called kings and rulers come to be sufficiently inspired with a genuine desire for wisdom; unless, that is to say, political power and philosophy meet together, while the many natures who now go their several ways in the one or the other direction are forcibly debarred from doing so, there can be no rest from troubles for states, nor yet for all mankind. (5.473)

At first the young men are shocked, and if they hanker after security their dismay is not unjustified. For if by philosophers we mean the sophists, then we must admit that they are either worthless or exert a corrupting influence; and if we think of Socrates as the paragon, then we know that they are the least qualified to give us the desired relief. For through their critical attitude they tend to undermine whatever sense of security a man may enjoy. And they lay no claim to infallible knowledge, much less to a panacea for the ills of society.

Under the pretense of defining the philosopher, Socrates seemingly tries to allay their fears by transforming the philosopher from a seeker after wisdom into one who is in possession of the truth.[21] This transformation in turn makes it necessary to convert the tentative hypotheses which result from the second-best method, as described in the *Phaedo*, into insight into essences. Furthermore, he must replace the changeable realities of human experience as objects of knowledge, by the eternal, immutable forms. And finally he has to attribute to the philosopher the ability to gain access to the *Idea of the Good*, the supreme principle of intelligibility and being. Only in a world of fully constituted realities, made transparently knowable by an ultimate principle of intelligibility, is infallible knowledge possible, and only if they possess such knowledge are philosopher-kings qualified to perform the function they are meant to perform.[22]

This bare enumeration of the results of the discussion which Socrates now undertakes and which extends over several books of the *Republic*, should arouse the suspicion that we are dealing here not with a conviction of either Socrates or Plato, but with an exercise of Socratic irony. Before the philosophers can take control so that "the state and individuals will have rest from trouble" (6.500), they must first be transhumanized and acquire an unearthly wisdom, which in turn would make them fit only to rule over an ideal realm and not the transient situations of the world which we inhabit. So far from describing how the ideal city can come about, Socrates seems to call attention to the impossible conditions which would have to be satisfied, and thus warn the individual that he can never hope to escape personal responsibility for his own welfare or for that of the state.

Outlining the knowledge which would be appropriate for philosopher-kings, Socrates starts with ordinary experience which reveals two components in the knowing process, namely things or events, and ideas in terms of which they are understood:

> Since beauty and ugliness are opposite, they are two things; and consequently each of them is one. The same thing holds of justice and injustice, good and bad, and all the essential Forms: each in itself is one; but they manifest themselves in a great variety of combinations, with actions, with material things, and with one another, and so each of them seems to be many. (5.476)

Now all men make use of ideas of some sort or other; otherwise they could not understand anything at all. Those of the philosophers may be more carefully worked out, and therefore clearer and more precise. But at best they too are mere approximations of what things really are. Socrates, however, pictures the non-philosopher as devoid of all ideas, and the philosopher as in the possession of the truth of things.[23] The philosopher, he says, "can discern the essence as well as the things that partake of its character," while the other is in a dream, for "he mistakes the semblance for the reality it resembles" (5.476). He acknowledges the experience of things, but denies the ideas on which they depend for their intelligibility.[24]

Knowledge, of course, depends on its objects. "Only the perfectly real," says Socrates, "is perfectly knowable" (5.476). And he draws a sharp distinction between realities which are "for ever in the same unchanging state" (5.480) and those which are not. The former alone serve as objects of knowledge as he understands it. The objects found in ordinary experience do not qualify. "Be so good as to tell me," asks Socrates, "whether of all these beautiful things there is one which will not appear ugly? Or of these many just or righteous actions, is there one that will not appear unjust or unrighteous?" (5.478). These are the objects of *doxa*. If we accept the customary translation of doxa as "opinion" or "belief," then we must keep in mind that while opinion and belief can become knowledge as we gather sufficient evidence, *doxa* can not. For the uncertainty of *doxa* is caused by the instability of its objects. Those who concern themselves with these changing realities are "adrift in a sort of twilight between pure reality and pure unreality" (5.479); they are "lost in the mazes of multiplicity and change" (5.484). The philosophers, by contrast, "are those who can apprehend the eternal and unchanging" (6.484). They are in possession of ideal standards, and this is why "knowledge and belief are not the same . . . for there would be no sense in identifying the infallible with the fallible" (5.477).

How will these Guardians, with their fixed standards, rule the state and educate the citizens by developing their capacities and drawing out what is best in them? This is how Socrates describes the process:

> These Guardians must . . . have in their soul . . . a clear pattern of perfect truth, which they might study in every detail and constantly refer to, as a painter looks to his model, before they proceed to embody notions of justice, honour, and goodness in earthly institutions . . . (6.484) He will mould other characters besides his own and shape the pattern of public and private life into conformity with his vision of the ideal. (6.500)

The individual seems to play no part in the formation of his character. For what we are witnessing here resembles more an act of creation than an educative process. This becomes even more evident in the following:

> He will take society and human character as his canvas, and begin by scraping it clean. That is no easy matter; but as you know, unlike other reformers, he will not consent to take in hand either an individual or a state or to draft laws, until he is given a clean surface to work on or has cleansed it himself. . . . He will reproduce the complexion of true humanity, guided by the divine pattern. He will rub out and paint in again this or that feature, until he has produced, so far as may be, a type of character that heaven can approve. (6.500)

This godlike activity of the Guardians removes them from the human situation and simultaneously condemns the subjects to the level of the subhuman.[25]

The infallible knowledge which the Guardians must possess to justify their rule has so far been identified with insight into the essences or forms of the various virtues. It requires little reflection, however, to realize that these forms by themselves alone are not sufficient. Devotion to a cause may be sincere and the cause itself appear deserving of the sacrifices which are brought in its name. But goals judged worthwhile at one time often turn sour as unforeseen consequences work themselves out in later years. So unless the Guardians are familiar with an ultimate goal toward which all humanity can be made to strive and which at the same time constitutes the goal of the whole universe, they cannot render infallible judgments. For they cannot be certain whether their deepest devotions are not placed in the service of an ultimately worthless and perhaps even evil cause. The aspiring Guardian, therefore, must be tested not only "by hardship and danger and by the temptation of pleasure; his strength must also be tried in many forms of study to see whether he has the courage and endurance to pursue the *highest kind of knowledge*, without flinching as others flinch under physical trials" (6.502–3).

The young men express surprise. "Are not justice," they ask, "and the other virtues we have discussed the highest? Is there something still higher to be known?" "There is," replies Socrates, "and of these virtues themselves we have as yet only a rough outline" (6.503).

When pressed to reveal this "highest kind of knowledge" Socrates speaks, not as if he were introducing them to a great secret, but as if he merely had to recall to their minds something with which they were only too well familiar:

> You have often been told that the highest object of knowledge is the *essential nature of the Good,* from which everything that is good and right derives its value for us. You must have been expecting me to speak of this now, and to add that *we have no sufficient knowledge of it.* I need not tell you that, *without that knowledge,* to know *everything else,* however well, would be of *no value to us,* just as it is of no use to possess anything without getting the good of it. What advantage can there be in possessing everything except the good, or in understanding everything else while of the good and desirable we know nothing. (6.504) [Italic added]

That from which "everything that is good and right derives its value for us" is evidently the ultimate goal of human aspirations and therefore the absolute standard of judgment. And what could be further removed from what we really know? And yet there is a sense in which it can be said to be most familiar to us, not in itself but in its effects. For it manifests itself in the anxiety which springs from our awareness of its remoteness, and the desperate need we feel for it. Must we not all admit that unless there is some ultimate purpose toward which our various chosen goals converge, all our efforts in the end are doomed to frustration? So if the philosopher-kings are to cure us of our insecurity and eliminate the risks which our own judgments always involve, they must perceive with clarity where we see "as through a glass darkly":

> A thing, then, that every soul pursues as the end of all her actions, dimly divining its existence, but perplexed and unable to grasp its nature, with the same clearness and assurance as in dealing with other things, and so missing whatever value those other things might have—a thing of such supreme importance is not a matter about which those chosen Guardians of the whole fortunes of our commonwealth can be left in the dark. (6.505)

Socrates is obviously right when he remarks that our commonwealth will not be "perfectly regulated unless it is watched over by a Guardian who does possess this knowledge" (6.505).

Socrates' friends urge him to make more explicit what he means by this supreme good which is the object of the highest knowledge and which the Guardians must discover before they can properly exercise their function. Socrates, understandably, expresses great hesitations. "I am afraid it is beyond my power," he says, "and with the best will in the world I would only disgrace myself and be laughed at" (6.506). Finally he agrees to speak about it indirectly.

In this indirect approach to the *Idea of the Good* four phases can be distinguished, each of which stresses a different aspect while implying all the others. One is based on simple analogy, another on analogy of proportionality, the third and least explicit on a process of extrapolation, and the last takes the form of an allegory.

As on a previous occasion, when introducing the distinction between knowledge and *doxa*, Socrates begins by referring his listeners to two aspects of the knowing process, namely things or events and ideas in terms of which they are understood:

> Let me remind you of the distinction we drew earlier and have often drawn on other occasions, between the multiplicity of things we call good or beautiful, or whatever it may be and, on the other hand, Goodness itself or Beauty itself and so on. Corresponding to each of these sets of many things, we postulate a single Form or real essence, as we call it. (6.506–7)

Next he describes sight. "You may have the power of vision in your eyes" he says, "and try to use it, and colour may be in the objects; but sight will see nothing and the colours will remain invisible in the absence . . . of light" (6.507). Now the ultimate source of light is the sun. "The Sun," he says, "is not vision but the cause of vision, and also is seen by the vision it causes" (6.507–8). Thus we have two processes, seeing and knowing, of which the former is the better and the latter the less well known. Three factors in one correspond to three factors in the other: What a being endowed with sight, visible objects, and light are to seeing, a being endowed with intelligence, intelligible objects, and ideas are to understanding. In the case of seeing, the better known process, there is in addition an ultimate source of light, namely the sun, which is also visible. If the analogy between the two processes is genuine, then it should hold even with reference to factors observed only in the better known process, that is, there ought to be an ultimate source of intelligibility, the *Idea of the Good*, corresponding to the ultimate source of light, the sun:

> It was the Sun that I meant when I spoke of that offspring which the Good has created in the visible world, to stand there in the same relation to vision and visible things as that which the Good bears in the intelligible world to intelligence and intelligible objects. (6.508)

In knowing, therefore, things are conceived as manifesting themselves to the understanding when irradiated by ideas and ultimately by the *Idea of the Good*, as things become visible to the eye in the presence of light, which ultimately originates in the sun.

This reasoning by analogy does not, of course, demonstrate the existence of the *Idea of the Good,* nor does it reveal anything definite about its nature. It merely suggests it as a possibility. Even if seeing and knowing can be regarded as similar, they must also have differences; otherwise they would be identical, which they clearly are not. One of these differences might well be that the ultimate source of light in seeing has no counterpart in knowing. In any event, it is not discovered in experience. And this raises the question of how it can in any meaningful sense be spoken of, even as a possibility.

The analogy of proportionality serves to solve this paradox. It shows how a man can in fact reach beyond his experience and reach out for a sheer possibility. It accomplishes this by establishing a relationship between a higher and a lower reality, both of which are known. In the *Phaedo* myth, for instance, Socrates relates the wider experience of a man to the obviously more restricted experience of a frog at the bottom of a pond. What man's experience is to that of a frog, a possibly wider experience than man's would be to man's experience: $M/F = X/M$. Again X is established merely as a possibility. Now when Socrates divides reality as one might divide and subdivide a line, he once more operates with analogy of proportionality, although of a more complex type. He extends the levels of reality from two to four. Beginning with the original division into the visible and the intelligible, he divides each section again: the visible into things and their reflections or shadows; the intelligible into ideas or forms and the *Idea of the Good.* Just as shadows are dependent on things both for their being and their intelligibility, so things are said to be dependent on ideas, and ideas in turn on the *Idea of the Good:* $T/S = F/T = G/F$. Again G or the *Idea of the Good* emerges as a sheer possibility.

Extrapolation, the third approach, attempts to anchor the *Idea of the Good* in human experience, so that, although transcendent in nature, it can be said to be empirical in origin. The process in question is not explicitly carried through in the dialogue, but it is set in motion and can easily be brought to a conclusion. Twice, as we have seen, Socrates calls attention to the fact that "corresponding to each . . . set of many things, we postulate a single Form or essence" (6.507). From this it appears that brute facts are transformed into reasoned facts by being shown to follow from or constitute instances of one and the same idea. Thus elements on one level of experience are explained through elements on a higher level. But when Socrates says that of the Forms "we have as yet only a rough outline" (5.503), he suggests that these Forms constitute a plurality of facts on a higher level, and that these facts must look to a still higher realm for their principle of explanation. And no matter how few or how many levels we may suppose to exist, unless there is an ultimate level, a supreme idea or principle, there is no possibility for genuine knowledge in the strict sense of the term.

Thus the movement of human inquiry, which aims at more and more comprehensive principles of explanation, if allowed to reach its consummation, ought to arrive at some such principle as Socrates' *Idea of the Good*.

What practical benefits can be derived from a sheer possibility which transcends experience, even if it has empirical roots? The answer to this question is supplied by the *Allegory of the Cave*.—The prisoners, chained neck and leg so that they cannot move about, see only the moving shadows which through the fire behind are cast upon the wall in front of them. And since their experience is restricted to shadows, they mistake them for genuine realities. Some of the prisoners are released from their chains and allowed to dwell outside where concrete things are seen in the light of the sun. When they return to the cave, they for the first time recognize the shadows as shadows. And what formerly passed for wisdom is now revealed as of far lesser value:

> They may have had a practice of honouring and commending one another, with prizes for the man who had the keenest eye for the passing shadows and the best memory for the order in which they followed one another, so that he could make a good guess as to which was going to come next. Would our released prisoner be likely to covet those prizes or to envy the men exalted to honour and power in the Cave? Would he not . . . endure anything rather than go back to his old beliefs and live in the old way? (7.516)

Perhaps it can be said that the imaginative descent into the cave, that is, the movement from a wider to a more limited experience, produces the same effect as the ascent to a transcendent, that is, to a possible richer experience. For both movements bring into sharper focus something which before was only vaguely seen. This can be shown through a closer look at the division of the intelligible world according to the *Line*. The lower part of this section is occupied by a kind of knowledge which is not grounded. Socrates uses mathematics to illustrate the point. The mathematician, he says, starts with unproved postulates and then proceeds by deduction to a set of conclusions. Even if these conclusions logically follow from the postulates, they cannot be said to be necessarily true: "Because the mathematicians start from assumptions without going back to first principle, you do not regard them as gaining true understanding about those objects, although the objects themselves, when connected with first principle, are intelligible" (6.511). Until mathematics is grounded in the first principle, the truth of its conclusions has not been established, and this principle still remains to be discovered. It may even be of such a nature that it cannot be discovered at all. Thus even mathematics, the most precise and, for the Greeks, the most developed of all sciences is still unfinished and its results do not constitute absolutely reliable truths. And so the thought of the mere possibility of an ideal science, that is, one which is based on first principle, has called attention to the imperfection of the most advanced science, and in this manner has made us more keenly aware of the extent of our ignorance.

Let us now yield to the promptings of Socrates in the *Allegory of the Cave* and the *Line* and see whether the outward movement of our thought toward the *Idea of the Good* should not also be followed by a return to the theme at hand, namely, the training of the philosopher-kings and their acquisition of the "highest knowledge." The return of the prisoners to the cave unmasked seeming realities as mere shadows, and in the light of the perfect although unrealized science, the most advanced of the actual sciences appeared greatly defective. What will be the complexion of the task of establishing the perfect common-wealth when it is viewed in the light of the *Idea of the God?*

Scientific inquiry as actually practiced and more or less as described by Socrates in the *Phaedo* proceeds by way of hypotheses which basically are guesses as to what the structure of things might be. These hypotheses are judged by the amount of order and consistency they introduce into the universe and the measure of control they afford. It is obvious that two different hypotheses might be equally successful, although neither has a secure claim to truth. Perfect knowledge, on the other hand, would have to seize the actual structure of things, and the supreme principle would have to be identical with the structure of the very ground of the universe:

> The Sun not only makes the things we see visible, but also brings them into existence and gives them growth and nourishment; yet he is not the same as existence. And so with the objects of knowledge: these derive from the Good not only their power of being known, but their very being and reality; and Goodness is not the same as being, but even beyond being, surpassing it in dignity and power. (6.508)

While we cannot be certain whether we have gained access to the nature of a single thing, the philosopher-kings, before they can lay claim to perfect knowledge, must succeed in going beyond reality and penetrate to the very ground of being. The abyss which separates ordinary human knowledge from that required for the establishment of the perfect city must now appear well-nigh unbridgeable.[26]

If, however, we are willing to follow Socrates' lead, we can take one more step forward. As we have seen, human knowing always understands the lower in terms of the higher, and extrapolation has shown that if the world is radically intelligible and if perfect knowledge lies within the realm of possibilities, then there must be an ultimate principle of intelligibility in terms of which all there is can be understood. But how is this ultimate principle itself to be understood? The attempt to turn to a still higher principle, even if successful, would not solve the problem but merely create it anew. And so the ultimate principle of intelligibility, although it is the cause of all knowing and knowability, must, at least for the human mode of knowing, remain unintelligible:

> The Form or essential nature of Goodness . . . is the cause of knowledge and truth; and so . . . you will do well to regard it as something beyond truth and knowledge. (6.508)

And so the last ray of hope that men in possession of infallible knowledge will ever govern the city, and that there will ever be rest from trouble both for individuals and for the state, has now definitely been extinguished. Under the pretext of showing how the ideal city can come into being, Socrates has really exposed the impossibility of the conditions which would have to be satisfied prior to its realization.[27] And if we are alert to the hints and suggestions which Socrates offers in the dialogue, we cannot agree with those who see in the reflections on the *Idea of the Good* the manifestation of a dogmatism which Plato, forgetful of the true liberal spirit of Socrates, puts illegitimately into the mouth of his master. For they now appear rather as a more sophisticated expression of the same liberalism which animates the early dialogues.

As if fearful that the desire to find security in a perfect social organization might have blunted the critical ability of his readers, Plato has Socrates launch a more obvious and less subtle attack against the possibility of surrendering one's personal and civic responsibilities. Socrates assumes that the impossible has become possible and that the philosopher-king with his infallible knowledge is in power. This is how the ideal ruler will go to work:

> He will take society and human character as his canvas, and begin by scraping it clean. . . . (6.500)[28]

The philosopher-king has set his sight on the ultimate goal or purpose of the universe and in its light all past achievements of mankind must appear as the outcome of mere bungling, and not worth preserving. But that the individual should also have to be stripped of whatever characteristics or qualities he has acquired for himself is much more disturbing. He is as if reduced to formless clay so that the ruler can mould both state and individual into whatever shape he sees fit:

> He will sketch in the outline of the constitution. Then, as the work goes on, he will frequently refer to his model, the ideals of justice, goodness, temperance, and the rest, and compare with them the copy of those qualities which he is trying to create in human society. Combining the various elements of social life as a painter mixes his colours, he will reproduce the complexion of true humanity, guided by that divine pattern whose likeness Homer saw in the men he called godlike. He will rub out and paint in again

this or that feature, until he has produced, so far as may be, a type of human character that heaven can approve. (6.500)

Habits are powerful forces, and once firmly established can become almost ineradicable. Only young children can be bent to the will of the ruler through a conditioning process which causes them to respond automatically and unquestioningly to commands whose intent they need not, and frequently cannot, understand. Therefore, they must be taken in hand while they are still malleable and before the older generation has had a chance of corrupting them beyond repair:

> They must send out into the country all citizens who are above ten years old, take over the children, away from the present habits and manners of their parents, and bring them up in their own ways under the institutions we have described. (7.540)

With this ludicrous counsel alone, the mock seriousness of Socrates stands exposed. It should have been enough to warn interpreters against taking the discussion of the *Idea of the Good* and its accessibility at its face value.

No less absurd than the rustication of the adult population before the philosopher-king can undertake his reform, are the reasons given for the banishment of the artist from the ideal commonwealth. For Plato has Socrates declare art of any kind as worthless or harmful in education, and then testify to the pedagogical efficacy of poetry by letting him conclude the discourse with a myth. The very absurdity and paradoxical nature of the attack should prompt us to look beyond the attack itself and in the direction to which it points.

First Socrates criticizes art from the point of view of knowledge of reality. Earlier it was agreed that the perfectly real is perfectly knowable and the imperfectly real is imperfectly knowable. Since only the eternal forms are regarded as truly real, they alone can serve as the objects of knowledge. The ordinary things in our experience were said to be merely objects of *doxa,* or belief. Using the painter as an illustration, he asks: What type or degree of reality is the object of his art? Clearly not the form, and not even the concrete object, but only an appearance of a single aspect of it. Hence the reality the painter deals with is said to be "at the third remove from the essential nature of the thing." "The tragic poet, too," Socrates continues, "is an artist who represents things; so this will apply to him: he and all other artists are, as it were, third in succession from the throne of truth" (10.597).

To the modern reader, this criticism appears shockingly naive and based on a complete misconception of the object and function of poetry. It is difficult to see how a Greek reader could have found it otherwise.

Socrates' second form of criticism may have appeared somewhat less unreasonable to his contemporaries. There he questions the poet's ability to promote the moral improvement of his readers. Now it is true that the Greeks often looked to their poets for moral guidance. And some seemed to have believed that in order to write well about technical matters, the poets must have had an intimate knowledge of them. The rhapsode Ion, for instance, in the dialogue by the same name, claims that his expertness in Homer qualifies him to serve as a competent general in warfare. As in the first instance, however, Socrates' complaint is directed against the low degree of reality of the objects of poetry:

> I should imagine that, if he had any real understanding of the actions he represents, he would far sooner devote himself to performing them in fact. The memorials he would try to leave after him would be noble deeds, and he would be more eager to be the hero whose praises are sung than the poet who sings them. (10.599)

From the point of view of reality and literal truth, the poets are of little account. "We may conclude," says Socrates, "that all poetry, from Homer onwards, consists in representing a semblance of its object, whatever it may be, including any kind of human excellence, with no grasp of the reality" (10.600).

Now it might have been possible to convince Socrates' contemporaries that the poets had failed them as moral teachers, as scientists or dialecticians; but that would scarcely have induced the men who attended the dramatic festivals to regard them as worthless or perhaps even so harmful as to require their expulsion from the city. They might even have been willing to admit that what they took with them from witnessing a performance did not consist in rules of moral conduct or truth about reality, either of the mutable or the immutable kind. When further questioned as to what they had gained, they might have been unable to answer. Unless, of course, they were of the highly intelligent and articulate kind, such as Aristotle, for instance. He maintained that "the poet's function is to describe, not the thing that has happened, but a kind of thing that might happen."[29] With this claim, Aristotle removes the foundation from the criticism of Socrates: poetry does not lead to reality and truth, because possibility and not reality is its proper concern. In fact, the unacceptable conclusions which follow from the position taken by Socrates may well be Plato's way of pointing to its opposite, namely, from what is to what might be as the object of poetry. And so Plato and Aristotle would be found in agreement in regard to the outcome of their teaching, although they differ so radically in method. This still would leave us with the question of whether the poets could then be conceived as performing a useful function in the ideal city.

Turning to the third criticism we find that Socrates refers to the poets not only as worthless but as psychologically injurious. To the complaint that the creations of the poet "are poor things by the standards of truth and reality," he now adds that "his appeal is not to the highest part of the soul, but to one which is inferior" (10.604). At first glance it is difficult to see why Socrates should regard an appeal to the emotions as necessarily harmful. Those emotions which in the *Phaedrus* are symbolized by the noble steed and in the analysis of the soul in the *Republic* are identified with the spirited element, can be powerful allies of reason. The vicarious experiences and feelings produced by the playwright may make us tolerant of others and inclined to sympathize with their trials and tribulations. But in reasoning in this manner we forget that Socrates is not talking about an ordinary city. In the one which he has imaginatively constructed, citizens have from their earliest youth been carefully conditioned so that they submit unquestioningly to the will of the ruler, and "preserve in all circumstances . . . the conviction implanted by the education which the law-giver has established" (4.428–29). Neither their will nor their critical intelligence has been given an opportunity for development. Their characters have been shaped by outside forces under the control of the state, and if we expose them to powerful influences, especially those of the great tragedians, we are likely to "endanger the order established in their soul" (10.607).

Now if the broadening effect which exposure to dramatic art tends to produce in the spectator is a threat to the brittle constitution of the carefully conditioned subject, would not the presentation of possibilities, which Aristotle sees as the function of the poet, wreak even greater havoc? Becoming aware of alternative courses of action, the individual might begin to reflect and weigh their relative advantages. He might become insecure and unable to continue in his blind trust in the infallibility of the rulers. He might reassert his inherent right to think and judge for himself. So the poets are harmful precisely because they tend to make men out of the robots which inhabit the "ideal" city. Their expulsion, with the inevitable impoverishment of the cultural life of the people, should have aroused the suspicion of the reader as to the seriousness of Socrates' criticism of the arts. If the reader should have failed to detect the thinly veiled irony underlying the argument which led to the condemnation of the poets, Socrates now issues a final warning to rethink the whole matter before agreeing to such a drastic step:

> If dramatic poetry . . . can show good reason why it should exist in a well-governed society, we for our part should welcome it back, being ourselves conscious of its charms. . . . We should allow her champions . . . to plead for her . . . that she is no mere source of pleasure but a benefit to society and human life. We shall listen favorably; for we shall clearly be the gainers, if that can be proved. (10.607–8)

Plato's way of simultaneously concealing and disclosing his thoughts, in order to induce and direct the reflections of the reader, makes it all too easy for the interpreter to read his own ideas into the dialogue. In the present case, the objection might be raised that we have foisted Aristotle's conception of poetry on

Plato, who nowhere claims that the poet is concerned with the possible instead of the real. Fortunately, since Plato himself often acts the poet, we can find out whether Plato practices what Aristotle preaches by looking at some of his own creations.

The myth in the *Phaedo,* it will be recalled, concludes the conversation in which Socrates engages his friends only hours before he drinks the fatal hemlock. The discussion, as we have seen, concerns itself less with the immortality of the soul than with the difficulty of maintaining a free faith against the threats of both dogmatism and skepticism. Socrates urges those present to enter imaginatively the world of such creatures as ants and frogs. They know nothing of our wider experience, whose existence is not in the least affected by their ignorance. So may not we in turn be part of a still vaster world of whose existence we are ignorant? The awareness of the sheer possibility, however, of such a world casts doubt on all the truths derived from human experience and reduces them to various degrees of probability; for whatever seems certain within our limited experience runs the risk of being found false or inaccurate on a wider view. This awareness discourages dogmatism and inclines one to tolerate the beliefs of others, even if one should find them unacceptable for oneself. It also serves as a protection against despair, for where there is uncertainty there is also the possibility of hope. And so the faith which Socrates exhibits in the *Phaedo* when he lies down to die as if he were retiring for a night's sleep, if it is to be genuine, must spring from a free choice, unsupported by a false sense of security.

The *Protagoras* myth, far from constituting a cultural history, also impresses upon its readers a possibility, namely that of men completely devoid of any sense of justice and therefore altogether incapable of survival. This possibility, even more clearly than that of the *Phaedo* myth, is capable of making its presence felt in human experience. For there is an observable correlation between the degree to which the sense of justice is developed in a given community and the quality of community life. The myth, by carrying this correlation to its logical limit, suggests the frightful possibility that the sense of justice might degenerate to a point where human society collapses into chaos. The thought of the possibility of such a catastrophe serves to bring men to the realization that social life cannot be taken for granted. It requires their sustained effort and vigilance. The Zeus of the myth has conferred upon them merely the capacity for social living. Its realization is their own responsibility, which they may meet or fail to meet. Thus the possibility which the myth has conjured up shows that the life of the community, and hence human life itself, rests on the will of the individual, almost as the medieval world was thought to rest on the will of God.

The *Phaedrus* myth directs attention toward an element already implicit in the truths conveyed by the other two myths, namely, transcendence. Without the ability to reach beyond the present moment, a man could not engage in the typically human activity of drawing upon *past* experience and in its light project goals into the *future* which give direction and meaning to his behavior *now*. This three-dimensional temporal transcendence of man can be observed in an ordinary attempt at recollection. For this process shows him engaged at the *present* moment in seeking out an event which occurred in the *past,* in the hope that at some *future* time it will reappear in his consciousness. Socrates extends recollection mythically and reaches not only beyond a present moment in his experience, but behind his actual existence to a possible previous existence, and forward again to a possible life beyond the grave. He thus holds up to view a transcending activity on a large scale. In the *Phaedo* we have been shown this same transcendence through Socrates' dream of a life in which all men's desires have found their fulfillment. There it served Socrates to exhibit the uniqueness of the human mode of being, and thus allay the fear of death which springs from a conception of the psyche as just another material thing. In the *Phaedrus,* as we shall see, transcendence, in the form of projection of goals, is revealed as the condition for the possibility of genuine love, for only in the sharing of significant goals can the desire of lovers to become one be realized.

Myth-making as such reveals man's most basic characteristic of transcendence, which Heidegger calls *existence* (using the term in its original meaning of 'standing out'). It is in this sense that Heidegger can say that "the essence of Dasein lies in its existence" (67). By enticing him with possibilities, poetry makes man realize that he does not have to be content with what is given but can venture into the unknown, or, more basically, that he need not act out an essence or nature but can, within certain limits, set his own goals and let these goals determine his behavior. Poetry, therefore, is "no mere source of pleasure but a benefit to society and human life" (10.607–8). The benefits it is able to confer, however, and the authentic individuals it helps to constitute are not welcome in a society of rigidly controlled subjects. Such a society does not allow for the assumption of personal responsibility for acts freely chosen among available alternatives, for the earliest education of the child sees to it that the will of the subject is made subservient to that of the ruler. Transcendence is allowed to atrophy, for it is the exclusive right of the ruler to set goals and thereby shape the lives of the citizens. New possibilities are not to be explored, for "those who keep watch over the commonwealth must take care not to overlook the least infraction of the rule against innovation" (4.424). All the elements which go into the makeup of a society of free and responsible individuals, the imaginary commonwealth of Socrates would subvert. Small wonder that the poets must be sent into exile.

Our reflections on the nature and function of the myths have strengthened the belief in the ironic character of Socrates' advocacy of the rule of philosopher-kings who are in possession of the *Idea of the Good*. As we have seen, Socrates leads to this absolute principle of intelligibility in the same way that Protagoras establishes the state of nature, namely, through a process of extrapolation. And as the *Protagoras* myth points to the lowest depths of community life, if not its utter destruction, so Socrates' doctrine of the philosopher-kings with their infallible wisdom moves in the direction of its greatest height or full perfection. But both the state of nature and the ideal city point away from themselves to the human condition. If the one puts us on the alert against the destructive forces which threaten community life, the other produces an awareness of the immense distance which separates the synthesizing process inherent in human knowing from its ideal consummation. In the light of this ideal possibility, which seems altogether out of reach of human endeavor, we feel less tempted to endow others, no matter how gifted they may be, with infallible knowledge and thereby create at least a semblance of justification for surrendering our responsibility to them.

On a literal interpretation the various stages of the fall from the ideal state furnish a vivid contrast to the ideal state itself. In books 7 and 9, Socrates describes the increasing enslavement of both ruler and ruled as they fall victim to the excessive ambition of the timocratic man, the greed for riches of the oligarch, the unbridled appetite and the lawless license of the democratic man, and finally the lust for power of the despot. And when it comes to the final comparison of the just and the unjust, Socrates identifies the first with "the happiest man . . . who is also king over himself" (9.577), seemingly forgetful of the fact that such self-mastery is reserved for the few philosopher-kings. The second, the unjust man, is depicted as in bondage:

> Just as the state enslaved to a tyrant cannot do what he really wishes, so neither can a soul under a similar tyranny do what it wishes as a whole. Goaded against its will by the sting of desire it will be filled with confusion and remorse. (9.577)

Now it is easy enough to see that a man may lose his freedom under a despot or that he may become enslaved by passion or deeply rooted habit. It is much more difficult to detect the subtle threat which comes from a highly intelligent and well intentioned ruler, and this may be the reason why Socrates placed him in the center of attention in the *Republic*, while the despot and his like are relegated to a less important section toward the end of the dialogue. Precisely because of his superior capabilities and his deep concern for those under his charge, such a ruler may be tempted to act for his subjects, But he cannot lift the burden of responsibility from their shoulders without at the same time robbing them of genuine selfhood.

This point is brought home in the *Myth of Er* which concludes the dialogue. Those who start a new cycle of existence choose a mode of life in one fell swoop. In reality it is accomplished through innumerable, often seemingly insignificant decisions. "To know how to choose always the middle course that avoids both extremes" (10.618)—this, according to Socrates, is man's most vital task. To select the mean, however—that is, the most appropriate course of action under the circumstances—implies a choice among possible alternatives. To give this choice at least a chance of success, a man must detach himself from the present in order to survey what might be. This ability to stand aloof for a moment, even in the face of an urgent call to action, had been lost by the man in the *Myth of Er* who had the first choice with all the possible lives spread out before him. Apparently, decisions had been made for him, for Socrates describes him as "one of those who had come down from heaven, having spent his former life in a well-ordered commonwealth and become virtuous from habit only" (10.619). When the great power in the life of a despot caught his eye, it overwhelmed him. "In his thoughtless greed he was not careful to examine the life he chose at every point and did not see the many evils it contained" (10.619). Those, on the other hand, Socrates continues, "who had come up out of the earth, having suffered themselves and seen others suffer, were not hasty in making their choice" (10.619). The task of the ruler, therefore, is not to remove the burden of responsibility from his subjects, but to help them carry their own burden. For, as Heidegger says, through "the solicitude . . . which takes away 'care' from the Other and puts itself in his position . . . the Other can become one who is dominated and dependent" (158). Genuine solicitude, he claims, "helps the other to become transparent to himself *in* his care and to become *free for it*" (159). The *Republic* is not interested in teaching a doctrine, either about education or government or human knowledge and aspiration. At the center of Plato's concern, however, there is always the free human spirit. This spirit is as precious as it is fragile. It is threatened not only by lack of education, but also by the wrong use of it, not only by the despot bent on self-aggrandizement, but also by the benevolent ruler willing to take his subjects' responsibilities upon himself. If we now return in thought to the beginning of the dialogue we find that we have no answer to the question suggested by the opening scene: How far should a man yield to the pressures and demands made upon him by his friends, by society, the world at large, and perhaps even the gods? Neither custom nor rule of law, nor man in authority, no matter how wise and well-intentioned, can be wholly relied upon as guides. But it may well be that this is the most significant lesson for an individual to learn. For only if he has been made aware of the futility of seeking security in a world essentially precarious and full of risks, will he be inclined to throw away all crutches and at last stand on his own feet. Only then is he ready for the supreme test, the choice of a way of life. And how can he be a genuine self, unless he succeeds in choosing his own life? So the great flaw of the character of the *Myth of Er* is not that he made a horrible choice—despite the fact that he had lived in a good community and spent a thousand years in heaven—but that he acted without deliberation, impelled by greed (10.619), and that as a consequence the life he seized was not his own.[30]

Once we discover the Socratic irony at play, then what seems to be an illustration of Heidegger's "leaping in" on a grand scale metamorphoses itself into a "leaping ahead." Instead of advocating the rule of philosopher-kings who would disburden us of the need to make vital decisions in an uncertain situation, we find Socrates trying to sharpen our wits so that we might learn to make such decisions ourselves. The main body of the *Republic* is now seen to be no less aporetic than the controversial first book, and the dialogue as a whole can no longer be cited as evidence that the liberal spirit of the master has given way to a pernicious dogmatism in the mind of the disciple. The Socratic method has merely become more sophisticated and is making heavier demands on our critical intelligence.

NOTES

1. As an illustration of this type of view, note that of Paul Shorey: "The Republic, in which Plato explicity states his solution of these problems, is a marvelous achievement of mature constructive thought" (p. 68). "The *Republic* does definitely meet and try to answer nearly every problem raised and left unanswered in the Socratic dialogues" (*What Plato Said* (Chicago: University of Chicago Press, 1968) p. 71. See also: "The*Republic* is as close as Plato comes to a comprehensive statement of his philosophy. . . . Throughout the argument, Socrates is open and positive to a degree that we have not seen in any of the dialogues taken up in previous chapters. Since he discusses most of the problems that those dialogues deal with, we find in the *Republic* answers to many of the questions which they left unresolved." Michael J. O'Brien, *The Socratic Paradoxes and the Greek Mind* (Chapel Hill, N.C.: The University of North Carolina Press, 1967), pp. 150–51.

This literalistic interpretation is not restricted to Plato scholars, as may be seen by the following: "I am content merely to point to the unmistakable difference between the Socrates of the *Apology* and the Socrates of the *Republic*. The former does not know all the answers but teaches men to keep asking the first and last questions, insisting that 'the unexamined life is not worth living': he chose to die rather than to sacrifice his own conscience to the state. The latter not only is more dogmatic but prescribes an unexamined life for almost all his citizens; he lays down principles that justify the execution of the historic Socrates." Herbert J. Muller, *The Uses of the Past* (New York: Alfred A. Knopf, 1952) p. 128, n. 12.

2. See for instance Karl Popper: "Again we find that the various forms of existing governments are explained as debased copies of the true model or Form of the state, of the perfect state, the standard of all imitations." *The Open Society and its Enemies* (Princeton, N.J.: Princeton University Press, 1950) p. 45.

3. Paul Friedländer is an advocate of this position: "It is practically certain, on the basis of an analysis of form and content as well as on the grounds of verbal statistics, that the first book of the *Republic* originally was a separate dialogue, written down as a whole or in part, or, at least carefully planned and far advanced in the mind of its author as an integral part of the early group of aporetic dialogues." *Plato*, vol. 2, translated from the German by Hans Meyerhoff (New York: Random House, 1964), p. 50. For a dissenting

opinion, note: "There is nothing in the dialogue to support any of the fanciful modern speculations about . . . the possible existence of the first book as a 'dialogue of search.' " A. E. Taylor, *Plato: The Man and His Work* 6th ed. (London, Methuen & Co., 1949) p. 264. For a list of the views of various Plato scholars on this subject, see Friedländer, *Plato*, vol. 2, p. 305. Even if it were definitely established that Book 1 is an earlier composition, we would still be faced with the problem of determining what Plato thought to gain by adding it to the *Republic*.

4. *The "Republic" of Plato*, translated with Introduction and Notes by Francis MacDonald Cornford (New York: Oxford University Press, 1945). All quotations from the *Republic* refer to this edition.

5. Since the visit to the Piraeus was motivated not only by piety but also by curiosity, that is, to watch the procession, Leo Strauss suggests that Socrates, at least in part, went for the sake of Glaucon, in order to have an opportunity to teach the young man. *The City and Man* (Chicago: Rand McNally & Co., 1964), p. 64. Plato, however, gives no indication to this effect, although it would have been easy for him to do so. Kitto's warning in connection with the *Antigone* seems apropos: "If we bring into our interpretation of the play . . . something which demonstrably is not there . . . we are making it more difficult to notice what *is* there." *Form and Meaning in Drama* (London: Methuen & Co., 1968), p. 148. But despite this addition, which is distracting, at least as far as my point of view is concerned, Leo Strauss, who is interested in different aspects of the *Republic*, recognizes the same or a similar tension: "We owe the conversation on justice to a mixture of compulsion and persuasion. To cede to such a mixture, or to a kind of such mixture, is an act of justice. Justice itself, duty, obligation, is a kind of mixture of compulsion and persuasion, of coercion and reason." *City and Man*, p. 64.

6. Note the pregnant formulation of this notion by Martin Heidegger: "Der Tod 'gehört' nicht indifferent nur dem eigenen Dasein zu, sondern er *beansprucht* diess als *einzelnes*. Die im Vorlaufen verstandene Unbezüglichkeit des Todes vereinzelt das Dasein auf es selbst. Diese Vereinzelung ist eine Weise des Erschliessens des "Da" fuer die Existenz. Sie macht offenbar, dass alles Sein bei dem Besorgten und jedes Mitsein mit Anderen versagt, wenn es um das eigenste Seinkönnen geht. Dasein kann nur dann *eigentlich es selbst sein*, wenn es sich von ihm selbst her dazu ermöglicht." *Sein und Zeit*, 6th ed. (Tübingen: Neomarius Verlag, 1949), p. 263.

7. Leo Strauss seems to express the same thought when he says: "The identity of the honest guard and the thief follows necessarily if one considers only the knowledge, the intellectual part, of their work, and not their opposite moral intentions." *City and Man*, p. 72.

8. The notion that justice extends over all human activities and springs ultimately from the will of the individual is stated explicitly later in the dialogue: "The just man will not allow the several elements in his soul to usurp one another's functions. . . . Only when he has linked these parts together in a well-tempered harmony and has made himself one man instead of many, will he be ready to go about whatever he may do, whether it be making money and satisfying bodily wants, or business transactions, or the affairs of state. In all these fields when he speaks of just and unjust conduct, he will mean the behavior that helps to produce and to preserve this habit of mind" (4.443).

9. R. C. Cross and A. D. Woozley, *Plato's Republic: A Philosophical Commentary* (London: Macmillan & Co., 1964), pp. 20–21.

10. Kitto comments on an analogous situation in his interpretation of Sophocles' *Antigone*. When speaking of the so-called "double burial" of Polyneices, he says: "We should not ask, 'Why did Antigone go back?' as if it were a real situation into which we are enquiring; we should ask 'Why did Sophocles make Antigone go back, without giving a clear reason for it?' " *Form and Meaning*, p. 140.

11. Strauss, *City and Man*, p. 80.

12. Cross and Woozley, *Plato's "Republic,"* p. 48.

13. Ibid., p. 50.

14. Gregory Vlastos, following Ernest Nagel, calls this procedure "intuitive induction." *Plato's "Protagoras "* (New York: Library of Liberal Arts, 1956), p. xxix, note 18.

15. Cf. also: "The artisan in the strict sense proves to be concerned, not with his own advantage, but with the advantage of others whom he serves: the shoemaker makes shoes for others and only indirectly for himself. . . ." Strauss, *City and Man.*, pp. 78–79.

16. Karl Popper comments on this passage as follows: "This social nature of man has its origin in the *imperfection of the human individual*. In opposition to Socrates Plato teaches that the human individual cannot be self-sufficient, owing to the limitations inherent in human nature . . . The state therefore must be placed higher than the individual since only the state can be self-sufficient ('autark'), perfect, and able to make good the necessary imperfection of the individual" (*Open Society*, p. 76). "The Socratic doctrime of *autarky* is mentioned in *Republic* 387D–E (cp. *Apology* 41ff . . .) This is only one of the few scattered passages reminiscent of Socrates' teaching; but it is in direct contradiction to the main doctrine of the *Republic*. . . ; this may be seen by contrasting the quoted passage with 369Cff., and very many similar passages." Ibid., p. 515.n.25.

Popper's statement is open to three objections:

(1) In *Republic* 369C, Plato has Socrates speak about economic interdependence: "having all these needs, we call on one another's help to satisfy our various requirements." This interdependence is not incompatible with the detachment which Socrates counsels in *Republic* 387D–E. There he refers to excessive lamentations at the loss of a friend, a son, or a brother. In the first case, we make use of another, such as a physician or a craftsman. In the second case, we surrender excessively to another who, if he should die, cannot be replaced in the same way a craftsman can.

(2) In *Apology* 41C, Socrates says that "nothing can harm a good man either in this life or after death. . . ." Again this moral independence is not in conflict with an economic or social dependence. I am dependent on law enforcement agencies for protection against thieves who may be after my possessions, but I need no such protection as far as morality is concerned. Whether my acts are morally good or evil depends exclusively on myself; otherwise they would not be *moral* at all.

(3) One cannot but applaud Popper when he critizes admirers of Plato for glossing over obvious aberrations in the *Republic*. Why does he himself, however, become uncritical when reading the early dialogues? In the *Crito*, for instance, he could discover even more drastic conflicts between what he calls Socratic and Platonic elements. 46B stresses the independence of the individual: "I am and always have been one of those natures who must be *guided by reason*, whatever the reason may be which upon reflection *appears to me* to be the best." But only a few paragraphs later Socrates subjects this same individual to the state: "Since you were brought into the world and educated by us, can you deny in the first place that you are *our child and slave*, as your fathers were before you? And if this is true, you are not on equal terms with us, nor can you think that you have a right to do to us what we are doing to you" (50E). (Italics added)

Would Popper be willing to say that the passage last quoted from an early dialogue foreshadows the dogmatic and real Plato of the later ones, as the liberal passages of the later dialogues are said to be traces of the real and liberal Socrates? The sharp contrast between these two passages, which seem to stand on an equal footing, would obviously make such a facile interpretation quite absurd.

It seems that Popper's eagerness to portray Socrates as liberal and humanistic and Plato as dogmatic and totalitarian, has blinded him to obvious distinctions and has made him prone to overlook, especially in the early dialogues, passages which seriously threaten his theory.

17. Although fully aware of the dehumanizing effect of this conception of justice, Herbert J. Muller is not deflected from his literal interpretation of the *Republic:* "The warriors are carefully educated but are not allowed to have minds or lives of their own; their reading and their music are rigorously censured. Only the philosophers may become rational, responsible human beings; they are given a thorough training because they must do all the thinking for society. Briefly, Plato's *Republic* incorporates the ideal bee-hive, in which there is no freedom, no individualism, no desire for self-realization but only the unthinking devotion to the prescribed task." *Uses of the Past,* p. 127.

18. Gerhard Krüger describes the well ordered individual as follows: "Darin zeigt sich im *Staat* das Wesen der *Gerechtigkeit:* der Mensch "duldet nicht, dass . . . die Arten der Seele gegenseitig Übergriffe machen, sondern er hat sein Haus wirklich wohl geordnet, beherrscht sich selbst . . . (*Staat* 443D–E)." (Einsicht und Leidenschaft, 3rd ed. [Frankfurt am Main: Vittorio Klostermann, 1963], p. 248). But he does not recognize that in the *Republic* such authentic selfhood is reserved for the philosopher-kings who "combine philosophical study with political leadership, while the rest of the world should accept their guidance and let philosophy alone" (*Republic* 5.474).

19. George Sarton, who admittedly is under the influence of Karl Popper, offers the following explanation: "The Athens of Plato's day was not pleasant to contemplate. Sparta and Crete in the distance seemed better. When he was writing the *Republic,* he was already disillusioned and was escaping from reality into a utopian dream." *A History of Science: Ancient Science through the Golden Age of Greece* (Cambridge: Cambridge University Press, 1952), p. 409. Elsewhere Sarton calls the *Republic* "the work of a disgruntled fanatic." Ibid., p. 412. Sarton thus accuses Plato of having fallen victim to a flaw against which, from another point of view, Plato might be said to have tried to warn his countrymen. Just as Sophocles took the popular conception of Oedipus as fated, or of Ajax as the ideal of heroic virtue, and revealed their true nature, so Plato's *Republic* could be understood as an attempt to expose the false image of the ideal state which some Greeks saw in Sparta and Crete. This theme has been developed by John H. Randall, "Plato on the Good Life and the Spartan Ideal," *Journal of the History of Ideas* 28, no. 3 (July-September 1967): 307–324. In this connection note also: H. G. Wolz, "The *Republic* in the Light of the Socratic Method," *Modern Schoolman* 22 (January 1955): 115–142, and "The Protagoras Myth and the Philosopher-Kings," *Review of Metaphysics* 17, no. 2 (December 1963).

20. Cf. Herbert J. Muller: "Today Plato's ideal is still seductive, as many are again being frightened by the riskiness of the democratic adventure." *Uses of the Past,* p. 128. If this was true in the early fifties, it seems to be even more so a decade or two later.

21. "If we are to elude those assailants you have described, we must, I think, define for them whom we mean by these lovers of wisdom who, we have dared to assert, ought to be our rulers. Once we have a clear view of their character, we shall be able to defend our position by pointing to some who are naturally fitted to combine philosophic study with political leadership, while the rest of the world should accept their guidance and let philosophy alone" (5.474).

22. Karl Popper has called attention to this shocking transformation which takes place before our eyes:

"If ever Socrates claimed that statesmen should be philosophers, he could only have meant that, burdened with an excessive responsibility, they should be searchers for truth, and conscious of their limitations.

How did Plato convert this doctrine? At first sight, it might appear that he did not alter it at all when demanding that the sovereignty of the state should be invested in the philosophers; especially since, like Socrates, he defined philosophers as lovers of truth. But the change made by Plato is indeed tremendous. His lover is no longer the modest seeker, he is the proud possessor of truth. . . . Plato's ideal philosopher approaches both to omniscience and to omnipotence. He is the Philosopher-King. It is hard, I think, to conceive a greater contrast than that between the Socratic and the Platonic ideal of a philosopher. It is the contrast between two worlds—the world of a modest rational individualist and that of a totalitarian demigod" (Open Society, pp. 130–31).

It is the great merit of Popper to have courageously faced these difficulties. But he also bears eloquent testimony to the absurd consequences of a literal interpretation, which he is unwilling to surrender.

23. A similar leap into dogmatism occurs in the *Phaedo*, as Socrates passes from an exposition of his method to its application in the final demonstration for the immortality of the soul. For there he identifies the provisional postulates with the eternal forms and proceeds as if they permitted him to gain insight into the very nature of the soul.

24. "Now if a man believes in the existence of beautiful things, but not of Beauty itself, and cannot follow a guide who would lead him to a knowledge of it, is he not living in a dream?" (5.476).

25. Sarton, consistent with his literalistic interpretation, heaps scorn on the philosophy of Plato:

"Plato's subordination of the individual to the state was so complete that his philosophy became almost inhuman. And yet his self-delusion was so deep that he gave to the *Republic* the alternative title of Justice, and a good part of the book is devoted to the discussion of abstract justice. . . .

It was a betrayal not only of Athenian democracy but also of the master who had been his first guide and whom he had loved. Indeed, many of the arguments against democracy were put in the mouth of Socrates. Plato made his old master say the very opposite of what he had taught. Was Plato's power of self-illusion so deep that he could no longer distinguish between the real Socrates and the Socrates created by his own fancy?

"Can there be a deeper betrayal than that? . . . Socrates' main purpose was to teach self-criticism, and he was always ready to recognize his ignorance; Plato, on the contrary, was the master who knew, the philosopher-king who must be obeyed implicitly, the creator of the *Republic* that is perfect by definition and therefore cannot change without disgrace." (pp. 418–19)

Even Herbert J. Muller, who points out that Plato "thought habitually in terms of tale, myth and symbol rather than dogma" (*Uses of the Past*, p. 124) and who considers it unfair to regard Plato as a "Fascist philosopher," nevertheless thinks that "Plato was in line with Fascism in rejecting the principles of liberty and equality, tacitly denying the dignity and worth of the individual, and anticipating the technique of deliberately lying to the common people." Ibid., p. 127.

26. Incredible as it may seem, Plato scholars have traditionally shown no hesitation in accepting Socrates' utterances here at their face value. The following may serve as a typical illustration: "Those few who will be the rulers obeyed by the rest . . . must have the philosopher's immediate knowledge of the Good. . . . The knowledge of the Good, on which well-being depends, is now to include an understanding of the moral and physical order of the whole universe. As the object of a purpose attributed to a divine Reason operating in the world, this supreme Good makes the world intelligible, as a work of human craftsmanship becomes intelligible when we see the purpose it is designed to serve. . . . The apprehension of it is . . . to be thought of as a revelation which can only follow upon a long intellectual training." Cornford, *Plato's Republic*, pp. 212–13.

27. Gilbert Ryle's interpretation of this passage may serve as an illustration of the kind of approach which disregards the possible dramatic function of difficulties found in the dialogues and seeks their solution in factors extrinsic to the context in which the difficulties appear: "This stretch of Republic VI on the Idea of the Good and the Divided Line does not seem to be unduly weighty for its role in the current argument, which opens at 487B. For Socrates is here trying only to explain the notorious worldly worthlessness of actual philosophers. Part of his explanation is that they are dazzled by the superior realities with which Thought acquaints them. The analogy of the Sun is used to illustrate this dazzlement. Ostensibly this is all that the analogical exposition of the Idea of the Good is brought in for. But it had surely been composed for a much more positive end. *It does not natively belong in the apologetic and diagnostic discussion-context where we find it. It was inserted into that context to 'preserve it from oblivion.'* " *Plato's Progress* (Cambridge: Cambridge University Press, 1966), p. 248. (Italics added) The meagerness of the results obtained would seem to bear eloquent enough testimony for the fruitfulness, or lack of it, of such an approach.

28. Popper is keenly aware of the absurdity inherent in Socrates' description of the reformation to be undertaken by the philosopher-kings, but he fails to recognize the underlying Socratic irony: "If they were really to clean the canvas, they could have to destroy themselves, and their utopian plans. (And what follows then would probably not be a beautiful copy of the Platonic ideal, but chaos.)" *Open Society*, p. 163.

29. *Poetics*, 1451a, 1.36, in *The Basic Works of Aristotle*, ed. Richard McKeon (New York: Random House, 1941), p. 1463.

30. Note that he himself disowns his act: "When he had time to look more closely, he began to beat his breast and bewail his choice, forgetting the warning proclaimed by the Interpreter; for he laid the blame on fortune, the decrees of the gods, anything rather than himself" (10.619). But not even on the assumption that he was controlled by habit does he completely escape responsibility. For he is responsible for having allowed the habit to gain control.

7

A Trilogy on Love and Friendship

On what ground can the three dialogues be called a trilogy? The fact that they deal with the same topic does not necessarily constitute them a whole. A whole, according to Aristotle, must have "beginning, middle and end," a beginning from which the middle follows as a consequence, which in turn leads to the end (De Poetica 1450b). In other words, there must be some sort of logical connection between the various parts. In the first dialogue, the *Lysis*, Plato through a series of paradoxes indicates the inadequacy of concepts applicable to things when used to describe the human mode of being. In the *Symposium*, Plato furnishes illustrations of numerous threats to genuine selfhood or authenticity in connection with the relationship between lovers and friends. He thus provides a better understanding of why substance ontology is unsuitable when dealing with human beings. The third dialogue, the *Phaedrus*, after contrasting authentic and inauthentic love, points to transcendence as the condition for the possibility not only of love and any sort of communication, but even of knowing. Transcendence therefore appears as an essential characteristic of man, without which he could not be what he is. The three dialogues are thus seen to probe progressively deeper into the problem of selfhood. In regard to all three, Heidegger carries the inquiry a step farther: by working out the existentials or human characteristics in contrast to Aristotle's categories; by laying bare the structure of man which makes love and friendship possible; and finally focusing on transcendence, that is, the ability to reach beyond anything that is and take his stand in Nothing, which Heidegger calls the veil of Being.

LYSIS: SUBSTANCE ONTOLOGY VERSUS EXISTENCE

I

Western philosophy, from its earliest beginning among the ancient Greeks to this very day, according to Heidegger, has been dominated by substance ontology. This view of the being of things recognizes only substance as the basic entity may undergo. "The seemingly new beginning," Heidegger maintains, "which Descartes proposed for philosophizing has revealed itself as the implantation of a baleful prejudice, which has kept later generations from . . . coming to grips critically with the traditional ancient ontology" (46).[1] Substance as such is not knowable according to Descartes; it becomes accessible only through some distinctive property. As his experiment with a piece of wax shows, for corporeal substance the property in question is *extension*. For this is all that remains unchanged when a hard piece of wax is heated. Similarly, the *cogito* alone is able to resist the destructive power of the *malin génie* conjured up by Descartes's methodical doubt and thus satisfy the definition of substance as *that which constantly remains*. Nor does Kant, despite his efforts, in the opinion of Heidegger, succeed in freeing himself from substance ontology:

> Even though in theory he has denied that the ontical foundations of the substantial apply to the 'I', he still slips back into *this same* inappropriate ontology. . . . The 'I' is a bare consciousness, accompanying all concepts. . . . It is the form of apperception, which clings to every experience and precedes it (366). . . . The 'I' is . . . the subject of logical behavior, of binding together. All binding together is an 'I' bind together. In any taking-together or relating, the 'I' always underlies—the *hypokeimenon*. [Although] Kant sees the impossibility of ontically reducing the "I" to a substance . . . he takes the "I" as subject again, and he does so in a sense which is ontologically inappropriate. For the ontological concept of the subject *characterizes not the Selfhood of the 'I' qua Self, but the selfsameness and steadiness of something which is always present-at-hand*. (367)

For Heidegger, substantiality or presence-at-hand is only one of several modes of the being of things. And since the term substance is traditionally used to refer to any entity, he uses the designation present-at-hand *(Vorhanden)* whenever the substance ontology is properly applied.

The present-at-hand, according to Heidegger, is not the reality which first comes to our attention. We become aware of things 'proximally' to the extent to which they can be put to some use. So his analysis starts with tools, with items of equipment, which he calls ready-to-hand *(Zuhanden)*. It is obvious that there cannot be such a thing as *a* tool, a single item of equipment. Tools have meaning only in a context, in a "world." Heidegger illustrates this point by referring to simple craftsman conditions. Merely looking at a hammer in isolation would never reveal its being. To understand a hammer as a hammer we must approach it with a prior awareness of an equipmental totality, the carpenter's craft, or that of the blacksmith, the tailor, etc. "In laying hold of an item of equipment, we come back to it from whatever work-world has already been disclosed" (404). The referential context or world, under normal working conditions, is not explicitly known. The tool itself becomes inconspicuous during the smooth operation in which it is employed. But when the tool is reality in which other modes, such as quantity, quality, relation, etc., inhere; and substance is held to be that which endures through all the changes which an damaged, for instance, it becomes conspicuous and the work-world is lit up. The damaged tool falls out of the referential context and stares at the beholder as a mere thing, substance or a present-at-hand.

Now we have discovered an additional mode of being, so that substantiality can no longer be regarded as the exclusive mode; in fact it is known only by way of readiness-to-hand. Of the present-at-hand we can speak in terms of properties. The hammer, as a mere thing, can be said to be heavy, in the sense of having weight, of being subject to the law of gravity, so that, if the surface on which it rests is removed, it falls. The hammer as a tool, a ready-to-hand, can be heavy only in the sense of its weight being appropriate or inappropriate for a certain task. "Its properties are, as it were," says Heidegger, "still bound up in the ways in which it is appropriate or inappropriate, just as presence-at-hand, as a possible kind of being for something ready-to-hand, is bound up in readiness-to-hand" (115).

Subjecting the referential context to a thorough analysis, Heidegger finds that it consists of a series of "in-order-to" relationships, ending ultimately in a "for-the-sake-of":

> . . . with this thing, for instance, which is ready-to-hand and which we accordingly call a "hammer," there is an involvement in hammering; with hammering, there is an involvement in making fast, with making fast, there is an involvement in protecting against weather; and this protection 'is' for the sake of [umwillen] providing shelter for Dasein—that is to say, for the sake of a possibility of Dasein's Being. (116)

Thus it appears that the meaning of the being of the ready-to-hand ultimately rests with a for-the-sake-of, i.e., with a purpose or goal, which only a human being can project. Beginning his analysis with our everyday activities, with the use of tools, Heidegger has discovered not only a distinction between readiness-to-hand and presence-at-hand, but he has been led to the most significant component of the human mode of being, namely *existence* (using this term in its etymological meaning of 'standing out'). For it is this trait, this ability to project goals and act in the light of these goals which makes it possible for a man to contribute to the constitution of his own being. And only by making this contribution authentically, that is, free from external and internal pressures, can he call himself a genuine self.

The human mode of being thus turns out to be radically different from that of the ready-to-hand and the present-at-hand, especially the latter. A rock, for instance, is what it is, and has no responsibility for and contributes nothing to its being. It can be understood in terms of substance and its properties. Of course, a man can also be addressed by means of the Aristotelian categories. He can be said to be tall or short, weak or strong, have brown eyes or black hair, and other such characteristics which are not within his control. But then the specifically human element is left out of account. The Epimetheus of the *Protagoras* myth, it will be recalled, failed to equip men with qualities and Prometheus corrected the error not by supplying them but by providing capabilities whose development was left to man's discretion.

Heidegger is undoubtedly right in maintaining that Descartes reenforced the traditional substance ontology and that Kant did not really succeed in surpassing it. But the reference to the *Protagoras* myth raises a doubt whether its reign in the history of philosophy is as exclusive as he would have us believe. A thorough analysis of the *Lysis*, it is hoped, will show that the numerous paradoxes, which have been a source of perplexity and outright despair to many commentators, could not have been constructed without a fairly clear awareness of the difference between presence-at-hand and existence.

II

On the surface, the *Lysis* has all the appearances of a typical early dialogue. Its opening scene, very much like those of the *Laches* and the *Charmides*, with which it is usually grouped together, presents the reader with a charming picture of the life of Socrates and of his concern for the education of the young. He is on his way from the Academy to the Lyceum, following the road outside the city wall, when he is accosted by some of his young friends and asked to join them in a discussion in a nearby palaestra. As usual on such occasions, Socrates is easily deflected from his course. When he discovers that one of the young men is in love, he proposes to give an exhibition of how the lover ought to converse with the object of his love.

During the ensuing discourse on friendship, definition after definition is proposed and found wanting. This, too, is typical of the early dialogues. What is unusual, however, is the intensity of the confusion which Socrates manages to create. For he makes the discussion run into seemingly insurmountable obstacles at every turn. And as we watch the thoughts of the participants moving now in one direction now in the other, merely to find each passage blocked, and becoming bewildered and frustrated like rats in a maze, the suspicion arises that Socrates is playing some wild joke, not only with the young boys, but also with us, the readers. The sense of absurdity is in fact foreshadowed at the beginning of the dialogue with the description of the behavior of the "ridiculous Hippothales" (205D),[2] who is hopelessly in love with and foolishly in pursuit of the fair Lysis. And the playfulness of the whole encounter is underscored at the end, when the slightly intoxicated attendants break up the discussion by calling the boys away, as from a game, in order to take them home.

That Socrates should play a game is in keeping with his character; that he should do so without a serious purpose is not. And he who lets himself be intimidated by the surface absurdity of the proceedings is likely to miss a rich treasure hidden underneath.[3] We would therefore be well advised to heed the warning of Alcibiades in the *Symposium:*

> His words are like the images of Silenus which open; they are ridiculous when you first hear them; he clothes himself in language that is like the skin of the wanton satyr—for his talk is of pack-asses and smiths and cobblers and curriers, and he is always repeating the same words, so that any ignorant or inexperienced person might feel disposed to laugh at him; but he who opens the bust and sees what is within will find that they are the only words which have a meaning in them, and also the most divine . . . and of the widest comprehension. (221E–222A)[4]

If Alcibiades correctly describes the method of Socrates, and if the *Lysis* can be said to exemplify it, then one would expect to be introduced to an ordinary life-situation (where smiths, cobblers, and curriers are at work), which Socrates proposes to explore. Before reaching a satisfactory conclusion, Socrates would give the argument a turn toward the ridiculous, and it would then be the task of the reader to disentangle the difficulty and discover the truth for himself. The foreground in the *Lysis*, as we shall see, is in fact always pregnant with philosophical implications. But in order not to make it too easy for the reader to uncover them, Socrates, so to speak, casts a spell over the argument to make its outcome appear paradoxical if not outright absurd. He usually produces this effect by employing a logic operating with Eleatic entities. The conflict between the rigidity and immutability of these entities and the fluidity of human existence gives rise to perplexities which form the obstacle course through which the reader must run if he wishes to penetrate to the inner reaches of the thought of Socrates. Borrowing two terms from Martin Heidegger, we may distinguish between the ontic, which constitutes the point of departure, and the ontological or underlying structure; while the logic curiously enough is employed, not for purposes of elucidation, but for diversionary tactics, to confuse the reader just enough so that he cannot rely on Socrates to do his thinking for him.

These three aspects or levels can be differentiated already in the first interchange between Socrates and Lysis, although they become more obvious in subsequent discussions. Under the prodding of Socrates, Lysis presents of himself the picture of a typical boy, whose impulses propel him hither and thither, who would now seize the reins of the horses pulling the race chariot, now insist on handling the mule team, and then become fascinated and try to meddle with his mother's loom. Following the lead of Socrates, we allow ourselves to be transported into the world of the child with its almost exclusive concern for the moment and its disregard of future consequences. We see Lysis no longer as a being engaged in a process of becoming but as sheer presence, as incapable of or not in need of development. It is the conflict between the seemingly timeless world of the child, and the more genuinely temporal, future-directed world of the adult which creates the paradox: While his parents manifestly love him and therefore should do anything to make him happy, they will not let him do what he wants. And how can a person be happy if he is restrained from doing what even a hired servant or a slave is allowed to do? Furthermore, tutor and teacher are set in authority over him, and Socrates exclaims in mock dismay:

> Whatever is the reason, then, that they hinder you, in this shocking manner, from being happy, and acting as you please, and keep you, all day long, in a state of bondage to someone or other? (208E)

His parents obviously do not allow him the liberty he craves, because his will is too short-ranged and too variegated; he lacks unity of purpose and above all foresight. It also becomes clear that he is in bondage not so much to the servants and slaves who have been assigned to him, as to the goals which his parents have chosen for him and in the direction of which they are trying to promote his development. To say that the child is immature now appears to mean that he is not quite himself; he will have grown to anything resembling manhood only after he has consciously and freely embraced the goals which give direction to his life. And so recoiling from the paradox constructed by Socrates and trying to solve it, we have in fact arrived at a rudimentary conception of man. It is, to use once more an expression of Heidegger, that of a being whose essence it is to be concerned with its own being (231).

Of course, a being can take part in and be responsible for its own constitution only if it is initially deficient in essential respects and is aware of this deficiency. It is, therefore, no coincidence that earlier in the dialogue, Socrates should have chided Hippothales for singing the praises of Lysis by reciting the deeds of the boy's ancestors. Instead of directing him toward the future, Hippothales has encouraged the youth to look to the past; instead of urging him on to self-realization, he tempts him to fill the void he experiences within himself by treating the achievements of his forefathers as if they were his own, and thus "become gorged with pride and arrogance" (206A).

Socrates, on the contrary, has succeeded in "humbling and checking Lysis, instead of puffing him up and pampering him" (210E), as Hippothales has been trying to do. The next step would be to give some indication as to what, if anything, the youth ought to do to overcome his shortcomings. Lysis himself suggests that he is simply "not old enough" (209A), which means that he suffers from a lack which time will remove without effort on his part. Socrates corrects him; it is not your lack of years, he says, but your lack of knowledge. For your parents will not interfere with your behavior when it is a question of reading or writing or playing the lyre; that is, in all matters where you show understanding. Socrates then speaks of the crafts: cooking, healing, managing a house or a city. "All matters of which we have a good idea," he continues, "will be put into our hands by all people, whether Greeks or barbarians, men or women" (210B). But as Socrates has chided Lysis for not going far enough, so Socrates' suggestion needs correction. And the need for such correction is brought home to the reader by way of a paradox. To stay on the level of craftsmanship and the resultant utility, as Socrates himself admits, would make parental affection impossible:

> Will anyone count us his friends, will anyone love us in those matters in which we are of no use? . . . Not even you are loved by your own father, nor is anyone else by anyone else in the world, in so far as you or he is useless. (210C)

His parents, however, do love him, although, from a practical point of view, he is in fact still useless to them. So they must love him not for what he is, but for what he may become. Through their feeling toward their son, they confirm Heidegger's claim that "Dasein . . . is existentially that which, in its potentiality-for-Being, is not yet" (186–87).

In his conversation with Lysis, Socrates has played a curious game of simultaneously revealing and hiding the truth. He lets us see the child from the child's point of view, absorbed in his concern with the present. But then he distorts the life of the child by treating it as if its concern with the present were sufficient and as if it were not in need of development. It is this distortion of what we have called the ontic situation which allows him to draw the paradoxical conclusion that the parents, who love the child, tyrannize him. To remove the paradox we must move back to the life of the adult, where the parents are seen to be lovingly heedful of the child's future, to which his present welfare and pleasure must to some extent be sacrificed. The paradox thus causes us to move back and forth, from the mature to the immature and back to the mature point of view, thus bringing both into sharper focus. The child is seen as a plaything of directionless impulses for which the parents must substitute their will. And by bringing about a keener awareness of what it means to be a child, Socrates has conveyed indirectly something of the essence or ontological structure of adulthood. For the child does not come truly in possession of himself until he succeeds in replacing the will of the parent by his own free resolve.

At this point Menexenus, who had been called away before Socrates began his interrogation, rejoins the company. During his absence the inquiry dealt, appropriately, not with friendship as such, but with the conditions for its possibility. Before we can effectively speak of such a relationship, we must have some notion of the individuals related. Now the discussion so far has disclosed a resolve which, through the choice of proper goals, confers a measure of unity upon the individual. This may not give us a fully developed conception of what it means to be a man, but it does point to a fundamental dynamism as a necessary, though not sufficient, condition for genuine selfhood. It is from a violation of this dynamism that Socrates draws most of the paradoxes with which he startles his audience during the remainder of the dialogue.

Socrates, addressing Menexenus who takes the place of Lysis, now states the main theme of the dialogue:

> I count you most happy, at your being able, at your years, to acquire this treasure with such readiness and ease—in that you, Menexenus, have gained so early a true friend in Lysis, and he the same in you—while I, on the contrary, am so far from making the acquisition, that *I do not even know how one man becomes the friend of another*, but wish on this point, to appeal to you as a connoisseur. (212A. Italics added)

The two boys are friends—this is an undisputed fact. But how is one to account for this fact? How must one conceive such a relationship? The road from the ontic to the ontological, from friendship as an experienced fact to the underlying structure, will be dotted with obstacles which Socrates constructs in the form of paradoxes in order to call forth a strenuous intellectual effort on the part of the participants to the discussion.

Anyone who is not forewarned, or who reads the argument which follows out of context, could gain the impression that Socrates intends to demonstrate the impossibility of friendship. To be friends means to be fond of *(philein)*, and so the question arises whether the love involved in friendship need or need not be mutual. There are, according to Socrates, three possibilities: (a) both must be fond of or love each other; (b) the one who loves is the friend; (c) the one who is being loved is the friend. The three alternatives are seemingly exhaustive and Socrates proceeds to show that all of them lead to unacceptable conclusions. Let us follow Socrates as he considers them one by one:

(a) "Unless both love, neither are friends" (212D)

    (1) The assumption conflicts with the use of language. We speak of lovers or friends of horses *(philippoi)*, or quails *(philortuges)* or of dogs *(philokynes)* or of wine *(philoinoi)* or of gymnastics *(philogymnastai)*, and finally of wisdom *(philosophoi)*. Surely it is absurd to demand that in all these cases the friend or lover be loved in return.

    (2) The assumption would make parental love impossible. But it is a generally recognized fact that "quite young children, who are either not yet old enough to love, or who are old enough to feel hatred when punished by father or mother, their parents, all the time even that they are being hated, are friends in the very highest degree" (212E–213A).

(b) "The lover is the friend" (213A)

> If we say that loving makes a friend, we must also admit that hating makes an enemy. It may, therefore, happen that if A loves B, he becomes his friend, and if at the same time B hates A, B is A's enemy. From this it follows that A loves his enemy and B hates his friend. "But surely, my dear friends," says Socrates, "it were grossly unreasonable, nay, rather, I think altogether impossible, for a man to be a friend to his enemy, and an enemy to his friend" (213B).

(c) "The object of love is the friend" (213B)

> If being loved makes a friend, then being hated makes an enemy. If, then, B is loved by A, he is A's friend, and if at the same time A is being hated by B, he becomes B's enemy. From this we must infer that A is being hated by his friend, and B is being loved by his enemy.

At the conclusion of the three-pronged argument, Socrates cries out in despair:

> What are we to do if neither those who love are to be friends, nor those who are loved, nor, again, those who both love and are loved? Are there any other people besides these that we can say become friends to each other? (213C)

Again Socrates does not dispute the fact of friendship but blames the argument for the impasse which the discussion has reached. "If we had conducted our search properly," he maintains, "we should not have lost ourselves in this manner" (213E). For the resumption of the argument he makes the following suggestion:

> Let us proceed on this line of inquiry no longer . . . but let us go back again to that point at which we turned aside, and follow the steps of the poets. (213E–214A)

But we wait in vain for him to lead us back to where the argument went astray. Instead he seems to move forward by exploring a suggestion of the poets and starting an entirely new argument. Now we cannot go forward and backward at the same time. Since Socrates himself goes forward, the impression imposes itself that he means to follow him only after we have retraced our steps and sought out the flaw in the argument.

Now if we reflect on Socrates' discussion of the first alternative, namely, that "unless both love, neither are friends" (212D), we shall find that it moves on the ontic level: people do in fact love horses or dogs, and young children do at times hate parents who have their best interests at heart. What then are the ontological implications of the situation with which Socrates has confronted the reader? The first instance (a1) suggests various kinds of desires for the satisfaction of which horses, dogs, quails, or wine can be used. Love of gymnastics implies a need to develop the body, love of wisdom to develop the mind. In the second instance (a2) we witness the opposite movement, away from one's own to another self. Parents devote themselves to the welfare of their children, whether their love is requited or not. The conception of being which thus emerges from the discussion is of one which can make part of its surroundings subservient to itself and even show utter self-concern; but it is also one which can serve its surroundings and its fellow-beings, and perhaps even lose itself in them, forgetful of its own vital interests. A being capable of fluctuating between such widely separated poles can certainly not be said to possess a fixed and rigid structure.

With Socrates' discussion of the second and third alternatives we find ourselves abruptly and without warning transported into an altogether different world. In the former we encountered beings who experienced needs which they could try to satisfy with things in their environment or by means of their fellow beings, who could use or abuse others, or let others use or abuse them. These beings which were inextricably involved with each other have suddenly given way to timeless, changeless entities, replicas of the Parmenidean One. In such a world a friend is a friend, an enemy an enemy, without possibility of change, and under such circumstances it is, of course, absurd to insist on loving one who inexorably responds with hatred. In a world in which beings are less rigidly constituted, love in response to hatred tends to reduce hatred and has even a chance of producing mutual affection, just as hostility meeting with its kind becomes intensified. As Bias, one of the Seven Sages is said to have counseled: "Treat a friend as an enemy, an enemy as a friend."[5] For the most trusted friend may one day forsake you and your fiercest enemy become your staunchest ally. In the real world of temporal beings, parental love does not militate against the rule that "unless both love, neither are friends." For this can be regarded as an ideal formulation of friendship, the goal at which parental love aims. The child, being punished and coerced, may well hate the parents now. But as he matures and understands the motives of his elders, he may forgive or even fully approve of their past actions toward him. And although the earlier relationship was defective because of the child's immaturity, it contained the seeds of, and may now have blossomed into, a genuine friendship.[6]

The resolution of the paradox which resulted from the argument with Menexenus has led us from a static back to a dynamic conception of man. We are now ready to rejoin Socrates who, addressing himself again to Lysis, is engaged in an examination of the statement of the poet to the effect that "like men to like God ever leads" (214A). This claim, he maintains, can only apply to the good. Either the poet is only half right or he means to exclude the wicked from the like as a matter of course. The reason why there can be no friendship with the wicked is said to be twofold:

[1] The nearer wicked men come to each other, and the more they see of each other, the greater enemies they become. For they injure each other. And it is impossible, I take it, for men to be friends, if they injure and are injured in turn. (214 B–C)

[2] The good are like and friendly with the good, but *the bad ... are not even*

like themselves, but are variable and not to be reckoned with. And if a thing be unlike and at variance with itself, it will be long, I take it, before it becomes like to or friendly with anything else. (214 C–D. Italics added)

The exclusion of the wicked, however, will not diminish our difficulties. For whether we use the like or the good in our argument, in either event will the outcome be unacceptable

[a] Is there any good or harm that a like thing can do to a like thing, which it cannot also do to itself? Is there any that can be done to it, which cannot also be done to it by itself? And if not, how can such things be held in regard by each other, when they have no means of assisting one another? And if a thing be not held in regard, can it be a friend? (214E–215A)

[b] Will not the good man, in so far as he is good, be found to be sufficient for himself? And if sufficient, he will want nothing so far as his sufficiency goes. And if he does not want anything he won't feel regard for anything either. And if he does not feel regard for, he cannot love. And if he does not love, he won't be a friend. (215 A–B)

In the discussion with Menexenus, the paradox resulting from the second and third alternatives could be resolved by reflecting on and drawing the implications from the first alternative. For it could then be seen that Socrates had shifted surreptitiously from a dynamic to a static conception of man. In the present case, a variation of the same procedure is in evidence. Socrates first describes the wicked as always injuring one another. Then, by giving the reason for their doing so, he passes from the ontic to the ontological. "They are variable," he says, "and not to be reckoned upon" (214 C–D). Presumably they do not exercise sufficient control over themselves to restrain their impulses and refrain from infringing upon the rights of others. They have not gained possession of themselves, and this is why Socrates can say that the wicked "are not even like themselves" (214C). If this is what Socrates means by the wicked, then we need only change the signs, so to speak, to discover his conception of the good. The good man is in full possession of himself and hence capable of exercising the necessary control over his appetites. This restraint is based on his will, on a free resolve. The goodness of a man, therefore, is not a quality which is fixed and determined once and for all,ʼ but rests on a sustained effort. The gap which separates this conception of man from that which Socrates uses to contrive his paradox should now be evident. The good men, as the opposite of the wicked above described, are not self-sufficient and in need of nothing and no one, as Socrates would have us believe for the purpose of creating the paradox. They can be serviceable *(opheilos)* to each other; they can encourage each other to persevere; they can set examples to each other; and each, by practicing the virtues of self-control and justice in himself and by encouraging them in others, contributes and helps the other to contribute to a richer and more successful community life which is in the interest and to the benefit of both.

Since Socrates has been able to conceive friendship neither between the like nor between the good as self-sufficient, he decides to try the unlike and the needy. He claims to have heard from someone that "the nearer two things resemble one another, the fuller they become of envy, strife, and hatred—and the greater the dissimilarity, the greater the friendship" (215D). Then Socrates confronts us with what is really an ontic or life situation where needs are felt and relief is sought, where means are chosen for desired ends. Here people are bound together, the poor to the rich, the sick to the physician, the ignorant to the wise. None of these can be said to be simply poor, sick, or ignorant, for they are presumed to have a capacity for the opposite. But the inherent dynamism is quickly destroyed, and that in two ways. In the first place it is destroyed by extracting the rule that contraries are friendly to each other and raising it to a cosmic principle. "My informant," says Socrates, "proceeded with increased magnificence of position to assert . . . that everything craves for its contrary— the dry craves for moisture, the cold for heat, the bitter for sweetness, the sharp for bluntness, the empty to be filled, the full to be emptied, and everything else follows the same rule" (215E). Through this excessive generalization, which finds its parallel in the speech of Eryximachus in the *Symposium*, the specifically human factor is lost sight of. In the second place, the rule is made useless by sharpening the obvious difference between that which desires and the object of its desire into a dichotomy of opposites. As Socrates points out, if we claim that contraries are friends to each other then we will be compelled to say that "friendship is a friend to enmity or enmity to friendship, . . . justice a friend to injustice, temperance to intemperance, good to evil" (216 A–B).

The lesson to be learned from this little exercise would seem to be that in order to render intelligible the structure of friendship as something specifically human, the relationship between possessor and object of desire must be made as intimate as possible, without losing sight of the obvious difference between them. And the misconception of the relationship, the excessive separation of these two factors, constitutes the source which henceforth supplies Socrates with his pedagogical paradoxes.

Unmistakable signs point to a significant break in the discussion at this point. So far Socrates has been concerned with loosening up the rigidity which tends to adhere to our conception of human personality; now he sets in motion a gradual process of interiorization of desire and object of desire, so that both become vital components of one and the same individual. The importance of this shift is indicated by the way in which Socrates introduces the new set of arguments. Previously he appealed to poets or unnamed informants when he could not induce one of the boys to make a fresh suggestion. Now he establishes the point of departure by what to all outward appearances is a formal argument.

Socrates distinguishes three groups between which the relation of friendship might exist: the good, the evil, and that which is neither good nor evil. If we let F stand for the relation, g, e, n for good, evil, neither good nor evil, respectively, then we can represent the six possible relationships which Socrates enumerates as follows:

(1)		(2)		(3)		(4)		(5)		(6)
Fgg	V	Fee	V	Fge	V	Fng	V	Fnn	V	Fne

Nos. 1, 2, and 3, he says, have been eliminated by the previous arguments. Of the relationships in which n is a factor, no. 5 would constitute friendship between like and like, which also has been shown to be impossible, while no. 6 is ruled out because "nothing can be friendly with evil" (216E). It follows then, he concludes, "that friendship can exist only between good and that which is neither evil nor good" (217A).

As noted earlier, demonstrations serve Socrates as a means, not of leading directly to the truth, but of pointing to some factor or misconception which blocks inquiry and conceals the truth. The present argument is no exception to this rule. By enumerating all possible relations, and passing in review the arguments on the authority of which five out of the six relationships were declared impossible, the reader is provided with the opportunity to determine the general nature of the flaws which made a proper conception of friendship impossible. Now nos. 1 and 5 on the one hand, and nos. 2, 3, 6 on the other, offer an interesting contrast. The elements of the first group, dealing with the good and the like, were *conceived* too rigidly; the elements of the second group, dealing with evil, were found to be insufficiently *constituted* ("at variance with themselves" 214D). In other words, the first group suffers from excessive stability in conception; the second from deficient stability in constitution, the flaw in one case being logical, in the other ontological. For the first, Socrates is to blame, and we if we follow him uncritically; for the second, the being itself is responsible. The implication should be obvious: friendship is possible only between two beings which are adequately self-constituted, and the problem for the philosopher is to devise a conception which reflects the structure or the mode of such beings without doing violence to its inherent vitality.

The manner in which Socrates analyzes the "neither evil nor good" suggests that to arrive at such a conception is the task he has now set himself. The "neither evil nor good" is not simply different from the evil and the good, but rather has something of both; or, to use Platonic terms, it suffers the presence of both good and evil. Speaking first about the presence of evil, Socrates shows that this presence can occur in two distinct ways. If Lysis's golden locks, for instance, were dyed with white lead, whiteness would be present to them; they would *appear*, but not really *be*, white, as they would be if old age had turned them white. Sickness, an evil, also may be present to a body in two ways. The body may suffer from an incurable disease and therefore *be* evil; or it may be ill while retaining the capacity of overcoming the illness with the aid of medicine. Again, a man may be simply ignorant or foolish; or he may be ignorant but desirous and capable of overcoming his ignorance. In this last instance, the evil is not something extrinsic to that to which it is present, as the dye to the hair, but the being itself is both good and evil, evil in as much as it suffers a lack, good in so far as the awareness of the lack incites a desire for or a striving toward the removal of the lack. Between the seemingly exhaustive opposites of good and evil, which led to the various paradoxes in the previous discussion, Socrates has now established a third alternative which in some sense is both good and evil:

> Those who are already wise are no longer friends to wisdom, be they gods or be they men, nor, again, are those friends to wisdom who are so possessed of foolishness as to be evil, for no evil and ignorant man is a friend to wisdom. . . . And thus, you see that it is those who are neither good nor evil as yet that are friendly to wisdom or philosophers. . . . (218A–B) For though evil be present, this very presence of evil makes them desirous of good; but the presence which makes them evil deprives them, at the same time, of their desire and friendship for good. (217E–218A)

With this hybrid notion of the "neither evil nor good," Socrates now attempts a formulation of the relationship under scrutiny. He starts out with a concrete situation:

> A body which is neither good nor evil . . . is compelled, because of sickness, to embrace and love the medical art. (217B)

From this he then abstracts the general formula or structure:

> That which is neither evil nor good becomes friendly with good because of the presence of evil. (217B)

Leaving the presence of evil for further consideration at a later time, Socrates now enlarges the formula. Parallel to the *because of (dia)*, the motive power at the beginning, there is also a *for the sake of (heneka)* at the end. The medical art, in our illustration a good, is befriended or loved, not only because of the presence of evil, but also for the sake of health and hence a good to which the body is also a friend. The new formula now reads as follows:

> That which is neither good nor evil is a friend to good because of [dia] an evil to which it is a foe, for the sake of [heneka] a good to which it is a friend. (219B)

Thus far Socrates has been willing to lead the way. Now he seems to think it time for the reader to put forth some effort of his own. The thought provoking medium is provided by two paradoxes which Socrates constructs on the basis of the dia and the heneka, the because of and the for the sake of.

From the above formula it appears that the neither good nor evil is friend to A for the sake of B. It is also said to be friend to B. And if it is friend to B in the same way as it is friend to A, it must be friend for the sake of a third, say C, to which it is also friend; and being friend, it is so for the sake of a fourth, say D. Unless we discover a final or ultimate good which does not lead any further, we have an infinite regress on our hands:

> Can we possibly help, then, being weary of going on in this manner, and is it not necessary that we advance at once to a beginning, which will not again refer us to friend upon friend, but arrive at that to which we are in the first instance friends, and for the sake of which we are friends to all the rest? (219C–D)

All values and thereby all friendships are now put in jeopardy. Whatever we prize for the sake of another depends for its value on the other, and without that other it is no good to us. And so we are using the terms good and friendship improperly if we apply them to objects which are valued for the sake of another:

> When we say we are friendly to things for the sake of a thing to which we are friendly, do we not clearly use a term with regard to them which belongs to another? And do we not appear to be in reality friendly only with that in which all these so-called friendships terminate? (220A–B)

This, then, is the dilemma with which Socrates has confronted us: we must either declare all so-called values as pseudovalues and regard friendship as impossible, or we must discover a final or ultimate good, which, however, appears to be nowhere in sight. Do we have to ascend to and explore a realm of transcendent, absolute values, before we can become genuinely friends with a fellow human being?

Actually, Socrates in his puckish manner had already suggested a way out of the dilemma even before he had fully developed it, at a time when most readers were perhaps no more than dimly aware of an impending difficulty. He did it by

pointing to an actual life situation, by citing an example of how people do in fact
come by a basic or ultimate good. Such a good is not so much the outcome of an
inquiry or a discovery, as it is the result of a choice:

> If a man sets a high value upon a thing—for instance, if, as is frequently the
> case, *a father prizes a son above everything else he has in the world*—may such
> a father be led by the extreme regard he has for his son to set a high value
> upon other things also? Suppose, for example, he were to hear of his son
> having drunk some hemlock; would he not set a high value on wine, if he
> believed that wine would cure his son? And on the vessel also which
> contained the wine? (219D–E. Italics added)

Men do not and cannot wait until some absolute good imposes itself upon their
choice. They select some one thing, or perhaps some day become aware that
there is such a thing which, for better or worse, they "prize above everything
else in the world" (219D). Most fathers, when asked why they chose their son as
the highest good, would be astonished at the question. The more articulate
might point out that he is so "close" to them, that he plays such an important
part in their lives, that he is in fact part and parcel of it. So to choose a son is
almost like choosing a way of life. Can there be a more basic, a more significant
choice? Before the son, however, can play such an important part in the father's
life, the father's life must be truly his own. Hence to choose oneself, to take
possession of oneself, is the most fundamental of all choices. The self, and not
some far-off good, is the ultimate object, the final "for the sake of." This is not
asserting a supreme egotism, but merely to recognize that the choice, the taking
possession of oneself, is the condition for the possibility of all genuine choices.

This complete interiorization of the *for the sake of (heneka)* is followed by that
of the *because of (dia)*. Again Socrates provokes the reader into independent
thinking by way of a paradox. Earlier, he says, we agreed that "the good is loved
because of evil" (Dia to kakon to agathon phileitai) (220B–C). So if evil were
removed from our lives, the good would no longer be of any use to us. "This,
then," he concludes, "appears to be the nature of the good. It is loved because
of evil by us who are intermediate between evil and good, but in itself, and for
itself, it is of no use" (220D). If we apply the same reasoning not to the relative
but to the ultimate good, then the paradox becomes even more embarrassing:

> The original thing to which we are friendly, that wherein all those other things
> terminate to which we said we were friendly *for the sake of* [*heneka*] another
> thing, bears to these things no resemblance at all. For to these things we
> called ourselves friendly *for the sake of* another thing to which we were
> friendly, but that to which we are really friendly appears to be of a nature
> exactly the reverse of this, since we found that we were friendly to it *for the
> sake of* [*heneka*] a thing to which we were unfriendly, and, if this latter be
> removed, we are, it seems, friendly to it no longer. (220D–E)

At first glance this looks like a very artificial difficulty. The word *heneka* appears three times in the passage; twice it is employed properly, but the third time its use seems illegitimate. For when Socrates previously spoke about evil as a factor in the relationship, he used not *heneka*, but *dia*, not *for the sake of*, but *because of*. Is he now trying to deceive the reader by failing to make a distinction which he clearly made before, namely, between cause and end in view? What possible advantage could accrue to the argument by such sophistical trickery? If we take a more careful look at the English and the Greek words and compare their meanings, the paradox loses its artificial character. *Because* means literally "by cause," and cause to the modern reader rightly or wrongly suggests efficient cause; *sake* in *for the sake of* indicates purpose, interest, regard. Now if we can trust Greek scholarship, then *dia* and *heneka* did not have such clearly distinguishable meanings. *Dia* means causally "through, by aid of, by means of, by reason of." The meaning of *heneka* is "on account of, for the sake of, because of."[7] The meanings of *dia* and *heneka* overlap to some extent. Perhaps the English expression "by reason of" retains the vagueness of the Greek terms. If we now reread the passage quoted, substituting "by reason of" for "*for the sake of*," we will find that the paradox persists on a more profound level: the *raison d'être* of the relative or lesser good is derived from a good (toward which it tends); that of the basic or final good must be sought in an evil (which gives rise to it).

As in the previous instance, when he dealt with the interiorization of the *for the sake of*, Socrates has already provided the material for the solution of the paradox. When discussing the nature of the *neither good nor evil* (217B–218B), he distinguished, as we have seen, between evil which has taken full and complete possession of a thing, and evil which can be overcome or eliminated: the whiteness of hair due to old age and the whiteness caused by a dye which can be washed off; the illness which is incurable and the one which can be cured; ignorance which is satisfied with itself, and ignorance which gives rise to the desire or love of wisdom. These three illustrations of the manner in which evil can be present to a thing, also point to an increased intimacy or interiorization: the white dye is the most external; the illness can be conceived as coming from without but capable of affecting and operating within the body; the ignorance is completely within the individual. Now we can take this ignorance as the illustration par excellence of the *neither good nor evil*. For it can be evil pure and simple if no desire is felt to overcome it. But it can also arouse the *desire* for wisdom and lead to a good. So here we have a good, namely, love of wisdom, which derives its *raison d'être* from an evil, namely ignorance. To say that evil serves as the ground for good is paradoxical only if we conceive good and evil in the Eleatic manner as static and immutable and as radically distinct and separate. But the good and evil involved here are neither dichotomous nor unchangeable. Ignorance itself, the evil, can lead to a desire to overcome the ignorance; love of wisdom, the good, is not the consummation of the search, but the search itself. As Socrates has said in the discussion of *neither good nor evil:*

> Those who are already wise are no longer friends to wisdom, be they gods, or be they men, nor, again, are those friends to wisdom who are so possessed of foolishness as to be evil, for no evil and ignorant man is a friend to wisdom. (218A)

So in *desire*, be it for wisdom or anything else, the evil and the good, that which gives rise to striving and that at which the striving aims, have found an intimate, dynamic union. For desire is based on an evil or lack; but despite this origin it strives toward and brings about a good.

In confirmation of the general correctness of the direction which our thoughts have taken, we can point to the fact that through them we have now again caught up with Socrates, and thus established a link between the previous discussion and the one which is about to begin with apparent abruptness. After stating the paradox about the ultimate good being dependent upon evil, he pretends to make a new start. He says he now regards desire, which is neither good nor evil, as the cause of friendship:

> Desire is the cause of friendship, and whatever desires is friendly to that which it desires, and friendly at the time it is feeling the desire. And was all that, which we previously said about being friendly, mere idle talk, put together after the fashion of a lengthy poem? (221D)

His young friend answers: "I am afraid it was"; but we now know that it contained the seeds of what Socrates is saying now. In trying to resolve the paradox we were led to a dynamic interdependence of good and evil in desire, and when Socrates now bases friendship on desire, he has not eliminated evil as the *because of*. But he has reduced its sharp distinction from good, and, what is even more important, he has interiorized the *because of* as he previously interiorized the *for the sake of*. At that time it was found that the ultimate *for the sake of* is the individual himself who must first take possession of himself before he can legitimately be called a self at all. But before a man can contribute to his own self, he must first encounter himself as deficient in essential respects. So here again we find an evil, in the form of a lack, which is the *because of* or gives rise to a good, namely authentic selfhood, and this evil or lack resides at the very core of the human mode of being.

A basic lack giving rise to a desire to remove the lack, might well be recognized as the condition for the possibility of authentic selfhood, and authentic selfhood in turn as a prerequisite for genuine friendship. But how does such a lack bind two people together so that in some sense they become one?

The relevant and crucial statement of Socrates, as might be expected, does not give the unequivocal, unambiguous answer to the question that one would like to receive:

> That which feels desire feels desire for that which it is in want [endees]. . . . But that which is in want is friendly with that of which it is in want and becomes in want of that of which it suffers deprivation. . . . That then which belongs to a man [to oikeion] is found, it seems, Lysis and Menexenus, to be the object of his love and friendship and desire. . . . If, then, you two are friends to each other, *by some tie of nature you belong to each other* [Hymeis ara ei philoi eston allelois, physei pe oikeioi esth' hymin autois]. . . . And so in general, if one man, my children, is desirous and enamored of another, he can never have conceived his desire, or love, or friendship, *without in some way belonging to the object of his love*. (221D–222A. Italics added)

What is that of which a man is deficient, although it properly belongs to him? That which is his own in the most intimate sense, is his selfhood; it is not given to him outright, but only as a possibility.[8] This is the reason why Heidegger calls it "Dasein's ownmost potentiality-for-Being [Eigenstes Seinkoennen]." And just because it is given only as a possibility can it, in a genuine sense, become his own. Does not this self, however, once acquired, belong to him uniquely and exclusively, so that it cannot be also acquired and possessed by another and thereby constitute a bond between two individuals, as Socrates seems to suggest? The cause of the difficulty with which we are here confronted is the same as that which gave rise to all the paradoxes throughout the dialogue. It is the tendency to yield to the influence of an ontology which considers as real only that which *constantly remains*, the present-at-hand, and fails to give recognition to a radically different mode of being, that of Dasein, which constantly projects possibilities and then understands itself and acts in the light of these possibilities. At the beginning of the dialogue we were puzzled by the paradoxical behavior of Lysis's parents who seemed to love and yet tyrannize him. Upon reflection, we found that Lysis's parents were concerned not only with what he was, but even more with what they felt he should aim to become. Now the physical being of a man cannot be shared, but it is quite otherwise with his aspirations, which give direction and a measure of unity to his life. The ideals which he loves and attempts to realize in his own being can also be loved by, and realized in the being of, another. They and they alone can constitute the "tie of nature" by which two friends "belong to each other" (221E). To see this possibility, we had to relinquish the absolute dichotomies of friend and enemy, good and evil, like and unlike,[9] and come to understand the intimate interdependence of good and evil in desire, and the union of that which desires and that which is desired in the authentic self. And so we must likewise rid ourselves of our customary concept of the individual as a being tightly closed in upon itself. Man reaches out into the future for goals and ideals which determine his actions and thereby shape the pattern of his life. This openness to future possibilities makes him accessible to other individuals who by sharing his aspiration become one with a vital portion of his own personality.

Our thoughts have carried us beyond what Socrates explicitly says in the *Lysis*. In fact we have somewhat anticipated the *Phaedrus*, where Socrates mythically pictures the awful vastness of man's longing projection by having the human psyche soar to the very abodes of the gods and with them to the place above the heavens where true beauty and wisdom and goodness reside. In the present dialogue, Socrates has long since gone into hiding behind the mask of the Sophist who plays his game of logic with the lifeless Eleatic entities which enable him to turn out innumerable paradoxes. He wonders whether that which belongs (to oikeion) differs from the like, for if it does not we would have to say that like is friendly with like, and this our earlier discussion, he claims, has shown to be absurd. We cannot well say that that which belongs differs from that to which it belongs, and if we maintain that it is the same, then the good is friendly with the good and the evil with the evil, both of which relationships were demonstrated to be impossible:

> What other way is left for us of treating the subject? Clearly none. I, therefore, like our clever pleaders at the bar, request you to reckon up all that I have said. If neither those who love or are loved, neither the like nor the unlike, nor the good, nor those who belong to us, nor any other of all the suppositions which we passed in review—they are so numerous that I can remember no more—if, I say, no one of them is the object of friendship, I no longer know what I am to say. (222E)

Of course, we can be deceived no longer. The puzzles which Socrates parades before us are simply warnings that unless our mind holds fast to the inner dynamism of the human personality it will be sucked in by the quicksands which surround the notion of friendship.

The dialogue ends, as it began, on a note of foolishness. Hippothales, the awkward lover of the opening scene, is matched by the uncouth attendants (paidagogoi) who rudely break up the gathering and in a faulty Greek call out to the boys that it is time to go home. Socrates, in the last moment, comes out of hiding and returns to the world of change and brute fact:

> Lysis and Menexenus, we have made ourselves ridiculous today, I, an old man, and you children. For our hearers will carry away the report that though we believe ourselves to be friends with each other—you see I class myself with you—we have not as yet been able to discover what we mean by a friend. (223B)

Friendship, he seems to say, and life in general, no matter how absurd and inconceivable they appear to be, can go on without philosophy; but philosophy divorced from life turns into an empty game.

A nagging doubt is likely to linger in the mind of the thoughtful reader as he puts the *Lysis* aside. Has not Socrates casually dropped a final paradox at the very moment when he left the stage? How can Socrates, an old man (geron aner) call himself a friend of mere children? They might have some trivial interests which are genuinely their own and which they can share. Their life goals, however, are still those their parents have chosen for them. Perhaps Plato is trying to suggest that the distinction between child and adult, as the many other distinctions considered in the dialogue, must not be drawn too sharply. The two young boys have not yet reached genuine selfhood, but, as Heidegger insists, neither have many adults. And even a truly mature man, as Socrates may be presumed to be, can never be secure in the possession of himself. What the children, with the aid of their elders, must continually strive to attain, Socrates must make every effort to preserve. For many are the pitfalls which not only hinder the achievement of authenticity but threaten to cause its loss.

III

In retrospect, Socrates' words, which, according to Alcibiades in the *Symposium*, "are ridiculous when you first hear them" (221E), should now have yielded their hidden treasure. For now we see that the perplexities which they created in our minds were due to the interplay of two radically different conceptions of man, one static and the other dynamic. Can these two conceptions, to which Socrates only points and leaves nameless, be more or less equated with the notions of substantiality and existence which Heidegger works out explicitly and in great detail? This concordance, which has been suggested all along, stands now in need of some reenforcement.

As noted earlier, Heidegger objects to the traditional categories as inadequate when applied to Dasein or the human mode of being. This entity he insists on characterizing in terms of existentials, of which the most basic ones are *existence*, *thrownness* and *fallenness* or inauthenticity. "The formally existential totality of Dasein's ontological structural whole," he says, "must therefore be grasped in the following structure: The Being of Dasein means ahead-of-itself-Being-already-in-(the-world) as Being-alongside (entities encountered within-the-world)" (237). Can this structure, at least in rough outline, be detected in the *Lysis?*

Despite the difference in approach, one indirect and the other direct, Plato and Heidegger at times show a remarkable similarity in the manner in which they evoke the phenomena to be scrutinized. Heidegger's image of the craftsman confronted with a damaged tool "brings to the fore the characteristic of the presence-at-hand in what is ready-to-hand" (104), and at the same time lights up the referential context or "world" which, together with the tool, must remain inconspicuous in the normal exercise of the craftsman's skill. Through the malfunction of the tool, three different realities are made to appear simultaneously: ready-to-hand, present-at-hand and world.

In analogous fashion, Plato presents the two boys in a *deficient* mode, having their life goals set, not by themselves, but by their parents. They thus exhibit an extreme case of inauthentic projection, but still of projection or *existence*, of Dasein as "being-ahead-of-itself." Another aspect of their behavior reveals their having *fallen captive* to their environment, "being-alongside-(entities encountered within-the-world)," when they yield to whatever attraction offers itself in the form of the race chariot, the mule team, or a mother's loom. And finally, the ritual which is in process when Socrates joins them shows them "already-in (the world)," *thrown* into a specific society, namely, that of Athens, with its cultural, political and familial institutions and the norms to which they must conform, endowed with certain natural gifts of bodily beauty and intelligence or the lack of them.

From Heidegger's point of view, the stage is properly set. The basic existentials, namely, *existence, thrownness*, and *fallenness*, are clearly present in the situation, although not specifically designated. Will Plato make use of them in order to delineate a proper conception of man which alone can give the inquiry into the nature of friendship a chance for success?

There are two basic realities, according to Heidegger. "An entity," he says, "is either a 'who' (existence) or a 'what' (presence-at-hand in the broadest sense)" (71). In the discussion of the first set of possible descriptions of friendship, Plato makes the distinction visible by pitting the first alternative in terms of 'who,' against the second alternative in terms of 'what.' Analyzing the statement "unless both love, neither are friends," Plato suggests that language, through such terms as *philippoi, philoinoi, philortuges* and *philokynes*, reflects the fact that man has, in Heidegger's terminology, been "abandoned to the world . . . and concernfully submitted to it" (465), that is, that he has been made dependent on things in the world which he must use in order to further his own being. Both body and mind are in need of development as indicated by the words *philogymnastai* and *philosophoi*. And as he uses things, so he can allow others to use and abuse him, as parents frequently do by loving and caring for children who often do not requite the love and perhaps even repay them with hatred. Here Plato treats man clearly as a 'who,' in Heidegger's terms as "an entity for which, in its Being, that Being is an issue." (236) But in the examination of the other two alternatives, "the lover is the friend" and "the object of love is the friend" (213A–B), the lover and the beloved, he who hates and the hated, are treated as a 'what,' having a property which "enduringly remains" (128), like Descartes's 'extension' and his *cogito*, and which can be predicated of them once and for all. Only then does it become absurd to love one who leaves that love unrequited or repays it with hatred.

Socrates plays basically the same game with the evil on the one hand and the good and like on the other. Again the members of the second group are inappropriately conceived as substances, as good or alike pure and simple, so that they need not and cannot receive any help from another and make friendship completely useless. The evil in their turn are brushed aside as obviously incapable of becoming friends. By describing them, however, as "not even like themselves" (214C), he suggests that they are capable of becoming themselves, of losing or gaining their own selfhood. "Because Dasein," according to Heidegger, "is in each case essentially its own possibility, it *can*, in its Being, 'choose' itself and win itself; it can also lose itself and never win itself" (68). Ironically, the very deficiency to which Socrates points as the reason for the impossibility of friendship in the evil, contains the seed for this very possibility. "For only in so far as it is essentially something which can be *authentic*—that is, something of its own—can it have lost itself and not yet won itself" (68). And, of course, only a genuine self can enter into a genuine relationship of friendship with another self.

The third discussion centers around the statement that "friendship can exist only between the good and that which is neither evil nor good" (217A). While earlier the inappropriateness of referring to human beings in terms of fixed properties was brought to light by showing that it makes friendship inconceivable, it is now demonstrated more directly. Socrates distinguishes openly between a characteristic which can be called evil pure and simple, and one which can be called neither or both. He uses three examples of increasing complexity: Lysis's hair artificially colored white or turned white through old age; a body inflicted with an incurable disease as against one which can be cured by means of medicine; and finally and most importantly, an ignorant individual who is content with his foolishness as against one who has the desire to overcome it. This second type of ignorance constitutes a deficiency which makes it evil; but it also contains the spur which incites the individual to seek wisdom, and to that extent it is good. This second type of ignorance does not constitute an enduring quality. Its possessor lends support to the view which Heidegger expresses by saying that "the characteristics which can be exhibited of this entity are not 'properties' present-at-hand of some entity which 'looks' so and so and is itself present-at-hand, but are in each case possible ways for it to be" (67).

Subjecting to further analysis this desire which is caused by an evil and motivated by a good, and therefore defies qualification by either opposite, Plato arrives at the same series of 'in-order-to' relationships which, according to Heidegger, characterizes man's concernful activities. And like Heidegger, he points out that they all end in a 'for-the-sake-of' *(heneka—umwillen)*, a final end which is radically different from the means employed in arriving at it. For this 'for-the-sake-of' gives meaning to the various 'in-order-to', so that the latter must be described, not in terms of properties, but rather in terms of appropriateness and inappropriateness in relation to the end which they serve. When Plato has Socrates speak of "that to which we are in the first instance friends, and for the sake of which we are friends to all the rest" (219C–D), he seems to have the same thought in mind which Heidegger expresses when he says:

> The primary 'toward-which' is a 'for-the-sake-of-which.' But the 'for-the-sake-of-which' always pertains to the Being of Dasein, for which, in its Being, that very Being is essentially an issue. We have thus designated the interconnection by which the structure of an involvement leads to Dasein's Being as the sole authentic 'for-the-sake-of-which.' (116–17)

Thus Socrates' analysis of the "neither good nor evil," similar to Heidegger's examination of Dasein's concernful activities, reveals three kinds of realities: one which can be described in terms of categories and which Heidegger calls present-at-hand; the ready-to-hand which has its properties still concealed in appropriateness and inappropriateness; and finally, the human mode of being which, through existence, that is, through the projection of a *heneka*, a 'for-the-sake-of,' creates a refential context or 'world,' giving meaning to the second type of being.

The nature of the *heneka* to which, Socrates says, we must go back as to a beginning (219C) is still undetermined. All we are told by Socrates is that this ultimate good bears to the relative goods "no resemblance at all" (220D). Commentators are quick to refer to the *absolute* good and beautiful mentioned in the *Symposium* and the *Phaedrus*.[10] If they are right, then according to Socrates friendship among ordinary people would be impossible; it would be reserved to those rare individuals, if there are any, who have access to absolute truth and beauty. Socrates issues a veiled warning against such extravagance when he speaks of the father who "prizes a son above all else he has in the world" (219D), and thus elevates him to his own particular *heneka* about which his life revolves.

Such a father's choice may be authentic or inauthentic. It may be a free choice, or more likely, his paternal affection simply got the better of him. If the choice of the *heneka* is not the father's own, then the life to which it gives meaning is not his own either. But what could more belong to a man in the most intimate and the most rigorous sense than his own life, his own self? Is this what Socrates means when he speaks of the *oikeios*, as "that which belongs to a man," this same *oikeios* which is said to be "the tie of nature" by which two friends "belong to each other" (221D–222A)?

Socrates has temporarily gone into hiding, and we are left to our own resources or we must seek help elsewhere in order to answer the question which Socrates has bequeathed to us: What is that something which belongs uniquely to each individual and still can serve as a bond between two friends?

As so often, what Plato hides in a paradox, Heidegger states explicitly:

> The Being-with-one-another of those who . . . devote themselves to the same affair in common, is determined by the manner in which their Dasein, each in its own way, has been taken hold of. They thus become *authentically* bound together, and this makes possible the right kind of objectivity (die rechte Sachlichkeit), which frees the Other in his freedom for himself. (159)

Existence in the authentic mode, that is, the free choice of significant life goals, makes for genuine selfhood. And the sharing of such goals constitutes true friendship, a friendship which binds two people together and still leaves each individual free. In the light of Heidegger's conception of man, the perplexing talk about the *oikeios*, in typical Socratic fashion, conceals and reveals *existence* rather than *substantiality* as the essence of man, and *existing*, in the sense of *projecting*, as the condition for the possibility of friendship.

As mentioned at the beginning of this chapter, Heidegger maintains that the earliest thinkers of our philosophic tradition understood the being of entities in terms of substance ontology. He refers to the famous Parmenides fragment: *To gar auto noein estin te kai einai*. This he interprets to mean that "Being is that which shows itself in the pure perception which belongs to beholding and only by such seeing does Being get discovered" (215). The type of being which is discovered in this manner is the present-at-hand. "Our understanding of Being," Heidegger argues, "is such that every entity is understood in the first instance as present-at-hand," because from the very beginning "presence-at-hand has been equated with the meaning of Being in general" (268). This may well be so, and Heidegger may also be right in maintaining that Descartes and Kant, two of the most significant figures at crucial moments in the history of philosophy, uncritically followed the tradition, so that this understanding of the meaning of being is "the one that prevails, and which even today has not been surmounted explicitly and in principle" (Ibid.). If, however, our interpretation of the *Lysis* is correct, then Heidegger's contention that the tradition has been unbroken to this very day finds a stumbling block in Plato's dialogues. For the paradoxes of the *Lysis*, as we have seen, find their solution only in the recognition that a substance ontology is inadequate for a conception of the human mode of being. The tradition appears unbroken only to an excessively *literal* reading of the dialogues and a failure to see that for Plato the paradox is one of the most important means of teaching by indirection. Then it could be said that in distinguishing between substance and existence, Heidegger is not so much engaged in breaking new ground as he is in making explicit and appropriating an ancient tradition.

SYMPOSIUM: LOVE AND LOSS OF SELFHOOD

The *Symposium* was composed at a time when Plato was at the height of his dramatic powers. On this point the scholarly commentaries on the dialogue seem to be in full agreement. And it could hardly be otherwise. For who would fail to admire the exquisite skill with which Plato recreates an historical scene, namely the gathering of prominent Athenians who celebrate a young play-wright's first triumph by singing the praises of the god Eros. But the philosophic yield, as it is presented by the various commentators, does not appear at all to be commensurate with the genius of Plato. We are urged to see the dialogue simply as a series of speeches describing various types and degrees of love, for the most part homosexual in character; or, if we insist on some unifying principle, we are invited to conceive the speech of Socrates as dealing with a mystical experience and as constituting the climax toward which all others lead and in which they lose themselves.[11] But the quick ascent from ordinary human love to an *amor mysticus* is particularly out of tune with the intellectual climate of our day. And if it were found to be the main thrust of this celebrated dialogue, then the relevancy of Plato's thought to our own vital concerns would have suffered a serious corrosion.

The modern reader seems to be confronted with the choice of relegating the philosophical aspects of the dialogue to the realm of purely historical interests, or to seek a new approach in the hope of penetrating to a living core which lies hidden from view beneath the crust of traditional interpretations.

The possibility and the fruitfulness of a new approach suggests itself from the neglect suffered by the dramatic aspect of this most dramatic of Plato's dialogues. A consummate artist, who is also a great thinker, is not likely to limit the dramatic elements to the mere byplay; they may be expected to permeate and determine every phase of the expression of his thought. And so the great stumbling block in the way of a proper access to the dialogue may have been a too literalistic attitude. In view of the so-called doctrine of *Platonic Forms,* we may have been too intent upon finding models to imitate and ideals to pursue, where we should have looked for aberrations, for pitfalls to avoid. Not unlike Aristotle surveying and analyzing the work of the great tragedians, we should have searched out the tragic flaw which must be capable of arousing feelings of pity and fear for ourselves. Perhaps we should make no less stringent demands upon Plato's dramatic dialogues and not be content until they too touch us in the very core of our being.

It is noteworthy that a similar loss of significance has occurred in some of the plays of Sophocles, the most philosophical of the Greek tragedians. If we believe the interpreters of the *Ajax,* for instance, then its protagonist, through his suicide, fully restores his stature as a heroic personality. In the name of some ideal of heroic virtue we are asked to forget the degrading act, the murder of the Greek generals, which he would have committed had not Athene intervened in the nick of time; we are to disregard the fervent pleas of Tecmessa not to leave wife, child, brother, and companions at the mercy of his cruel enemies, a plea to which he seems not wholly insensitive; we are not to hold it against him that he leaves the burden of all his problems on the shoulders of his brother Teucer. And yet it seems relatively easy to rescue the play from this insufferable confusion, if we only have the courage to break with the traditional interpretation and let our own deeper feelings be our guide. For who has not seen men fall captive to the role they have chosen to play in life. And if we see Ajax as a victim of his own image, then we understand why he should strike out so furiously against the Greeks who refused to award him the arms of Achilles, why he could not face the world once his image had been shattered through his slaughter of the animals while under the spell of Athene, and why he should be willing to give his life if that sacrifice might possibly refurbish his image in the eyes of posterity. Then we need not feel obliged to find his behavior praiseworthy against strong feelings to the contrary, nor need we blame him. What is then called for is pity, for it is so easy to fall victim to one's own aspirations, and fear, because the same fate might befall any of us. But through the experience gained vicariously in witnessing the play, we have also come to a better understanding of ourselves and thus have increased the chances of avoiding the misfortune which has struck down Ajax.

In the attempt to make the play more significant for ourselves, we may also have brought it closer to the lives of the ancient Greeks. For Aristotle speaks of the arousal of pity and fear as one of the objectives of great tragedies, and he sees the hero as possessed of the tragic flaw, that is, of something which the spectator is urged to avoid. In transforming Ajax from an ideal to be imitated to an example to be avoided, we may, after all, not have broken away but rather returned to the genuine tradition.

Perhaps a similar transformation of the types of love eulogized in the various speeches of the *Symposium* will succeed in pointing to a basic insight and thus restore the philosophic significance of the dialogue as a whole. But in order not to do violence to the spirit of the text while working the transformation, the reader must hold himself open and receptive to all the prompting and influences which Plato the dramatist will bring to bear upon him.

The dramatic byplay at the beginning of a dialogue, as we have seen, often creates a mood or atmosphere which suggests the general theme or at least the manner in which it will be approached. In the *Symposium* this mood points to excess. The dialogue is narrated by "Apollodoros the madman" who is "always raging against [himself] and everybody but Socrates" (173E.)[12] He has heard the story from Aristodemos who attended the banquet and who, at the time, is said to have been the most "devoted admirer of Socrates" (173B). Aristodemos encountered Socrates bathed and sandalled, apparently an unusual sight, on the way to the house of Agathon to celebrate the young playwright's first victory. He lets himself be persuaded to come along uninvited on the responsibility of Socrates. Before they reach the house, Socrates "drops behind in a fit of abstraction" (174D), and Aristodemos, without realizing Socrates' absence, enters the house without the one on whose urgings he came. Agathon asks his servants to dish up whatever they please without being ordered. "I have never left you to yourselves," he says, "but on this occasion imagine that you are the hosts, and that I and the company are your guests" (175B). Finally there is the agreement that instead of the drinking bout for which the occasion would normally call, there should be speeches in praise of the god Eros.

Everything indicates a deviation from the customary, from the norm, a relaxing of the reins, sufficient to raise the spirits as befits the occasion, without ending in licentiousness, without completely losing sight of the proprieties of social life. And so in the speeches which follow there can be expected a measure of exaggeration, a degree of excess, just enough to startle the reader and make him wonder where, between the extremes, the truth may be found.

Phaedrus opens the round of encomia. He makes a brief reference to Eros as "the eldest of the gods," who, according to the poets, came into being without parents. Then he abruptly turns from the mythical to the empirical and speaks of the benefits which accrue to the young man and his lover alike, inasmuch as they incite each other to acts of honor and courage:

> A lover who is detected in doing any dishonorable act, or submitting through cowardice when any dishonor is done to him by another, will be more pained at being detected by his beloved than at being seen by his father, or by his companions, or by any one selse. The beloved, too, when he is found in any disgraceful situation, has the same feeling about his lover. And if there were only some way of contriving that a state or any army should be made up of lovers and their loves, they would be the very best governors of their own city, abstaining from all dishonor, and emulating one another in honor, and when fighting at each other's side, although a mere handful, they would overcome the world. (178D–179A)

Phaedrus is impressed by the great power of love which shows itself in such behavior, and uncritically he calls it good, without inquiring into the inner springs of its outward manifestations. Socrates cannot object until his turn comes, but Plato can drop a warning hint. "The veriest coward," Phaedrus is made to declare, "becomes an inspired hero equal to the bravest . . . when Love of its own nature infuses into the lover that courage which, as Homer says, the god breathes into the souls of some heroes" (179A–B). If the lover thus acts as if possessed, if he cannot help performing deeds of valor, whether he be a brave man or a coward at heart, how can he earn merit? Why, then, does Phaedrus cite Alcestis and Achilles, who were ready to die for husband and friend respectively and whose sacrifice the gods rewarded by allowing Alcestis to return to earth and transplanting Achilles to the Islands of the Blessed? The paradox inevitably calls for reflection.

First it must be noted that the irresistible power of Eros in Phaedrus's lovers operates through the image of each one of them in the eyes of his beloved. There is no real concern on the part of one for the welfare of the other. Each one is in love not with the other, but with the beautiful image of himself in the mind of the other. Their love is still on a low level; it is in fact no more than a kind of self-love. The lovers have not succeeded in breaking through the narrow circle of their selfhood to a community of shared goods, where the self is forgotten and absorbed in the WE. But if it is a self-love, why this concern not with the self but with the image which the other forms of it? Does it not appear as if the very existence of the individual had shifted from that individual to the image in the mind of the other and thus were thrown upon the mercy of that other who entertains the image? We cannot help thinking of Ajax, who found life unbearable once his reputation as the bravest of the Greeks before Troy had been damaged beyond repair. To Phaedrus's lover, as to Ajax, this image is dearer than life itself. For "he would be ready to die a thousand deaths rather than endure its destruction" (179A). The object of Phaedrus's admiration is therefore neither a true lover nor a man of genuine courage.

Then there is a second consideration: If Achilles and Alcestis were deserving of reward for moral excellence, as the legend maintains, their sacrifice must have been free from coercion. Phaedrus's lovers are under the domination of Eros and cannot help themselves. For them, therefore, merit is out of the question, for it is incompatible with lack of freedom. But despite the fact that they have lost control over their *present* behavior and therefore are not responsible for it, they are responsible for having surrendered to Eros and forfeited their responsibility. From the contradiction between compulsion and merit, which emerges from Phaedrus's comparison of his lovers with Achilles and Alcestis, we have arrived at a merely seeming incompatibility between loss of freedom and responsibility. And so, contrary to Phaedrus, we must conclude that Eros is not an unmitigated boon to mankind, for he now stands exposed as a possible threat to man as a moral being. But whether Eros will in fact be helper or destroyer ultimately rests on a decision of the individual: will he allow Eros to gain control over him, or will he make himself the master of Eros?

The harm which may come to a man from the image which he has formed of himself should not be unfamiliar to the modern reader. Jean-Paul Sartre, for instance, explores this problem in *The Flies*. Aegisthus, the King of Argos, is presented in the play as a real person who has allowed himself to become reduced to a mere symbol of fear in the hearts of his subjects; Zeus, on the other hand, a mere symbol, exercises great power over men. But both king and god are at the mercy of the people of Argos and can function only as long as their subjects remain forgetful of their freedom and power.[13] Thus Plato, as Sophocles before and Sartre after him, can be said to recall men to their responsibility by presenting instances of the loss of responsibility.

The next eulogy, offered by Pausanias, is governed by a conception of love which, at first glance, constitutes a considerable improvement over that of Phaedrus. Lover and beloved are no longer locked into the narrow confines of their individual selfhood and rigidly controlled by their own image. Their relationship is based on a prior choice between two loves, one noble and the other common, the first allegedly descending from a heavenly, and the second from an earthly, Aphrodite:

> The love who is the offspring of the common Aphrodite is essentially common, and has no discrimination, being such as the meaner sort of men feel . . . and is of the body rather than the soul . . . and does good and evil quite indiscriminately. . . . Those who are inspired by [the offspring of the heavenly Aphrodite] turn to the male, and delight in him who is the more valiant and intelligent nature. . . . They love not boys, but intelligent beings whose reason is beginning to be developed. . . . And in choosing young men to be their companions, they mean to be faithful to them, and pass their whole life in company with them. . . . (181B–D)

Despite the reference to the gods, the quality of the love is determined by the individual lover. The right kind of love presupposes typical human endowments: intelligence, freedom, and the ability to exercise proper choice.

There is also a greater awareness of the complexities which surround the love relationship, as reflected in Pausanias's account of the diverse customs governing the public attitude toward lovers. In Elis and Boeotia and "in countries having no gift of eloquence," love of youth is simply condoned. In Ionia, on the other hand, and "generally in countries which are subject to the barbarians, the custom is held to be dishonorable; loves of youths share the evil reputation in which philosophy and gymnastics are held, because they are inimical to tyranny" (182C). In Athens, by contrast, the rules about love are said to be very perplexing. The lover is encouraged in the pursuit of his beloved, and no matter how foolishly he acts and to what extremes he goes to obtain his ends, he is not being reprimanded. "And what is the strangest of all," says Pausanias, "he only may swear and forswear himself, and the gods will forgive his transgression, for there is no such thing as a lover's oath" (183B). While the lovers are thus granted unusual liberties, the youths are kept under strict surveillance by parents and tutors to prevent them from associating with their admirers. Love of youths, therefore, appears as something honorable when seen from the lover's side, and something disgraceful from the beloved's point of view. Now the real reason, according to Pausanias, for urging one to pursue and one to flee is to gain time during which to test both lover and beloved. The lover must not be interested in a fleeting attachment for the sake of bodily pleasures, and the beloved must not be attracted by wealth, prestige, or political power. A genuine relationship of this type is said to be rooted in a desire on the part of the beloved to acquire an education in virtue and wisdom, and in the willingness of the lover to provide such an education:

> When the lover and the beloved come together . . . the one capable of communicating wisdom and virtue, and the other seeking to acquire them with a view to education and wisdom . . . then, and then only, may the beloved yield to the lover. (184D–E)

This time Plato issues no warning against the possible hidden shortcomings in Pausanias's conception of love. And there would seem to be no need of it, for our experience with the first speech should have put us on our guard against too ready an acceptance of the second. But for those readers who have been taken in by its surface plausability, Plato has prepared a rude awakening from their intellectual slumbers. Since this occurs much later in the dialogue, nothing less than a shock is required to make the reader go back and reconsider his judgment. The agreement between lover and beloved which Pausanias finds so noble and praiseworthy, is utterly discredited by the report of Alcibiades on how he once tried to strike just such a bargain with Socrates and failed miserably. Alcibiades met all the requirements laid down by Pausanias: he was young, intelligent, and eager to exchange his bodily charms for the other's wisdom. Socrates, however, is said to have spurned the offer in his usual ironical manner:

> Alcibiades, my friend, you have indeed an elevated aim if what you say is true, and if there really is in me any power by which you may become better; truly you must see in me some rare beauty of a kind infinitely higher than any which I see in you. And therefore, if you mean to share with me and exchange beauty for beauty, you will have greatly the advantage of me; you will gain true beauty in return for appearance—like Diomede, gold in exchange for brass. But look again, sweet friend, and see whether you are not deceived in me. The mind begins to grow critical when the bodily eye fails, and it will be a long time before you get old. (218D–219A)

Socrates refuses to agree to the exchange which Alcibiades suggests, not only because he does not desire what his young friend has to offer but also because he could not deliver his part of the bargain, the communication of wisdom. "How I wish," he had said earlier, "that wisdom could be infused by touch out of the fuller into the emptier man as water runs through wool out of a fuller cup into an emptier one." [175D]

A critical look at the speech itself uncovers additional defects. Why, for instance, is the lover in the initial stages given complete freedom while severe restrictions are imposed on the behavior of the other party to the relationship? Does it not suggest great vulnerability on the part of the younger member? Are they really, as Pausanias would have us believe, equals "in the work of their own improvement" (185B)? It would undoubtedly be closer to the truth to say that the lover will tend to impose his goals, his ideals upon the beloved in order to make him as much like himself as possible. Thus the younger man's life is not really his own, and he has fallen victim to a bondage, no less vicious for its subtlety and for going unnoticed. In any event, the teacher-student relationship is not one between equals, as a genuine love relationship between two persons should be, neither one of whom ought to lose his identity through subjection to the other.

Finally the speech contains an almost casual remark which points to the openness and vulnerability of all men, young or old:

> In countries which are subject to the barbarians, the custom is held to be dishonorable; loves of youths share the evil repute in which philosophy and gymnastics are held, because they are inimical to tyranny; for the interests of rulers require that their subjects should be poor in spirit and that there should be no strong bond of friendship or society among them, which love, above all other motives, is likely to inspire. (182B–C)

One may well imagine that high-spirited youths might prove troublesome to tyrants and refuse to buckle down under heavy-handed authority. But why should this be particularly true of lovers? Now we may think of the self-centered love of Phaedrus, where the lover loves his own image in the mind of the beloved, or of the more genuine love at which Pausanias aims but does not quite reach, where both lover and beloved strive for a common ideal in terms of which they understand themselves. Whatever conception of love we entertain, it is obvious that the image plays a vital part. For such lovers to submit to tyrannical rule would mean to rid themselves of their idealized image and substitute the picture of a helpless pawn in the hands of the ruler. And while the idealized image inspires love, be it self-love or love of the other, the depraved image can only breed hatred. And so tyrannical rule, if fully successful, reaches down to the very core of a man and corrupts him both as an individual and in his relation to his fellowmen. This is why Jean Genêt has one of his young Negro characters exclaim:

> I began to hate you when everything about you would have kindled my love and loving would have made the world's contempt unbearable, and their contempt would have made my love unbearable.[14]

The tyrannical rule here described, which is said to make love impossible, is merely an extreme case of the violation of a person standing under the authority of another. As we have seen, the teacher also exercises authority, and he too can inflict irreparable harm on his students no matter how well-meaning he may be, if he imposes his ideals instead of simply helping them pursue their own.[15] Small wonder that Socrates in the *Theaetetus* should be so insistent in maintaining that he knows nothing, but that those who converse with him profit (150D).

Pausanias's eulogy is now unmasked as a warning against a threat to the proper formation of a human being, a formation which is a prerequisite for the possibility of a genuine love relationship, and the theme of Pausanias's discourse is revealed as a variation of that of Phaedrus. For while the latter presented the individual victimized by his own image, the former shows him in danger of falling prey to the image imposed by another.

The next to speak is Eryximachus, the physician. It is actually the turn of Aristophanes, the famous comedian; but he is suffering from the hiccups at the moment and he has asked the physician to cure him or to take his place. Eryximachus promises to do both. The remedy he prescribes proves effective; the scientific speculations in which he indulges are much less so.

It would, of course, be pedantic to seek a profound significance in all of the comic byplay in every dialogue. But it is difficult to resist the temptation to interpret this reversal of roles as an attempt on Plato's part to deflate somewhat the exaggerated prestige which physicians have probably enjoyed in all ages. The jester one would not be inclined to take seriously. But everyone would listen to the physician, for "one learned leech is worth the multitude," as Alcibiades quotes Homer as saying.[16] As it turns out, the physicians's speech is philosophically of much less importance than that of the jester. And Plato might thus be said to present Eryximachus as a living example of those who, in the words of Socrates in the *Apology*, "on the strength of their technical proficiency claim a perfect understanding of every other subject, however important" (22D).

Eryximachus rightly criticizes the two preceding speeches for the narrowness of their outlook, for they would restrict the love relationship to that between a young man and a youth. This defect his speech proposes to correct:

> Seeing that Pausanias made a fair beginning and but a lame ending, I must endeavor to supply his deficiency. I think that he has rightly distinguished two kinds of love. But my art informs me that the double love is not merely an affection of the souls of men toward the fair, or toward anything, but is to be found in the bodies of all animals and in productions of the earth, and I may say in all that is; such is the conclusion which I seem to have gathered from my own art of medicine, whence I learn how great and wonderful, and universal is the deity of love, whose empire extends over all things, divine as well as human. (186A)

As a physician, he says, he recognizes different desires, such as those of the healthy and those of the unhealthy body, corresponding to the loves mentioned by Pausanias; the first of these desires can be indulged in while the second must be eradicated or converted into the other type. Then there are opposite elements which the physician must try to reconcile, "such as hot and cold, bitter and

sweet, moist and dry, and the like." Going beyond his own field, he sees the
same need for reconciliation of opposites in music, inasmuch as "harmony is
composed of differing notes of higher and lower pitch which disagreed once . . .
and rhythm is compounded of elements short and long, once differing and now
in accord; which accordance, as in the former instance medicine so in all these
other cases music implants, making love and unison to grow up among them"
(187C). And as the reconciliation of "the hot and cold, the moist and dry"
brings health to the human body, so it produces abundant crops and a rich
livestock in husbandry. All this, says Eryximachus, is the work of the god of
love, whereas "hoarfrost and hail and blight spring from excess and disorders of
these elements" (188A–B). Even in such fields as astronomy and men's
relationship with one another and the gods, love is said to reign supreme.

On the surface, Eryximachus's theory reflects a genuine empirical outlook.
There is the physician's eye for observed facts: conflicting desires in the human
body which need to be harmonized. To extend the theory, reference is made to
typical human activities, such as music, husbandry, astronomy; to basic
experiences such as the effect which excessive heat or cold, the wet or the dry
have on the crops and on the lives of man and beast. But then his desire for
generalization gets the better of him and love is turned into a harmonizing
principle of the whole universe. Eryximachus ends up with a fanciful construct
which is of little if any theoretical or practical significance. Worst of all, love as
a distinctively human trait has been lost sight of.[17] Viewed from the theory of
Eryximachus, man sees himself simply as one among all the other things in the
world which have a fixed nature and which merely need act out that nature. And
instead of helping him break up the molds into which an earlier upbringing and
the pressures of society have forced him, Eryximachus's theory encourages the
'tendency to mistake these molds for his real self and their rigidity for the
stability of his own nature.

When Eryximachus has concluded, the hiccup of Aristophanes has also come
to an end, but only after he has applied the most radical of the cures prescribed
and provoked a sneeze or two by tickling his nose. Aristophanes teases
Eryximachus by pointing to the discrepancy between his cosmic theory of love
as a harmonizing principle, and his homely but effective remedy of a hiccup,
and he "wonders why the harmony of the body has a love of such noises and
ticklings" (189A).

The function of the jester is to entertain and make the audience laugh, and
yet Aristophanes, more than any of the previous speakers, captures something
of the pathos and the tragedy of human existence. Again, while his art allows
him complete freedom in the use of fancy, he manages to put it to such use that
it brings about a clearer understanding of the life of man. He achieves this result
not by appealing at the outset to empirical evidence, but by starting boldly and
unabashedly with a myth, his myth being such that it lets some truth about man

shine forth in its own light. Men, he says, were originally double of what they are now. They had two faces looking in opposite directions, set on one head and a round neck, with four eyes and ears, and also four arms and legs, and all the other parts to match. They could walk erect in all directions, or, at great speed, tumble over and over on their four feet and four hands. Sexually they were self-sufficient, and the sexes were three in number: man, woman, and man-woman. They were powerful in mind and body, and in their arrogance decided to scale heaven and lay their hands upon the gods. At first the gods were perplexed; they could not let such impudence go unpunished, but if they destroyed men they would deprive themselves of their worship and sacrifices. Zeus finally hit upon the idea of cutting them in two, "like a sorb-apple which is halved for pickling, in order to humble their pride and improve their manners" (190C). He threatened to split them again and make them hop on one leg, should they persist in their insolence. Once they were so divided, the various halves ran about looking for the remainder. When they had found each other they forgot to eat and drink and everything else, in their eagerness to stay together. They were in fact threatened with extinction had not Zeus taken pity on them and invented a new plan:

> He turned the parts of generation round to the front, for this had not been always their position, and they sowed the seed no longer as hitherto like grasshoppers in the ground, but in one another; and after the transposition the male generated in the female in order that by the mutual embraces of man and woman they might breed, and the race might continue; or if man came to man they might be satisfied, and rest, and go their ways to the business of life: so ancient is the desire of one another which is implanted in us, reuniting our original nature, making one of two, and healing the state of man. Each of us when separated, having one side only, like a flat fish, is but the indenture of a man, and he is always looking for his other half. (191B–D)

No one should be tempted to take Aristophanes' tale as a seriously intended theory of the origin of man. Through the deliberate and undisguised use of a myth, Aristophanes forestalls any distractive concern about the truth or falsity of his report. The myth points not to the past but to the present: in its light man appears deficient in the very core of his being, a deficiency for which he must take responsibility and make amends, AS IF it were the result of a punishment for some wrongdoing on his part. The notion of guilt incurred and punishment suffered could not, of course, produce the feeling of inadequacy and the sense of obligation to take corrective measures. But if these are already present, it can bring them into sharper focus, making them more keenly felt, and thereby increase the likelihood of their being translated into action. The myth does not impart any new information or any new facts with which the reader has not long been familiar. But men have a way of concealing their shortcomings and shirking their responsibility for self-improvement. The myth thus serves as a mirror which is held up to the reader in the hope that the sight of himself will set in motion the powers which lead to a better and more satisfactory existence. Thus while the theory of Eryximachus encouraged man to look away from himself and his specifically human mode of being, Aristophanes' myth tries to recall him to himself.

Aristophanes thus brings the discussion of Eros back to its proper point of departure, to the recognition of love as a desire which touches man in his very being as a man. The next step should be a determination of its proper object. It is here where the myth of Aristophanes begins to bog down. Aristophanes' lovers are as possessed of a desire without a clear awareness of the object of the desire. They are pictured as being lost to their impulses very much as Phaedrus's lovers appeared lost to their images:

> They could not explain what they desired of one another. For the intense yearning which each of them has toward the other does not appear to be the desire of lovers' intercourse, but of something else which the soul of either desires and cannot tell, and of which she has only a dark and doubtful presentiment. (192C–D)

The "presentiment" might suggest a transcending tendency, a vague reaching beyond. But Aristophanes' lovers are so earthbound that if pressed they would admit to a desire for a union of a literally physical character:

> Suppose Hephaestus, with his instruments, to come to the pair who are lying side by side and to say to them, "What do you people want of one another?" they would not be able to explain. And suppose further that when he saw their perplexity he said: "Do you desire to be wholly one; always day and night to be in one another's company? For if this is what you desire, I am ready to melt you into one and let you grow together, so that being two you shall become one, and while you live, live a common life as if you were a single man, and after your death in the world below still be one departed soul instead of two—I ask whether this is what you lovingly desire, and whether you are satisfied to attain this?"—There is not a man of them who when he heard the proposal would deny or would not acknowledge that this meeting and melting into one another, this becoming one instead of two, was the very expression of his ancient need. (192D–E)

Even if the god were able and willing to forge them into one, he still would not produce the unity of two individuals, a genuine WE in which the two selves are somehow preserved. As Aristotle has pointed out, "one or both would certainly perish."[18] But if man's most deep-rooted cravings prove impossible of fulfillment, then the conclusion seems inescapable that man, in essential respects, is absurd.

Socrates, of course, does not allow the round of discourses to reach such an impasse. An unbridgeable gap, however, seems to separate the ultimate and total frustration to which the myth of Aristophanes has led, from the promise of complete fulfillment in the subsequent speech of Socrates. The chasm appears somewhat less untraversable if we take into account that it is the professional jester who has given us a picture of man. If he is successful, then, as Aristophanes himself remarks, he will make us laugh with him and at ourselves, and the man he portrays will not only be frustrated but also ludicrous:

> Zeus (after having cut men in half) bad Apollo give the face and the half of the neck a turn in order that the man might contemplate the section of himself: he would thus learn a lesson of humility. Apollo was also bidden to heal their wounds and compose their forms. So he gave a turn to the face and pulled the skin from the sides over all that in our language is called the belly, like the purses which draw in, and he made one mouth at the center, which he fastened in a knot (the same which is called the navel); he also moulded the breast and took out most of the wrinkles, much as a shoemaker might smooth leather upon a last; he left a few, however, in the region of the belly and the navel, as a memorial of the primeval state. (190E–191A)

To laugh at something is to rise above it. And Aristophanes could not have succeeded in making his friends laugh at themselves if in some sense they had not already transcended the human condition. As the word *Galgenhumor* ("gallows humor") suggests, men believe that they need not be bound and hence can rise above even the most desperate conceivable situation.

To explore that transcending tendency would seem to be the next logical step in the discussion. The mere talk about a transcending element in man, however, is paradoxical. If it is truly beyond actual experience, or even human experience in general, how can it be spoken of? Such logic would be fatal only if we were concerned with a reality which simply is, without fuzzy fringes. But the human beings with which the various speeches were concerned, appear extraordinarily fluent and difficult, if not impossible, to force into a conceptual mold. Phaedrus's lover seems to attach more significance to the image of himself in the eyes of the beloved than to his own existence and thus has become alienated from himself. Pausanias's beloved was found to be in danger of losing his being to his lover by following the other's goals and thus leading not his own life but that of another. And if we laugh with Aristophanes at ourselves, we stand outside ourselves; and we could not be aware of the inadequacy of our condition unless we were able to view it from a point beyond our actual achievement, from the possibility of a more satisfactory condition which makes it appear unsatisfactory. But if man is thus always ahead of himself, the possibility or goal at which he aims and from which he understands himself is part of his very being, and while this transcending quality of man may be paradoxical, it is nonetheless a fact.

To aim at a goal, that is, to reach beyond the present moment into the unknown future, is never without risks. The tenuous thread which binds the present to the future is easily broken. If the goal pursued is too far removed from the individual's capacity, it will cause frustration and perhaps a complete breakdown of personality. If it is not rooted in experience at all, it becomes a vacuous dream. Ideals can be powerful motivating forces; but if severed from reality they wither and die, and all that remains are husks of empty words.

This aberration into pure verbiage, divorced from all experience, is illustrated by the speech of Agathon. While the preceding speakers paid their respect to the god and then turned to human experience, Agathon proposes to dwell on the nature of the god. His eulogy has been characterized as "a brilliant but passionless and fanciful tissue of jewelled conceits."[19] All his command of language, all his skill in achieving prettiness cannot fill the bottomless emptiness that yawns beneath the elegant phrases. The purported demonstrations of the divine qualities show barely a trace of experienced reality. Love is said to be the youngest and therefore the fairest because he "flees out of the way of old age, who is swift enough, swifter truly than most of us like" (195B); "he is the softest for he walks not upon the earth . . . but in the hearts and souls of both gods and men, which are of all things the softest"; he is "exceedingly temperate, for temperance is the acknowledged ruler of the pleasures and desires, and no pleasure ever masters Love, and if he masters them he must be temperate indeed" (196C–D). In the same vein he attributes to the god justice, wisdom, and courage. And finally the discourse erupts into a gush of words:

> This is he who empties man of disaffection and fills him with affection . . . who sends courtesy and sends away discourtesy, who gives kindness ever and never gives unkindness; the friend of the good, the wonder of the wise, the amazement of the gods; desired by those who have no part in him, and precious to those who have the better part in him; parent of delicacy, luxury, desire, fondness, softness, grace; regardful of the good, regardless of evil; in every word, work, wish, fear—saviour, pilot, comrade, helper; glory of gods and men, leader wisest and brightest: in whose footsteps let every man follow, sweetly singing in his honor and joining in that sweet strain with which love charms the souls of gods and men. (197D–E)

Plato underscores the inane prettiness of Agathon's oration by having Socrates exclaim in mock alarm that he was almost struck dumb, especially by the beauty of the concluding words, and that he who was next in line to speak could not possibly match such artistry. And then Plato has him object to the type of eulogy offered by all the previous speakers:

> In my simplicity I imagined that the topics of praise should be true, and that this being presupposed, out of the true the speaker was to choose the best and set them forth in the best manner. And I felt quite proud, thinking that I knew the nature of true praise and should speak well. Whereas I now see that the intention was to attribute to Love every conceivable greatness and glory, whether really belonging to him or not, without regard to truth or falsehood—that was no matter. (198D–E)

If they insist on their way of eulogizing Eros, Socrates is made to continue, he must ask to be released from his promise to participate, "but," he adds, "if you like to hear the truth about Love, I am ready to speak in my own manner" (199B).

In spite of his professed concern with the truth, it would be a mistake to expect Socrates to deliver a dissertation on the nature of Eros. There is no reason to believe that he suddenly abandoned his views on the communicability of truth, as expressed earlier in the *Symposium*, or his function as a gadfly and a midwife as described in the *Apology* and the *Theaetetus*. If the speech of Socrates represents the climax of the *Symposium*, it will be the climax not only in content, but also in the use of the Socratic method and the dramatic approach to philosophy. The reader must, therefore, be especially on his guard to distinguish truth explicitly stated from hints and challenges inviting him to penetrate beneath the surface meaning and search out the truth for himself.

During the interrogation of Agathon which serves as an introduction and at the beginning of the actual speech, which takes the form of a narration of a conversation with the stranger-woman Diotima, Socrates abruptly reduces Eros the god, to Eros a human desire. Some of the previous speakers, especially Eryximachus and Aristophanes, came close to identifying love and desire, but they all maintained an ambiguous relationship with divinity. Now this connection is definitely and irrevocably broken. Love, says Socrates, has an object toward which it aspires. But that which desires something lacks what it desires; and if Eros desires beauty, wisdom, or excellence of any sort, he cannot himself be beautiful, wise or good, and hence cannot be a god at all. From the fact that Eros is neither wise nor good, it does not by any means follow that he is ignorant, evil, or ugly, for he is a mean between two extremes. The real evil of ignorance, for instance, lies in this, that "he who is neither good nor wise is satisfied with himself" (204A). Eros, however, is ignorance seeking wisdom, discontentment seeking satisfaction, deficiency seeking beauty and perfection in body and soul. It is through Eros that men experience the attraction, the pull of the transcendent, the ideal. This is why Diotima refers to him as "the mediator who spans the chasm which divides . . . gods and men, and conveying and taking across to the gods the prayers and sacrifices of men, and to men the commands and replies of the gods" (202E). The picture drawn is not that of a god but that of man stretched out between what he lacks as expressed in "his prayers," and the call of the ideal, "the commands of the gods," promising fulfillment.

Eros as a symbol thus points to man as essentially deficient and aware of his deficiency, a condition which has been described as *la grandeur et la misère de l'homme*, the greatness and the misery of man. For if man is to be able to call himself legitimately an 'I', and to call his life in a genuine sense his own, then whatever reality he possesses cannot have been given to him once and for all. In essential respects his being must be the outcome of his own conscious efforts.

His very impoverishment leads to his richness and the nature of this wealth demands that it arise out of deprivation. In his deficiency he shows his descent from Penia or Poverty according to the myth of Diotima; but since he is not restricted to a fixed and immutable nature, since he can reach beyond what he actually is at any given moment toward a richer experience, a fuller realization of his capacities, he resembles his father Poros or Plenty. And so the dark clouds which in Aristophanes' account gathered at the horizon of human existence now appear adorned with a silver lining. For man's basic wants, which Aristophanes presented mythically as a form of punishment, have now gained positive significance in the Diotima myth in as much as they appear as the condition for the possibility of authentic humanity.

Some of man's decisions, therefore, concern his very being. They appear even more momentous if we consider that man is finite. If he had endless time at his disposal, he might retrace his steps once he found he had chosen the wrong way. As it is, every chance may be the last, every opportunity may be lost for ever.

Plato creates a sense of that finitude by having Diotima draw a vivid picture of man as engaged in a desperate and futile struggle to overcome it and gain immortality. Love, says Diotima, according to the report of Socrates, desires the possession of the beautiful or good leading to happiness, "and not only the possession, but the everlasting possession of the good" (206A), and therefore, she concludes, "all men desire immortality together with the good" (207A). Animals, as well as men insofar as they are animals, achieve a kind of immortality through procreation, which "leaves behind a new existence in place of the old" (207D). "See you not," Diotima is quoted as saying, "how all animals, birds, as well as beasts, in their desire of procreation, are in an agony when they take the infection of love, which begins with the desire of union, whereto is added the care of offspring, on whose behalf the weakest are ready to battle against the strongest even to the uttermost, and die for them, and will let themselves be tormented with hunger or suffer anything in order to maintain the young?" (207B).

This desperate attempt to gain immortality is merely the other side of a keen sense of the instability and perishability of all that is mortal:

A man is called the same, and yet in the short interval which elapses between youth and age, in which every animal is said to have life and identity, he is undergoing a perpetual process of loss and reparation—hair, flesh, bones, blood, and the whole body are always changing. Which is true not only of the body, but also of the soul, whose habits, tempers, and opinions, desires, pleasures, pains, fears, never remain the same in any one of us, but are always coming and going; and equally true of knowledge. . . ." (207D–208A)

Diotima's generalization of this straining for immortality, unlike the generalization of love on the part of Eryximachus, does not bring the love operative in man and beast on the same level. On the contrary, it serves to mark an essential difference. For the road to immortality through procreation, open to animals and men insofar as they are animals, is contrasted with another way which is possible only to human beings, namely, immortality through fame. To beings which merely act out their nature, the preservation of the species through procreation may be sufficient. But for men, who have no fixed nature, who in some measure are responsible for their own mode of being, procreation which substitutes a new for an old existence, is not enough. They aim at the preservation of some individual uniqueness, and hence must resort to other means. They can choose and seek to live up to a certain exalted image of themselves and then try to impress that image on the memory of their fellowmen in the hope that it will be handed down from generation to generation and thus afford them a kind of immortality:

> Think only of the ambition of men, and you will wonder at the senselessness of their ways, unless you consider how they are stirred by the love of immortality of fame. They are ready to run all risks greater far than they would run for their children, and to spend money and to undergo any sort of toil, and even to die, for the sake of leaving behind them a name that will be eternal. (208C)

The futility of this attempt to attain to the everlasting possession of a good is obvious. For those who seek fame place themselves at the mercy of the good will of other men. As Aristotle will remark later, on the same subject, "honor depends on those who bestow it rather than on him who receives it, but the good we divine to be something proper to man and not easily taken from him."[20] Plato himself seems to call attention to the questionable character of this search for happiness by having Diotima make an obviously exaggerated claim. "All men," she says, "do all things, and the better they are the more they do them, in the hope of glorious fame of immortal virtue; for they desire the immortal" (208E). Furthermore, she specifically refers to Alcestis, Achilles, and Codrus, already mentioned in one of the preceding speeches as having been rewarded by the gods in recognition of their devotion to husband, friend, and subjects respectively. But if Diotima were right, then the very paragons of love would have acted solely out of a desire for immortality, that is, for selfish reasons, and Socrates' discourse on love would have reached the unfortunate conclusion that men cannot go beyond self-love and that any kind of genuine friendship is impossible.

If we do not wish the argument to founder on this rock, we must take the trouble of laying bare the kernel of truth encased in the extravagance of Diotima's assertion. We cannot agree that all men seek immortal fame—for few are immodest enough or gifted enough to hope for so much—but all do in fact try to establish for themselves some kind of stability or identity by living up to and maintaining an image. This reduced claim does set the argument afloat again. For the next logical question is: by what process does this identity establish itself? And it is to this question that Diotima does in fact give an answer:

> Souls which are pregnant . . . conceive . . . wisdom and virtue in general . . . But the greatest and fairest sort of wisdom by far is that which is concerned with the ordering of states and families, and which is called temperance and justice. And he who in his youth has the seed of these implanted in him and is himself inspired, when he comes to maturity desires to beget and generate. He wanders about seeking beauty that he may beget offspring . . . And when he finds a fair and noble and well-nurtured soul . . . to such a one he is full of speech about virtue and the nature and the pursuits of a good man; and he tries to educate him; and at the touch of the beautiful which is ever present to his memory, even when absent, he brings forth that which he had conceived long before, and in company with him he tends that which he brings forth; and they are married by a far nearer tie and have a closer friendship than those who beget mortal children. . . . (209A–C)

The search, be it for immortality or mere stability, has now become socialized, for the seeker shows at least a concern for another human being. The older is willing to share what is dearest to him with the younger. He is eager to raise him to his own higher level. But what guarantee does he have that the younger will carry on in pursuit of their common ideals after his influence has ceased with his death, or that others will take over when the younger has died? Furthermore, nothing is said as to how the older obtained his ideals of excellence. Were they uncritically taken over from a previous generation and are his virtues based on habit only? But even if they are genuinely his own, the ideals and goals which tie the older and the younger together are not the common offspring of them both. For it is the older who "brings forth that which he conceived long before," and so the life they lead is at best that of the older. The transmission of ideologies from the older to the younger generation is vital to a community in the interest of continuity and stability. But inherent in it is the risk of neglecting the idiosyncrasies of the individual, of failing to develop his own unique potentialities, of molding him after an idea which may be that of another, or, even worse, may long have ceased to correspond to real needs. And so the lover in his eagerness to confer a measure of stability on himself and his beloved may have succeeded merely in sharing with him his own inauthentic selfhood. And before trying to perpetuate himself by raising another in his own image he had better make sure that his image is really his own. What then must a man do to become truly himself?

In the myth, Diotima has described Eros as destitute and homeless, as having "no shoes, nor a house to dwell in," as lying "on the bare earth exposed under the open sky, or at the doors of houses." For this dogmatic assertion she has now supplied the empirical confirmation by pointing to the fruitless attempts men make to find a permanent dwelling place in their children, or in the memory of future generations, or by educating a youth in their own image. There seems to be nothing in human experience capable of stilling man's craving for fulfilment, and of providing a place where he can come to rest. Is it conceivable that man is destined to seek salvation in a transcendent world, and if so, are there discernible signs in human experience which might serve as a guide to this higher realm?

Diotima in fact leads the way from the love of a single beautiful body to the love of absolute beauty. After a more detailed presentation, she sums up the ascent as follows:

> The true order of going, or being led by another, to the things of love, is to begin from the beauties of earth and mount upwards for the sake of that other beauty, using these as steps only, and from one going to two, and from two to all fair forms, and from fair forms to fair practices, and from fair practices to fair notions, until from fair notions he arrives at the notion of absolute beauty, and at last knows the essence of beauty. (211C–D)

It seems that the higher is distinguished from the lower in terms of permanence. The beauty of an individual body is less lasting and therefore less dependable as an object of love than the beauty of all bodies; beauty of soul is more enduring than bodily beauty; institutions and laws outlive generations, and these in turn are outstripped by knowledge with its concern for things eternal, so that the love which attaches itself to their beauty is still more firmly secured. Even the highest beauty so far considered is, however, relative to the thing in which it inheres, and so the mind must make one last effort to conceive beauty independent of everything else, that is, beauty absolute. Beauty so conceived transcends human experience and can be expressed only *via negationis:*

> It is a nature which in the first place is everlasting, not growing and decaying, or waxing and waning; secondly, not fair in one point of view and foul in another, or at one time or in one relation or at one place fair, at another time or in another relation or at another place foul, as if fair to some and foul to others, or in the likeness of a face or hand or any other part of the bodily frame, or in any form of speech or knowledge, or in heaven, or in earth, or in any other place; but beauty absolute, separate, simple, and everlasting, which without diminution and without increase, or any change, is imparted to the ever-growing and perishing beauties of all other things. (211A–B)

At each step of the ascent, according to Diotima, the recognition of the higher depreciates and loosens the attachment to the lower. When the lover, for instance, perceives "that beauty in every form is one and the same," she maintains, "he will abate his violent love of the one, which he will despise and deem a small thing," and recognizing the beauty of the sciences he will see himself as "being not like a servant in love with the beauty of one youth or man or institution, himself a slave mean and narrow-minded" (210C–D). And as the notion of absolute beauty appears on the horizon, his detachment from all that ordinary experience has to offer should be complete. At the same time there looms in the distance a supernatural object promising satisfaction to all that man desires:

> "This, my dear Socrates," said the Stranger of Mantineia, "is that life above all others which men should live, in the contemplation of absolute beauty. . . . Remember how in that communion only, beholding beauty with the eye of the mind, he will be enabled to bring forth, not images of beauty, but realities, and bringing forth and nourishing true virtue to become a friend of God and be immortal, if mortal man may be." (211D–212A)

Man's fate now seems to depend upon the chances of gaining access to this absolute; if it should prove inaccessible, then man's existence is absurd, possessed as he is of a desire for the impossible. Socrates only says: ". . . such were the words of Diotima, and I am persuaded of their truth" (212B). But he is in the habit of hiding the truth, at least in part, and even if he really were persuaded, we still would have to seek conviction for ourselves.

Before taking a stand on the question of the existence and accessibility of such an Absolute, or deciding whether such a question can be legitimately asked in the context of the dialogue, it might be useful to recall briefly the nature and function of two similar Absolutes which we encountered in some of the other dialogues.

While the *Symposium* refers to an Absolute which provides the richest possible experience, the myth of the *Protagoras*, as we have seen, describes a condition which is absolute in the sense that it renders human existence impossible. The myth arrives at this condition by imagining men without a sense of justice so that, as social beings, they can live neither in isolation nor in society. Underlying the myth we found a process of extrapolation which carries the correlation between the sense of justice and the quality of the community life to its absolute limit.

The argument, no less than the myth, fails to establish the actual existence of a primitive asocial state. Since such a state is said to be destructive of human life, perhaps it is even impossible as an event in the past, since men have in fact survived. But both argument and myth point to its possibility as a continued threat to social living. They bring home the fact that the maintenance of an adequate level of community life is a responsibility which men can shirk only at the risk of self-destruction.

In the *Republic*, the Absolute appears as the ultimate principle of intelligibility and being. Socrates, it will be recalled, establishes it by the simple analogy with the sun, by the multistoried analogy of proportionality in the so-called *Line* which moves from shadows to the *Idea of the Good*, by the *Allegory of the Cave*, and again by a process of extrapolation which carries the synthesizing process inherent in human knowing to its ultimate limit. These various ways, far from demonstrating the existence and accessibility of the Absolute, were found to underscore the distance which separates it from the realm of possible human achievement. In fact, our previous reflections have shown that the way in which it would have to be known, namely, by direct intuition, would place it irrevocably beyond the reach of human endeavors. But if the *Idea of the Good* is inaccessible, then the philosopher-kings are not infallible and they cannot really relieve us of the burden of having to make our own decisions.

It seems, therefore, that the absolute asocial state in the *Protagoras* and the absolutely perfect city in the *Republic* are merely devices which Plato uses to block all possible escape from reality and to induce men resolutely to face the human condition and to accept the agonizing responsibilities which it imposes. Can a similar function be assigned to the idea of Absolute Beauty in the *Symposium?*

As a warning against the temptation to draw too close a parallel between the *Republic* and the *Protagoras* on one hand, and the *Symposium* on the other, it might be said that in the former Plato establishes the absolute by means of myth, allegory, and analogy, while in the latter he explicitly uses a straightforward argument. With such an argument one should perhaps not take the liberties that one might feel justified in taking with the less logical literary devices. On closer examination it appears, however, that the various steps of the "ascent" to absolute beauty are not linked by any logical necessity. The arguments which can be constructed on the basis of the hints in the *Protagoras* and the *Republic* contain at least a hypothetical necessity: *If* the correlation holds even when the terms are carried to the limit, *then* when one term is reduced to zero, the other reaches zero also; or: *If* the synthesizing process were to reach its ultimate consummation, *then* it would arrive at an all-embracing principle as the source of all reality and intelligibility. But why should a man's love of a single beautiful body pass to the love of beautiful bodies in general, and from there to love of institutions and laws, and thence to love of knowledge? And once this stage has been reached, by what logic does Absolute Beauty reveal itself? If Plato had been interested in establishing the existence of an absolute as the end of man's desire, he would have been more effective by using the good rather than the beautiful as a basis for his argument. Diotima herself does not hesitate to "put the word *good* in the place of the *beautiful*" (204E) when Socrates has difficulty in answering a question. In the *Lysis* Socrates characterizes the *beautiful* as "something soft and smooth and slippery" and conjectures that this may be the reason why "it slides and slips through our fingers so easily" (216C–D). He also suggests how from the experience of any good one might arrive at the notion of an absolute good. A man, says Socrates, who prizes his son above all else in the world, on discovering that he has drunk hemlock and believing wine to be a cure, would come to value a measure of wine and even the pot which contains it. But clearly the vessel is valued only for the sake of the wine and the wine for the sake of the son. Thus we get a kind of hierarchy of values. It would be easy to ask the further question as to the value of the son, and an answer might be given by referring to the important role he plays in the life of the father. The process could be continued indefinitely, and we are faced with a choice between an infinite regress of relative values, and therefore ultimately no values at all, or the postulation of an absolute good or value by which all others are sustained.

It would, therefore, be difficult to maintain that Plato chose out of ignorance the weaker of two possible foundations for his argument in the *Symposium*. Beauty, however, constitutes the weaker foundation only if we assume that it was meant to support the establishment of the existence of an absolute. If Plato did in fact choose it, with full awareness of the alternative at his disposal, then the suspicion arises that the purpose he had in mind was quite different from that which is usually attributed to him.

We have had several occasions to observe that it is a disservice to the understanding of the dialogues, if in our admiration for Plato we slur over logical fallacies in his arguments or inconsistencies and weaknesses in his position. For the correction of an argument and the criticism of a position has often brought us closer to the insight which gives meaning to the dialogue as a whole. Such seems to be the case with the present stage of our interpretation of the *Symposium*.[21] As we saw before, the steps of the ascent to Absolute Beauty seems to lack a logically necessary connection. Whether a man passes from one to the other is a question not of logic but of desire or will. The higher step is not related to the lower as its logical consequence, but as a means of exposing the unsatisfactory character of the lower and thus loosening the attachment of the will. And what each step does to the one preceding it, the absolute does to all the steps together. This detachment as the effect of the "ascent" had to be accepted earlier on the authority of Diotima's explicit statement. Now it is seen to be supported by the way in which the various steps are linked together. The *existence* of the absolute is not so supported. Unless we are willing to resort to a blind leap of faith, there is now extinguished the last spark of hope that Eros might find a home outside the individual. And within the individual the only stable element that remains is man's *resolve*, his determination to choose what *he* thinks right, to pursue goals which *he* has set for himself, for only in this way can he be truly himself. Thus, more basically than in the *Protagoras* and the *Republic*, the absolute in the *Symposium* serves as a means of throwing the individual back upon himself, of reminding him that he must exercise unflagging vigilance, not only in regard to matters political, but even and more importantly in regard to his very being. Not until he has acquired, and is able to maintain, such an existence has he laid the proper foundation for a sound relationship with other human beings.

In the *Republic*, the last lingering doubt about the impossibility of a literal interpretation is eliminated by the myth of Er with its report of an individual who, as we saw before, had enjoyed an education equivalent to the best the philosopher-kings could offer and yet failed in his most important function as a man, i.e., in the choice of his own life. Now it is not difficult to attribute to the Alcibiades scene at the end of the *Symposium* a similar significance. The appearance of the drunken Alcibiades is usually seen exclusively as a device used by Plato to sing the praises of his beloved friend and master Socrates, and it is undeniably true the Alcibiades pays him a tribute such as can hardly be surpassed. He sees him as a brave soldier, patient and uncomplaining in the endurance of hardships, but also capable of great enjoyment in the company of friends. He describes the inner beauty of the man hidden beneath an ugly exterior, his effectiveness as a speaker far surpassing that of a Pericles and of the great Athenian orators, the influence he exerts on others, and above all the uniqueness of the man as an individual:

> There are many more quite wonderful things that I could find to praise in Socrates. But although there would probably be as much to say about any of the other of his habits, I select his unlikeness to anybody else, whether in the ancient or in the modern world, as calling for our greatest wonder. You may take the character of Achilles and see his parallel in Brasides or others; you may couple Nestor, Antenor, or others I might mention, with Pericles; and in the same order you may liken most great men; but with the odd qualities of this person both in himself and in his conversation, you would not come anywhere near finding a comparison if you searched either among men of our day or among those of the past, unless perhaps you borrowed my words and matched him, not with any human being, but with the Silenuses and satyrs, in his person and his speech. (211C–E)[13]

Alcibiades, despite his admiration for Socrates, gained a very evil reputation. One would think that he did not turn out as good a man as he might have been because he lacked the will power to live up to the high example which fate had set before him. But the truth of the matter, as Plato presents it, seems to have been the very opposite. He had to exert all his efforts to maintain his own against the powerful personality of Socrates:

> This Marsyas has often brought me to such a pass that I felt as if I could hardly endure the life which I am living (as, Socrates, you will admit); and I am conscious that if I did not shut my ears against him, and fly as from the voice of the siren, my fate would be like that of others,—he would transfix me, and I should grow old sitting at his feet. (216A)

If Alcibiades had to struggle so desperately against being submerged by the powerful personality of Socrates, what chance would a man have if he were confronted with absolute beauty? Might he not find its attraction irresistible?

Now, says Diotima, the presence of fair youths "entrances you; and you and many a one would be content to live seeing them only and conversing with them without meat or drink, if that were possible—you only want to look at them and be with them. *But what if a man had eyes to see the true beauty—a divine beauty, I mean, pure and clear and unalloyed. . . ?"* (211D–E) (Italics added) Does not Diotima's thought lead to the obvious conclusion that if bodily beauty can call forth such a state of inebriation and self-forgetfulness in an individual, absolute beauty would completely overwhelm him? Since it would serve as "the final cause of all our former toils" (211A) and would determine all subordinate goals, we would no longer have to grope more or less blindly in the dark, projecting and pursuing goals which time and circumstance may later reveal as ill conceived.[23] But where would there be room for legitimate choice, for the courage to make decisions on inadequate evidence, for the willingness to take responsibility—in a word, for authentic existence? Would it not seem that such existence is possible only in the twilight zone of ordinary human knowledge? And so it appears that just as the philosopher-kings, in possession of the *Idea of the Good*, or absolute knowledge, would prevent their subjects from becoming free and responsible citizens, so absolute beauty, if it did exist and were accessible, would render the genuine human mode of being impossible. For if a man were at all able to resist the absolute, if he were to succeed in mustering enough strength to act counter to its dictates, would he not have to choose that which in the light of the absolute he knows full well to be not good and not rational? Like the mythical Lucifer, closest to God and hence to truth and goodness, he could assert his individuality only by willfully turning to evil.

If Plato had said nothing further about Alcibiades, it would be tempting to regard him as some sort of existential hero who is willing to sacrifice even his moral qualities if these constitute the price he must pay to attain to a unique and genuine selfhood. Such an interpretation might find support in the *Lesser Hippias* where Socrates maintains the paradoxical claim that there is a sense in which it is true to say that "those who do wrong voluntarily are better than those who do wrong involuntarily" (375D). Perhaps it could even be said that in a sense the man who does evil voluntarily is better than the one who does good involuntarily: before an act can be moral at all, it must be the individual's own act and not simply the result of habit, custom, passion, or social pressure.[24] Plato, however, does not allow Alcibiades to gain such heroic proportions. For no sooner has Alcibiades escaped the attractive force of Socrates that he is drawn into the orbit of another:

And therefore I run away and fly from him, but when I leave his presence the love of popularity gets the better of me. (216B)

The Alcibiades scene casts a retrospective light on the dramatic approach as well as on the main theme which has been in evidence throughout the dialogue. The need for a moral being to become the sole source of his acts is effectively demonstrated by presenting a powerful personality who struggles but fails to attain to freedom and genuine selfhood. Alcibiades is strongly reminiscent of Haemon in Sophocles' *Antigone*, who alone among the characters of the play is not guilty of a rigid attitude of mind and is willing to consider the various aspects of a situation before passing judgment and reaching a decision. But in the critical moment he too fails. For when he finds Antigone "by twisted cord suspended," he is overcome by his grief, attempts to kill his father, and failing in this throws himself upon his sword.

While Haemon and Alcibiades thus have their brief moment of freedom in which they see their true self, although they fail to attain it, the other speakers, not unlike the characters of the Sophoclean tragedies, are locked in a sterile self-righteousness. Phaedrus praises the condition of men who have fallen captive to the image they have formed of themselves; Pausanias eulogizes the student-teacher relationship, unaware of the vulnerability to corruption of the young who are in a process of formation; the pseudoscientific generalizations of Eryximachus destroy the radical dynamism of the human mode of being and see man as just another thing in the universe; Aristophanes' laughter belies the totally earthbound nature he attributes to the characters in his myth; and Agathon's pretty garland of empty conceits mocks the transcendence without which man is inconceivable. Even Socrates is in part made to play the devil's advocate. It is true that by unmasking the deity and revealing Eros as a typical human desire, he puts the inquiry on a sound empirical basis. But when the question arises as to the object of this desire, he follows Diotima, who in a few simple steps leads to an absolute goal, in which all man's aspirations would find their ultimate consummation, without mentioning that it would also deprive his decisions of all significance and leave nothing for him to achieve on his own.[25] And as Sophocles characters protray men as they ought *not* to be, so the various discourses in the *Symposium* move about a common ground, namely genuine selfhood as a condition for the possibility of love, without touching it. Thus, while the young boys in the *Lysis* are not yet in possession of goals of their own, the various speakers of the *Symposium* eulogize men who appear to have let the goals possess them. But an individual could not lose himself, unless he also had the capacity of finding himself. In order to put him on the right road, Plato blocks all avenues of escape by exposing the fruitless attempts men make to find stability and significance outside themselves. Only when a man is thus forcibly thrown back on himself is there a chance that he will courageously face the human condition. And only through such acceptance can he constitute himself as an authentic self, and only then is he ready to enter into a genuine union with another human being equally constituted. But neither authenticity nor inauthenticity, neither gain nor loss of selfhood would be possible if men did not have the ability to reach beyond the present into the future, beyond what is to what is not. To shed some light on this aspect of the human mode of being is a task reserved for the last member of Plato's trilogy dealing with love and friendship.

PHAEDRUS: TRANSCENDENCE AS THE GROUND OF LOVE AND FRIENDSHIP

In the *Lysis,* Socrates speaks to young boys who, as is typical of their age, find it difficult to project too far into the future. By taking the world of the child with its excessive concern for the present moment, as if it were that of the adult who is ready to sacrifice much of the present to the future, Socrates creates countless paradoxes about friendship, for which the ability to transcend is indispensable. And suppressing this transcendence, he makes it conspicuous through its absence. In the *Symposium,* Socrates uses the opposite approach. As befits the festive occasion, there is an exuberance which permeates the various speeches in praise of Eros, including that of Socrates. The transcending tendency is allowed free rein, and as a result the several discourses go to excess in all directions. But while doing so they move away from, and circle about, a common center and thus indirectly reveal that center, namely genuine selfhood. The *Phaedrus,* the last of the three discourses on love and friendship, sheds more light on selfhood, which has transcendence as its most significant characteristic, and it reveals transcendence as capable of striking a bridge between one person and the other so as to bring them into a genuine union, without infringing on the individuality of either.

As usual, the mood which prevails in the opening scene and its byplay is apt to furnish significant hints as to the direction which the discussion will take. Phaedrus is a mature man, but considerably younger than Socrates, and there is in fact still some of the playfulness of the *Lysis*. The young man has spent the morning with Lysias, an Athenian rhetorician, whose discourse on love he has committed to memory. He would now like to practice his skill of recitation on Socrates, who is only too eager to listen. But Socrates insists that Phaedrus first show what he holds in his left hand, which is hidden under the cloak. And when he discovers that it is the actual speech of Lysias, he demands that Phaedrus read it to him. This harmless little deception is paralleled by a similar, but more serious one in the second speech of Socrates. His real view will be scarcely hidden below the surface. But unless we pay close attention we will miss the genuine article and go away, if not with a counterfeit, at least with an inadequate conception of love and friendship.

Another incident of seemingly small importance foreshadows a matter of considerable consequence later in the dialogue. While looking for a shady place on the banks of the river where they might sit down, Phaedrus conjectures that thereabouts might be the spot where Boreas was said to have seized the maiden Orithyia, and he asks Socrates whether he believes the story to be true. Socrates takes the occasion to criticize those "clever, industrious people" (229D)[26] who would trace all legends and myths to natural events. Presumably he believes that they thereby deprive them of their specific function, which is to lead us imaginatively beyond human experience in order that we may return to it more clear-sighted than before. As long as he is in ignorance of himself, he says, he has no time to busy himself with such matters, and so, when later in the dialogue the famous recollection myth appears, it is likely to serve Socrates primarily as a means of gaining a better understanding of himself and only secondarily, if at all, to advocate a doctrine concerning prenatal existence and life after death.

Perhaps even more significant is the contrast of the opening scene with that of the *Lysis*. There Socrates barely ventures outside the city walls to take a short cut between one part of Athens and the other; and the ensuing discussion takes place within the narrow confines of the palaestra, suggestive of the restrictive world of the young. Now we find Socrates, quite contrary to his wont, outside the city, expressing his delight at the sounds and sights of the countryside, sensitive to the influence of the animate and the inanimate, the mortals and the gods. His openness to this world stands in sharp contrast to the self-centered individual who appears in the speech of Lysias. Such self-encapsulation makes genuine communication well-nigh impossible, for, as Heidegger says, "others are encountered environmentally" (515), and it is only in a world shared in common that people can reach out for each other.

As soon as the two friends have found a suitable spot under a huge plane tree by the banks of the Illisus, Phaedrus begins to read the speech which he has with him. Its author, Lysias, develops the paradoxical theme that it is more expedient for a boy to grant favors to a nonlover than to a lover. He harps on the sanity and reliability of the nonlover, as against the fleeting passion which dominates the lover. Association with the lover adversely affects the boy's social life: the lover is prone to boast of his success and thus causes embarrassment to his beloved; any meeting between them, even when harmless, will be eyed with suspicion by family, friends, and townspeople, and thus damages the boy's reputation. Other ill effects are even more far-reaching: the lover is not in control of himself and subjects the object of his love to the craving to which he himself is in bondage; in his jealousy he will try to isolate his beloved from the influence of others, especially those who are superior in wealth and wisdom. The nonlover, by contrast, is said to be concerned with the betterment of the youth. "If you listen to me," the nonlover is made to say, "my intercourse with you will be a matter of ministering not to your immediate pleasure but to your future advantage" (233B).

Lysias, however, has left the essential points undeveloped. The sickness of the lover is not adequately diagnosed; the harm that comes to the beloved is not exhaustively determined, nor is the discourse clear as to the nature of the "betterment" and the "future advantage" which will accrue to the boy from his association with the nonlover. These points will receive an unexpected depth of development in the two speeches of Socrates. The first will deal with the dreadful injuries inflicted by the lover who is the slave of his passion; the second, with the benefits conferred, not by the nonlover, but by the genuine lover, who is in control of himself.

After Phaedrus has finished reading, Socrates pretends to share his friend's enthusiasm, but when pressed he admits that he was carried away by the reader's ecstasy rather than by what was read. He is willing to praise the author's "lucidity and terseness of expression, and his consistently precise and well-polished vocabulary" (234E). But he thinks the whole speech repetitious and superficial, and he believes he has heard a better speech somewhere, which he is willing to rehearse for the benefit of Phaedrus. Later in the dialogue, in connection with the discussion of rhetoric, he points to the absence of a definition of the subject matter and to the lack of "any cogent principle of composition which the author observed in setting down his observations in this particular order" (264B). But the most devastating criticism is offered by the contrast between the shallow cleverness of the sophist and the profundity of the two speeches of Socrates, which leave the reader with a better understanding, or at least with a greater awareness, of the complexity or even mystery of his own self.

Socrates begins his speech by remedying the first defect, the absence of a definition. For the word love, as he later points out, is one of those words about which "we diverge and dispute not only with one another but with our own selves" (263A). But the procedure which he follows is not exclusively logical.

The term love is subsumed under the general term of desire and is then further restricted to "an innate desire for pleasure" (237D). The desire for pleasure, in turn, is divided into one which is controlled by "an acquired judgment (doxa) that aims at what is best" (237D). This mastery is called temperance. The uncontrolled desire, on the other hand, which "drags us irrationally toward pleasure, and has come to rule within us" (238A), is called wantonness (hybris). Wantonness has many forms, such as gluttony in the matter of food, drunkenness in the matter of drink. When the excess concerns sex, it is called love:

When irrational desire, pursuing the enjoyment of beauty, has gained the mastery over judgment that prompts right conduct, and has acquired from other desires, akin to it, fresh strength to strain toward bodily beauty, that very strength provides it with its name: it is the strong passion called eros. (238B–C)

It is obvious that Socrates has moved from logic to morality by designating the mastery over the innate desire as temperance. But temperance is a moral excellence, and hence must be within the power of the individual. Socrates in fact says that it is based on an "acquired judgment," which therefore constitutes the condition for the possibility of morality. And now he reaches the ontological level, for not only does he distinguish between the *innate* desire and acquired judgment, that is between facticity and transcendence, to use modern existential terms, but he recognizes that the control or the absence of control will determine two opposing modes of being, namely authenticity or inauthenticity.

The desire for food, drink, etc., need not of course degenerate into wantonness. And the same can be said to be true of sex. So it seems arbitrary for Socrates to declare *eros*, without proof, to be a form of excess which involves loss of selfhood. The error, however, is intentional, for it serves to foreshadow the reason for the recantation in the second speech.

The condition of the lover, which Lysias simply calls a sickness, as might befall a man through no fault of his own, now takes on moral connotations and endangers the very selves of lover and beloved:

> He who is the victim of his passion and the slave of pleasure will of course desire to make his beloved as agreeable to himself as possible. Now to him who has a mind diseased anything is agreeable which is not opposed to him, but that which is equal or superior is hateful to him, and therefore *the lover will not brook any superiority or equality on the part of his beloved; he is always employed in reducing him to inferiority*. (238E–239A,J) (Italics added)

The lover will try to deprive his beloved of his wealth, alienate him from his family and friends, and, worst of all, "he will debar his beloved from the advantages of society which would make a man of him, and especially of that society which would have given him wisdom, and thereby it cannot fail to do him great harm" (239B,J). And thus the lover, like a beast of prey, feeds on the beloved: "As wolves love lambs so lovers love their love" (241D,J). In fact he is worse than a beast of prey; for he preys not only on the body, but also on the soul of the beloved being "hurtful to his spiritual development, which is assuredly and ever will be of supreme value in the sight of gods and men alike" (241C). Thus while the lover is depicted as enslaved to his own passion, the beloved appears subject to the passion of another; and while the former has forfeited his selfhood, the latter is never allowed to mature into a genuine personality.

During the interlude between the first and the second speech, Plato makes Socrates suddenly come to the realization that through his warning against the lover he has committed a great wrong:

> At the moment when I was about to cross the river, there came to me my

familiar sign—which always checks me when on the point of doing something or other—and all at once I seemed to hear a voice, forbidding me to leave the spot until I had made an atonement for some offence to heaven. (242B–C)

What has gone wrong? The description of the lover who not only has lost control over himself but tries to enslave the beloved and the dire consequences which follow for both seemed accurate enough. So why does Socrates describe the speech as "foolish and somewhat blasphemous" (242D)? At least a partial answer is suggested through Socrates' reference to "a man of generous and human character, who loved or had once loved another such as himself" (243C). Such a man, says Socrates, would "utterly refuse to accept our vilification of love" (243D). So Socrates' error would seem to consist in the identification of one aspect or form of love with the whole of it.[27] But the man who completely rejected the type of love described by Socrates would also be wrong; he could be accused of a similar if opposite narrowness of conception. Instead of calling attention to the danger of arriving at an erroneous conception in the opposite direction, Plato, to all appearance, has Socrates disguise it from the reader. "Do you not hold love to be a god, the child of Aphrodite?" Socrates asks Phaedrus. "If love," he continues, "is, as he is indeed, a god or divine being, he cannot be an evil thing: Yet this pair of speeches treated him as evil. That then was their offence toward Love" (242D–E).

Can Socrates seriously entertain this view? Has he not in the *Symposium* reduced Eros from a divinity to a human desire? If love were a god, then the lover, possessed by the gods, would not be an authentic self any more than the man who is in the grip of an uncontrollable passion. And if love as divine were destructive of authentic selfhood, would it not also be ruinous to man as a moral being? And if it has this effect, how can it be wholly good? The reader would be well advised to keep these questions in mind when listening to Socrates' second speech. Socrates, in any event, creates the impression that he had spoken sheer folly before. This, he says, is the reason why at the beginning of the first speech he covered his head in order not "to break down for shame" (273A). Now he claims to be committed to speak the truth:

I shall attempt to make my due palinode to love before any harm comes to me for my defamation of him, and no longer veiling my head for shame, but uncovered. (243B)

But since, contrary to his claim, he has not been altogether wrong in the first speech, can he be trusted to speak the truth and be altogether right in the second?

Appropriately, Socrates opens his second speech with a discussion of madness *(mania)*. Love always involves a condition of being in some sense possessed, of being beside oneself. If such madness were invariably evil, he says, then love would be evil, and it would be true to say that "when a lover is at hand favor ought rather to be accorded to one who does not love, on the ground that the former is mad, and the latter sound of mind" (244A). Socrates, however, can cite the prophetess at Delphi, the priestesses at Dodona, and others who in a state of madness have been able to guide men aright "through the power of inspired prophecy" (244B), and delivered certain families "from grievous maladies and affliction" which beset them "by reason of some ancient sin" (244D). In a state of sanity they were powerless. And the same can be said of poetry: "If any man comes to the gates of poetry without the madness of the Muses, persuaded that skill alone will make him a good poet, then shall he and his works of sanity with him be brought to naught by the poetry of madness" (245A).

In all the cases mentioned, however, the good in question is a good conferred on others. Nothing is said of the benefit, if any, which prophetess, priestess, or poet might derive from the state of being possessed. Socrates, therefore, correctly states the problem when he maintains that he must prove love to be "a thing sent from heaven for the advantage of both lover and beloved" (245B). What is this advantage? Obviously, if the lovers, like the priestess and the prophetess, were possessed by a divine power, would they not suffer the most grievous harm, namely the loss of their very selves? Such questions cannot be answered without first taking a closer look at the kind of being which the human *psyche* really is. This Socrates now proceeds to do.

The way he goes about this task, however, is quite astonishing. First he attempts to demonstrate the immortality of the soul by means of two arguments, one of which is deductive and the other based on analogy. The demonstration is followed by a description of the soul which is also twofold. It is presented first in the form of an allegory and then in the form of a myth. What significance, if any, is to be attached to this movement from the purely formal, the deductive argument, to the purely imaginative, the myth? Do these disparate modes of procedure share a common element to which Socrates attempts to call attention? And if there is such an element, what is its possible relevance to the problem of the nature of love?

It now becomes necessary to analyze each item carefully in the hope of detecting an underlying sameness which proves essential to a genuine love relationship.

In connection with the demonstration, we must determine first whether the demonstration is valid, and second whether the premise on which it rests can be accepted as true.

This is how Socrates presents the first argument:

All soul is immortal; for that which is ever in motion is immortal. But that which while imparting motion is itself moved by something else can cease to be in motion, and therefore can cease to live; *it is only that which moves itself that never intermits its motion, inasmuch as it cannot abandon its own nature* (245C). . . . Now that we have seen that that which is moved by itself is immortal, we shall feel no scruple in affirming that precisely *that is the essence and definition of soul, to wit self-motion.* (245E) (Italics added)

The italicized portion of the argument can be formally expressed in this manner:

I. (a) A self-moving being which ceases its motion is a being which abandons its nature.
   (b) No being abandons its nature.
   (c) Therefore, a self-moving being does not cease its motion.
II. (a) A being which does not cease its motion is ever in motion.
   (b) A self-moving being does not cease its motion.
   (c) Therefore, a self-moving being is ever in motion.
III. (a) A self-moving being is ever in motion.
   (b) The soul is a self-moving being.
   (c) Therefore, the soul is ever in motion.
IV. (a) That which is ever in motion is immortal.
   (b) The soul is ever in motion.
   (c) Therefore, the soul is immortal.

Let us make the following substitutions:

S = a being which is self-moving
C = a being which ceases its motion
A = a being which can abandon its motion
E = a being which is ever in motion
P = Soul or *psyche*
I = a being which is immortal

In symbolic form, the argument would read:

I.	(a)	$(x) [(S_x \cdot C_x) \supset A_x]$	Premiss
	(b)	$(x) \sim A_x$	Premiss
	(c)	$(x) \sim (S_x \cdot C_x)$	I_a and I_b (Modus Tollens)
	(d)	$(x) (S_x \supset \sim C_x)$	I_c (Equivalence)
II.	(a)	$(x) (\sim C_x \supset E_x)$	Premiss
	(b)	$(x) (S_x \supset \sim C_x)$	Premiss (I_d)
	(c)	$(x) (S_x \supset E_x)$	II_a and II_b (Hypothetical Syllogism)
III.	(a)	$(x) (S_x \supset E_x)$	Premiss (II_c)
	(b)	$(x) (P_x \supset S_x)$	Premiss
	(c)	$(x) (P_x \supset E_x)$	III_a and III_b (Hypothetical Syllogism)

IV. (a) (x) (E$_x$ ⊃ I$_x$)   Premiss
     (b) (x) (P$_x$ ⊃ E$_x$)   Premiss (III$_c$)
     (c) (x) (P$_x$ ⊃ I$_x$)   III$_a$ and III$_b$ (Hypothetical Syllogism)

From the above it appears that the argument is valid. Its conclusion, therefore, is true, that is, the statement that the soul is immortal is true, if all the premises are true. If a single premise is false, nothing can be said about the truth value of the conclusion. Now the following premises are unaccounted for:

I$_a$—A self-moving being which ceases its motion, is a being which abandons its nature.

I$_b$—No being abandons its nature.

II$_a$—A being which does not cease its motion is a being which is ever in motion.

III$_b$—The soul is a self-moving being.

IV$_a$—That which is ever in motion is immortal.

If it can be shown that any one of these statements is false or not necessarily true, then the conclusion is not necessarily true.

Premise I$_a$ raises the question of the meaning of a "self-moving being." It is conceivable that such a being might initially have received a certain amount of energy, which is gradually being dissipated. Such in fact is Cebes' objection against one of Socrates arguments for the immortality of the soul in the *Phaedo*. Once the stock of energy has been exhausted, the motion ceases and the being is destroyed. In such a case would it not be true to say that the being itself "abandoned its own nature?"

In answer to the objection it might be said that a being is not really self-moving unless it is the source of, and in complete control over, its own motion, in other words, unless it is self-moving by nature. If there is a being which is self-moving by nature, then it would perhaps be true that if it were to cease its self-motion, it would thereby abandon its own nature.

Now when premise III$_b$ asserts that the soul is a self-moving being, self-moving must be understood in the sense of self-moving by nature. In fact Plato has Socrates expressly state that "we shall feel no scruple in affirming that . . . self-motion . . . is the essence and definition of the soul" (245E).

The success of the demonstration of the immortality of the soul is now seen to depend on man's access to the essence or nature of things. Those who interpret Plato's dialogues literally tend to maintain that Plato thought such knowledge possible, at least for the philosopher who in the *Republic*, for instance, is said to have insight not only into the forms, but the form of forms, the *Idea of the Good*. If the dramatic aspects of the *Republic* are taken into account, this view becomes highly dubious. Fortunately, the question need not be argued here, for at the end of the two demonstrations Plato sees fit to forestall any claim to certainty as far as the result of the demonstration is concerned. This, in any event, is the effect of the flat declaration of Socrates:

> As to the soul's immortality then we have said enough, but *as to its nature* there is this that must be said: what manner of thing it is would be a long tale to tell, and most *assuredly a god alone could tell it*. (246A) (Italics added)

Now assuming that Plato was fully aware of what he was doing, these questions impose themselves: Why should he have Socrates undermine his own argument by denying the one factor on which the truth of the conclusion depends, namely, knowledge of the nature of the soul? Why should he think it necessary to block the thought of the reader which naturally tends to see in the demonstration a means of establishing a truth expressed in the conclusion, namely, the immortality of the soul? What is left once our attention is diverted from the outcome of the demonstration?—The answer is obvious: what remains is the demonstration as an act, as a performance. Now a demonstration is an attempt to reach beyond what is actually known; and a demonstration for the immortality of the soul, whether successful or not, reaches beyond human life itself in so far as it is experienced. It constitutes a grand act of transcendence, and in performing this act man manifests himself as a transcending being, in Heidegger's terminology, as a being whose "essence lies in his existence" (68).

At present this interpretation must be regarded as highly tentative. Before passing judgment let us see whether it finds confirmation in the second argument, as well as the allegory and the myth which immediately follow, and above all, whether transcendence can be shown to play a vital role in human love.

In the second argument the transcending tendency is made more conspicuous. It is an argument based on analogy. As such it is an endeavor to extend the border of what is known by conceiving the less well known in terms of the better known. Two similar things are compared, A_1 and A_2. A_1 is observed to possess qualities a_1, b_1, c_1, d_1. In A_2 the corresponding qualities a_2, b_2, d_2 are also found. c_2 cannot actually be observed. But since A_2 is observed to possess qualities which correspond to a_1, b_1, d_1 in A_1, it is assumed that it also possesses c_2 corresponding to c_1 in A_1.

With this model in mind, let us examine the second argument (245C–E). It may be summarized as follows:

A. (1) The first principle, of its very nature, must be a self-mover and the source of all motion.
   (2) A first principle cannot come into being, for if it did it would come from a first principle and not itself be a first principle.
   (3) The first principle must be imperishable, for its destruction would involve the destruction of all that is.
   Conclusion: The first principle is uncreated and imperishable.

B. (1) The first principle is a self-mover.
   (2) The soul is a self-mover.
   (3) The first principle is uncreated and imperishable.
   Conclusion: The soul is (or ought to be) uncreated and imperishable.

If the first principle and the soul have, of their very nature, self-motion in common, then it is not unreasonable to assume that they share the other essential characteristics of the first principle, namely, imperishability and uncreatedness. A not unreasonable assumption, however, is far from being an established truth. An argument from analogy may help a scientist to set up a hypothesis which he can tentatively accept and act upon, until he discovers evidence to the contrary. But in regard to a first principle and the soul, verification or confirmation may not even be possible. A first principle ought to exist if the world is radically intelligible, that is, conformable to human reason. But what assurances do we have that it is? And Socrates himself questions the knowability of the soul as far as man is concerned. The actual outcome of the argument is again of so little value that we are perforce thrown back upon the argument as a performance, that is, as the manifestation of a transcending activity.[28]

Aside from transcendence, there is another factor which makes its presence known in the second argument, namely, imagination. The unobserved factor in the less well known is imagined to be present on the analogy of the better known. Thus imagination appears as the indispensable tool of transcendence. When the mind reaches out blindly into the unknown, the imagination populates the void with the creatures it has constructed by rearranging elements found in actual experience. In retrospect we can now find the imagination at work even in the first argument. For when we spoke of the nature of the soul, we did so without having any clear idea of it. It may well be that whenever we refer to natures we have in reality tentative guesses and hypotheses which at best express various degrees of probabilities. But we imaginatively extends these probabilities upward in the direction of certainty and then treat the hypotheses as if they reflected the actual structures of things. So both arguments are found to manifest transcendence together with imagination, its handmaiden. And we can now give at least one reason why Plato should have chosen the demonstration of the immortality of the soul rather than any other demonstration. For in this demonstration, the powers of transcendence and imagination are particularly conspicuous. Witnessing the death of a human being, we are struck by its impenetrable mystery. Unable or unwilling simply to accept what we find, namely an inert body, and refusing to believe that the self which controlled the body has dissolved into nothingness, we transcend the world we know and imaginatively create another world in which this self finds continued existence.

As we pass from demonstrations, both deductive and analogical, to allegory and myth, transcendence and imagination become increasingly more prominent. But now a problem confronts us from the other direction. For these more imaginative devices tend to break off contact with reality and lose themselves in a world of pure fancy. As Socrates has indicated in connection with the Boreas-Orithyia legend, such flights of the imagination are of no interest to him unless they contribute to his knowledge of himself. The myth, to be more than mere play, must not be allowed to sever its links with experienced reality. But what are these links and what light does the myth shed on the human personality?

We get a first and fairly simply indication of the proper use of a myth when Socrates speaks about the human soul or self (psyche). He has just acknowledged that we do not know its nature and that in describing it he must resort to an image:

> Let it be likened to the union of powers in a team of winged steeds and their winged charioteer. Now all the gods' steeds and all their charioteers are good, and of good stock; but . . . with us men . . . one of the steeds is noble and good . . . while the other has the opposite character . . . Hence the task of our charioteer is difficult and troublesome. (246A–B)

It will have been noticed that the passage contains both allegory and myth. In view of its one to one correspondence, the allegory keeps close to experience. Reason is easily regonized in the guise of the charioteer, as well as the supporting and the opposing emotions, with which we are familiar from the *Republic*, in the noble and the ignoble steed respectively, while the wings symbolize striving or desire. In his first speech, Socrates defined love as "some sort of desire" (237D); it was a desire which had gotten out of control and had enslaved its possessor. Here desire is different or at least takes a different direction. It is not drawn toward pleasures but toward that "which is fair and wise and good, and possessed of all other such excellence" (246E). There is a suggestion that man's development is not spontaneous; he may realize or fail to realize his potentialities. For "by these excellences," as Socrates puts it allegorically, "the soul's plumage is nourished and fostered, while by their opposites, even by ugliness and evil, it is wasted and destroyed" (246E).

The allegory thus does little more than describe the human condition. Its picturesque language creates a more intense awareness and frees the expression from distracting detail not directly relevant to the main issue to be brought before the reader. By contrast, the brief reference to the gods in the above passage is mythical. There is nothing in experience which correspondence to the complete control which the gods have over themselves, the perfect ease with which their being responds to their will. The myth is an idealization of the human constitution which Socrates has described in the allegory. But while it thus goes beyond what actually is, it reflects back on human experience. For by its very perfection it brings into sharp relief the imperfection on the human level: "Hence the task of our charioteer is difficult and troublesome" (246B).

The movement from the real to the ideal and back to the real is repeated when Socrates describes the activity which corresponds to the constitution: smooth and effortless for the gods; laborious and perilous in the case of man:

> But at such times as the souls go to their feasting and banquet, behold they climb the steep ascent even unto the summit of the arch that supports the heavens; and easy is that ascent for the chariots of the gods, for they are well-balanced and readily guided; but for the others it is hard, by reason of the heaviness of the steed of wickedness, which pulls down his driver with his weight; except that driver have schooled him well. (247A–B)

The world above the heavens is now populated with the extrapolations of the achievements of human aspirations:

> It is there in that place beyond the heavens that true being dwells, without colour or shape, that cannot be touched; reason alone, the soul's pilot, can behold it, and all true knowledge is knowledge thereof. Now even as the mind of a god is nourished by reason and knowledge, so also is it with every soul that has a care to receive her proper food; wherefore when at last she has beheld being she is well content, and contemplating truth she is nourished and prospers, until the heaven's revolution brings her back full circle. And while she is borne round she discerns justice, its very self, and likewise temperance, and knowledge, not the knowledge that is neighbour to becoming and varies with the various objects to which we commonly ascribe being, but the veritable knowledge of being that veritably is. (247C–E)

The uncertain truths which men pursue have been turned into perfect insights into absolute reality; the objects of knowledge have become immutable, so that whatever is found true remains true for ever; human goals, which either are not attained or, when attained, fail to bring satisfaction, are pictured as easily accessible and capable of providing complete contentment.

Against this background of clear visions of perfect goals, and of easy consummation of all striving, human life stands out in stark contrast with its agonizing strife and struggle which so often ends in futility and frustration;

> Such is the life of the gods: of the other souls that which best follows a god and becomes most like thereunto raises her charioteer's head into the outer region, and is carried round with the gods in the revolution, but being confounded by her steeds she has much ado to discern the things that are; another now rises, and now sinks, and by reason of her unruly steeds sees in part, but in part sees not. As for the rest, though all are eager to reach the heights and seek to follow, they are not able; sucked down as they travel they trample and tread upon one another, this one striving to outstrip that. Thus confusion ensues, and conflict and grievous sweat. Whereupon, with their charioteers powerless, many are lamed, and many have their wings all broken; and for all their toiling they are baulked, every one, of the full vision of being, and departing therefrom, they feed upon the food of semblance. (248A–B)

Yet all is not gloom in the human condition as it appears when projected against divine perfection. There is a ray of light which issues from its own reality and which is not found in its idealized image. The gods achieve their easy success by virtue of their divinity. Men have no corresponding human nature to rely on for success; they are threatened with complete failure by the unruly steed. But they also have a chance of gaining control and achieving success, not through their nature, but through an effort initiated by a free resolve. And it is this ability to take charge of themselves against great odds which distinguishes them from the gods and from all other creatures. For they alone, in Heidegger's words, are "beings for whom their Being is an issue."

> Like a racer recoiling from the starting rope, the driver jerks back the bit in the mouth of the wanton horse with an even stronger pull, bespatters his railing tongue and his jaws with blood, and forcing him down on legs and haunches delivers him over to anguish. (254E) And so, if victory is won by the higher elements of mind, . . . the power of evil in the soul has been subjected, and the power of goodness liberated,—and he has won self-mastery and inward peace. (256B)

Before introducing the reader to a proper conception of love, Plato, as we have seen, thought it necessary to inquire into the human mode of being, and show transcendence, imagination and free resolve at work in the basic human activities. For without this dynamism inherent in the human personality, without this openness of man, it is inconceivable how two human beings, in any significant sense, should be able to become one.

The manner in which Plato now approaches the question of the possibility and the nature of genuine love constitutes a particularly thorny problem.

Since the lover referred to in the first discourse is characterized by extreme selfishness, it is perhaps natural to expect that the second will deal with a lover who is concerned about the welfare of the beloved. And then the first type of human relationship could be called evil and the second good. Although one would think this black and white approach to be quite foreign to Socrates, he does in fact lend credence to this view when he uses his two speeches to illustrate the method of division later in the dialogue:

> Our two discourses alike assumed, first of all, a single form of unreason; and then . . . the speaker proceeded to divide the parts until he found in them an evil or lefthanded love which he justly reviled; and the other discourse leading us to the madness which lay on the right side, found another love, also having the same name, but divine, which the speaker held up before us and applauded and affirmed to be the author of the greatest benefits. (266A,J)

Furthermore, there are numerous passages which show that the shameless abuse of the beloved in the first speech is matched in the second by the utter devotion of the lover to the beloved, who "like a god has received every true and loyal service from his lover, not in pretence but in reality" (255A,J).

Would it not, however, be a violation of the Socratic method, as we now understand it, if the author of our dialogue were to state his views in so forthright and dogmatic a manner, if he were to separate the good from the bad so sharply as to leave nothing to the reflection of the reader? Would it not be more in keeping with the intellectual midwifery reportedly practised by Socrates, if Plato were to lead the reader surreptitiously from one excess to another and thus force him to seek his own solution by aiming at a precarious mean between the two extremes?

If the reader applies a modicum of critical intelligence, he will become aware of the excess in the description of love in the second speech, as easily as Socrates detected the actual speech of Lysias which Phaedrus had tried to conceal under his cloak. For if the first love is characterized by the shameless use which the lover makes of the beloved, the second is vitiated by the complete subjection of the lover to the object of his love. Several passages from the dialogue make this self-abuse of the lover abundantly clear:

> Every one chooses his love from the ranks of beauty according to his character, and *this he makes his god,* and fashions and adorns as a sort of image which he is to fall down and worship. (252D,J)
>
> *The qualities of their god they attribute to the beloved,* wherefore they love him all the more. (253A,J)
>
> Looking upon the face of his beloved as of a god he reverences him, and if he were not afraid of being thought a downright madman, *he would sacrifice to his beloved as to the image of a god.* (251A,J)
>
> The rules and proprieties of life, on which he formerly prided himself, he now despises, and is ready to sleep like a servant, wherever he is allowed, as near as he can to *his desired one, who is the object of his worship.* (252A–B,J) (Italics added)

Socrates has started his second speech with the promise to show that "love is . . . for the advantage of lover and beloved" (245B). Now the interest of the lover has been completely lost sight of. A man may decide, with an initially free resolve, to help another in the attainment of his goals. But he may get carried away by this commitment to such an extent that his service to the other becomes compulsive and that he becomes completely neglectful of his own goals. But since these goals, as we have seen, are part and parcel of the human personality, such self-neglect may lead to the surrender of his own personality to that of the other. It is obvious that if one ought never to use another person as a means toward one's own ends, then one is under obligation never to allow one's own person to be used merely as a means. A man owes responsibility also to himself. "As I am convinced that I never wronged another intentionally," says

Socrates in the *Apology*, "I will assuredly not wrong myself" (37A–B). And so it seems that even altruistic love has its excess, that it too carries within itself the possibility of evil.

What shall we now make of Socrates' division into a good and a bad love, which were said to be the subject of his first and second speech respectively? It now appears that this simple division represents a challenge to the readers' critical abilities rather than an expression of the view of Socrates. The division into good and bad gained a measure of plausibility from the fact that one speech dealt with self-regarding and the other with altruistic love. The first speech, however, criticized the lover not only for being selfish but also for being in the grip of an uncontrollable passion. This suggests a new principle of division which, when applied to the right-handed love, produces two altruistic loves, one which is under the control of the lover and one which is not. It will be recalled that Socrates used the same division in some of the dialogues previously discussed. His demand for a definition of piety, for instance, seemed at first glance the proper opposition to Euthyphro's appeal to superstition, until it was found to imply undue reliance on logic in moral matters; the rule of the philosopher-kings in the *Republic* was proposed as the cure for the excesses of democracy, merely to exhibit excesses of an even more dangerous kind; obedience to law, though a civic virtue, may turn out to be a shirking of responsibility; even innocence and guilt could not be pressed into the dichotomy of good and bad as shown in the *Lesser Hippias*. In all these cases, a conventionally "good" word served to cover up a potentially evil reality, because the division "on the right side" had not been carried far enough.

The recognition of potential evil in both self-regarding and altruistic love does not of itself reveal a proper conception of love. In fact it does not even tell us whether a genuine love relationship between two free individuals is at all possible. Would it not seem that in order to become in some measure one, the lover must be subject to the beloved or the beloved to the lover, and that the two loves described by Socrates are not simply excesses suggesting a mean, but real contradictories allowing of no middle term? Then it would be true to say, as Eliot does in one of his plays, that we can merely make "use of each other, each for his purpose, that we are all in fact unloving and unlovable";[29] and Plato would have anticipated Jean-Paul Sartre who maintains that "unity with the Other is . . . unrealizable . . . , for the assimilation of the for-itself and the Other in a single transcendence would necessarily involve the disappearance of the characteristic of otherness in the Other.[30]

It is true that we have not found a conception of genuine love in Socrates' second speech, despite Socrates' promise. The reason for this failure, however, may lie exclusively with our naive expectation of having the idea spoon-fed to us, without any effort of our own. Instead of looking for a ready-made answer, we should search out the elements with which to construct an answer.

Now the most significant material which we have so far left unused is Socrates' anatomy of the basic structure of the human mode of being. That he should have chosen to clothe it in the language of the myth detracts nothing from its significance. The fact that he introduces it prior to the direct approach to the problem which forms the topic of his discourse suggests the belief that he regarded an understanding of this structure a condition for the possibility of arriving at a proper conception of love.

It will be recalled that according to the myth the being of man appears as radically different from that of anything else in our experience. A thing simply acts out its nature; it is lost in being what it is. Only man is able to stand away from himself and to opt among various alternatives offered by his innate capacities and the circumstances in which he finds himself. The alternatives, freely chosen in the ideal case, become goals which determine and give direction to his various activities and thereby shape his character. Thus man, at least in part, constitutes himself.

In such a dynamic conception of personality, the goal appears as an integral part of the very being of the man. Therefore one cannot love such a man without loving the goal or ideal to which he aspires. But to love an ideal is to pursue it, to endeavor to realize it as far as possible in the realm of concrete existences. "To love things as they are would be a mockery of things," as Santayana has said, "for to love things . . . means to love the love in them, to worship the good which they pursue."[31] This fundamental openness of man, and the corresponding goal which is constitutive of his being, make genuine communion possible. For goals can be shared without loss to either party; they do not require subjection of one to the other. Each one, striving toward a common goal, joins and rejoices in the activities of the other and still surrenders nothing of his being, since the subjection to the goal is merely a subjection to one's own ideal possibilities.[32]

Is this interpretation faithful to Plato? Fortunately, we can let the text speak for itself. It shows that the lover is confronted with two successive choices. First, he must select an appropriate god or ideal to follow:

And *he who follows* in the train of *any* other god, while he is unspoiled and the impression lasts, *honours and imitates him* as far as he is able; and after the manner of his god he behaves in his intercourse with his beloved. (252C,J)

Then he will choose a like-minded person as a beloved:

The followers of Zeus desire that their beloved should have a soul like him; and therefore they *seek out someone of a philosophical* or imperial *nature*, and when they have found him, they do all they can to confirm such a nature in him, and if they have no experience of such a disposition hitherto, they learn from anyone who can teach them, and themselves follow in the same way. (252E,J)

And finally, lover and beloved must take care that the goal they pursue is rooted in their being as a capacity:

> If they draw their inspiration from Zeus, they pour out their own fountain upon him, *wanting to make him as like as possible to their own god*. But those who are the followers of Here seek a royal love, and when they have found him they do just the same with him; and in like manner the followers of Apollo, and of every other god *walking in the ways of their god, seek a love who is to be made like him whom they serve*, and when they have found him, *they themselves imitate their god, and persuade their love to do the same,* and educate him in the manner and nature of their god as far as they can; for no feelings of envy or jealousy are entertained by them toward their beloved, but *they do their utmost to create in him the greatest likeness of themselves and of the god whom they honour*. Thus fair and blissful to the beloved is the desire of the inspired lover. (253A–C,J) (Italics added)

Platonic love, then, appears as the mutual assistance in the realization of one's capacities through the pursuance of a common ideal or goal, and one cannot help thinking of Socrates for ever urging his companions to become better men by joining him in the pursuit of truth.

It will probably not have gone unnoticed that we have appealed to one and the same speech of Socrates for support of a proper as well as an improper conception of love. In fact most of the passages used for both purposes appear more or less in the same paragraphs, namely, 252 and 253. These paragraphs contain indeed a curious mixture of propositions: some of them refer to a relationship which involves the subjection of one person to another, and some outline a relationship which grants equal status to both partners. And so it seems that we have overcome one obstacle merely to be confronted with an even greater one. For what right do we have to regard one type of relationship as Platonic and the other as un-Platonic? Again we must recall Plato's purpose which, in accordance with the Socratic method, is not to impart his own views to the reader of the dialogue, but through his paradoxical presentation arouse the thought of the reader so that he can see for himself. And if the reader does respond properly and can be induced to reflect, then he will have to admit that what we have called the genuine conception is able to explain and shed light on the improper one, but not the latter on the former. The first set of quotations which refer to the lover as willing to "sacrifice to his beloved as to the image of a god" (251A,J), as attributing to him the qualities of the god (253A,J), as making "his desired one . . . the object of his worship" (252A–B,J) describe a psychological error, an error which is understandable enough in the light of the conception derived from the second set. For if a man is a being moving toward an ideal, then it is all too tempting for a youthful enthusiasm to mistake the ideal, which the other can only approximate, for the stage of development he has actually reached. [33]

Needless to say that Plato has led us to an ideal love which is rarely if ever realized. As suggested in the myth by the symbol of the horse of "ignoble breed" (246A,J), the transcending tendency itself may be challenged, and in fact overcome, by the opposite tendency toward physical pleasure. Or the disillusionment which comes with advancing age may cause us to lose sight of ideals and let the soul "sink beneath the double load of forgetfulness and vice" (248C,J). Or again the beloved may fall in love with the idealized picture which the lover has of him, so that what seems to be love of the other is merely a disguised self-love: "The lover is a mirror in whom he is beholding himself, but he is not aware of this" (255D,J). And finally there is the difficulty of communicating ideals which in the first place are only "seen as through a glass dimly" (250B,J). But the benefits which love makes possible are well worth running all these risks and far outweigh those which the nonlover has to offer. And so Socrates concludes his address to the young man who is confronted with a choice,:

> Thus great are the heavenly blessings which the friendship of a lover will confer on you, my youth. Whereas the attachment of the non-lover, which is alloyed with a worldly prudence and has worldly and niggardly ways of doling out benefits, will breed in your soul those vulgar qualities which the populace applaud, and will send you bowling around the earth during a period of nine thousand years, and leave you a fool in the world below. (256E,J)

With the end of the recantation, about the middle of the dialogue, an abrupt change of tone takes place. Socrates' second speech was inspiring; he himself calls it a "mythical hymn of praise, in due religious language, a festal celebration, of . . . that god of love who watches over the young and fair" (265C). The subsequent discussion is prosaic in comparison, critical and coldly analytical. It begins by pointing out the defects in the speech of Lysias, calling attention to the absence of a proper definition, its poor organization, the lack of a method of analysis and synthesis. Then speech-writing in general comes under scrutiny: The claim of the rhetoricians that they need not know the truth but only what the audience holds to be true, which according to Socrates amounts to the laughable attempt of the blind leading the blind; the indispensability of the truth even for those who want to mislead the audience; the superficiality of the rhetorical manuals which speak in highfaluting terms, such as preamble and recapitulation, refutation and allusion, reduplications, maxims, similes, and many others. All these, says Socrates, deal with the preliminaries only, and he who is familiar with them has still to learn how to apply them effectively. And finally, Socrates launches a devastating attack upon the false pretenses of the rhetoricians by describing the impossible conditions which would have to be satisfied before rhetoric could call itself a genuine science:

> Oratory is the art of enchanting the soul, and therefore he who would be an orator has to learn the differences of human souls. . . . Next he divides speeches into their different classes:—"such and such persons" he will say, "are affected by this or that kind of speech in this or that way," and he will tell you why. The pupil must have a good theoretical notion of them first, and then he must have experience of them in actual life, . . . When he understands what persons are persuaded by what arguments and sees the person about whom he was speaking in the abstract actually before him, and knows that this is the man or this is the character who ought to have a certain argument applied to him in order to convince him of a certain opinion . . . and knows also when he should speak and when he should refrain, and when he should use pithy sayings, pathetic appeals, sensational effects, and all the other modes of speech which he has learned;—when, I say, he knows the times and the circumstances of all these things, then, and not till then, he is a perfect master of this art; and if he fail in any of these points, . . . and yet declares that he speaks by rules of art, he who says, "I don't believe you", has the better of him.
> (271D–272B,J)

Exposing the implied requirements of a position in order to show that its advocate could never hope to meet them is simply a more subtle version of Socrates' way of reducing his opponent's views to absurdity. We have seen him use this device against Protagoras's exaggerated claims to success in teaching, against Euthyphro's assurance that in prosecuting his father he is doing the will of the gods, against the tendency in time of crisis to surrender personal responsibility to the rule of the powerful and benevolent ruler in the *Republic*, and against the temptation to regard a successful hypothesis as the essence of things in the *Phaedo*. The attentive reader should therefore be prepared to detect the irony in Socrates' description of oratory. For he will recall the remark made about the soul earlier in the dialogue to the effect that "what matter of thing it is . . . most assuredly a god alone could tell" (246A). Such enigmatic and elusive entities as human souls do not lend themselves to being typed and classified and matched with specific speeches according to fixed rules which a genuine "art of oratory" would demand.

Aside from this ironic episode, the discussion so far has been quite explicit. After so much straight talk, however, we may expect a final challenge before the dialogue comes to a close.

The challenge appears in the form of a condemnation of written discourses. Such discourses, says Socrates, are quite incapable of conveying the truth from one person to another:

> He must be exceedingly simple-minded . . . [who] imagines that written

words can do anything more than remind one who knows that which the writing is concerned with. (275C–D)

The historical Socrates might well have maintained that the written discourse is useless as a tool of instruction. For he left nothing in writing and restricted himself to teaching by word of mouth. But how could Plato agree to such a view in one of his numerous, carefully constructed written discourses? Is he trying to give Socrates the lie through the creation of supreme masterpieces of written works, or are we confronted with one of those paradoxes which are to set our thought processes in motion?

A glimpse of the way out of the difficulty may be found in the following passage:

> Nothing that has ever been written whether in verse or prose merits much serious attention—and for that matter, nothing that ever has been spoken in the declamatory fashion which aims at mere persuasion without any questioning. . . . In reality such compositions are, at best, a means of reminding those who know the truth. (277E–278A)

The disparagement is now extended from the written to at least a certain type of oral discourse, which leads to the suspicion that the uselessness of the written words is to be found not in the word itself, but in some defect to which it is more prone than the spoken word. What is this defect? According to Socrates, it is the inability to answer questions:

> Written words . . . seem to talk to you as though they were intelligent, but if you ask them anything about what they say, from a desire to be instructed, they go on telling you the same thing forever. (275D)

Neither the speaker nor the writer can be sure whether he is understood, although the speaker, because of his ability to ask questions, has a better chance, according to Socrates, "to plant and sow words founded on knowledge" (276E).

What are we to understand by "words founded on knowledge?" If we briefly remind ourselves of Heidegger's conception of truth and project Socrates' enigmatic remarks against it, they might reveal the insight which Plato is hiding behind them.

Heidegger first shows the current theory of truth as agreement to be beset by unsolvable problems; then he develops a theory of truth as unconcealment; and finally he works out a theory of truth as agreement which is derivative from the theory of truth as unconcealment.

Those who hold that truth consists of the agreement between ideas or representations in the mind with the corresponding objects outside, maintain that truth lies in the judgment. "In judgment," Heidegger says, "one must distinguish between the judging as a *real* psychical process, and that which is judged, as *ideal* content." It is between the *ideal* content of the judgment and the *real* thing which is judged, that the relationship of agreement is said to exist. With regard to what can such radically different beings agree? "If it is impossible for *intellectus* and *res* to be equal, because they are not of the same species," Heidegger wonders, "are they perhaps similar? But knowledge is still supposed to 'give' the real thing *just as* it is" (259).

The problems thus raised, according to Heidegger, are pseudoproblems, for they arise from a misconception of the being of truth. In order to arrive at a proper conception he invites us to witness a situation in which truth becomes phenomenally explicit. Consider, he suggests, a man with his back toward the wall making the assertion: The picture on the wall does not hang straight. The assertion is found to be true if, in facing the wall, the man *discovers* the picture in the condition described. Truth, therefore, is primarily *being uncovering*, which is a characteristic of Dasein, and secondarily *being uncovered* of the things known. The assertion does not refer to representations or images in the mind, but to a thing in a concrete situation and nothing else. This is true even if the thing spoken about is not actually present. "Interpretation," Heidegger insists, "in which something else is here slipped in, as what one supposedly has in mind in an assertion that merely represents, belies the phenomenological facts of the case as to that about which the assertion gets made. Asserting is a Being-toward the thing itself that is. [Das Aussagen ist ein Sein zum Seienden selbst.]" (260). In the discussion of the meaning of the word phenomenology Heidegger defines the word *phenomenon* as "that which shows itself in itself, the manifest" (51) and *logos* as "that which lets us see something from the very thing which the discourse is about" (56). Thus phenomenology means "to let that which shows itself be seen from itself in the very way in which it shows itself from itself" (58). Of course, things can also show themselves as what they are not, what they merely seem. Preconceptions, prejudices, inappropriate approaches can prevent the thing from showing itself, or disguise or hide itself altogether. But for Heidegger there can be no question of something inside the mind having to correspond with something outside.

Now truth as unconcealment yields a conception of truth as agreement which is free from the problems of the old theory. In the case of a simple assertion Dasein not only points to the entity which shows itself, but lets another Dasein share in "the Being-toward the entity uncovered." What is thus uncovered can be preserved in the assertion and passed on from person to person. Those others can take over what is said in the assertion, without themselves uncovering the entity in question. They have lost contact or have never made contact with the thing itself, but are concerned only with what is said about it. "In large measure, the uncoveredness gets appropriated not by one's own uncovering, but rather by hearsay of something that has been said . . . that which has been expressed as such takes over Being-toward those entities which have been uncovered in the assertion" (266–67). It is only at this point that the theory of truth as agreement comes into play: the assertion is true if its contents correspond to or are in agreement with the thing itself. But such agreement presupposes that the thing has been uncovered in the first place.

Frequently we have to be satisfied with this kind of truth. We are all born into a society in which certain views are held to be true, and there is no possibility for an individual to trace them all down to their origin in order to see whether they spring from an actual experience, or whether they started from a surmise or even misunderstanding and were uncritically passed along from generation to generation. But the substitution of what is *said* in the assertion for what the assertion is about may lead to a degenerate kind of communication. Heidegger calls it *Gerede* or idle talk. "What is said-in-the-talk as such," according to Heidegger, "spreads in wider circles and takes on an authoritative character. Things are so because one says so . . ." (212). [34] Writing may suffer from the same groundlessness and become *Geschreibe*, if "it feeds upon superficial reading" (212). Both types of communication, *Gerede* and *Geschreibe*, produce a pseudoerudition:

> Idle talk is the possibility of understanding without making the thing one's own. If this were done, idle talk would founder; and it already guards against such a danger. Idle talk is something which anyone can rake up; it not only releases one from the task of genuinely understanding, but develops an undifferentiated kind of intelligibility, for which nothing is closed off any longer. (213)

Thamus's objection to Theuth's invention of writing now appears in a clear light. For the description of its possible effects bears a remarkable resemblance to Heidegger's account of *Gerede* and *Geschreibe:*

> It is not true wisdom that you offer your disciples, but only its semblance; for by telling them of many things without teaching them you will make them seem to know much, while for the most part they know nothing, and as men filled, not with wisdom, but with the conceit of wisdom, they will be a burden to their fellows. (275A–B)

If Heidegger's philosophy has helped us to a better understanding of Plato, it has, paradoxically, also shown us that Heidegger did not understand Plato as well as he might have, if he had read him less literally. For through Thamus's objection to the art of writing it has now become manifest that Plato was more fully aware of and made more use of truth as *aletheai* than Heidegger, in several of his writings, gives him credit for. More will have to be said about this later.

In retrospect we can see how the various parts of the dialogues balance each other. There is a main division between speeches on love in the first part and the critique of speech writing in the second. The first part is further divided into the speech of Lysias and the first speech of Socrates on the one hand and the second speech of Socrates on the other. In the former, the lover is portrayed as in bondage to his own passion and as making use of the other for the satisfaction of his own desires. This self-love stands in contrast to the altruistic love of the second speech of Socrates. This seemingly good love, when carefully analyzed, reveals itself as in need of further division, namely between authentic and inauthentic devotion. In the latter, the lover subjects himself to the beloved, while in the former both retain their individuality unimpaired. Now while the first half of the dialogue is devoted to the intimate relation between lover and beloved, the second half deals with communication between individuals in general, a relationship which is presupposed by the first half. As the lover of the first section, of the first half, is motivated by pure self-interest, so the rhetoricians discussed in the second half are shown to be interested neither in the truth nor in the good of the audience. They are driven by their lust for power, as Lysias's lover by his sexual passion, and both harm themselves as well as those with whom they deal. But goodwill on the part of the speaker is not enough, just as devotion, even of the altruistic kind, can miscarry. Again a division is called for. Ostensibly, it is between written and oral discourses. In reality, and as Socrates does not tell but indirectly suggests, it is between discourses "telling them of many things without teaching them" (275A), and "those lessons," whether written or oral, which are "veritably written in the soul of the listener" (278A). The division corresponds to Heidegger's distinction between discourses which succeed in letting the phenomena show themselves so that the listener or reader sees the truth for himself, and *Gerede* or *Geschreibe*, that is, discourses which merely pass along what has been said or written, for these too make men "seem to know much, while for the most part they know nothing" (275A–B).

What then are the conditions for the possibility of genuine communication in general and love and friendship in particular? First there must be a common world. World as here used is to be understood not as the sum of all entities, but in the sense of the world of the artist, the farmer, the housewife, etc., which for Heidegger is an essential characteristic of Dasein. It can range from the culture of a vast group such as "the Western world," to the narrow confines of a craftsman in his shop. To communicate means to light up various aspects within a particular world, aspects which are implicitly known and through discourse are made explicit. Within a wider world, the same term may take on different meanings dependent upon whether it is used in one subworld or another. Love as understood by a man who frequents "some haunt of sailors" would be quite different from that experienced by one who is "himself of a noble and gentle nature and who loved or ever had loved a nature like his own" (243C–D,J). Second, there must be a being who is capable of transcending the present situation, and who, by reaching into the future, tries to realize the various possibilities offered by the world into which he has been *thrown*. According to the talents and dispositions with which he is endowed, an individual *exists*, that is, projects goals and ideals and patterns his life in conformity with them. These goals, which are part and parcel of a man's being and which can be shared with another, make it possible for two individuals to become one in essential respects. The union of two individuals, based on the pursuit of common goals, can appear in the *inauthentic* and the *authentic mode*. The former we have encountered, not only in the selfish lover, in the grip of an uncontrollable passion, but also in the altruistic lover who fell captive to his beloved and forfeited his individuality. The latter appears in the form of a myth:

> We beheld with our eyes that blessed vision, ourselves in the train of Zeus, others following some other god. . . . (205B) Thus the followers of Zeus seek a beloved who is Zeus-like in soul; wherefore they look for one who is by nature disposed to the love of wisdom and the leading of men, and when they have found him and come to love him they do all in their power to foster that disposition . . . as they follow up the trace within themselves of the nature of their god . . . in so far as man can partake of god. (252E–253A)

But the most beautiful and impressive view of friendship emerges from the dialogue as a whole. As if to outdo the Chinese proverb which says that one picture is worth a thousand words, Plato creates a picture with words which shows the two friends, Socrates and Phaedrus, enjoying a simple walk into the country, charmed by the clear water of the stream which cools their bare feet, the soft grass on which they rest in the shade of a tall plane tree in full bloom, listening to the chirping of the cicadas, sensing the presence of the gods who spur them on to search into the mystery of life as far as man may. Thus they share a rich and beautiful world, united in the pursuit of truth, and asking for material goods, of gold, "so much of it as only a temperate man might bear and carry with him" (279C).[35]

Ideals to be approximated and pitfalls to be avoided—these are the prime constituents of Plato's discourses on love and friendship in the *Lysis*, the *Symposium*, and the *Phaedrus*. As such, they are more a call to action than a body of tenets set forth for our acceptance or belief. And Plato's view of man, as being forever straining to transcend itself, instils, as we have seen, the hope that the desire for union with others, for a life of peace and harmony with our fellowmen, is not foredoomed to frustration as long as the world offers us common goals to pursue. Thus these discourses have an astonishingly modern ring and are far removed from the mysticism which has been traditionally associated with Plato's conception of love. For they address themselves to men who believe that whatever the conditions in which circumstances beyond their control have thrown them, they are in important respects responsible for their own mode of being. And they achieve that self-realization not by leaving the human experience behind and seeking refuge in another-worldly mysticism, but by inquiring into the real possibilities which it has to offer and by joining with others in a common effort to bring them to fruition. [36]

Has Plato exhaustively dealt with the role which transcendence plays in the human mode of being? He has shown that without it neither love and friendship nor communication in general would be possible. He has even suggested its indispensable presence in intellectual activities ranging from fantasies and myths to logical arguments. The very thoroughness, however, with which Plato discusses transcendence creates the impression that it meant more to him than he explicitly stated, and that for artistic reasons, for the sake of the unity of his dramatic dialogues, he thought it necessary to restrict himself in the main to a discussion of the relevance of transcendence to love and friendship.

Be that as it may. In any event, for Heidegger, "every essential answer is only the beginning of a responsibility. In it, the question arises with greater originality. Hence the genuine question is not stilled by the answer found."[37]

Heidegger does in fact carry the discussion of transcendence beyond the position reached by Plato. In *Being and Time* he calls attention to its presence in our most ordinary daily activities. These become intelligible only in terms of goals projected into the future. This is the reason why he can say: "The essence of Dasein lies in its existence" (67), understanding *existence* in its original meaning as "standing out," i.e., reaching into the future and letting that future determine present activities.

Such future goals, however, are not yet, and the "standing out" in question, the transcendence, is a standing in Nothing.

How about this Nothing? This is a question which Heidegger tackled in his inaugural lecture at the University of Freiburg in Breisgaw in 1929 under the title *What is Metaphysics?* The members of the faculty, especially the scientists among them, must have been struck with amazement upon hearing their new colleague speak of Nothing. Or perhaps they merely saw in his talk another confirmation of the popular notion that there is nothing too useless and too absurd to serve philosophers as a subject matter for discussion.

Heidegger, anticipating their possible objections, dwells on the seemingly insurmountable difficulty which such a discussion presents. The very question: What is Nothing? appears impossible, for it converts that which *is not* into something which *is*. And the answer, if it could be found, would have to say: Nothing *is* such and such, thereby destroying its object, for it is impossible of Nothing to say that it *is*.

Heidegger is quick to point out, however, that if, according to the standards of logic the inquiry into Nothing is self-contradictory and therefore impossible, the attitude of the scientist is no less untenable. For the scientist declares that he relates himself to the world of entities and nothing else; that he takes his direction from such entities and nothing more; that he inquires into these entities and nothing beyond. Thus, in circumscribing his domain he calls upon Nothing for aid. Nevertheless, he rejects Nothing. But is he not, by this very rejection, admitting it? How can he, however, speak of an admission, if he admits Nothing? Still, there remains the undeniable fact that science, in determining itself, invokes the aid of Nothing. "What it rejects, it calls upon for aid. What sort of schizophrenia is this?" (W. i. M., p. 27)

Thus the philosopher and the scientist find themselves in an equally embarrassing position. They both speak and therefore think of Nothing. But to think is to think of something. Their speaking and their thinking simultaneously affirms and denies and thereby violates a principle of reason, namely, the principle of noncontradiction. (W. i. M., p. 28)

The absurdity involved in the talk about Nothing presupposes a recognition of the supremacy of logic, the science of reason. This supremacy, it would seem, cannot be challenged. Nothing is generally defined as the negation of the totality of things. Any reference to Nothing, therefore, presupposes reason, for according to this definition Nothing is derived from negation, an activity of reason.

Heidegger, however, boldly asserts the opposite, namely, that "nothing is more original than the not and negation" (W. i. M., p. 28), and he sets out to prove this thesis.

He begins by questioning the traditional definition of Nothing as the negation of all there is. Before such a negation can take place, the totality of things must first show itself. Now it is obvious that we cannot comprehend this totality, but it can be said that we find ourselves in the midst of it. This awareness, Heidegger claims, comes to us in the mood of boredom—not when we are bored about this or that thing, but when all things, other men, and we ourselves assume a strange indifference. When our mind roams about and can find nothing of interest, it is still concerned with being. The mood of boredom, Heidegger concludes, makes us aware that we are in the midst of the totality of things, but it does not reveal Nothing. (W. i. M., pp. 30–31)

As a phenomenologist, Heidegger must bring the object to be investigated before us. But where can we find Nothing? And how can it be made to reveal itself?

From *Being and Time* and from our discussion of the *Phaedo* we know that Nothing becomes manifest in the mood of anxiety, provided we have the courage to face that mood and do not convert it into fear. In fear we recoil from a threatening entity or situation encountered in the world; in anxiety Dasein is torn out of the world in which it feels at home, and as a result things appear devoid of all significance. The analyses of anxiety in *Being and Time* and *What is Metaphysics?* are essentially the same, except that in the latter Heidegger is less concerned with what this mood reveals about Dasein and more with what it shows about Nothing:

All things and we ourselves sink into a sort of indifference, not in the sense of a mere disappearance, but in their moving away they turn toward us. This moving away of things in their totality, which crowds about us in anxiety, is what oppresses us. There remains nothing to hold on to. All that remains and comes over us—in this slipping away of entities—is this Nothing (W. i. M., p. 32)

Of this Nothing we cannot say that it *is*. And yet it functions by letting things slip away. It keeps them at a distance; it makes them appear strange, unrelated to any of our interests. They have fallen out of the world in which they normally function and are familiar to us. Heidegger calls this process nihilating *(nichten)*. In keeping the totality of things separate from Dasein, so that Dasein itself feels suspended from itself, this Nothing creates the open space, the clearing, in which entities, including Dasein, can show themselves as they are in themselves, stripped of all relations to human concerns. So it appears that when Dasein approaches things in regard to their being, it comes from out of Nothing. (W. i. M., p. 35)

The phenomenon of the nihilating function of Nothing does not reveal negation as an act of understanding. Dasein is powerless in the face of the totality of things, staring at it in cold indifference. Furthermore, the understanding can deny only if there is something to deny, that is, after Nothing has made it possible for things to show themselves in their being. Thus the primacy of negation as the source of not and Nothing is broken. And the earlier claim that the inquiry into Nothing is absurd on the ground that it violates a principle of the understanding, is now itself absurd; for the operation of the understanding presupposes the prior functioning of Nothing. As Heidegger expresses it:

Herewith we have proved the above thesis in all essentials: Nothing is the source of negation, not the other way about. If this breaks the sovereignty of reason in the field of inquiry into Nothing and Being, then the fate of the rule of "logic" in philosophy is also decided. The very idea of "logic" disintegrates in the vortex of a more original questioning. (W. i. M., pp. 36–37)

Similarly, the scientist who laughs at the inquiry into Nothing, makes himself ridiculous:

Only because Nothing is revealed in the very basis of our Dasein is it possible for the utter strangeness of what is to dawn on us. Only when the strangeness of what is forces itself upon us does it awaken and invite our wonder. Only because of wonder, that is to say, the revelation of Nothing, does the "Why?" spring to our lips. Only because this "Why?" is possible as such can we seek for reasons and proofs in a definite way. Only because we can ask and prove are we fated to become inquirers in this life. (W. i. M., p. 41)

A final objection must be dealt with: If only by standing into Nothing can Dasein relate to entities and if only anxiety reveals that Nothing, then it would follow that we continuously suffer anxiety. Heidegger himself, however, has admitted that anxiety is a rare mood. But since we all relate to entities, it would seem that Nothing, and the anxiety which reveals it, are not necessary. We are familiar with the answer to this objection from *Being and Time*, where Heidegger characterizes fallenness as a flight from Nothing into the world of things, to which it clings and which it does not let slip away. "And yet," Heidegger continues, "this perpetual if ambiguous reversion from Nothing accords, within certain limits, with the essential meaning of Nothing. It— Nothing in its nihilation—relegates us to entities. Nothing nihilates unceasingly, without our knowing about this happening through the knowledge which guides our daily concerns" (W. i. M., p. 36).

In the dialogues earlier considered, Socrates' attitude toward the laws and toward the gods, toward the state, toward education and toward death, suggested a conception of man which could not be contained in so rigid a framework as that supplied by what later went under the name of the Aristotelian categories, such as substance, quality, quantity, relation, etc. Its dynamism found a more adequate expression in Heidegger's existentials of thrownness, existence, fallenness, and anticipatory resoluteness. All these existentials point toward transcendence: thrownness by offering possibilities to be developed, existence as the projection of these possibilities, anticipatory resoluteness as holding oneself in suspense and open for the demands of the concrete situation, and fallenness as the countermovement in which Dasein clings to the present, letting itself be controlled by it and not allowing transcendence full play. In the trilogy on love and friendship, especially in the *Phaedrus*, transcendence is presented as the condition for the possibility of interpersonal relationships. Plato, at least by implication, thus touches the very roots of the human mode of being, while Heidegger, in an even more far-reaching inquiry (extending an analogy which he borrows from Descartes), reaches the soil in which these roots find their nourishment:

> Dasein means: Projection into Nothing. Projecting into Nothing Dasein is already beyond the totality of entities. This being beyond entities we call transcendence. If Dasein in the very ground of its being, did not transcend, i.e. if it were not in advance holding itself into Nothing, then it could not relate to entities and therefore not even to itself. Without the original manifestation of Nothing there is no selfhood and no freedom. (W. i. M., p. 35)

Only through Nothing, that is, the opening which it provides, are entities enabled to show themselves to us in their being. Nothing, therefore, is the condition for the possibility of things. Heidegger calls it Being *(Sein)*, which in anxiety manifests itself as Nothing, the wholly other than what is:

This, the pure Other than everything that is, is that-which-is-not [das Nicht-Seiende]. Yet this Nothing functions as Being. It would be premature to stop thinking at this point and adopt the facile explanation that Nothing is merely nugatory, equating it with the non-existent [das Wesenlose]. Instead of giving way to such precipitate and empty ingenuity and abandoning Nothing in all its mysterious multiplicity of meanings, we should rather equip ourselves and make ready for one thing only: to experience in Nothing the vastness of that which gives every being its warrant to be. That is Being itself. (W. i. M., pp. 45–46)

It is obvious that the search for selfhood, at this stage, is far from having reached a final conclusion. A full comprehension of the human mode of being is not possible, unless the ground on which Dasein rests has been elucidated. And this in turn would involve an understanding, not only of the being of entities, nor of Being as the ground of entities, but the meaning of Being as such, as it is in itself. In the mood of anxiety, the most significantly revelatory of all moods, Being manifests itself as Nothing. Heidegger, therefore, most appropriately, calls this Nothing "the veil of Being" (W. i. M., p. 51). The attempt to lift this veil is a task which occupied Heidegger to the very end of his life.

Again we find confirmation of Heidegger's claim that every significant answer is merely the beginning of a renewed questioning. But incomplete as the inquiry may be, there is a clear line of development visible from Plato's dialogues, over Heidegger's Dasein analytic, to Heidegger's search for the meaning of Being in general. This last quest is of such enormous proportion that even Heidegger, on his own admission, could do no more than prepare the way.

NOTES

1. Quotations from Martin Heidegger's *Being and Time* refer to the translation by John Macquarrie and Edward Robinson (New York: Harper & Row, 1962).

2. All quotations from the *Lysis* refer to the translation by J. Wright in *The Collected Dialogues of Plato*, edited by E. Hamilton and H. Cairns, Bollingen Series 71 (Princeton, N.J.: Princeton University Press, 1971).

3. Note for instance: "The *Lysis* [is] a rather dreary early work with only two or three really interesting moments." Thomas Gould, *Platonic Love* (New York: Free Press of Glencoe, 1963), p. 1. Paul Shorey gives a rather rough paraphrase of the dialogue and concludes that it "plays baffingly with [various] distinctions to no specific result." *What Plato Said* (Chicago: University of Chicago Press, 1968), p. 115.

4. *The Dialogues of Plato*, trans. B. Jowett, vol. 1 (New York: Random House, 1937).

5. Quoted by F. M. Cornford, *The "Republic" of Plato* (New York: Oxford University Press, 1945), p. 173.

6. Of course, it can also go in the opposite direction, that is from approval to disapproval, or even from love to hate, as George F. Kennan put it so engagingly in a speech at Swarthmore College on the *Radical Left on the American Campus Today:*

In most of the reproaches with which our children shower us, there is of course an element of justification. There is a point somewhere along the way in most of our adult lives, admittedly, when enthusiasms flag, when idealism becomes tempered, when responsibility to others, and even affection for others, compel greater attention to the mundane demands of private life. There is a point when we are even compelled to place the needs of our children ahead of the dictates of a defiant idealism, and to devote ourselves to the support and rearing of these same children—in order that at some future date they may have the privilege of turning upon us and despising us for the materialistic faintheartedness that made their maturity possible.

7. Liddell and Scott, *Greek-English Lexicon*, 7th ed., s.v. "heneka."

8. A. E. Taylor interprets *to oikeion* as a "natural good" and ultimately "the true supreme good" on the common pursuit of which "the full and perfect type of friendship can only be based." *Plato* (London: Methuen & Co., 1949) p. 73. But *that which belongs* to each individual in the most basic sense is his own self, and to gain possession of his own being is his primary task, not the pursuit of an absolute reality.

9. Paul Friedländer points in this direction: "The reality of life is not as rigid, it appears, as the two theses between which it moves, and their refutation is not as radical as it seemed to be." But he does not show in sufficient detail how the paradoxes lead to that realization. Furthermore, instead of seeing in the dialogue the outline of a proper conception of man as the condition for the possibility of friendship, he links the friendship of the *Lysis* to the love in the *Symposium*, which he conceives as having the absolute for its object: "Lysis . . . desires wisdom because he does not have it; subjectively speaking he loves Socrates. The same relationship is repeated on a higher level. Socrates himself is not a wise man but a lover of wisdom, because he lacks perfect wisdom which, according to the *Symposium* (203 et seq.) and the *Phaedrus* (246D) is a prerogative of the gods." *Plato*, vol. 2, trans. H. Meyerhoff (Princeton, N.J.: Princeton University Press, 1964), p. 98. If friendship and love tend to lose themselves in the absolute, are they not stripped of their character as a relation between one person and another? For G.M.A. Grube, too, friendship in the *Lysis* is directed to the absolute and not to another human being: "Already we catch a glimpse . . . of an absolute object of desire, loved for its own sake, an ultimate good and beauty. . . . From all this there begins to emerge the Socratic conception of mutual love as a means to joint search for supreme truth." *Plato's Thought* (Boston: Beacon Press, 1961), pp. 95–96. Richard Robinson states dogmatically that "the explicit question of the *Lysis* is not what friendship is but what its condition is." *Plato's Earlier Dialectic*, 2nd Ed. (Oxford: Clarendon Press, 1953), p. 49. But it is not clear whether he takes this condition to be the absolute or a particular structure of the human mode of being.

10. See notes 8 and 9, above.

11. ". . . Socrates takes the floor and reduces all previous speeches to insignificance." Paul Friedländer, *Plato vol. 1, An Introduction*, trans. H. Meyerhoff (Princeton, N.J.: Princeton University Press, 1958), pp. 56–57.

12. Unless stated otherwise, all quotations from the *Symposium* refer to *The Dialogues of Plato*, trans. B. Jowett, vol. I (New York: Random House, 1937).

13. Aegisthus exclaims: "Since I came to the throne, all I said, all my acts, have been aimed at building up an image of myself. I wished each of my subjects to keep that image in the foreground of his mind, and to feel, even when alone, that my eyes are on him, severely judging his most private thoughts. But I have been trapped in my own net. I have come to see myself only as they see me. I peer into the dark pit of their souls, and there, deep down I see the image that I have built up. I shudder, but I cannot take my eyes off it. Almighty Zeus, who am I? Am I anything more than the dread that others have of me?" But the god to whom Aegisthus appeals is no better off. Zeus too complains:

"And I—who do you think I am? I, too, have my image, and do you suppose it does not fill me with confusion? For a hundred thousand years I have been dancing a slow, dark ritual dance before men's eyes. Their eyes are so intent upon me that they forget to look into themselves. If I forget myself for a single moment, if I let their eyes turn away . . . Once freedom lights its beacon in man's heart, the gods are powerless against him." *"No Exit" and "The Flies,"* English version by Stuart Gilbert (New York: Alfred A. Knopf, 1952), pp. 134, 136.

14. *The Blacks,* trans. Bernard Frechtman (New York: Evergreen, 1960), p. 36. Basically the same phenomenon finds a different expression in one of Sartre's novels. Daniel has freely confessed to his friend Mathieu that he is a homosexual. Seeing himself as such in the eyes of his friend, a fierce hatred begins to flare up in him: "Suddenly the silence grew burdensome; Mathieu said to himself: 'Daniel is looking at me,' and he hurriedly raised his head. Daniel was indeed looking at him, and with so venomous an expression that Mathieu's heart contracted. 'Why are you looking at me like that?' he asked. 'You know,' said Daniel, 'there is someone who knows.' " Jean-Paul Sartre, *The Age of Reason,* translated from the French by Eric Sutton (New York: The Modern Library, 1947), p. 392.

15. Eugene Ionesco's *The Lesson* has been interpreted as dealing with an extreme form of this tendency of the teacher to violate the person of the student: "There is more about language in *The Lesson* than a demonstration of the futility of communication. Here language is also shown as an instrument of power. . . . Pierre Aimand Touchard has argued that *The Lesson* expresses in caricature form the spirit of domination always present in teacher-pupil relationships. . . . It is all authority, therefore, which is shown up in its sexual, sadistic nature. What Ionesco is saying is that even behind such apparently harmless an exercise of authority as the type of teacher-pupil relationship, all the violence and domination, all the aggressiveness and possessiveness, the cruelty and lust are present that make up any manifestation of power." Martin Esslin, *The Theatre of the Absurd* (New York: Doubleday Anchor, 1961), pp. 95, 96, 97.

16. *Symposium* 214B. *Plato,* with an English translation by W.R.M. Lamb, vol. 5, Loeb Classical Library (Cambridge, Mass.: Harvard University Press, 1961).

17. Instead of a loss, G.M.A. Grube sees a gain: "Its main contribution from our point of view is to broaden the conception of Eros and to insist on its essential kinship, if indeed not identity, with the forces at work in the whole of nature, a step that can but deepen its significance." *Plato's Thought* (Boston: Beacon Press, 1961), p. 99.

18. *Politics,* 2, chap. 4, 1262b.

19. A. E. Taylor, *Plato: The Man and his Work* (London: Methuen & Co., 1949), p. 216.

20. *Nicomachean Ethics,* B. 1, chap. 5, 1095b.

21. G.M.A. Grube senses the difficulty correctly, but instead of exploring it dramatically, he puts the blame on Plato: "As we follow the philosopher on his upward journey we feel that something has gone wrong, that passionate oratory has somehow left love behind; that in the contemplation of supreme beauty the philosopher may indeed find a sublime satisfaction, but we would hardly call this the satisfaction of love which must surely be limited to relations between individuals. If we look closer we shall find that the point where we should part company with Plato is when Diotima reaches the beauty of 'laws and institutions.' Love, we feel, must have and retain some sort of physical basis and Plato has here . . . been carried away on the tide of his own magnificent metaphors." *Plato's Thought,* pp. 114–15.

22. *Plato,* trans. Lamb, vol. 5.

23. "Thither looking, and holding converse with the true beauty simple and divine

. . . he will be enabled to bring forth, not images of beauty, but realities (for he has hold not of an image but reality), and bringing forth and nourishing true virtue [he will] become a friend of God and be immortal, if mortal man may be" (211E-212A).

24. This notion seems to be implied in the following exchange between Socrates and Crito:

Crito: But you see, Socrates, that the opinion of the many must be regarded, for what is now happening shows that they can do the greatest evil to any one who has lost their good opinion.

Socrates: I only wish it were so Crito; and that the many would do the greatest evil; for then they would also be able to do the greatest good—and what a fine thing this would be! But in reality they can do neither . . . and whatever they do is the result of chance. *Crito*, 44D, in *The Dialogues of Plato*, ed. B. Jowett, pp. 428–29.

25. Hartmut Buchner (*Eros und Sein* [Bonn: H. Bouvier u. Co. Verlag, 1965]), a former student of Heidegger's restricts his inquiry almost exclusively to the conversation between Socrates and Diotima. He justifies his disregard of the preceding speeches on the ground that they deal with the traditional conceptions of Eros. These views, he maintains, are not those current today, and the speeches which refute them have lost the pedagogical function which they had for the Greeks (p. 19). This restriction places Buchner's book, interesting as it is in many respects, outside the scope of this inquiry. For it makes him miss the dramatic interplay of excesses of which the Socrates-Diotima exchange is a part. It also hides the contrast between the absolute beauty in which the individual loses himself and the unique individuality of Socrates which emerges from the eulogy of Alcibiades.

26. Unless otherwise indicated, quotations from the *Phaedrus* refer to the translation by R. Hackforth in *The Collected Dialogues of Plato*, ed. E. Hamilton and H. Cairns, Bollingen Series 71 (Princeton, N.J.: Princeton University Press, 1961.) When the Jowett translation seemed preferable, the reference is followed by the letter 'J'. *The Dialogues of Plato*, trans. B. Jowett (New York: Random House, 1937), vol. 1.

27. It has been pointed out that the dramatic situation also points to narrowness as the flaw in the definition: "The fictional speaker, who is attacking lovers, is in reality a lover himself only pretending to be a non-lover. . . . Does his definition of love fit his own case? If so, he is undercutting his own chances of success with the boy. Given his cleverness, it seems much more likely that, although he is a lover, his definition of love is not descriptive of his own feeling for his beloved. In other words, he is motivated by a different kind of love than the kind he defines. But this implies that even before the definition is presented Phaedrus and the reader are being told indirectly that the definition of love (along with the following argument) is inadequate since it does not cover all cases of love." Herman L. Sinaiko, *Love, Knowledge and Discourse in Plato: Dialogue and Dialectic in "Phaedrus," "Republic," "Parmenides"* (Chicago: The University of Chicago Press, 1965), pp. 31–32. Note also: "And here, as is not infrequent, Plato's humour has misled most of his commentators. The blasphemy was only in giving the name of Eros to the kind of passion described. Hence the palinode. Of the substance of his magnificent indictment of mere physical erotic madness which is ruthlessly possessive and profoundly selfish he does not need to retract a single word for it gives us an understanding of what real Eros is not, which is essential to the understanding of the true nature of the god of Love." G. M. A. Grube, *Plato's Thought* (Boston: Beacon Press, 1961), p. 108.

28. This may be the reason for the fact, to which Sinaiko has called attention, that "immortality and functioning as an arche of motion, the two attributes that are most strongly emphasized in the 'proof,' are hardly mentioned in the body of the myth." *Love*,

Knowledge and Discourse, p. 298, n. 25. The myth manifests transcendence in its own particular way.

29. T. S. Eliot, *The Cocktail Party* (New York: Harcourt, Brace and Co., 1950), p. 92.

30. Jean-Paul Sartre, *Being and Nothingness: An Essay on Phenomenological Ontology*, translated with an Introduction by Hazel E. Barnes (New York: Philosophical Library, 1956), pp. 365–66.

31. George Santayana, "Ultimate Religion," in *The Philosophy of Santayana* ed. Irwin Edman (New York: C. Scribner's Sons, 1936), p. 581.

32. Sartre seems to recognize this kind of communion when, in a later work, he defends himself against the charge that his philosophy, as expressed in *Being and Nothingness*, lacks social relevance: "Notre *être commun* n'est pas en chacun *une nature identique*; . . . je ne reconnais pas mon essence inerte en tant qu'elle est manifestée dans un autre exemple. . . . La fraternité est le lien réel des individus communs, en tant que chacun vit *son être* et celui de l'Autre. . . . Le groupe constitué est produit en chacun par chacun comme *sa propre naissance d'individu commun* et, en même temps, chacun saisit dans la fraternité sa propre naissance d'individu commun comme produit au sein du groupe et par lui. . . ." Jean-Paul Sartre, *Critique de la Raison Dialectique*, vol. 1, *Théorie des ensembles pratiques* (Paris: Librairie Gallimard, 1960), pp. 453–454.

33. Gerhard Krüger (*Einsicht und Leidenschaft*, 3rd ed. [Frankfurt am Main: Vittorio Klostermann, 1963], p. 28), speaks in the same breath of the "Vergötterung des Geliebten" and his education "nach dem Urbild des Zeus oder eines anderen Gottes" as if they constituted one and the same process. Following the traditional view, he regards the second speech of Socrates as simply "good," and as a result slurs over the hidden conflict between the *idealization* of the beloved and his *education* in the light of the ideal. He thus misses the pitfalls which are contained in the second speech, or, to put it differently, the need for a division into good and bad of the attitude toward the beloved even in the second speech.

34. Jacob Klein recognizes the distinction between authentic talk and *Gerede* in the *Meno* when he says: "Gorgias might well *know what arete is*, while Meno might merely *know what Gorgias said it is*." A *Commentary on Plato's "Meno"* (Chapel Hill, N.C.: University of North Carolina Press, 1965), p. 45.

35. This scene is reminiscent of Heidegger's conception of world as expressed in "Das Ding": "Wir nennen das ereignende Spiegel-Spiel der Einfalt von Erde und Himmel, Göttlichen und Sterblichen die Welt." In *Vorträge und Aufsätze* (Pfullingen: Neske, 1959), p. 178.

36. In the *Phaedrus* myth, the need to have regard for what is given appears in such statements as these: "We philosophers following in the train of Zeus, others in company of other gods" (250B,J); "Every one chooses his love from the ranks of beauty according to his character" (252D,J). This suggests that the ideal cannot be chosen arbitrarily but must be rooted in the disposition and capacity of the chooser. In the myth of *Er*, in the *Republic*, lots are drawn to determine the sequence in the selection of a new life, which means that some men have a wider range of opportunities than others. But it is made clear that the important things is not what is given to them, but what they do with the lives laid out before them: "Even for the last comer, if he chooses wisely and will live diligently, there is appointed a happy and not undesirable existence" (619B). This paradoxical twofold obligation of man, namely, to accept himself and not to accept himself, to respect what is given but to endeavor to go beyond it by unfolding its potentialities, is expressed in Martin Heidegger's pregnant formulations: "Und als geworfenes ist das Dasein in die Seinsart des Entwerfens geworfen." *Sein und Zeit*, 6th

ed. (Tübingen: Neomarius Verlag, 1949), p. 145. Cf. also: "Die Seinsverfassung des Daseins [ist] geworfener Entwurf." Ibid., p. 223.

37. Translated from Martin Heidegger, *Was ist Metaphysik?* *(W.i.M.)*, 8th ed. (Frankfurt am Main: Vittorio Klostermann, 1960), p. 44.

Conclusion

For Heidegger, as we have seen, truth in its primary sense does not consist in an agreement between knowing and its object. "To say an assertion is true," he maintains, "signifies that it uncovers the entity as it is in itself. Such an assertion asserts, points out, 'lets' the entity 'be seen' (apophansis) in its uncoveredness" (261). This does not mean that all entities lie open before us. They can show themselves differently according as we view them from one perspective or another. Truth does not thereby become completely relative to the viewer, for while he can choose the point of view, he cannot control the way in which the entity responds. Some approaches may reveal it in significant ways, while others uncover only its trivial aspects or even prevent it from showing itself at all.

Now an entity, and especially a work of art such as a Platonic dialogue, offers innumerable aspects, and these can form the basis of a variety of interpretations. Perhaps no single interpretation can cover all aspects. But the worth of a specific approach can be judged in terms of the significance of the insights it reveals and by the extent to which it leads to a better understanding not only of the thoughts of the author, but of our own selves and the world in which we live.

Has the interaction of Heidegger's Dasein analytic and Plato's dramatic dialogues born fruit, or has it been a futile exercise? A brief reminder of some of its results should help the reader to decide the issue for himself one way or the other.

The image of the sleeping Socrates, Crito's excessive concern with the opinion of the many, and the paradoxical wish of Socrates that the many could do the greatest evil—all these have been mentioned only casually by commentators of the *Crito*, if they have been mentioned at all. Now they are seen to point to the distinction between authentic and inauthentic selfhood, which is presupposed in Socrates' choice between life and death, between escaping and submitting to the judgment of the Athenians.

The *Euthyphro* no longer appears as an exercise in the logic of definition, in which piety plays only an accidental part. Piety as doing the will of the gods is now the central theme. It is understood as constituting oneself an authentic

293

human being, and this is the great work of which Socrates speaks as requiring the genuine cooperation of gods and men. For the gods can give no more than the capacity, while its realization is the exclusive task of the individual man.

This same notion of authenticity underlies the paradoxes of the *Hippias Minor*, where Socrates claims that the voluntary evildoer is better than the involuntary one. This is literally true, not on the moral but on the ontological level, in as much as the one has constituted himself a genuine self while the other has not.

The *Phaedo* has gained renewed vitality and relevance to modern concerns. Its purpose is no longer seen as furnishing a logically convincing proof for life after death. On the contrary, it shows that certainty in such matters is unattainable and it thereby opens the way for a genuine faith which, while not unreasonable, must be based on a free choice fully aware of the risk involved. Genuine faith presupposes genuine selfhood. The opportunity for the choice of self, according to Heidegger, is offered by anxiety arising in the face of imminent death. Plato tries to call forth this anxiety by letting the reader vicariously witness the dying of Socrates. Heidegger pursues the same end through a phenomenological analysis of "Being-toward-death." When read with this analysis in the background, the death scene which concludes the *Phaedo* takes on added significance.

The proofs for the unity of the virtues in the *Protagoras*, which on purely logical grounds appear so unacceptable, become meaningful as a refutation of Protagoras's guarantee that he can make anyone who comes to him a better man. He would do this by molding the young in conformity with the values handed down by tradition. To tradition Socrates opposes critical intelligence. Heidegger in turn shows how tradition and critical intelligence complement each other and how their interplay must be conceived so as to enhance rather than crush the freedom and responsibility of the individual.

The *Idea of the Good* and the philosopher kings in the *Republic* can no longer be cited as evidence of the growing dogmatism of Plato. For they serve as a mirror which reflects the uncertainty of human knowledge and the impossibility of shirking responsibility by following a leader no matter how well-meaning and competent. The *Republic* thus illustrates on a large scale Heidegger's distinction between *leaping in* and *leaping ahead*, that is, between the solicitude which relieves the other of his responsibility and thus makes him dependent, and the solicitude which helps to make him free by preparing him for carrying his own burden.

In the light of Heidegger's differentiation between substantiality and *existence*, Shorey's criticism that "the *Lysis* plays bafflingly with [various] distinctions to no specific results," appears wholly unjustified.[1] For the dialogue calls attention to the dynamism of the human mode of being without which friendship would be inconceivable, and it restricts the applicability of the Aristotelian categories, even before they were formulated, to beings other than men.

The mysticism which commentators have frequently claimed to have found in the *Symposium* has given way to a series of concrete illustrations of the dangers which threaten genuine love and friendship.

The *Phaedrus* in various ways demonstrates transcendence and the sharing of goals and insights as the condition for the possibility of communication in general and the realization of the lovers' desire in some sense to become one. Goals can be shared only in a common world. Heidegger therefore uses various devices to make this phenomenon appear before us, while Plato suggests it with a charming picture of two friends amusing themselves with philosophical discussion while enjoying a beautiful summer day in the countryside.

From the perspective of Heidegger's Dasein analytic, all the dialogues considered converge on a single point: the most important choice a man can make, the choice of his own self. And in accordance with the Socratic method, this choice is presented indirectly. Since men are reluctant to assume responsibility for themselves, Plato eliminates all excuses, exposes all hiding places, such as those behind the prescriptions of the law, or the will of the gods, or science, logic and philosophy, or tradition, or men in authority no matter how wise.

Plato can only offer the opportunity to make this choice. Compulsion of any sort is obviously out of the question. As we have seen, this self-possession, which Heidegger calls anticipatory resoluteness, consists in an effort to hold oneself open for whatever demands the concrete situation may make upon an individual. It is totally inconsistent with the rigid adherence to a specific resolve, and for that matter to any doctrine such as those with which Plato has been traditionally saddled. Only on a literal interpretation of certain statements, or if taken out of context, can these doctrines be attributed to Plato.

The doctrine of the impossibility of the voluntary evildoer, for instance, appears in the *Protagoras* as an implication of the Sophist's guarantee of the effectiveness of his teaching. Socrates exposes the preposterous nature of this boast by showing that it would entail the elimination of a difference as important to the Athenians as that between a man who stands fast in the face of danger, and one who takes to his heels. Both Shorey[2] and Taylor[3] refer to the *Laws* in support of their contention that Plato upheld the doctrine to the very end of his life. The Athenian in the *Laws*, however, speaks as the legislator to whom the main function of the law is to teach men to become good citizens. To the extent to which he considers the law to be effective, he believes that the mere presentation of what is right and wrong will induce men to pursue the one and shun the other. He knows, however, that not all men are easily persuaded and that in some instances the law must "both teach and constrain those who have done wrong" (862D). The doctrine as used by the Athenian expresses merely a hope, a faith that most men are willing to cooperate with the authorities. Protagoras, on the other hand, who *guarantees* to make a man better through instruction, must assume that the mere presentation of the right course of action will be sufficient, and this can be true only if it is in the nature of man not to pursue evil if the good is accessible to him. The doctrine also appears in the *Gorgias* when Socrates asks Polus whether a man "would choose the more evil and shameful in preference to the less." To this Polus replies: "Not according to this argument, I think" (475D–E). But as Callicles points out later, Polus has merely been shamed into admitting that "it is more disgraceful to do than to suffer injustice" (482E), and he would presumably also be ashamed to say that he or any other decent person would willfully choose the shameful. From this it can hardly be concluded that we are here confronted with a Platonic doctrine.

The doctrine of recollection also plays diverse roles in a variety of dialogues. In the *Phaedrus* Socrates speaks of the human soul as having dwelled with the gods and there caught a glimpse of the ideals or forms. Once enshrined in the body, the soul forgot the divine visions but is reminded of them through their traces in earthly things. Filled with yearning, she sets out to recapture them and seeks a companion to join her in that pursuit. Of course, one can take this myth literally and attribute to Plato a doctrine of recollection with its implied belief in a prenatal existence of the human soul. But one can also see it as a grand case of transcendence, which reaches not only from the present to the past, but from this life to a previous existence. Socrates is then understood to offer a dream, a free invention of the creative spirit, to *demonstrate*, in the literal sense of this word, man's power to reach beyond what is to what might be or might have been. Thus he illuminates the fact that man can transcend his condition, an ability which, according to Heidegger, is indispensable to man's most ordinary activities and therefore a necessary element in the constitution of Dasein. This transcendence is also the condition for the possibility of genuine love and friendship, and since the dialogue inquires into the nature of eros in all its forms, the empirical interpretation would seem to be the more appropriate and the more profitable one. In the *Meno*, the doctrine of recollection appears in a different context and serves a somewhat different purpose. Meno, a disciple of Gorgias the rhetorician, has raised a sophistical difficulty which would seem to make the search for truth an impossible undertaking. "You argue," says Socrates, summing up Meno's position, "that a man cannot inquire either about that which he knows, or about that which he does not know; for if he knows he has no need to inquire; if not, he cannot; for he does not know the subject about which he is to inquire" (80E). Socrates resolves the paradox by appealing to a previous existence of the soul when she was in possession of all knowledge, so that her present ignorance is merely a state of forgetfulness and the learning process a case of recollection. And therefore, he concludes "there is no difficulty in eliciting or as men say learning, out of a single recollection all the rest, if a man is strenuous and does not faint; for all inquiry and all learning is but recollection" (81D). Just as his heavy reliance on myth in the *Phaedrus* serves to disparage preexistence as a literal truth, so now he refers vaguely to "certain wise men and women who spoke of truth divine" (81A). In fact it is not the recollection of a previous existence which refutes the sophist, but any case of recollection, of which the myth simply presents a fantastic instance on a grand scale. For when I am trying to recall a past event, I do not know it, for otherwise I would not try to recall it. But if I were completely ignorant of it, I would not think of trying to recover it in memory. This is why prior to recollection, for example, it is true to say that I do not know the person I am trying to recall. But although I cannot give a description, I may yet be able to say that such and such is not the person I have "in mind." And when the person does appear, I can often make the identification, usually with considerable assurance. So while I am trying to recall, I both know and do not know. And if the sophist wants to use this paradoxical characteristic to declare inquiry impossible, he should, to remain consistent, deny the possibility of recollection as well. But to deny recollection is to make all mental activity impossible. In the *Phaedo*, Cebes, one of the young Pythagoreans, invokes the doctrine of recollection in support of the belief in immortality. And when his friend Simmias asked to be reminded of the relevant proofs, Socrates points to the fact that our recognition of the approximate equality of things presupposes an awareness of absolute equality which is not found in sense experience. And this is true, he says, not only of equality, "but of all absolute standards . . . such as absolute beauty, goodness, uprightness and holiness" (75C–D). Things of our experience, he continues, "have a tendency to be like something else, but fall short and cannot be really like it, only a poor imitation" (74D). Again we can take a literalistic and perhaps naive view of the matter, or we can take the argument as a device to call attention to the unsatisfactory nature of human existence and man's tendency to reach beyond to an imaginary world where his deepest desires may be stilled, a tendency which provides Socrates not with a proof, but accords his faith at least a measure of reasonableness.

Despite the diversity of uses to which Plato puts the doctrine of recollection, he appears motivated by a single purpose. The dream of the perfect world of the gods in the *Phaedrus* brings into sharper focus the imperfect and seemingly circular nature of human inquiry as described in the *Meno* and man's discontent with his earthly existence as referred to in the *Phaedo*. In this manner, Plato illuminates the human condition and confronts the reader with the choice between a view which offers his existence at least a chance of being meaningful in the long run, and one which makes it absurd.

The doctrine of ideas is the one which, from ancient Greece to the present day, is most intimately associated with Plato, and to question it seems almost like heresy. According to it, Plato is said to have divided the world into two realms: an upper world of perfect entities and a lower one occupied by changing things which only seem real. Socrates' pronouncements in several dialogues can be cited in support of this view—but only if they are taken out of context and if we forget that Socrates' avowed purpose is to provoke the reader, and not to indoctrinate him. Whatever he says must be interpreted in the light of the context in which it appears.

An early reference to the doctrine of ideas is said to be contained in the *Euthyphro,* when Socrates asks for a definition or idea of virtue which he might use as a standard for judgment in moral matters. But, as we have seen, Socrates' request is a challenge to Euthyphro. Only if in possession of such a definition could he justify his claim to be certain about the pious nature of his proposed act, namely, to prosecute his own father for murder. Furthermore, Socrates' appeal to logic in moral matters is merely the counterpart or opposite extreme of Euthyphro's blind adherence to an old and antiquated tradition. For looking to principles alone will never reveal the greater or lesser evil or good which are relative to the situation in which they occur.

It is noteworthy that when Socrates tries to prove to Protagoras that virtue cannot be taught, he appeals not to a definition or idea of virtue, but to the behavior of the Athenians in the assembly and to the attitude of the great statesmen toward the education of their sons. Their behavior makes sense in the light of a *tentative hypothesis* that virtue cannot be taught. And Protagoras is made to respond in the same general way by coming forward with a more comprehensive and more firmly established hypothesis. The question is not so much of true or false, but of a more or less adequate attempt at explanation. It will not do to say that because of his relativistic outlook on life, Protagoras cannot acknowledge the existence of forms which would convey absolute truth, and that Plato has Socrates do battle on the ground of his opponent. For there is too great a similarity between the way to two men argue in the *Protagoras,* and Socrates' second-best method as expounded in the *Phaedo.*

A clear appeal to the ideas is made in Socrates' rigorous proof for the immortality of the soul in the *Phaedo.* But this proof is based on insight into essences and necessary connections between things, which the preceding exposition of Socrates' second-best method and the subsequent geographic myth make impossible. If we take the argument at its face value, then it supports the view that Plato believed men have access to absolute truths. But then it becomes necessary to accuse him of gross and obvious inconsistency between his method and the final proof. On the other hand, if it is taken as a dramatic mimicry of the tendency to take hypotheses, which at best approximate the truth, as expressions of the essences of things, then this part of the *Phaedo* is compatible with the rest and testifies to the same liberal attitude.

The *Republic,* more than any other dialogue, seems to abound in evidence supporting the doctrine. Socrates starts sensibly and empirically enough by pointing to two aspects of the knowing process: things and actions on the one hand, and on the other an idea in terms of which they are understood. But the ideas again form a multiplicity which find their unifying principle on a higher level. This tendency toward more and more general principles Socrates carries imaginatively to its logical consummation when he speaks of the idea of all ideas, which he calls the *Idea of the Good*. Knowledge of this principle he makes a prerequisite for the rule of the philosopher-kings in the ideal city. If we take the words of Socrates at their face value, then we must ascribe to him the preposterous claim that the cleverest among the young men, if only kept long enough in school, will eventually come to know the ultimate principle of intelligibility of the whole universe, in the light of which they can render infallible judgments about all phases of life. In view of these consequences of a literal interpretation, we may prefer to see the Socratic irony at work. Then we understand him to say that nothing less than the possession of absolute truth would justify our complete surrender to philosopher-kings. And since this is an impossible condition to meet, we will simply have to carry out our responsibilities by relying on our own meagre resources and muddle along as best we can in our affairs both private and public.

In all three dialogues, which are principally mentioned in support of the doctrine of ideas, we have the option of regarding Plato as a dogmatist, or as one who is engaged in combating dogmatism. If we choose the second alternative, then we see Socrates mimic the all too frequent inclination men show to attribute excessive probative power to arguments in order to secure their faith, to shirk responsibility by appealing to absolute ethical standards which may express no more than their own preferences and prejudices, and to avoid the agony of choice in an uncertain and complex political situation by submitting to a leader whom they endow with power of rendering infallible judgments.

The adoption of this second alternative involves a step beyond the one Socrates himself takes. He moves from the real to the ideal, from the empirical to the transempirical. The second step back to the real we ourselves must take. It now appears that the doctrine of ideas, as traditionally understood, can be attributed to Plato only if we follow Socrates as he moves into the supersensible world, but refuse to return to the world in which we live, and see it in a truer light. This return movement is clearly illustrated in the *Allegory of the Cave*. As Heidegger points out:

> The narrative in the story does not end, as one likes to believe, with the description of the highest stage one attains in his ascent from the cave. On the contrary, the narrative of the free man's return to those still enchained in the cave also belongs to the "allegory."[4]

Only the man who has been in the outer world recognizes the shadows as shadows.

Unlike the prisoners of the cave, men cannot escape from their world to a higher one and then return more clearsighted to their own. But if they are gifted, they can imaginatively create such a world, which then performs the same illuminating function as the outer world does for the prisoners. And since most men are not poetically gifted, Plato the poet-philosopher does that work for them. But to use the imaginary world and in its light survey the world in which they live, this is something they can and must do for themselves. And what does this survey reveal? That neither principle, nor logical demonstration, nor reliance on men in authority can relieve them of their responsibility of making their own decisions. The allegory of the cave thus gives a hint as to the way in which the doctrine of ideas should be understood and used. If we follow the hint, then the doctrine becomes an exemplary device in existential phenomenology: as *phenomenological* it provides us with a means to see; as *existential* it calls upon us to act responsibly in the situation as revealed. If we fail to take the hint, then we end up with the useless belief that Plato regarded the world in which we hope and suffer frustrations, into which we were born and eventually will die, as a phantom world, an image of a real world of which, unfortunately, we have no experience at all.

The two-phased movement from the empirical to the transempirical and back to the empirical is, as we have seen, also characteristic of the various myths. The *Protagoras* myth, for instance, moves from an observable degeneration of the sense of justice in a city to its complete absence. No one would claim that either Protagoras or Plato believed that a city whose citizens are devoid of justice could exist. On the contrary, the myth points to the fact that communal life is not god-given, but must be created, nurtured, and preserved if men are to survive at all. The geographic myth in the *Phaedo* does not point to the existence, but merely to the possibility, of a world wider than our own. But this sheer possibility suggests that our own experience is an unreliable basis for any argument aiming at irrefutable knowledge. The *Phaedrus* myth describes the easy movement of the gods toward ideals, not for its own sake but in order to focus on the laboriousness of all human endeavors, which because of that laboriousness lead to genuine achievement. In all cases there is a movement away from the human situation in order to gain distance and thereby a better view of it. Is the distance thus brought about, the *opening* which Heidegger in some of his later writings gives the name *aletheia:*

> We must think *aletheia*, unconcealment, as the opening which first grants Being and thinking and their presencing to and for each other. . . . *Aletheia*, unconcealment, in the sense of the opening may not be equated with truth. Rather, *aletheia*, unconcealment thought as opening, first grants the possibility of truth. For truth itself, just as Being and thinking, can only be what it is in the element of the opening.[5]

Aletheia understood as opening, says Heidegger, was mentioned at the beginning of philosophy by Parmenides. Subsequent thinkers, he claims, spoke about that which appears in the opening, but not the opening itself. Plato is said to have known that without light there is no appearance, but failed to mention the traversable opening which light needs. Perhaps Plato knew more than he was willing to communicate explicitly. It might be that he tried to help his readers, in various ways, to stand in the opening so that they could see more clearly, as in the *Phaedo* he placed before them the opportunity to see themselves as sheer *potentiality-for-Being* by letting them vicariously be present at the dying of Socrates. Plato thus acted as if he were aware of the opening as the condition for the possibility of truth, as he seemed familiar with the revelatory power of *Being-toward-death*, although he did not specifically mention it. In other words, he made use of the opening, but shied away from exploring it any further. Heidegger's questioning, however, moves boldly forward:

> What does ground and principle and especially principle of all principles mean? Can this ever be sufficiently determined unless we experience *aletheia* in a Greek manner as unconcealment and then, above and beyond the Greek, think it as the opening of self-concealing?[6]

Do we create the opening by willfully moving beyond our situation and even beyond ourselves? Or do we, from the beginning and unknowingly, stand in the opening which is *granted?* Then we would have to ask with Heidegger:

> Where does the opening come from and how is it given?[7]

Thus the inquiry into selfhood of two great thinkers, Plato and Heidegger, ends with a question. This is properly so. For the human mode of being is inexhaustible in its aspects, and every conclusion reached is of necessity tentative and, in the opinion of Heidegger, must give rise to renewed questioning:

> The essential answer . . . is only the beginning of a responsibility where the asking arises with renewed originality. Hence even the most genuine question is never stilled by the answer found.[8]

Heidegger did not know how close he was to Plato. Had he been less tradition bound he might have discovered that his *existentials* were secretly at work behind the paradoxes of the *Lysis*. And he could not have maintained that the substance ontology dominated Western philosophy *uninterruptedly* to this day. He saw that the significance of the allegory of the cave in the *Republic* does not come into full view until the freed prisoner's return, for only then do the shadows reveal themselves as shadows. He should have taken the allegory as a hint of how the ideas, and especially the *Idea of the Good*, are to be regarded, namely, as tools in the service of *aletheia*. That he failed to do so is all the more surprising since he assigned to the ideas and to myths basically the same function, namely to provide the light in which entities can show themselves.[9] He should have realized that in order to perform this function, Plato need not give the ideas reality, especially since, as the discussion of the *Republic* has shown, such an assignment creates insurmountable obstacles. By following only the outbound movement from the entities of sense experience to the ideas, a movement which in the case of the allegory he considered insufficient,[10] he thought Plato made the ideas into superrealities to which things and our knowledge of things had to conform. This in turn led Heidegger to the claim that with Plato there occurred a change in the conception of truth from *aletheia* to *orthotes*, from unconcealment to correctness.[11] The allegory of the cave which suggests *aletheia* he regarded as the trace of an earlier tradition which increasingly fell into oblivion. In a later essay he withdrew the claim about the transformation of the conception of truth in the dialogues and acknowledged that truth as *orthotes* is found already in Homer.[12] Heidegger still maintained, however, that through the theory of ideas as realities Plato moved away from the "opening of presence" which grants being and truth. This made it possible for him to say that Plato ultimately tried to understand the being of things in terms of a superreality, the *Idea of the Good*, that is, to think Being as such onto-theologically.[13] If the ideas are understood as superrealities, then Plato's philosophy is diametrically opposed to Heidegger's. "With Heidegger," says Walter Biemel, "it is not a question of surpassing the highest being by setting up a yet higher entity, to explain the last principle by a finally ultimate ground."[14] On the other hand, if Plato took the *Idea of the Good* as a device to show that the conditions for the possibility of the philosopher-kings cannot be met, if he used the ideas to reveal the complexity, not of a supersensory realm, but of the world in which we live, then the road to Heidegger's philosophy would at least be left open. Could Heidegger then still claim that Plato set in motion the long process of the oblivion of Being which reached its culmination in Nietzsche's *Will to Power?*[15] Moreover, Plato's persistent emphasis on transcendence, especially in the *Phaedrus*, makes it less likely that he was unaware of the *opening* to which Heidegger now gives the name *aletheia*, meaning not truth but that which "first grants the possibility of truth."[16] Then it becomes also questionable whether we can say with Heidegger that while Plato knew that "eidos, idea, the outward appearance in which beings can show themselves" is not possible without light, the opening without which "there is no light and no brightness . . . remains unthought in philosophy."[17] However, Heidegger's "Die Metaphysik als Geschichte des Seins"[18] cannot therefore be called incorrect, provided we assign the role which the Plato of the dialogues is said to play to the Plato of the traditional interpretation, and it is this Plato after all who has left his indelible impress on the philosophy of the West.

NOTES

1. Paul Shorey, *What Plato Said* (Chicago: University of Chicago Press, 1968), p. 115.

2. Ibid., p. 89.

3. A. E. Taylor, *Plato: The Man and His Work* (London: Methuen & Co., 1949), p. 37.

4. Martin Heidegger, "Plato's Doctrine of Truth," in *Philosophy in the Twentieth Century*, vol. 2, edited with Introductions by William Barrett and Henry D. Aiken (New York: Random House, 1962), p. 260.

5. Martin Heidegger, "The End of Philosophy and the Task of Thinking," in *On Time and Being*, trans. Joan Stambaugh (New York: Harper & Row, 1972), pp. 68, 69.

6. Ibid., p. 71

7. Ibid., p. 73.

8. Martin Heidegger, "What is Metaphysics?—Postscript," in *Existentialism from Dostoevsky to Sartre*, ed. Walter Kaufmann (New York: New American Library, 1975), p. 259.

9. "Gewöhnlich meint der Mensch, er sehe eben geradehin dieses Haus und jenen Baum und so jegliches Seiende. Zunächst und zumeist ahnt der Mensch nichts davon, dass er alles, was ihm da in aller Geläufigkeit für das 'Wirkliche' gilt, immer nur im Lichte von 'Ideen' sieht." Martin Heidegger, *Platons Lehre von der Wahrheit*, 2nd ed. (Bern: Francke Verlag, 1954), p. 20. Compare this with what Heidegger has to say about the myth: "Im Grunde ist das Mythische noch kaum bedacht, vor allem nicht in der Hinsicht, dass der *mythos* Sage ist, das Sagen aber das rufende zum-Scheinen-Bringen." Martin Heidegger, "Moira," in *Vorträge und Aufsätze*, 2nd ed. (Pfullingen: Weske, 1959) p. 248.

10. Cf. also: "Dieses (das Dichterische) ueberfliegt und uebersteigt die Erde nicht, um sie zu verlassen und über ihr zu schweben. Das Dichten bringt den Menschen erst auf die Erde, zu ihr, bringt ihn so in das Wohnen." Martin Heidegger, ". . . dichterisch wohnet der Mensch . . . ," in *Vorträge und Aufsätze*, p. 192.

11. For further details see Henry G. Wolz, "Plato's Doctrine of Truth: Orthotes or Aletheia?" *Philosophy and Phenomenological Research* 27 (December 1966): 157–82.

12. "The End of Philosophy and the Task of Thinking," p. 70.

13. Cf. "Die Onto-Theo-Logische Verfassung der Metaphysik," in Martin Heidegger, *Identitaet und Differenz*, 3rd ed. (Pfullingen: Neske, 1957), pp. 35–74.

14. Walter Biemel, *Martin Heidegger: An Illustrated Study*, trans. J. H. Mehta, (New York: Harcourt Brace Jovanovich, 1976), p. 125.

15. Cf.: "Der Name Subiectität . . . nennt die eigentliche Geschichte des Seins als *idea* bis zur Vollendung des Seins als Wille zun Macht." Martin Heidegger, "Die Metaphysik als Geschichte des Seins," in *Nietzche*, vol. 2, 2nd ed. (Pfullingen: Neske, 1961), pp. 452–53.

Cf. also: "Anfänglich aber ist das *en* weder vom 'ich denke' noch von der *idea* her begriffen, sondern aus dem *nous* (Parmenides) und aus dem *logos* im Sinne von Heraklit als das entbergendbergende Versammeln." Ibid., p. 463.

16. "The End of Philosophy and the Task of Thinking," p. 69.

17. Ibid., p. 67.

18. Nietzsche, 2:399–457.

Bibliography

Anderson, Albert. "Socrates' Reasoning in the *Euthyphro*." *Review of Metaphysics* 22 (1969): 461–481.

Anselm, Saint. *Proslogium*. Translated by Sidney Norton Deane. Chicago: Open Court Publishing Co., 1925.

Aristotle. "Poetics." In *The Basic Works of Aristotle*. Edited by Richard McKeon. New York: Random House, 1941.

Bacon, Francis. "Novum Organum." In *Modern Classical Philosophers*, 2nd ed., compiled by Benjamin Rand. New York: Houghton Mifflin Co. 1936.

Biemel, Walter. *Martin Heidegger: An Illustrated Study*. Translated by J. L. Mehta. New York: Harcourt Brace Jovanovich (An Original Harvest Book), 1976.

Bluck, R. S. *Plato's "Phaedo."* Translated with Introduction Notes and Appendices. New York: Liberal Arts Press, 1955.

Boas, George. *Rationalism in Greek Philosophy*. Baltimore, Md.: Johns Hopkins Press, 1961.

Bridgman, P. W. *The Logic of Modern Physics*. New York: Macmillan Co., 1951.

Brown, John H. "The Logic of *Euthyphro* 10A–11B." *Philosophical Quarterly* 14 (1964): 1–15.

Buchner, Hartmut. *Eros und Sein: Erörterungen zu Platons "Symposium."* Bonn: H. Bouvier u. Co. Verlag, 1965.

Cohen, S. Marc. "Socrates on the Definition of Piety: *Euthyphro* 10A–11B." *Journal of the History of Philosophy* 9 (1971): 1–13.

Cross, R. C., and Woozley A. D. *Plato's "Republic": A Philosophical Commentary*. London: Macmillan & Co., 1964.

DeVogel, C. J. *Greek Philosophy*. Vol. 1, *Thales to Plato*. 2nd ed. Leiden: Brill, 1957.

Einstein, Albert, and Infeld, Leopold. *The Evolution of Physics*. New York: Simon and Schuster, 1951.

Eliot, T. S. *The Cocktail Party*. New York: Harcourt, Brace and Co., 1950.

Esslin, Martin. *The Theatre of the Absurd*. New York: Doubleday Anchor, 1961.

Friedländer, Paul. *Plato*. Translated by Hans Meyerhoff. 3 vols. Bollingen Series 59. Princeton, N.J.: Princeton University Press, 1958–1970.

Frutiger, Percival. *Les Mythes de Platon*. Paris: F. Alcan, 1930.

Furley, David. *Two Studies in the Greek Atomists*. Princeton, N.J.: Princeton University Press, 1967.

Gadamer, Hans-Georg. *Platos dialektische Ethik und andere Studien zur platonischen Philosophie*. Hamburg: Felix Meiner Verlag, 1968.

Gauss, Hermann. *Philosophischer Handkommentar zu den Dialogen Platos* in 3 Teilen. Bern: Verlag Herbert Lang & Cie., 1960.

Geach, P. T. "Plato's *Euthyphro*." *The Monist* 50 (1966): 369–82.

Genêt, Jean. *The Blacks: A Clown Show*. Translated by Bernard Frechtman. New York: Grove Press, 1960.

Gomperz, T. *Griechische Denker*. Leipzig: Voit & Co., 1896.

Gould, Thomas. *Platonic Love*. New York: Free Press of Glencoe, 1963.

Grube, G. M. A. *Plato's Thought*. Boston: Beacon Press, 1961.

Guthrie, W. K. C. *Socrates and Plato*. The Marcossan Lectures for 1957. Brisbane: University of Queensland Press, 1958.

Hackforth, R. *Plato's "Phaedo."* Translated with Introduction and Commentary. Cambridge: Cambridge University Press, 1955.

Heidegger, Martin. "Aus einem Gespräch von der Sprache zwischen einem Japaner und einem Fragenden." In *Unterwegs zur Sprache*, 3rd ed. Pfullingen: Neske, 1965.
Being and Time. Translated by John Macquarrie and Edward Robinson. New York: Harper & Row, 1962.
". . . dichterisch wohnet der Mensch . . ." In *Vorträge und Aufsaetze*. 2nd ed. Pfullingen: Neske, 1959.
"Das Ding." In *Vortraege und Aufsaetze*. 2nd ed. Pfullingen: Neske, 1959.
"The End of Philosophy and the Task of Thinking." In *On Time and Being*, translated by Joan Stambaugh. New York: Harper & Row, 1972.
"Die Metaphysik als Geschichte des Seins." In *Nietzsche*, vol. 2, 2nd ed. Pfullingen: Neske, 1961.
"My Way to Phenomenology." In *On Time and Being*, translated by Joan Stambaugh. New York: Harper & Row, 1972.
"Moira." In *Vorträge und Aufsätze*. 2nd ed. Pfullingen: Neske, 1959.
"Die Onto-Theo-Logische Verfassung der Metaphysik." In *Identitaet und Differenz*, 3rd ed. Pfullingen: Neske, 1957.
Phenomenologie und Theologie. Frankfurt am Main: Vittorio Klostermann, 1970.
Platons Lehre von der Wahrheit. 2nd ed. Bern: Francke Verlag, 1954.
"Plato's Doctrine of Truth." In *Philosophy in the Twentieth Century*, edited with Introductions by William Barrett and Henry D. Aiken, vol. 2. New York: Random House, 1962.

Sein und Zeit. 6th ed. Tübingen: Neomarius Verlag, 1949.

"Time and Being." In *On Time and Being*, translated by Joan Stambaugh. New York: Harper & Row, 1972.

> *Vom Ursprung des Kunstwerkes*. Stuttgart: Philipp Reclam, 1960.

> *Was ist Metaphysik?* 8th ed. Frankfurt am Main: Vittorio Klostermann, 1960.

> "What is Metaphysics? Postscript." In *Existentialism from Dostoevsky to Sartre*, edited by Walter Kaufmann. New York: New American Library, 1975.

Hoerber, Robert G. "Plato's *Euthyphro*." *Phronesis* 3 (1958): 95–107.

Huxley, Aldous. *Point Counterpoint*. New York: Modern Library, 1928.

James, William. *Principles of Psychology*. New York: H. Holt & Co., 1890.

Kanthack, Katharina. *Vom Sinn der Selbsterkenntnis*. Berlin: Walter de Gruyter & Co., 1958.

Kent Sprague, Rosamond. *Plato's Use of Fallacy*. New York: Barnes & Noble, 1962.

Kitto, H. D. F. *Form and Meaning in Drama*. London: Methuen & Co., University Paperback, 1968.

Klein, Jacob. *A Commentary on Plato's Meno*. Chapel Hill, N.C.: University of North Carolina Press, 1965.

Krüger, Gerhard. *Einsicht und Leidenschaft*. 3rd ed. Frankfurt am Main: Vittorio Klostermann, 1963.

Liddell and Scott. *Greek-English Lexicon*. 7th ed. Oxford: Clarendon Press, 1961.

Livingstone, Sir R. W. *Portrait of Socrates*. Oxford: Clarendon Press, 1946.

Loewith, Karl. An Interview in *Der Spiegel* 43 (1969).

Lucretius. *On the Nature of Things*. Translated by H. A. J. Munroe. Chicago: Henry Regnery Co., 1949.

Malraux, André. *La Condition Humaine*. Paris: Gallimard, Le Livre de Poche 27, 1955.

Muller, Herbert. *The Uses of the Past*. New York: Alfred A. Knopf, 1952.

Nietzsche, Friedrich. *The Portable Nietzsche*. Edited and translated by Walter Kaufmann. New York: Viking Press, 1954.

> *Werke*. Grossoktavausgabe, Nachlass, vol. 12. Leipzig: A. Kröner, 1926.

O'Brien, Michael J. *The Socratic Paradoxes and the Greek Mind*. Chapel Hill, N.C.: University of North Carolina Press, 1967.

Plato. *The Collected Dialogues of Plato*. Edited by Edith Hamilton and Huntington Cairns. Bollingen Series 71.

> *The Dialogues of Plato*. Translated by Benjamin Jowett. 2 vols. New York: Random House, 1937.

> *Plato*. With an English Translation by W. R. M. Lamb. Vol. 5. Loeb Classical Library. Cambridge, Mass.: Harvard University Press, 1961.

Plato's "Protagoras." Benjamin Jowett's translation, extensively revised by Martin Ostwald. Edited, with an Introduction by Gregory Vlastos. New York: Library of Liberal Arts, 1956.

The "Republic" of Plato. Translated with Introduction and Notes by Francis MacDonald Cornford. New York: Oxford University Press, 1945.

Popper, Karl R. *The Open Society and Its Enemies.* Princeton, N.J.: Princeton University Press, 1950.

Randall, Jr., John Herman. *Aristotle.* New York: Columbia University Press, 1960.

Plato: Dramatist of the Life of Reason. New York: Columbia University Press, 1970.

"Plato on the Good Life and the Spartan Ideal." *Journal of the History of Ideas* 28 (1967): 307–324.

The Role of Knowledge in Western Religion. Boston: Beacon Press, 1958.

Richardson, William J. *Heidegger: Through Phenomenology to Thought.* The Hague: Martinus Nijhoff, 1963.

Robinson, Richard. *Plato's Earlier Dialectic.* 2nd ed. Oxford: Clarendon Press, 1953.

Rosen, Frederick. "Piety and Justice: Plato's *Euthyphro.*" *Philosophy: Journal of the Royal Institute of Philosophy,* vol. 43, no. 164 (1968): 105–116.

Russell, Bertrand. "A Free Man's Worship." In *Mysticism and Logic.* New York: Doubleday Anchor Book, 1957.

Ryle, Gilbert. *Plato's Progress.* Cambridge: Cambridge University Press, 1966.

Santayana, George. "Ultimate Religion." In *The Philosophy of Santayana,* edited by Irwin Edman. New York: C. Scribner's Sons, 1936.

Sarton, George. *A History of Science: Ancient Science through the Golden Age of Greece.* Cambridge: Cambridge University Press, 1952.

Sartre, Jean-Paul. *The Age of Reason.* Translated by Eric Sutton, New York: Modern Library, 1947.

Being and Nothingness. Translated with an Introduction by Hazel E. Barnes. New York: Philosophical Library, 1956.

Critique de la Raison Dialectique. Vol. 1, "Théorie des Ensembles Pratiques." Paris: Librairie Gallimard, 1960.

The Flies. In *"No Exit" and "the Flies,"* translated by Stuart Gilbert. New York: Alfred A. Knopf. 1952.

Search for a Method. Translated by Hazel E. Barnes. New York: Alfred A. Knopf, 1963.

Scarrow, David. "*Phaedo* 106A–106E." *Philosophical Review* 70 (1961): 245–253.

Schleiermacher, Friedrich. *Einleitung zum "Protagoras."* Berlin, 1817.

Schwerin, Christoph. "The Officers' Plot: German Foes of Hitler." *New York Times,* 20 July 1974.

Shorey, Paul. *What Plato Said*. Chicago: University of Chicago Press, 1968.

Sinaiko, Herman L. *Love, Knowledge and Discourse in Plato: Dialogue and Dialectic in "Phaedrus," "Republic," "Parmenides."* Chicago: University of Chicago Press, 1965.

Strauss, Leo. *The City and Man*. Chicago: Rand McNally & Co., 1964.

Taylor, A. E. *Plato: The Man and His Work*. 6th ed. London: Methuen & Co., 1949.

Tillich, Paul. *The Courage to Be*. New Haven, Conn.: Yale University Press, 1953.

Wolz, Henry G. "Hedonism in the *Protagoras*." *Journal of the History of Philosophy* 5 (1967): 205–17.

"The Paradox of Piety in Plato's *Euthyphro* in the Light of Heidegger's Conception of Authenticity." *Southern Journal of Philosophy* 12 (1974): 493–511.

"Philosophy as Drama: An Approach to Plato's *Symposium*." *Philosophy and Phenomenological Research* 30 (1970): 323–53.

"Plato's Discourse on Love in the *Phaedrus*." *The Personalist* 46 (1965): 157–170.

"Plato's Doctrine of Truth: *Orthotes* or *Aletheia?*" *Philosophy and Phenomenological Research* 27 (1966): 157–82.

"The Protagoras Myth and the Philosopher Kings." *Review of Metaphysics* 17 (1963): 214–34.

"The *Republic* in the Light of the Socratic Method." *Modern Schoolman* 32 (1955) 115–42.

Index